THE LIVING HISTORY OF PAKISTAN

Judges & Generals in Pakistan

Volume-III

by

INAM R SEHRI

CONTEMPORARY HISTORY IS NOT
THAT WHAT HAS BEEN HAPPENING AROUND?
IT IS THE STATEMENT OF FACTS
ABOUT WHAT THE PEOPLE
CONSIDERED SIGNIFICANT

Grosvenor House
Publishing Limited

Re-Print   June 2017

This book is published by
P H P Grosvenor House Publishing Ltd
28-30 High Street, Guildford, Surrey, GU1 3EL.
www.grosvenorhousepublishing.co.uk

A CIP record for this book
is available from the British Library

[All page with usual statements ending with]

ISBN 978-1-78148-204-9

For

The
Oppressed
Broken & Depressed
Dejected & Subjugated
Demoralized & Disheartened
People of Pakistan
who are
continuously being exploited
for the last 66 years
in the name of

JUSTICE & DEMOCRACY

Other Books from

INAM R SEHRI

KHUDKUSHI
    (on Suicide) [in Urdu]   (1983)
    {Details of historical perspective of 'Suicide' in various societies; &
investigation techniques differentiating in Murder & Suicides}

WARDI KAY ANDAR AADMI
    (Man in uniform) [in Urdu]   (1984)
    {Collection of short stories keeping a sensitive policeman in focus}

AURAT JARAIM KI DALDAL MEIN
    (on Female Criminality) [in Urdu]   (1985)
    {Describing various theories and cultural taboos concerning Female
Criminal Behaviour}

POLICE AWAM RABTAY
    (on Police Public relationship) [in Urdu]   (1986)
    {Essays describing importance of mutual relationships}

DEHSHAT GARDI
    (on Terrorism) [in Urdu]   (1987)
    {Various theories and essays differentiating between Freedom
Fighting & Terrorism in Middle Eastern perspective}

QATL
    (on Murder) [in Urdu]   (1988)
    {The first book written for Police students & Lawyers to explain
techniques of investigation of (difficult) Murder cases}

SERVICE POLICING IN PAKISTAN
    [in English]   (1990)
    {A dissertation type book on which basis the PM Benazir Bhutto, in
1990, had okayed the Commissionerate System of Policing in Pakistan.
Taking Karachi as the pilot project, later, it was levied for all major cities
and still going on as such}

SHADI

(on Marriages) [in Urdu]   (1998)

{A detailed exposition of Marriage explained in various religions, cultures, countries and special groups; much applauded & commented upon on PTV in 1998-99}

All the above books were published by Pakistan's number one publisher

SANG E MEEL PUBLICATIONS,
25 - The Lower Mall LAHORE, Pakistan

And are normally available with them in latest re-prints.

Judges & Generals in Pakistan VOL-I
[in English]   (2012)

Judges & Generals in Pakistan VOL-II
[in English]   (2012)
{Collection of essays mostly published; dealing with Pakistan's chequered history of army rule and higher judiciary's gimmicks during 1971 to 2008; the military & judiciary's nexus made the politicians more corrupt.}

Published by

Grosvenor House Publishing Ltd
28-30 High Street, Guildford
SURREY UK GU1 3HY

It's me; my Lord!

INAM R SEHRI

- Born in Lyallpur (Pakistan) in April 1948

- First Degree from Government College Lyallpur (1969)

- Studied at Government College Lahore & got first Master's Degree from Punjab University Lahore (1971);

- Attachment with AJK Education Service (1973-1976)

- Central Superior Services (CSS) Exam passed (batch 1975)

- Civil Service Academy Lahore (joined 1976)

- National Police Academy Islamabad (joined 1977)

- LLB from BUZ University Multan (1981)

- Master's Degree from Exeter University of UK (1990)

- Regular Police Service: District Admin, Police College, National Police Academy, the Intelligence Bureau (IB), Federal Investigation Agency (FIA) [1977-1998] then migrated to the UK permanently.

A part-script copied from the earlier volumes:

Just spent a normal routine life; with hundreds of mentionable memoirs allegedly of bravery & glamour as every uniformed officer keeps, some times to smile at and next moment to repent upon but taking it just normal except one or two spills. During my tenure at IB HQ Islamabad I got chance to peep into the elite civil and military leadership of Pakistan then existing in governmental dossiers and database.

During my stay at FIA I was assigned to conduct special enquiries & investigations into some acutely sensitive matters like Motorway Scandal, sudden expansion and build-up of Sharif family's industrial empire, Nawaz Sharif's accounts in foreign countries; Alleged Financial Corruptions in Pakistan's Embassies in Far-Eastern Countries; Shahnawaz Bhutto's murder in Cannes (France); Land Scandals of CDA's Estate Directorate; Ittefaq Foundry's 'custom duty on scrap' scam,

Hudaibya Engineering & Hudaibya Paper Mills enquiries, Bhindara's Murree Brewery and tens more cases like that.

> [*Through these words I want to keep it on record that during the course of the above mentioned, (and also which cannot be mentioned due to space limits) investigations or enquiries, the then Prime Minister Benazir Bhutto, or [late] Gen Naseerullah Babar the then Federal Interior Minister, or G Asghar Malik the then DG FIA, had never never issued direct instructions or implicit directions or wished me to distort facts or to go malafide for orchestrating a political edge or other intangible gains.*
>
> *Hats off to all of them!*]

I should feel proud that veracity and truthfulness of none of my enquiry or investigation could be challenged or proved false in NAB or Special Courts; yes, most of them were used to avail political compromises by Gen Musharraf's government.

That's enough, my dear countrymen.

Contents

- Black Coat Revolution
- PM Gilani Brings Back Sharifs
- Pakistan's New Judicial Policy

My Apologies; Once More:

This volume-III carries more facts of compromises amongst the ruling elite and 'friendly' oppositions both at federal and provincial levels. It may be taken as a story of the contemporary Pakistan ruled by few feudal and industrial families; marked by all the characteristics of civil dictatorship in the name of democracy.

A note from the recent past:

The Supreme Court of Pakistan was surprised *on 8th February 2013* when Member Inspection Team's report revealed that some 300 to 400 police functionaries of Karachi involved in atrocious crimes had been facing trials in different offences and were enjoying field postings.

A bench of the apex court, headed by Justice Jawwad S Khawaja, while hearing the Karachi law and order case at the Karachi Registry, observed:

> *"Do not play game with the citizens of Karachi. We are going to initiate proceedings against the government functionaries who failed to make compliance with the court's directives despite the lapse of 16 months.*
>
> *It is an extreme indifference by the [sitting] government people. The city is burning but authorities concerned do not bother to perform their duties."*

16 people had been killed in the city a day before as per the media reports and no one was expecting any sign of improvement in the prevailing law and order situation. The apex court took exception to the non-compliance of the court directives by the federal government and observed that nothing had been placed before the court by the federal law officer [*Deputy Attorney General Javed Farooqui*] to show that it was fulfilling its constitutional obligations.

There were hundreds of observations and directions by the SC for which no reply was ever placed before the court. DIG Legal Ali Sher Jakhrani submitted that he was not in position to make a comment on it.

However, as a person, Nawaz Sharif was a changed man in later years. During the period covered in this book, he surfaced with vibrant

728

dimensions, in exciting colours, and showing vivacious leadership qualities. The people expected him to deliver better Pakistan after elections of 2013. Let us see how he deals with such non compliance of the SC observations by the federal government.

During Gen Musharraf's times: in Sialkot, Ch Anwar Aziz got success in the local elections through stern efforts because of his local influence as he was in politics since decades. The members of the District Council as a group came at his residence on the eve of the elections day with rose petals paying tribute to his victory and told him that 'all the members of the councils elected today have unanimously decided to choose you as *Zila Nazim* (Chairman District Council) to recognise your services for the people'. Ch Anwar Aziz thanked him, offered them food and future development plans discussed.

Suddenly an army jeep entered the compound; Pak-Army's Brigadier in uniform got down with a gentleman in civies; took Ch Anwar Aziz aside and talked for a minute or two. When they came out, the army Brigadier announced before the enchanting members that this gentleman [pointing towards the accompanying person] would be your new Chairman. He was some retired army officer. It happened during the army rule of Gen Musharraf because *in Pakistan there exists no rule of law but compromises and concessions.*

The legacy, however, continued.

In January 2011, Raymond Davis kills two persons in Lahore and one more killed by an American car at the scene of occurrence. On 29th January 2011, the then Foreign Minister Shah Mahmood Qureshi was contacted [while he was in Karachi] by the US Ambassador in Islamabad and the US Secretary Hilary Clinton with the requests [*later changed to threats*] to assign diplomatic status to the American killer which was refused. The matter was subjudice in the court.

Two days later, President Zardari summoned Mr Qureshi in presidency where the PM Gilani, DG ISI, Rehman Malik & Babar Awan were already sitting. The arguments developed between Mr Qureshi and Rehman Malik which ended in the resignation of the Federal Foreign Minister because *in Pakistan there exists no rule of law but compromises and concessions even for foreign killers.*

On *25th June 2011*, an armed group of local miscreant attacked Kolachi Police Station [*Kolachi is a town at 45 km away from Dera Ismail Khan*] during day light and killed eight police officers including their Inspector incharge. It took eight hours to get released the police station premises from the scoundrels after a fierce fighting in an operation headed by the DIG Police Imtiaz Shah himself.

The event should have been dealt with severely but nothing heard anything; perhaps they were poor [& corrupt?] 'pulsias'. *In Pakistan there exists no rule of law but compromises and concessions for many.*

In 2011, on the occasion of anniversary of 12th October's military coup, a debate on the Parliament's floor degenerated into mutual accusations between the PPP and the PML(N) with each side blaming the other for providing support to various military dictators in the past. PML(N) reiterated their demand for initiating a treason case against Gen Musharraf and accused the PPP rulers of providing protection to him under a clandestine deal and providing the General an honourable departure. They blamed Gen Musharraf for the security crisis the country was facing then and demanded that he should be hanged.

But, PPP's legislators wanted to know that why had the PML(N) singled out Gen Musharraf and spared others, including the judges who had allowed him in uniform to carry out changes in the Constitution.

Above all; when Gen Musharraf had physically landed back in Pakistan on 24th March 2013 and was arrested in April 2013 and was made to appear before the Supreme Court in the treason case, the same PML(N) did not utter a single word for the trial against Gen Musharraf.

Nawaz Sharif remained mum despite asking dozens questions [regarding trial of the General in treason case] from the media reporters and TV anchors at tens of occasions – because the Western lords had 'conveyed appropriate instructions' to the PML(N) leadership on the subject. In Pakistan there exists no rule of law but compromises and concessions for many.

One angry MNA from Sargodha Mr Gondal said the PML(N) should not claim the credit for the reinstatement of superior judiciary, including Chief Justice Iftikhar Chaudhry, who had been reinstated because of the intervention of the ISI and not because of the opposition's long march. '*Long march was just a drama and a circus. The judiciary was restored when the ISI wanted it,*' Mr Gondal mentioned. He asked the PML(N) why was it not demanding action against the army Generals who had been with Gen Musharraf in the past and were '*nowadays playing golf in Punjab*'.

Interestingly, the CJP Iftikhar Chaudhry also came under criticism in that session from the PML(N)'s Capt Safdar while questioning his inaction on the incident of 12th May 2007 in Karachi in which 43 people had been killed during the CJP's visit to the city. '*If the CJ does not provide justice to families of those killed for him, then one should not expect justice from the CJ,*' MNA Capt Safdar had announced.

> *But, since that day he was never seen speaking in the parliament, never heard in any media conference, never issued any press statement and the poor fellow was not even allowed to represent PML(N) in any live TV discussion for which he was known all over the country – **hats off to the party policy**.*

The whole house, however, kept an opinion that had the then PM Nawaz Sharif constituted a commission on Kargil, they would not have suffered the humiliation of 12th October 1999's military coup. Kh Sa'ad Rafiq, the PML(N)'s lawmaker admitted that '*it was Mr Sharif's mistake to appoint Gen Musharraf as the army chief, ignoring the seniority list*'.

Gen Ghulam Ahmed (Musharraf's Chief of Staff) also once stunned the audience when he said: '*But sir, first they [Gen Musharraf, Gen Mahmood, and Gen Aziz] will have to get out of the cage of Kargil, otherwise all their efforts will be reactive.*'

See another scenario below:

The PM Yousaf Raza Gilani, in saddles since 2008, had started his politics in Gen Ziaul Haq's military regime in 1980s under the able guidance of army. Referring to an **interview of Gen Hamid Gul** with Dr Shahid Masood in a live TV program **dated 5th February 2012**:

> [*PM Mr Gilani is also a product / discovery of a military dictator. In Gen Ziaul Haq's rule in 1980s, Mr Gilani was called in Islamabad to be made a cabinet minister to represent Multan; he was having long hair like 'hippys' as was a fashion in youngsters then. Gen Zia, before talking to him, handed him over to me to have his hair cut like 'gentlemen'.*
>
> *I took him out, had an army haircut, and we went before the General again in the evening and he was made a Federal Minister.*]

But then Mr Gilani changed his boat to uphold democracy and joined the PPP because then there was no likelihood of military rule again.

Now hats off to the slogans of democracy; after twenty years Syed Ahmed Mujtaba Gilani, the younger brother of the PM, was elected as Member Provincial Assembly of the Punjab in bye-election held on 5th June 2010 against the seat fell vacant after resignation of Ms Naghma Mushtaq Lang. The PM's eldest son Kadir Gillani was already a sitting MPA from PP-295. Since mid 2011, a very hot move to make Saraiki province was brought on cards so that PM's son Kadir Gilani be made first Chief Minister of the new province; just to make out a colourful family history. Democracy hurray!

On *6th February 2012*, 20th Constitutional Amendment Bill was placed before the Parliament; which was passed unanimously as usual with the PML(N)'s hidden bargain on it; again, through 'usual gimmicks' because it allowed the then PM's younger son Syed Musa Gilani to win the by-election seat of the National Assembly from Multan which was vacated by Shah Mahmood Qureshi, the former Foreign Minister.

All this game, allocating the parliamentary tickets to younger brother and two sons, was played in the name of democracy and in the name of *'greater interest of the nation'*.

The PM Mr Gilani has been waiting anxiously for some lady to vacate the 'women's reserved seat' on any pretext so that the PM's daughter Fiza Gilani could be brought in the parliament to make the democratic traditions stronger in Pakistan.

In Pakistan, every one is dying for democracy, the PPP has been ruling in the name of democracy. The people believed that after Z A Bhutto, they had voted for her daughter Benazir Bhutto for democracy; then to her husband A A Zardari to uphold democracy; Zardari's sister Faryal Gohar was voted for democracy; Faryal Gohar's husband Munawwar Talpur was brought in the Sindh Assembly for upkeep of democracy.

Zardari's son Bilawal was initially told to 'uphold democracy' from Lyari [*and was designated as the next prime minister through suitable Constitutional Amendment also; had the PPP won*]. Do not ask for Nabil Gabol who had been winning that PPP seat from Lyari since decades, but then forced to vacate the seat for Bilawal. Nabil Gabol had to join the MQM in utter distress but secured his seat back.

Gabol was being sacrificed for democracy or to give seat to Bilawal Bhutto - never mind; it is the same thing. Zardari's daughter Bakhtawar was made incharge women wing for nourishment of democracy; Zardari's second daughter Asifa was to hold PPP's next command to sustain democracy. In nut shell Pakistan's civil dictators would continue to make mockery of the country 'to uphold democracy' but no army dictator.

The fact remains that Gen Ziaul Haq and Gen Abdul Rehman's sons were also seen in the parliament and in cabinets successively but only after the death of both the Generals, not in their lives. Other Generals, Corps Commanders, or the ISI Chiefs seldom opted to strengthen the 'democracy in Pakistan' through this way. This prerogative always remained with the politicians whether belonged to the PPP, PML(N) or PML(Q) or similar heavy mandated parties including JUI(F).

As per report of UN Office on Drugs & Crime [2011], nine (9) million population of Pakistan was on narcotics & drugs at an annual increase of 0.6 million per year. Out of these nine million, women were 10% and 60% were educated people; but who cares – Pakistani politicians are there only to 'uphold democracy' for their sons and daughters.

During third week of December 2011, the PPP had spoken overtly of the military as a '*state within a state*' and criticized the Generals for illegal acts. Mediators prevailed; the president and the Generals met and agreed to back off on threats to reduce the military power. The Supreme Court, however, continued to examine abuses (allegedly murdering four detainees out of eleven) by the ISI.

During mid January 2012, there had been a great debate in the media, attacking the Pakistan Army and the ISI in particular. PM Gilani, the PPP cabinet members and Mr Zardari raised open remarks over the military. On 27th January 2012, the angry Generals directly pushed open threats of another military coup causing the president to pull back and retreat.

Hats off to Gen Kayani and his team again; he never opted to interfere.

(Inam R Sehri)
Manchester UK
May 2013

Scenario 57

ON JUDGES & JUDICIARY IN PAKISTAN:

Munir A Malik, former President SC Bar Association was once asked [*when he had taken stand against Gen Musharraf on Justice Chaudhry's dismissal in March 2007*] that Benazir Bhutto and Nawaz Sharif both humiliated and attacked the judiciary in their second terms of power, but there was no massive movement then. What was different this time?

Munir Malik had replied that:

> '*Historically, the judiciary [in Pakistan] has always been a collaborator with the ruling elite. It has been the 'B' team of the army. It retains the old, imperial mindset that it is there to serve the government. If a high court judge was called by the president, he would probably put on his best suit and take a camera with him; it would be an event for him to remember, that he has been summoned by the president or prime minister.*
>
> *In a white paper published after 1977, Zulfiqar Ali Bhutto in one of his side notes remarked, 'they [judges] will come to you for petty favours'; for a diplomatic passport, an admission for a child, a posting for a relative......'*
>
> *Basically, the judges were part of the establishment, they had no moral credibility. You could sense that if there was a case involving the corp commanders or cantonment land, the judge would think that before the commander says something to me, I should oblige him. Such judges did not inspire public support.*
>
> *This time however, the media brought to our drawing rooms a man saying 'no' to the establishment, a man standing up to the military, saying 'I will not resign, I am innocent'. So I think both the legal community and civil society felt they had to support him.*'

Judiciary in Pakistan remained mostly dormant. The higher judiciary seldom felt courage in initiating *suo moto* action against any influential functionary, private or government sponsored. In past it mostly remained subservient to the executive controls, whether there has been a political party in power or army dictator. History of Pakistan is replete with certain glaring examples.

Until it was suspended on 12th October 1999, the 1973 Constitution provided for an independent and impartial judiciary but this guarantee was immediately curtailed following the coup. On 14th October 1999 the military government issued a Provisional Constitution Order [PCO] which mandated that the judiciary would not issue "*any order against the Chief Executive or any person exercising powers or jurisdiction under his authority*".

The people of Pakistan were expecting that the apex judiciary would itself call a bench of available judges, might be in late hours of night, and would declare the said phrase 'unconstitutional' [*as they have been doing during CJP Sajjad Ali Shah's last days in November 1997 and also did later in the evening of 3rd November 2007*]. The Supreme Court was the custodian of the Constitution.

This order effectively insulated the military Government's actions from judicial scrutiny. The judiciary had to remain silent. But, on 26th January 2000, when the military rulers further increased executive control over the judiciary through the promulgation of the '*Oath of Judges' Order 2000* (which required judges of all Superior Courts to take a new oath to Gen Musharraf's regime) the whole judiciary could have refused to take such derogatory oath but the game continued.

The American media termed it as infamous '*General Pervez Musharraf's Oath*'; 13 out of 17 judges, who were not invited to take this oath, were thrown out of the Supreme Court of Pakistan. The reports of the '*Information Times*' dated 28th *January 2000* had used highly objectionable language for this event by saying that:

> '*Pakistan Supreme Court judges took the GPMO on Wednesday January 26, 2000 in accordance with orders issued by Pakistan's Chief Executive and Army Chief Gen Pervez Musharraf and swore to work like judicial clerks under the ruling Military Regime*'.

Moral and financial dishonesty are bad but the intellectual dishonesty is intolerable. It is recorded in Pakistan's history as to if the Judges tried to restore the lost honour of Judiciary by declaring Martial Law illegal and Law of Necessity as immoral ...... but .... *That had usually happened after the departure of every Military Regime and Military Dictator.*

Since 1988 till 1999, certain people like Habib Wahabul Khairi, M D Tahir and Al-Jihad Trust had allegedly blackmailed every civilian government in the name of 'Judicial Activism'. Whether it was true or not, the critics held that they had been doing so at the behest of their paymasters in the Pakistan Army. Facts and verifications are needed.

Another disappointment; that the first petition challenging illegality of the military coup of 12th October 1999 was filed in November 1999. On 12th May 2000 the Supreme Court, reconstituted by the military executive, unanimously rejected the petition, and endorsed the coup's legitimacy under the doctrine of State necessity, thus losing their own integrity in the eyes of general populace of Pakistan. Similarly:

> 'On 13th April 2005 the judiciary was blamed and more severely cursed by the people of Pakistan because on that day the Supreme Court had dismissed all petitions challenging the 17th constitutional amendment and the dual office of Gen Musharraf; the present incumbent Chief Justice Iftikhar M Chaudhry was the part of that bench.'

MAKING ANTI-TERRORIST COURTS:

Going a little earlier; the general public once hailed the decisions taken on merits only, irrespective of the fact that the ruling executive authority was on the loosing end. For example; PM Nawaz Sharif enacted the Anti-Terrorist Act (ATA) in August 1997 to *"provide for the prevention of terrorism, sectarian violence and for speedy trial of heinous offences and for matters connected therewith and incidental thereto"*.

Eleven courts were then set up under the ATA in Punjab and presiding judges for these were appointed after consultation with the Chief Justice of the Lahore High Court. In May 1999 several courts were set up in Karachi. Irony of fate was that many of such courts were presided by serving military officers as judges.

> [A life time tragedy was that Nawaz Sharif himself was tried by one of the same ATA courts constituted in Karachi.]

In May 1998, the Supreme Court ruled that a number of provisions of the ATA were unconstitutional. These provisions were concerning the lack of appeal in Anti-Terrorist Courts, the far reaching powers of police, and right of the police to shoot & kill. On a similar occasion the public unanimously hailed the Supreme Court of Pakistan and its realistic decision when two people were sentenced to death by a Military Court in Karachi in November 1998. The Supreme Court had decided in January 1999 to halt their executions pending the review of legality of the establishment of these Military Courts.

In February 1999, the Supreme Court gave a ruling unanimously that the establishment of the Military Courts in Karachi were "*unconstitutional, without lawful authority and of no legal effect*" and that the pending cases should be transferred to regular courts. The Anti-Terrorism Act was also amended accordingly.

The idea of curbing the terrorist trends based on sectarian affiliations was appreciable in fact; the intelligentsia had also hailed the step of Nawaz Sharif but the related law was not perfect. The law should have given the 'powers of summary trials' to specified Session Judges of regular cadre to meet that program. The Supreme Court had finished those courts but could not give alternative remedy to end centuries old slow trials by normal courts.

However, this decision changed the path of history in Pakistan. In the past, whenever there has been a military government, whether they came up through coup or malicious transfer of power, the first step adopted by the ruler used to be the establishment of military courts and tribunals generally without cogent provisions of appeals before the higher courts. In 1997 the situation was different and disgusting.

This time there was no military ruler to constitute the military courts. It was the PML(N), which had assumed power after having two third majority public vote in general elections of 1997. *A hard luck for Pakistani people that a democratic Prime Minister had ordered for establishment of Military Courts to rule them.*

This decision from the Supreme Court of Pakistan blocked the way of Gen Musharraf to make an announcement of military courts when he took reigns of the country in hands on 12th October 1999. Nevertheless the General made his way through by assigning extra powers to the then existing *Ehtesab Bureau* through amendments in law and changing the name of that establishment to '*National Accountability Bureau*' *(NAB)*.

The NAB did more than the (would be) military courts for the dictator and brought most of the political heads to his knees through coercion, threats of arrest, harassments, illegal custodies without any charges and baseless references (the practice continued till March 2009 at least). Joint teams of ISI and NAB then negotiated with characterless and allegedly corrupt politicians to help the military ruler announcing so called political approvals and consents but the judiciary remained silent over the whole process of this '*militarized trading*'.

In October 2000, a report detailing hundreds of **killings in "***police***
encounters" since 1990 was presented to the then Punjab provincial
government for further investigation. Some 967 criminal suspects were
reportedly killed in various police encounters between February 1997
and October 1999 in Punjab. The people generally praised the step
which was an indirect slap on the judiciary's face; showing mistrust in
the judicial proceedings and ultimately letting off the hardened criminals
because of 'lack of evidence' defined under colonial rule of 19th century
but still prevailing in Pakistan.

During this period Shahbaz Sharif was the Chief Minister of Punjab
and the head of provincial government. All the extra-judicial killings
were carried out apparently with his prior approval. It was an explicit
demonstration of miss-trust over the judiciary and open defiance of
judicial institutions. As per Police Rules, in Pakistan's administrative
set up there are provisions that each death in police custody and each
death in police encounter would be independently enquired into
through a 'judicial enquiry' conducted under the supervision of District
Magistrate. Though some judicial enquiries were also held but there was
no significant complaint whatsoever.

Because those killings were ordered or closely supervised by the Chief
Executive of the province, Shahbaz Sharif, a political uproar was seen
but due to ineptness of judiciary, it was all tolerated. Every killing was
reported in media and the political stalwarts from the respective districts
had also raised their cries in this respect. The federal government did not
respond because firstly, the then Prime Minister Nawaz Sharif was the
real elder brother of the then CM. Secondly, the laws and judiciary both
were weak [and still going so].

Judiciary never came up with suggestions to make out or amend the
150 years old laws through calling a body of retired judges or jurists
or bars or through their Judicial Academy, or through guiding the
Law Ministry or suggesting governments to make commissions or
parliamentary boards during the last 63 years; so the people were denied
speedy justice.

'Honour killings' (the tradition of punishing women who allegedly bring
dishonour to their families) is another area where the educated populace
of Pakistan has been expecting vocal stand by the state and the higher
judiciary both. This black act is prohibited under Pakistani law; however,
the practice has ever been *de facto* tolerated by successive governments
and even today, we read and listen news of honour killing in media

almost daily. Southern Punjab, Balochistan and Rural Sindh are known for these extra-judicial killings.

In April 2001, Pakistan's upper house, the Senate, had rejected a bill condemning the growing incidence of honour killings. The Senate had not even considered discussing the issue of honour killings by blocking a draft resolution condemning violence against women. It is on record of the house that two tribal Chiefs, who were representing Baluchistan in the Senate, had expressed their views in a sentimental way urging that 'this act of *Honour killing is their tradition and it cannot be abandoned*". Even higher courts could not take any notice of this tradition effectively since 63 years.

Gen Musharraf's Government had also made various declarations of intent against honour killings but to the extent of slogans only. The political will to combat this practice had always been lacking but the judiciary have never taken a serious notice of any such news published in the newspapers except *suo moto* notices in one or two events but that too, without any cogent result to make mention of it.

BENAZIR BHUTTO's VISION OF JUSTICE:

After landing in Pakistan on 18th October 2007, Benazir Bhutto was much concerned about judiciary, judicial crisis, Lawyer's agitations and boycotts of the courts etc then going on in Pakistan since about a year. This had paralyzed day to day life of her country. Pakistan was notoriously known in the world for its in-effective judicial procedures, lengthy hearings, corrupt and ineligible judges and their remarkable judgments always suitable to the sitting governments or military dictators.

Even then Ms Bhutto, endured it wishing for better tomorrow; she herself had been victim of that inept judicial system which had pushed them into exile for about a decade.

In a meeting with Nawaz Sharif, which was convened in London in May 2006 and '*Meesaq e Jamhooriat*' was signed, Benazir Bhutto had discussed judicial atrocities with him at length and they promised with the nation that they would leave no stone unturned to make institutions free of political pressures especially the judiciary. Ms Bhutto personally was not happy with judiciary on various counts like:

- In 1979, Z A Bhutto was judicially murdered by Maulvi Mushtaq, the then Chief of Lahore High Court (he does not deserve to be called as

739

Mr Justice; a stigma on judiciary) subsequently endorsed by the then CJP Anwar ul Haq, another stooge in military hands.

- In 1985, Benazir's brother Shahnawaz Bhutto was murdered in Canes city of France through his Afghani wife named Rehana as a result of conspiracy hatched by Gen Ziaul Haq. Bhutto family could do nothing being not in power.

- In September 1996, Benazir's brother Murtaza Bhutto was allegedly targeted by 'agencies' in association with or more precisely on the instructions the then President Farooq Leghari, the trial court later closed the case declaring 'not proved'.

- During Nawaz Sharif's regime, Chief Justice Lahore High Court (namely Rashid Aziz) and judge Qayyum Malik used to take directions from Saif ur Rehman, the then chief of *Ehtesab* Bureau. The said judge had announced decision against both, Benazir Bhutto and Zardari, which was dictated to them on phone.

Their conversations were tape-recorded and ultimately they both had to resign from their seats in 2001 because those tapes were procured and got their scripts published in '*The Sunday Times*' of London.

- These courts and judges kept Zardari in jails for eight years. They could not dare to announce even a single judgment against him on the charges of corruption [*though the corruption details were available with media*]. They were not courageous enough to even decide matters of bail on merit.

Those were the judges who used to ask the Deputy Commissioners for latest instructions from 'high ups'. They did not grant him bail in two cases unless they were not sure that the police was waiting outside the court with a fresh case registered against him.

- The judiciary of Pakistan had also given decision against Bhuttos in '*Nusrat Bhutto vs Pakistan case*' endorsing Martial Law of 1977.

There were many more examples. In Pakistan, the laws have been applied in a different way for higher status people and the under privileged; still the same system prevails. Rich, influential, or politically connected people are never sent to jails and only poor populace are awarded punishments by Pakistani mighty courts. This practice is going on since half a century; one can dig out that:

- How many big politicians, industrialists and feudal lords have been taking loans from banks especially from Agricultural Development Bank of Pakistan, Industrial Development Bank of Pakistan, National bank of Pakistan and others and how many have paid them back.

How much bank loans were condoned by Gen Ziaul Haq in 1980s, Nawaz Sharif in 1997, Gen Musharraf in 1999 and then PM Shaukat Aziz during his tenure? The condoners and beneficiaries were culprits in the eyes of law but did the judiciary have ever taken the cases seriously.

> [*The Supreme Court had initiated a suo moto action in 2009 against the loan defaulters since 1971, with high trumpeting strictures but ...... proved to be an 'eye wash'; hats off to the 'independent judiciary'.*]

- How many women have been killed or buried alive in events of *KaroKari* and honour killings in Sindh, Baluchistan, and southern Punjab. The judiciary has seldom taken notice of any event (though most of them are published) because they are unable to punish the feudal lords and tribal chiefs behind the curtain.

- How many cases of narcotics trafficking have been caught in the last 60 years? Has any drug lord been punished; is any one in jail now or has been.

- How many *Qabza* cases have been reported during the last 60 years? How many *Qabza* group leaders have been punished so far? Is there any one behind bars?

- How many industrialists or business tycoons have been punished by the courts that have been found guilty of taking false claims of customs rebate, excise duty, or income tax during the last 60 years?

One would find that all cases reported under the above heads had been heard by our courts and might be punished at times but the jails are filled by those poor people who had been associated with these tycoons as their drivers, carriers, clerks, supervisory managers, *patwaris* and security guards. Is it justice which our judiciary delivers daily?

Benazir Bhutto, when came in power in ending 1988, did not initiate criminal proceedings against those who had conspired for hanging of his father, Mr Bhutto. When Gen Ziaul Haq snatched PPP's government in

July 1977 and developed a conspiracy to kill Mr Bhutto, it was the judiciary who came forward to accomplish his plans.

Anwarul Haq, the then CJP and A K Brohi advocate used to visit Gen Ziaul Haq daily to talk about day to day proceedings in the Court and in chatting moods. The decision of hanging Z A Bhutto was also taken in those informal meetings.

Later, Gen Ziaul Haq himself once told Gen Zamin Naqvi and Dr Qadeer Khan (of Kahoota Nuclear Plant) that Anwarul Haq and Brohi used to visit him daily to assure that:

'*The job (of hanging Bhutto) would be done according to your wishes and the courts would not give decisions against your will*".

Justice Naseem Hasan Shah, former Chief Justice of the Supreme Court, himself had admitted on Pakistan TV in 1996 that there was a tremendous pressure on the judges to sign death penalty for Z A Bhutto though he was not guilty of such major punishment.

The same inept and hopeless attitude was shown by our judiciary when they approved the PCO of Gen Musharraf in 2000 and confirmed that the military dictator had done the right. Some of the judges of that bench were the same as sitting in the Supreme Court today with the change that then its Chief was Irshad Hasan Khan.

It was a planned and negotiated deal; Justice Irshad Hasan Khan had announced that decision only to get a slot as Chief Election Commissioner of Pakistan which he got immediately after his retirement. *In Pakistan, the superior judiciary has been believing in bargains and negotiations; keep it noted, though never for financial gains.*

CIVIL SOCIETY FOR IND JUDICIARY:

Often questions are asked about the 'emergence of 'Civil Society'; how 'Lawyers Movement' started in 2007; how scheme of 'Independent judiciary' was developed in contemporary history of Pakistan.

Taking light from *Harvard Law Review [2010] Vol 123, Page 1712-18*; one can recall that as defunct CJ Iftikhar Chaudhry's case continued [in 2007] before the Supreme Judicial Council [SJC], J Chaudhry developed an idea of giving a call for judicial independence to the Pakistani people.

He assembled a defence team of Pakistan's well-regarded attorneys, and embarked on a country tour speaking before local bar associations. In his speeches, J Chaudhry mostly discussed the reimbursement and benefits of judicial independence.

J Chaudhry's motorcade soon attracted large crowds, and inspired them often to the level of revolt. The lawyers eventually began accepting the support of other civil society groups. For example, lawyers in Lahore started meeting every week at the Lahore High Court with representatives from professional trade bodies and political parties and labour unions to plan protest activities. One could recall the eagerness of such groups to participate saying: *'Why didn't you call us sooner?'*

Thus the groups of doctors, engineers, professors, religious scholars, traders, and political party workers were showing up in force to support the lawyers at their weekly rallies. In addition, urban professional and student groups formed their own factions but towards a common goal.

One Ghazala Minallah explained how a protest group known simply as **"Civil Society"** grew out of a letter to a newspaper editor she sent shortly after the sacking of the Chief Justice:

'In response to that letter I got quite a few emails. . . . my dentist in Islamabad . . . gave me a phone call, "Okay great that you wrote this letter. . . . Are we just going to sit at home and watch what happens next on the news?" . . . We mutually agreed that we'd send out SMS messages to all our contacts, and tell them to forward it to everyone else, saying, "Let's meet in front of the Supreme Court at a fixed time."

That was the beginning. It was amazing turnout on that first day.'

During those early months of the lawyers' movement, J Chaudhry convinced many Pakistanis that at least one prominent jurist was willing, if not yet able, to serve as a watchdog against governmental abuses. When Justice Ramday's SC bench quashed the reference against J Chaudhry and reinstated him as Chief Justice on **20th July 2007**, the legal community, and much of the public, rejoiced.

On **3rd November 2007**, the SC was on the verge of ruling [*it was a general perception then; based on media discussions*] on the validity of Gen Musharraf's re-election as President when he suspended the constitution and declared emergency. 63 out of 95 judges of higher judiciary were sent home; many of them had refused to take new oath themselves.

After the imposition of emergency rule, the lawyers began to cooperate more directly with opposition parties. Protests became much larger and more diverse as a result. In addition, new protest groups emerged and came to include not only secular urban elites, but also some poorer and more religious Pakistanis. According to Minallah, "*It was a very interesting mixture. It was from every class. . . . Even people from the religious political parties . . . would be [protesting] with us outside the Supreme Court.*" Gen Musharraf had to end emergency rule in December 2007 under intense international pressure and continued protests.

Jumping to the days after general elections of 2008, taking over of PPP, Gen Musharraf's exit and taking over of President Zardari; J Chaudhry's team was not yet reinstated despite numerous promises and back-outs. Lawyers protests moved by and by on slow pace though continued through the fall and winter of 2008; the movement appeared to lose its momentum or it was being reported so.

Protests began to swell once again in early 2009, only after Zardari attempted to sideline Nawaz Sharif of PML(N) by declaring Governor Rule in Punjab. Shortly thereafter, the (CJ Dogar's) Supreme Court issued a ruling declaring Sharifs ineligible to run for office. In response, the lawyers planned a massive protest in cooperation with PML(N) and a number of opposition parties, promising to stage a sit-in in the capital Islamabad, until J Chaudhry and his team was restored.

With the Pakistani government seemingly on the verge of collapse, a last-minute flurry of negotiations led Zardari, to reinstate the deposed judges, including J Chaudhry, on 16th March 2009.

[*Complete details are given elsewhere in this Volume-III*]

So, in Pakistan it is there, the concept of **CIVIL SICIETY & INDEPENDENT** Judiciary originated from.

JUSTICE CHAUDHRY IN SADDLES AGAIN:

It was, no doubt, another page of our judicial history. Lawyer's movement of 2007-08 was going on, though its dimensions had apparently been shrugged. Though some lawyers had departed themselves from the movement but there hearts remained with J Chaudhry, the deposed judge. President Zardari was not inclined to reinstate Justice Chaudhry because he had certain reservations.

On 9th March 2007, the Chief justice Chaudhry had retaliated [*because the fire was going to turn his own home*] when Gen Musharraf had asked him to resign. Before that day he was as much a part of Pakistan's routine sub-survient judiciary as the others were, for example;

- Justice Iftikhar M Chaudhry was one of those judges who took oath on PCO in January 2000 allegedly betraying his Chief Justice Saeeduz Zaman Siddiqui and others.

- J Chaudhry was also one of those who did not consider Mr Zardari's bail petitions for years because he was an 'upright' judge in Gen Musharraf's books.

- On 11th February 2001, former Prime Minister Gillani was imprisoned in Adiala Jail by a military court instituted under Gen Musharraf on charges of corruption; released on 7th October 2006. The SC could have either declared the case false or had barred Mr Gilani to contest next elections of 2008. The CJP of the SC kept silent.

  [*However, on 3rd August 2007, a three-member bench of the Supreme Court under CJ Iftikhar Chaudhry granted bail to Javed Hashmi after serving approximately three and a half years in prison. Javed Hashmi was given 23 years imprisonment in a trial held in Adiala Jail Rawalpindi on charges of 'mutiny'*]

- J Chaudhry was the judge who had thrown out petition from a citizen challenging the house arrest of Dr Abdul Qadeer Khan Scientist. He should have taken *suo-moto* action on this gross misconduct on the part of the Chief Executive or the government but ignored being in parcel with the military government.

- J Chaudhry was on the apex court strength when three of the politicians named Neelofar Bakhtiar, Aftab Sherpao and Faisal Saleh Hayat, being equal culprits like so many others in *Ehtesab* files, were picked and raised to the level of federal ministers whereas others were made to lead miserable lives in jails.

Under the LFO Gen Musharraf announced amendments to the constitution which restored executive powers to the President, including Art 58(2)(b), the right to dismiss the National Assembly, appoint Governors and Service Chiefs and created a National Security Council (NSC).

After the **general elections of 10th October 2002**, PML(Q) and the MMA, an alliance of religious parties, emerged as the prime benefactors. In December 2003, the two parties in the Parliament, in association with certain independent members, gathered the two-third majority required to pass the 17th Constitutional Amendment which had validated almost all the previous unconstitutional military actions including the revival of Art 58(2)(b), the presidential power to dismiss the parliament.

Gen Musharraf later garnered a simple majority to pass the 'President to Hold Another Office Act 2004' (PHAA), vehemently denying the constitutional provisions in allowing him to retain the portfolio of the Army Chief in addition to the office of the President.

- **On 13th April 2005** [as has been mentioned earlier], in the *Pakistan Lawyers Forum* case, again a five member bench of the Supreme Court of which *Justice Iftikhar M Chaudhry was a member*, had validated both the 17th Amendment and the PHAA, based on an extension of the doctrine of state necessity.

In legitimizing the powers of the military and executive over the Parliament, this case further strengthened the popular perception of the subservience of the Supreme Court to the military regime.

However, luck favoured Justice Iftikhar Chaudhry because PPP's Aitzaz Hassan and Nawaz Sharif suddenly jumped forward to raise him up [*and later Sharifs got him en-cashed, too*]. Contrarily how Nawaz Sharif could forget that the same courts of Pakistan had announced for him fourteen years jail twice in plane-hijacking case. How Nawaz Sharif could turn a blind eye to the fact that his PML(N)'s Acting President, Javaid Hashmi was sent to jail for 23 years on a false case by the same judicial system.

Leaving it aside, one should admire Nawaz Sharif's political wisdom that he picked a slogan of reinstating Justice Chaudhry and his team back to 3rd November 2007's position. The PPP also used this issue as catch-phrase but either the PPP went a bit late or their voice remained at low pitch. Meetings of Zardari with Nawaz Sharif at Murree and Dubai were OK but PML(N)'s explicit commitment to the people, that the judges would be reinstated, provided an edge to the PML(N) and PPP lost the chance and thus the whole game.

PPP's advisors [*allegeaiy Farooq Naek and Rehman Malik, as per media claims*] betrayed the PPP and the strategy coined by them in this issue had not succeeded to get desired results. Mr Naek had approached and negotiated with certain judges of Justice Chaudhry's team, made them to join again as fresh entrants in judiciary but this technique had not demonstrated positive achievements because:

- Firstly Farooq Naek's invitation and some judge's acceptance would have proved that those judges were totally characterless, bland, and insipid. They were not having any commitment for the cause of justice and any ruler could dictate them any decision; their conscious was rotten, dead, or nearly dead.

- Secondly they would have been known as 'ready to work as judges but as an uninspiring lot and without courage'. They would not be loyal even to Mr Zardari or PM Gilani's government rather they would be at a look out to harm PPP and Mr Zardari's colleagues whenever a chance cropped up.

- Thirdly, how could they agree to Naek's proposal because they were like snakes whose tails were crushed by PPP's promises during the last nine months [till then]. They were, in fact, ready to attack and bite PPP as they were themselves hurt.

- Fourthly PML(N) had withdrawn their ministers from the cabinet in mid 2008. They were looking for a chance to attack politically on Mr Zardari and the PPP. Much weak that judiciary was, so there were all possibilities that those newly re-recruited judges would be exploited by the PML(N).

In fact, the PPP were going to create a circle of enemies in the judiciary in the form of those 'already disturbed' judges.

Pakistani people keep a short memory. They forget that once; in November 1997, the Supreme Court was raided and ransacked by a crowd loaded on thirty buses, sent from Lahore, carrying explicit instructions from the PML(N) leaders.

What the apex court did then. Case was heard; MsNA were identified; videos were displayed as evidence; news reporters were extensively examined in the court; lengthy hearings held and then the case was suddenly closed by Jusice Nasir Aslam Zahid's bench on some pretext because the sitting MsNA were on the front. However, police officers like

IGP, SSP and DSP were bullied enough and punished instead; *Pak-Judiciary Zindabad.*

Moreover, in the same apex court, in October 2007, serving police officers, mostly in uniform, were called and confronted with contempt of court charges, and were subsequently punished up to one month's jail though they all had tendered unconditional apology before the court.

Why so because the Chief Justice Iftikhar Chaudhry himself was allegedly manhandled on 9th March 2007; *bechari* police. The court had no waters to call the persons of authority who had ordered the police to manhandle, because they were khakis, so the Supreme Court won the award of bravery by punishing IGP, SSP and DSP of Islamabad Police. This was the way our judiciary used to settle their ego scores.

The same attitude was shown by the Supreme Court in Mehran Bank case where a retired Army Chief Mirza Aslam Beg had appeared in the said Court, openly got recorded his statement that he had ordered to snatch 140 million rupees from Mr Younus Habib, President of Mehran Bank, to be used by ISI as a secret fund in 1990. Gen Beg had also confessed that the money was used in elections to obstruct the possible win of PPP.

Gen Beg had given statement that their strategy was successful and consequently PML(N) had manoeuvred to win because it was then a pro-establishment political party.

Did Mr Beg or anyone else got punishment then. No; because Waseem Sajjad was immediately sent to the Supreme Court to dictate decision. The then sitting bench did sign it only.

In 2012, the SC had [*in Asghar Khan Case*] given judgment against Gen Beg on the same pretext; then was the Executive's turn to show their muscles, but nothing happened as usual.

This is Pakistani justice and these are our courts but it has a long history too, to recall:

- On 21st March 1955, Chief Justice Muhammad Munir of the Federal Court (the present Supreme Court of Pakistan) legalized the dissolution of the 1st Constituent Assembly. Only Justice A R Cornelius (a non-Muslim) of the Federal Court dissented.

- Once again, on 6-7ᵗʰ October 1958, the same Chief Justice called Iskander Mirza's dissolution of the 2nd Constituent Assembly & abrogation of 1956's Constitution, a 'legalized illegality'.

- On 7ᵗʰ & 20ᵗʰ April 1972, The Supreme Court of Pakistan declared Yahya Khan's martial law to be illegal but the bench was so 'courageous' that the decision was announced four months after the departure of that army ruler.

- On 22ⁿᵈ September 1977, Yaqub Ali Khan, the then Chief Justice of Pakistan, was forced to retire because he had dared to accept Begum Nusrat Bhutto's petition (against Gen Zia's illegal take over and arrest of Z A Bhutto) for hearing just three days earlier i.e on 19ᵗʰ September 1977.

Next day Anwar-ul-Haq, an officer of Administrative Cadre, a person who also lacked adequate judicial training, was appointed as the Chief Justice of Pakistan. So on 10ᵗʰ November 1977, the Supreme Court unanimously validated imposition of martial law over the country relying upon the 'doctrine of necessity' under that able Chief justice.

- On 5ᵗʰ November 1996, President Farooq Legahri dissolved National Assembly and dismissed PPP's government. When challenged this dissolution order, the Supreme Court initially returned Benazir Bhutto's petition with flimsy and insubstantial objections but finally admitted.

[See details of Mr Leghari's orders at the end of this chapter]

On 29ᵗʰ January 1997, the Supreme Court upheld Farooq Leghari's order dissolving the National Assembly and dismissing PPP's claims. These were the same judges who used to lick Mr Zardari's feet just three months earlier.

- On 3ʳᵈ November 2007, Gen Musharraf announced 'emergency' and played the same old trick of PCO oaths for High Court and Supreme Court judges. The judges were not able to unite themselves to say NO to an unconstitutional order. Out of 94 judges, 60 judges declined to take oath under that PCO, rest of the 34 survived and continued as such.

- On 21st November 2007, Gen Musharraf did numerous changes in the constitution issuing an executive order only. On the very next day (22ⁿᵈ November 2007), the new Supreme Court rejected a petition in which Gen Musharraf's competency to contest president's election was challenged. Next dat again (23rd November 2007), that puppet SC validated all the orders issued under the hand of Gen Musharraf including *Emergency.*

- **On 14th December 2007,** Gen Musharraf issued another executive order by virtue of which six more amendments in the constitution were done; the Supreme Court remained mum and silent.

- **On 14th February 2008,** the Supreme Court issued about 100 pages detailed decision of November's various announced short judgments.

One Tikka M Iqbal deposited a review petition on the same day. In a swift reaction, it was accepted and on the same day a 13 member's bench was constituted to deal with this review petition. Same day notices to the parties were issued to appear next day. It was purposefully done to strengthen the earlier decision taken in that context.

- **On 15th November 2008,** the 13 member bench of the Supreme Court announced to reject the review petition and upheld the validation of Gen Musharraf's executive orders for amendments in the constitution.

Never mind; the same judiciary ultimately held the flags of honesty and consciousness; slaughtered the 'wrong doer' and PCOed judges forgetting that once they were also amongst the same team, rather gone through alike privileged moments twice.

In the last week of July 2009, one Pakistani TV anchorperson Ms Aysha Tammy Haq was accusing Gen Musharraf in her program and then she suddenly asked that: *'Is there any country in the world where 60 judges are dismissed overnight* [referring to 3rd November 2007's Emergency probably]?' Next day one Shams Z Abbas sent an interesting questionnaire for her through a Dubai based internet media. Let us share some of the questions.

- "Is there any other country in the world where you don't need to pay lawyers when the Judges are available to the highest bidder?

- Is there any other country in the world where a reference is filed against a Chief Justice [*CJP Iftikhar Chaudhry's turmoil of 2007 referred*] accusing him of serious allegations, of getting undue personal favours for his son, but his fellow judges decide not to hear the reference to protect him?

- Is there any country in the world where a "Saeeduzzaman Siddiqi bench" is constituted to dismiss a sitting honorable Chief Justice namely Sajjad Ali Shah against whom there was no reference, simply because the prime minister [*Nawaz Sharif*] of the day wanted the judges to wage a 'Judges vs. Judges' battle?

- Is there any country in the world where a Supreme Court is physically attacked [*episode of 28th November 1997 is referred*] and the judges seek help from the Army which is denied [*Gen Jehangir Karamat's reply is referred*]?

- Is there any country in the world where the same leader becomes the torch bearer of a movement to restore a Chief Justice against whom office he had earlier ordered to attack the Supreme Court [*16th March 2009's Long March is referred*].

- Is there any country in the World where Maulana Aziz and Sufi Mohammad arrested by the law enforcing agencies are released by the judiciary to avoid attacks on its judges?

- Is there any country in the world where actions of Red Mosque operatives challenging the writ of the State are condoned without any answers to law & justice; where were the courts?

- Is there any country in the world where the people are so disgusted with their Judiciary that they want Islamic Sharia, as in Swat, which was then approved overnight by the Parliament?

- Is there any country in the world where the judiciary passes judgment for a serving army General to contest elections for presidency [*SC's shameful judgment of 28th September 2007 is referred*]?

- Is there any country in the world where a National Reconciliation Ordinance (NRO) is perforce issued because the NAB & judiciary could not decide the cases even in ten years?

I dedicate this article to the Pakistani middle and lower classes, the prisoners and litigants whose cases would never be decided in their lifetime; thanks to these judges and lawyers. *(Shams Z. Abbass through www.Ahmedqureshi.com)*"

May God The Almighty, give our judiciary enough strength to avoid such pinching [but factual] questions from ordinary citizens.

PRESIDENT LEGHARI's ORDER [1996]:

Referring to a thought provoking column of [late] Ardeshir Cowasjee appeared in **Dawn of 8th June 2001 and** a subsequent discussion in the same columns **dated 14th June 2001**, it was suggested that:

> *"The Supreme Court to examine former President Farooq Leghari [now he is also 'late'] under oath and finally come to conclusion as to the part played in the whole sordid episode [of killing of Mir Murtaza Bhutto] by various functionaries of the government including the Judges of the Supreme Court and President Rafiq Tarar....... the above mentioned were responsible for masterminding, engineering and storming the Supreme Court."*

In addition to that the intelligentsia also wanted Mr Farooq Leghari to be examined under section 540 of CrPC, by the trial court dealing with Murtaza Bhutto's murder case. In a seminar of Helpline dated 19th March instant, Mr Leghari had divulged the following details:

a) That Asif Ali Zardari told Farooq Leghari in the presence of Benazir Bhutto that the conflict between MMB and AAZ had reached such heights that only one of them would survive.

b) That Mr Leghari later advised Benazir Bhutto to resolve this conflict in her family, as she could not afford any further divide.

c) That the people who fired at MMB had been chosen by AAZ. Every child in Sindh knows who killed Murtaza Bhutto.

Here is the charge sheet issued (and read over to the nation) by the President Leghari against the then Prime Minister Benazir Bhutto **on 5th November 1996,** while dismissing her elected government. Amongst the other charges, the President also mentioned about killing of Murtaza Bhutto and the government's alleged lethargic attitude towards judiciary related matters. He said;

> *".........during the last three years thousands of persons in Karachi and other parts of Pakistan have been deprived of their right to life in violation of Article 9 of the Constitution.*
>
> *........ On 20th September 1996, Mir Murtaza Bhutto, PM's brother, was killed at Karachi along with seven of his companions including the brother in law of a former Prime Minister, ostensibly in an encounter*

with the Karachi Police. The Prime Minister and her Government claimed that Mir Murtaza Bhutto has been murdered as a part of a conspiracy.

Within days of Mir Murtaza Bhutto's death the Prime Minister appeared on television insinuating that the Presidency and other agencies of State were involved in this conspiracy. These malicious insinuations, which were repeated on different occasions, were made without any factual basis whatsoever.

A situation has thus arisen in which justice, which is a fundamental requirement of our Islamic Society, cannot be ensured because ....

On 20th March 1996 the Supreme Court of Pakistan delivered its judgment [in the Judges Case]; the Prime Minister ridiculed this judgment in a speech before the National Assembly which was shown more than once on nation-wide television.

The implementation of the judgment was resisted and deliberately delayed in violation of the Constitutional mandate ......

The directions of the Supreme Court with regard to regularization and removal of judges of the High Courts were finally implemented on 30th September 1996, with a deliberate delay of six months and ten days and only after the President informed the PM that if advice was not submitted in accordance with the Judgment by end September 1996 then the President would himself proceed further in this matter to fulfill the constitutional requirement.

The Government has, in this manner, not only violated Article 190 of the Constitution but also sought to undermine the independence of the judiciary guaranteed by Article 2A of the Constitution read with the Objectives Resolution.

The sustained assault on the judicial organ of State has continued under the garb of a Bill moved in Parliament for prevention of corrupt practices without informing the President as required under Article 46(C) of the Constitution.

The Bill proposes, interalia that on a motion moved by 15 percent of the total membership of the National Assembly, that is any 32 members, a judge of the Supreme Court or High Court can be sent on forced leave. Thereafter, if on reference made by the proposed special committee, the Special Prosecutor appointed by such Committee, forms the opinion that the judge is prima facie guilty of criminal misconduct, the special committee is to refer this opinion to the National Assembly which can, by passing a vote of no confidence, remove the judge from office.

The decision of the Cabinet is evidently an attempt to destroy the independence of the judiciary guaranteed by Article 2A of the Constitution and the Objectives Resolution.

Further, as the Government does not have a two-thirds majority in Parliament and as the opposition parties have openly and vehemently opposed the Bill approved by the Cabinet, the Government's persistence with the Bill is designed not only to embarrass and humiliate the superior judiciary but also to frustrate and set at naught all efforts made to combat corruption.

And; whereas the judiciary has still not been fully separated from the executive in violation of the provisions of Article 175(C) of the Constitution of Pakistan.

And, whereas the PM and her Government have deliberately violated, on a massive scale the fundamental right of privacy guaranteed by Article 14 of the Constitution through illegal phone- tapping and eaves-dropping techniques. The phones tapped and the conversations monitored in this unconstitutional manner include the phones and conversations of judges of the superior courts, leaders of political parties and high-ranking military and civil officers."

Then, in exercise of my powers under Article 58(2)(b) of the Constitution, Farooq Ahmad Khan Leghari, President of the Islamic Republic of Pakistan, dissolved the National Assembly. The Prime Minister Benazir Bhutto and her Cabinet were debarred to hold their offices.

Under the provisions of Article 48(5) of the Constitution he announced 3rd February 1997 as the date for next general elections.

Scenario 58

PAK – ARMY ON 'WAR ON TERROR' - I:

In the wake of 9/11 War on Terror, **Dr Paul Craig Roberts** [an Assistant Secretary of the US Treasury for Economic Policy and Associate Editor of the Wall Street Journal & a well known columnist for Business Week] had once written in his essay *'Taliban the Wrong Target' published on 13th November 2001* that:

> 'The war on terrorism has lost its focus. It has become a military campaign against the Taliban. The Taliban are not terrorists. Defeating them will have very little effect on terrorism.
>
> The Taliban are a group of Afghans focused on their own country, not on the West. We are [otherwise] Israel's ally and are perceived as the power behind a corrupt Saudi royal family.
>
> **If the U.S. becomes bogged down in an Afghan civil war between the Taliban and the Northern Alliance, we will achieve our own demoralization and embolden terrorists unimpaired by our efforts.'**

Dr Paul had further elaborated that by using the authority of Islam to create a national unity in place of tribal consciousness, the Taliban were engaged in what the Council of Foreign Relations, the State Department, and the World Bank called "nation building." *The Taliban did not participate in the attacks on the World Trade Centre and the Pentagon.* The anthrax letters were postmarked in the US not in Afghanistan.

Contrarily, most Americans believed that Muslim terrorists were not able to harm the US unless American Immigration Policy barred the Muslims from entering the US; it could have done better to protect the Americans than bombing the Taliban. In an arena of Nine-Eleven, President Bush had said that *'we [the Americans] are at war with terrorists, not with Islam.'* The fact, however, remained that about 25% of Muslims then found them at war with the US.

AN ERA OF NEW WORLD ORDER:

The American think-tanks and intelligentsia had warned the US ruling elite then quite well in time [*referring to the above paragraphs written in*

November 2001, a few days after President Bush had decided to wage WOT in the aftermath of Nine-Eleven episode] that '**America should not land on Afghan soils**'; but it could not desist. Let us travel a little back.

A general acuity prevails that when the Soviets attacked or entered in Afghanistan (25th December 1979), the Americans wanted to resist them because they did not want the Soviet presence in this South Asian region. It is commonly perceived that the Americans had used Gen Ziaul Haq, the then military ruler of Pakistan, to fight a proxy war on their behalf to expel the Russians from the Afghan soil. The record points out that it was not the whole truth.

The British libraries, Home Office, Foreign Desks and War Colleges keep the special notes on Afghan War but the general public holds a very basic sketch of Taliban on Afghan soils which the BBC had written for them. The British diplomatic briefs, perhaps based on BBC's unit of intelligence, contain that:

> *"During the recent years, more precisely in post 9/11 era, the re-emergence of the Taliban movement in Afghanistan posed a major threat to its own government; and also destabilised Pakistan through a series of bomb attacks and suicide killings. After withdrawal of Soviet troops from Afghanistan the Taliban emerged in the early 1990s in northern Pakistan which was predominantly a Pashtun movement; came to prominence in Afghanistan in the autumn of 1994.*
>
> *It is commonly believed that the Taliban first appeared in religious seminaries; mostly paid from Saudi Arabia to restore peace and enforce the Sharia once in power. In both countries they were to introduce Islamic punishments; men were required to grow beards and women had to wear the all-covering burka; a similar contempt for music and disapproved of grown up girls from going to school.*
>
> *Fact remains that many Afghans who initially joined the Taliban movement were educated in madrassas (religious schools) in Pakistan. Pakistan was also one of only three countries [along with Saudi Arabia and the United Arab Emirates (UAE)] which had recognised the Taliban [government] when they were in power in Afghanistan from the mid-1990s until 2001.*
>
> *The world knew the Taliban in Afghanistan more only after 9/11 episode in 2001 which were accused of providing a sanctuary to Osama Bin Laden (OBL) and the al-Qaeda movement. Soon after, the*

Taliban were driven from power in Afghanistan by a US-led coalition, although their leaders Mullah Omar and Osama remained at large. Later, the Taliban emerged in Pakistan as far stronger factions and groups.

The main Pakistani faction, known as Tehreek e Taliban Pakistan (TTP) was formed by Baitullah Mehsud (then) presently led by Hakimullah Mehsud. The Taliban in Afghanistan are still believed to be led by Mullah Omar and their early popularity was largely due to their success in stamping out corruption, curbing lawlessness and making the roads and the areas under their control safe for commerce to flourish. By 1998, they were in control of almost 90% of Afghanistan.

The Taliban were accused of various human rights and cultural abuses; in 2001, they went ahead with destruction of the famous Bamiyan Buddha statues in central Afghanistan.

On 7th October 2001, a US-led military coalition invaded Afghanistan and within two months the Taliban regime had collapsed. Mullah Omar and his comrades had evaded capture despite one of the largest manhunts in the world. Since then they have re-grouped in both Pakistan and Afghanistan, but are now under pressure in both countries, from the Pakistani army and NATO respectively."

It remained a general discernment all over Pakistan and in both military and civil societies that Gen Musharraf had taken 'personal' decision to join hands with Americans in the aftermath of 9/11 episode. However, in the '*Capital Talk*' program of **GEO TV *dated 7th December 2009*,** Gen Shahid loudly told the viewers that:

'*The US invasion of Afghanistan and our involvement in this war were very difficult events to handle. The U-turn after 9/11 was a complex and historic decision. There were great reservations within the Army with what we had to do.*

There was no formal agreement undertaken [after 9/11 event] by the Army for operations in Fata. If there was any such agreement at the government level, the GHQ was not aware of it. When decisions were made at the government level, departments concerned, including the Army, were informed of their part in the process.

All that transpired between Washington and Islamabad and the war on terror was not shared with the Army. This does not imply that the

757

*Army as an institution was kept in the dark. Regular corps
commanders' conferences were held in which the president talked at
length on these important issues'*

However, the detailed picture can be found elsewhere, including the
following paragraphs.

ANOTHER PICTURE OF THE PAST:

Referring to an Urdu column [written by Rauf Klasra] appeared in the
daily 'Jang' of 7th December 2009, one can understand the whole
philosophy of Afghan War; thus the sinking of a nation and country
named Pakistan in the sand-grave of greed and curse.

The present youth would not be able to know about those black
moments of early 1980s when a few Generals of Pakistan Army held a
mutual table talk and decided to conquer Afghanistan on various
pretexts like:

- *We want to save our Afghani Muslim Brothers from the Russia's
  attack.*

- *If Russia reached hot waters of the Arabian Sea, Pakistan would be
  their next target.*

- *Russia wants to make Kabul as their second capital; we should resist.*

- *The various Islamic countries around, especially the Saudi Arabia,
  would send their men [later called Taliban] to fight here in the name
  of jehad.*

- *Pakistan would manage those foreigners with American funds and
  ammunition.*

- *If America would be happy, we would get more financial aids from
  them under other heads.*

- *Afghanistan's Islamic rule would be copied and implemented in
  Pakistan, taking them as a role model.*

Tens of other similar reasons were added in the above agenda to make
the Pakistani nation fool through planned media campaigns. Pakistan
won that war in 1988, Russians preferred to quit, but left the two

countries in ruins making them a laughing stock for the whole world; and for the historians, too.

Those army Generals named Ziaul Haq, Akhtar Abdul Rehman and some others could not conceive that if they were going to spread bullets and gunpowder in their neighbouring country, the same kind of stuff would also be seen in their own regions of Pakistan. Later the poor people of Pakistan had to go through the same burning fires along with two more versatile nuisances; Kalashnikov culture and drugs in abundance. Pakistan's present youth has taken birth amidst the whiffs of the same two menaces of killing powders; they have never breathed the clean air as available to the rest of the world.

That group of few Army Generals had decided at their own, purportedly on behalf of the nation, that only that ruler would occupy the presidency in Kabul to whom they give the clearance chit, to whom they would allow to pass through the green signal; how innocent [*do not say them fools*] they were. They were wise enough to handle the bags full of American dollars which were continuously pouring in their villas in the name of 'war money'. Their few families were happy but they had pushed their *jawans* and the next generations into the hell of miseries, gloom, and depression amidst showers of blood and arson.

The lower hierarchy of army command knew that their Generals were keeping those bags of US dollars at their homes but they were assured that the same '*are to be sent at Pak-Afghan borders and inside Afghanistan because there are no banks to keep that foreign currency*'; those dollars were not to be sent away on borders and were never sent.

It was not a story of one General; every top General and his lower command got their shares but only those who had become part of that loot-game; the cruel philosophy in fact. They were wise enough to keep those looted bags for their own families and kinship not for the dying *jawans* or lower ranks of their own flanks.

The history would not be able to name even a single General or his brother or son who had died in Afghanistan in that 'holy war'; it was a dying field for *jawans* and officers belonging to poor and 'tail-less' families whose dependents were never shown those dollars. They were only given titles of '*shaheed*' [martyrs] dying for Islam & Pakistan. Those golden Generals had sent their sons and brothers to America and Europe from where they returned to become either industrialists or ministers nothing less; people hear them daily in press & the media.

The whole Pakistani nation has continuously been betrayed, till today even, with a brain-washing slogan that '*Pakistan's survival depends upon the Islamic rule in Kabul*'; that too sponsored by the Pakistan's few Generals not all. Mostly it was argued that '*Islamic rule in Afghanistan, with Pakistan's choice is vital to wrestle with India successfully*'. What a logic; no other country could buy Pakistan's that ideology, putting the western border on arson to control the eastern borders, but the poor nation was made to believe it; hats off to Pakistan's media also.

During the next decade, another army General Pervaiz Musharraf joined the same orchestra but with different notes in mind. This time the team joined America in the name of War on Terror [WoT] as there were no Russians around; but the destiny was the same.

The same game rules were played that Pak army *jawans* and low ranking officers should die there. $10.67 billions were begged and bagged from October 2001 till ending 2007 by some top Generals including Gen Musharraf. However, nation remained puzzled as before about the benefits they got out of those gimmicks; either termed Islamic war or WOT.

Ponder about that 'terror' and those terrorists. When Pak-Army wanted to tackle them in FATA or Swat or Balochistan, the Generals were dictated from Washington to hold on; those were not terrorists but '*our Afghan associates or the Taliban*'. When the same groups of terrorists attacked the Pakistani mosques killing dozens of innocent people, did bomb blasts in RA Bazars, in Charsadda, Hangu & Kohat; then the media was briefed that India or America or Afghan National Army had been sponsoring some miscreants. Height of agony it was.

Who was there to think for Pakistan being nationalist? Each times the compromises and conspiracy theories. Parliament remained impotent like ever, they never felt the necessity of making out effective laws. The judiciary always took refuge behind the barriers of '*insufficient admissible evidence*'; both were cowards in fact; the poor people suffered and continued to suffer since two decades at least.

The Pakistan's mighty Generals, on both occasions, preferred to conquer Kabul instead of marching towards Srinagar in Indian Occupied Kashmir.

In a live TV program, M Malick, editor '*the News*' once made a nice analysis on the situation:

'The irony of fate of this poor nation is that the three Generals who should have been behind the bars over the said Kabul Conquering Quest, are welcome on Pakistan's TV live programs as "defence experts". No one asks them about their blunders. Pakistan is going mad for playing role in Afghan-Peace negotiations but is unable to control terrorism within the country.

We still do not have good scanners, planning it for the last two years. Our intelligence agencies are zero; billions of funds are there but they don't have name of any terrorist on their lists. Our GHQ and air bases are attacked by them. We are unable to make the GHQ safe but are going to offer for Kabul's security – what a mockery of ourselves.'

Daily Jang's columnist, Rauf Klasra visited Bangladesh in early 2009. In those days there were some frictions, slogans and voices in one area claimed by some 'religious militants'. Klasra asked his host columnist that if that trend would be going to spread all over the country and how much time it would take. The Bangla columnist smiled and said;

'It will never make good news for you; it is not going anywhere. Soon it will die down; will be controlled by the people and police because our Bangla army do not support these extremists; no governmental policy or opposition party favours them.'

Klasra opined that since ten months we had never heard any *'Islamic extremist activity'* from the Bangladesh. However, whenever the innocent children are killed in Pakistani mosques, we discuss that:

'We are unable to take care of Rawalpindi Cantt area here; how we'll fulfil the commitment of controlling Kabul, if at all we are offered. Let us shun such wishful thinking; let us be realistic; let us think Pakistan first.'

ONE GENERALS' WISH-PAKISTAN RUINED:

It was Gen Ziaul Haq who was bent upon to fight the Soviets on the plea that:

'Pakistan would not tolerate presence of the white bear in its neighbourhood. The Soviets should not get an access to the hot waters of Arabian Sea through puppet 'un-Islamic' government in Afghanistan.'

761

The fact remained that all the army regimes in Pakistan since 1979 took the Afghan cause as their premier responsibility and extended all material, regimental and moral helps, openly and covertly, with aid from the foreign world and without, to their Afghan counterparts.

What the poor Pakistani nation got out of this long and tiresome operation; A gift in the shape of officially recorded three million *Afghan Muhajreen (un-officially ten million), devastated economy, gun culture, terrorism spread at their door steps, suicide bombers and second spill of Afghan War in which Pakistan lost thousands of their security officials since 2001.*

The Pakistan had spoiled all their business, industry and social set up as well as the international support by allowing a large influx of Afghan refugees into Pakistan. All of them and their generations have their 'SHANAKHTI CARDS' (National Identification Cards of Pakistan), Pakistani Passports, property ownership documents and substantial businesses in all major towns of the country. There lies 2100 miles unmanned border and a belt of Tribal Area in between the two countries which though exists geographically in Pakistan but no Pakistani law is applicable there by constitution.

On the event of Nine Eleven, Gen Musharraf decided to stand by America to expel Taliban from the government and their native soil but some Pakistani Generals only routinely denied that their army had any sympathy for the Taliban. In early September of 2003, US soldiers suddenly blamed, while chasing Taliban fighters in southern Afghanistan, that they had nabbed three regular Pakistani army officers.

First time the question appeared that whether Pakistan was on the side of US or of Taliban backed arrogant forces. Gen Musharraf kept mum. Pakistan was fingered at by al-Qaeda's top planner, Khalid Sheikh Mohammed, no body else. It is on record that Khalid Sheikh Mohammad, later an admitted mastermind of the 9/11 attacks, was caught in March 2003 inside a Pakistani army officers colony in Rawalpindi, suspected that he was sheltered there by a serving army major.

Lt Gen (Rtd) Talat Masood once told in live TV show that *'there exists a strong anti-US feeling in the army'*. After Gen Musharraf turned against the Taliban at US stance there was a sense of betrayal inside the armed forces, might not be visibly seen due to strict discipline.

A script, just for change, from *'Daily Times' of 16th November 2003:* that a Washington-based veteran journalist, Khalid Hasan and Amir

Ghauri of Prime TV were at the 11 Corps HQ in Peshawar [*The 11th Corps oversees all Army operations in the Pakistani Tribal Areas bordering the sensitive and challenging terrain with Afghanistan where the US Army has been desperately trying to fish out fugitive Al-Qaeda and Taliban fighters since more than a decade*] as guest of Lt Gen Ali Jan Orakzai on 23rd October 2003. Gen Orakzai told the horror he had to face when he travelled to Tampa, Florida for the inauguration of the new Centcom C-in-C, Gen Abizaid, who had replaced Gen Tommy Franks. He had gone on the invitation of the US Army. He reached London to take a flight to New York.

When he went in for briefing at the airline counter in London, he was asked to take off his shoes, his jacket and his belt; thoroughly screened and checked because he had Pakistani green passport. The same treatment was repeated at JFK. Gen Orakzai told the US Immigration he was a guest of the US Army, he himself was an army General and he had a flight to catch for Tampa which may leave without him if he was delayed; but no effect.

So Pakistan Army's Corps Commander was asked to take off his shoes, carry the shoes bare footed to the machines for screening and was asked whatever number of questions were relevant. The General openly told the media that he would never come to the US again.

Alleged news about sharing nuclear technology with North Korea and Iran played another role in parting of ways. Gen Musharraf disgraced Dr Abdul Qadeer, the veteran nuclear pride of Pakistan, by arresting him, torturing and forcing him to read over the dictation endorsed by the Americans. The graph of hatred against America was seen at 86% in general populace of Pakistan; some army Generals had also felt it but Gen Musharraf's army rule continued and American plans of extending harm to Pakistan got strength as well as wide appreciation both in the US and India [actually blended with criticism and betrayals].

Once in 2003, *The Time's editorial* concluded;

> "*Beneath the surface of Washington's new closeness with Islamabad, mutual suspicions continue to fester. ... Neither country has fully delivered what other expected. ... The Bush administration has withheld trade benefits Pakistan deserves. General Musharraf has failed to sever all links with international terrorism.*"

The partnership, however, continued.

Going back to early 1980; while deciding so, Gen Ziaul Haq did not bother to approach his populace but discussed the matter with his closest friend and the then DG ISI Gen Akhtar Abdul Rehman. When DG ISI agreed with him he placed his thinking and brief plans on the table in next Corp Commander's meeting. He had argued that to block the way of the Soviets, it was imperative to help the Afghan brotherhood. Then he approached the leaders of 'Islamic political parties' and certain 'Landlord politicians' to stand by him.

Then America was not happy with Gen Ziaul Haq's plans at all. The then American National Security Advisor Brzezinski had categorically told Pakistan's Military ruler that *'Pakistan should not interfere in affairs of the other governments; let the Afghanis deal with the Russians in a way they want to settle,'* but Gen Ziaul Haq did not heed to any sane advice.

A high level Commission sent by the US President Jimmy Carter had also recommended Gen Ziaul Haq to refrain from fighting with the Soviets at foreign soil; and that Pakistan should focus its attention on its own development instead, but the military head was hard on accepting it. Jimmy Carter had also offered some aid for Pakistan's development plans which Gen Ziaul Haq had discarded terming it as 'peanut' for him.

Getting frustrated from his American ally, Gen Ziaul Haq called Conference of Foreign Ministers of Islamic countries on 27th January 1980 and placed his proposal before them. They all agreed with his plans and especially the Saudi government had announced to bear major part of expenses. The matter was then taken to the UN Council which passed a resolution condemning the Soviet aggression against its neighbouring country. That was the moment when America jumped into the game.

The war continued for about seven years and ultimately the Soviets had to quit Afghanistan.

TALIBAN: WHO WERE THEY?

There was seen a point of difference amongst the senior officers of Pakistan Army on the issue of governing authority when the Soviets left Afghanistan. Jama'at e Islami (JI), which was once banned to be even named in Gen Ayub Khan's time of 1960s, had been covertly helping the army and Gen Ziaul Haq. JI was of the view that Pakistan government should help Hikmatyar Gulbadin and Burhanuddin Rabbani in

Afghanistan whereas the Pakistan's liberal army Generals were of the opinion to include all factions of Afghan fighters in making a new set up in Afghanistan. The days of interim set up and of *Mujahideen* were over.

It was a hard fact that all Afghan fighting factions, who had pushed out the Russians across their borders, were pure Islamic. Younus Khalis, G Hikmatyar and B Rabbani all were having Islamic way of governance in their minds with little difference but all they were fighting to establish their own government in Afghanistan not to bring Islam only.

For instance, the first battalion of *Mujahideen* or Taliban were consisting of all those pilots or artillery men who were with the Afghan President Najeebullah at one time. Then they let their beards grow long and joined Taliban while making necessary adjustments in their way of life.

{*An untold fact that the original 'Taliban' faction came into being in Kandahar province of Afghanistan due to internal frictions amongst members of Hizb e Islami (HI). Taliban were then encouraged and helped by all opponents of Mujahideen who were then ruling Afghanistan. For instance Rasheed Doostam (an Uzbec by origin) had not only given cash support to Taliban but also had sent trained pilots to fly war planes & helicopters based in Kandahar; American CIA immediately provided them strategic equipment and basic knowledge.*

Pakistan government was not happy with Rabbani's governance and Mujahideen; thus also started helping Taliban secretly. Not only had this, Pakistan asked Saudi and UAE rulers to extend them financial aid. In those early days Taliban were fighting to take control of mostly the Pakhtun areas which were under the influence of H Y Gulbadin [a political opponent of Rabbani, the then ruler of Afghanistan] so Rabbani, though was a Tajik by origin, had also opted to help Taliban.

What was the result the Taliban went stronger and started posing threat to all their helping hands. After dealing with Gulbadin, they first expelled Rabbani from Kabul, then launched unending battles with Rasheed Doostam, then brought CIA to senses by awarding the major pipeline contract to a company from Argentine [the American competitors] and in the last threatened Pakistan, too.

The rest has been the history still lingering on.}

Later, when Benazir Bhutto assumed power in 1988, the GHQ and ISI gave a detailed briefing to her on Afghan policy then going on. Benazir

765

Bhutto had got notes from the Foreign Office too. She noted down certain important points from the GHQ's briefing and then merged them in her write up. To go ahead according to her own perception she had constituted an '**Afghan Cell**' comprising of certain army officers and some from the Foreign Office. The GHQ had, for instance, suggested that Pakistan should recognize the then Interim set-up in Afghanistan but Ms Bhutto declined. Subsequent developments proved that Benazir Bhutto's political decision was correct.

In February 1989, in a meeting of the Afghan Cell headed by the then PM Benazir Bhutto, the Foreign Office Officials placed an 11 point agenda before all. The US envoy Robert B Oakley was also sitting in the meeting. These eleven points were basically meant for the Afghan *Mujahideen* as a future agenda because the Soviets had nearly moved out from Afghanistan. The underlined fact was that Pakistan was not inclined to recognize the interim government then in making in Afghanistan.

The ISI Chief Lt Gen Hamid Gul was then saved by Benazir Bhutto saying that *'it is too much for Gen Hamid Gul. He is not a General of Afghan army. May be that the Mujahideen do not agree with all terms or 11 points being coined by us.'* Benazir Bhutto told the meeting that there would be only three points to proceed further by Gen Gul:

- That the *Mujahideen* of the interim set-up should take control of any one city in Afghanistan and make a formal announcement of their government.

- That the *Mujahideen* should give a call to the Irani *Mujahideen* also to join them.

- That Zahir Shah, the former Afghan ruler, should also recognize the interim set-up.

The ISI Chief Gen Hamid Gul had to agree with the proposal because it was brought forward by the prime minister. Gen Gul told the meeting that in that cold weather it was not possible for the *Mujahideen* to take control of Kabul, however, Jalalabad could be the best option. It was agreed by all and Gen Hamid Gul was given green signal to go ahead.

On 5ᵗʰ **March 1989**, Jalalabad Operation was launched but the US Ambassador had played the double game. In the meeting he had promised 6000 tons of ammunition but in fact only 100 tons was supplied. Washington had changed their priorities and had not agreed with Robert B Oakley's recommendations in the back drop of Ojhri Episode of 1988 and more due to the fact that Soviets were already working on their planned quit. American government was not at all interested that *'who rules and controls Afghanistan'* after Russians quit. The operation failed.

It was in that background when the *Mujahideen* were raised in Afghanistan and subsequently termed as Taliban. Those were the local Islam-minded people gathered under the guidance of some Generals and certain ISI officers from Pakistan, equipped with financial aid, arms & ammunition supplied by the US through the then rulers of Pakistan, to continue with their activities.

The other historians have also reached a similar conclusion that *Mujahedeen*, no doubt, fought against Russians but they were under three different commands; under Ahmed Shah Masood, Gulbadin Hikmetyar and Burhanuddin Rabbani.

When the Russians announced for going back, the three leaders tried to eliminate each other to get hold of Kabul. To create harmony amongst those Afghan leaders, Lt Gen Hamid Gul had to go and stay in Kabul to bring them on one table. In the meantime, the fled away soldiers of these three factions gathered themselves in Kandahar and declared them as 'Taliban'.

Already there were seven *Jehadi* parties emerged when the Soviets left. To keep them together was a big problem because all they were always fighting over the dollars and ammunition supplied by the US and Saudi governments. Due to that inside sharing battles no one was seriously interested in making the government; the political process blocked. When at last, the Russians left Afghanistan, the Taliban took reigns of the country in hand and planned to impose their fundamentalist thoughts over the region; *those people, the original Taliban, were independent and not under any group at beginning.*

TALIBANIZATION COMES TO PAKISTAN:

On 18th October 2007, Benazir Bhutto's cavalcade was creeping through towards the Jinnah's mausoleum over an especially fortified, bullet-proof truck, waving hastily at her followers and occasionally wiping her tearful eyes. At 11.50 PM, when the cavalcade reached the Karsaz

Bridge, Benazir stepped down to use the makeshift washroom built in the lower deck of the truck. Just 20 minutes later someone tossed a grenade on the right side of Benazir's truck to break the three rings of security cordon through explosion. In the ensuing confusion, a suicide bomber sneaked under Benazir's truck from the left and detonated himself. Simultaneously, a sniper showered bullets on the truck's screen to ensure nobody could escape to safety. The cavalcade soon turned into a crying grave yard; human flesh and limbs flew around leaving 143 people dead.

Benazir Bhutto was not atop the truck at that fatal moment; the explosion was powerful enough to rip off a door of her truck. The assassination plan later revealed the prior knowledge of Benazir's security arrangements in detail; the suicide bomber had successfully evaded the jamming devices fitted into two vehicles immediately in front and behind Benazir's truck. 21-year old suicide bomber had 15-20 kg of an explosive mix of C4 and TNT on his body; for Benazir Bhutto, two police jeeps accompanying her got the whole burden and torn into pieces.

Al Qaeda, along with local militant groups affiliated to it, was suspected but did these groups had assistance or tacit approval of *jehadi*-minded elements in the administration? Benazir told the media next day that:

> '.... I had made it clear (to Gen Musharraf) that I won't blame Taliban or Al Qaeda if I am attacked, but I will name the three / four officials as I know quite well my enemies in the Pakistani military and intelligence establishment'.

The PPP insiders disclosed their identity to *Outlook* naming Brig (retd) Ejaz Shah DG IB; Ch Pervaiz Elahi-the CM Punjab; former DG ISI Lt Gen Hameed Gul and Hassan Waseem Afzal, a former official of the NAB.

Categorically named in Benazir's letter, Hassan Waseem Afzal was then Secretary to the Governor of Punjab; appointed to this post after he was removed as NAB's Deputy Chairman on Benazir's insistence during her Abu Dhabi meeting with Gen Musharraf in July 2007. Hassan W Afzal had incurred Benazir's wrath because he had made it his personal mission to pursue corruption cases against her in UK, Spain and Switzerland. On his instance and personal interest there were only two persons against whom the Interpol had issued 'Red Notices'; Benazir Bhutto & Inam R Sehri of FIA who had once arrested his real & only brother in law [named Javed Zia] in September 1995 in a cheat-cum-fraud case.

The FIR filed by Benazir Bhutto in Karachi carried as suspects *'those four names which were given to Gen Musharraf'*, neither of Taliban nor of any other *Jehadi*-group. However, the intelligence agencies believed that the *Jehadi* elements could be responsible. Inspired by those Taliban in Afghanistan, the Islamist groups in the border areas of Pakistan had also started regimentation and influencing the local folk residents especially in the tribal belt.

These local Taliban then started threatening the way of life of general populace particularly of the settled areas of NWFP like Swat & Dir. Later, they claimed their presence every where in Pakistan; for instance in Lahore as well where they, in 2008-09, bombed certain places of entertainment. Soon the government had reached the conclusion that the Taliban's brand of *Sharia* was anti-progress, anti-education, anti-culture, anti-entertainment and anti-women.

Due to government's ineptness, a large majority of people were unaware and oblivious to what had happened to a part of smoothly governed Pakistan, especially to Swat, and what was on its way. To protest or demonstrate or even comment on this threatening challenge emerging in the name of Islam and religion was not given priority neither by the governments in power nor by intelligentsia. Some media-men who propagated the cause of Taliban or those who criticized them being opposite to the prevailing norms of contemporary development theories; both sides either eliminated or severely attacked.

Local groups of Taliban flourished because in Pakistan a common man kept his lips tight while speaking against this new breed of clergymen because no one liked to be labelled as 'un-Islamic' or 'western-minded'. Taliban's apparent activities were 'Islamic' therefore the law enforcement agencies did not touch them. When these local Taliban started targeting video shops, TV show rooms, shops of barbers doing 'beard-shaving service' and coercing the people to keep their *'shalwars'* 6 to 9 inches high from their feet, the alarms were triggered in the higher echelons of the successive rulers; but it was too late then. Suddenly the situation deteriorated; had gone worse and out of control.

Both the government and the people went genuinely scared that had the Taliban succeeded, they would tolerate neither higher courts nor any parliament. The justice that they would dispense would be barbaric, and the proposed *Shura* [the Law Making Body] would have medieval rules and procedures. Where there was Talibanisation in some parts of Pakistan, mostly southern Punjab and scattered towns in un-educated northern belts, civil administration was non-existent and the armed forces started struggling to combat with the Taliban.

Religious *Madressahs* in Gen Ziaul Haq's era had started emerging like mushrooms, flourishing and producing young persons with obsolete and fundamentalist ideas. Some human rights groups and organizations started urging people to raise their voice against these extremist elements. Some were organizing demonstrations and marches to let these extremists know that the majority do not want them to succeed.

During 2008-09 there were numerous demonstrations by the women and girls in various parts of the country with play-cards carrying picture of a girl with a line saying, **"Save me, save Swat, Save Pakistan."**

AFGHAN TALIBAN – THE REAL FACTOR:

It may be kept on record that the Taliban of Afghanistan, who were fighting with President Hamid Karzai for the last eight years, welcomed the US President Obama in 2008 in an unfamiliar way. They asked Obama to close all evil US Detention Centres for militants; completely withdraw from Iraq and Afghanistan; reverse the 'satanic' policies of his predecessor George W Bush and stop defending Israel. The message was conveyed to President Obama through SITE Intelligence Group. The text also contained that:

> *'Obama's move to close Guantanamo Detention Centre is a positive step for peace and stability in the region and the world. If he wants real stability in the world, he should also void all those evil projects established in the light of Bush's satanic perspective of instability in the world.'* (**Ref: The News dated 30th January 2009**)

It is a matter of record that Mr Obama had, in his first week of take over, ordered to close all overseas torture and detention cells including the US military prison at Guantanamo in Cuba. Guantanamo was established in 2002, as a means to hold detainees beyond the reach of American courts and at the time of closure in 2009, it contained 245 prisoners. There was another detention centre at the US Airbase Bagram in Afghanistan which held hundreds of [610 till ending 2010] detainees. Dr Aafia Siddiqui was kept here before she was shifted to US after a media uproar.

The Afghan Taliban's above message was mainly focusing on this Bagram Centre urging that Mr Obama should have felt courage to close it too. Taliban's message further said that:

'If Obama is right, and according to his words, wants to open a new page based on peaceful interaction built on mutual respect with the Islamic world, the first thing he has to do to stop and annul all these (Middle East Policy) procedures which were created according to Bush's criminal policy.

He [Mr Obama] must completely withdraw all his forces from the two occupied Islamic countries (Iraq & Afghanistan) and to stop defending Israel against Islamic interest in the Middle East and entire world.

It is imperative that Obama, before he gets hit by the same fate as the communist empire in the past, must find potential ways to carry a message of peace and stability to the world.'

Michael Semple maintains [referring to his essay based on an interview with a Taliban Commander published in *New Statesman* of *11th July 2012*] that *'two other aspects of the Taliban's political practice are remarkable. First, they have maintained their internal cohesiveness for approaching two decades. Second, they manage to operate from behind an iron curtain, with tight central control over communications between the movement and the non-Taliban world.'*

The Taliban keep enough political thinkers within their ranks and their leadership speaks with authority and inside knowledge. Most leaders of the group had been held in Guantanamo for various intervals of time and then *'purposefully released'* to accomplish their assignments mutually negotiated with the American bosses.

Michael Semple answered certain cogent questions as per his own assessment and knowledge [one can differ with] but generally reflected the actual situation on the Afghan soils. For instance, to a question [Does the Taliban movement hope for military victory over the Afghan government?] he replied that *'it would take some kind of divine intervention for the Taliban to win this war'.*

For another question [NATO has clearly announced a timetable for withdrawal from Afghanistan, what is the justification for the Taliban to continue their armed campaign?] Semple relied that *'they also believe that over time they will become stronger than the Karzai regime. The Taliban are fighting to expel the foreign occupiers and to enforce Shariat.'*

How a head of the state be selected, is an interesting event. Last time the Taliban called 2.000 religious scholars, including people from every district, to elect Mullah Omar. The point of this election was to establish who can be a just ruler, who knows how to respect fellow Muslims, how to apply the Shariat and how to maintain peace and eradicate narcotics. Voting [might be informal] is very important in the Muslim tradition.

However, the Taliban also kept note that Afghans would not accept a repeat of the Taliban's effort to impose an '*Ameer*' and that; ultimately, democratic elections make sense for Afghanistan.

Taliban are criticised for their social policy; for banning female education and using force to make people comply with fundamentalist's rules but, according to their philosophy, '*the developed world has no right to ask them about their social policy*'.

The international community has failed miserably in everything they promised with Afghans; promises of making Afghanistan secure, prosperous and free of drugs. Instead, the country has gone the most insecure place in the world, has grown more poppy than ever before; seen utmost humiliation for getting their houses searched daily by Americans or NATO soldiers. Taliban's treatment of women, their harsh enforcement of beards and prayers were tolerated but not white soldier's harsh shouts.

Taliban were then prepared to hold talks with the Afghan government but the Kabul regime had no authority in the issues concerned with war – power and control of the armed forces; real authority still rests with the Americans. Afghani Taliban have established a political structure and they are running it. Michael Semple [referring to above essay again] quoted a Taliban leader saying boldly that:

> '*At least 70% Taliban are angry at al-Qaeda considering them a plague. Some even concluded that al-Qaeda are actually the spies of America. Originally, the Taliban were naive and ignorant of politics and welcomed al-Qaeda into their homes. But al-Qaeda abused our hospitality. Taliban who returned from Cuba have refused to let al-Qaeda operate in their provinces.*
>
> *Osama [Bin Laden], through his policies, destroyed Afghanistan. Had he really believed in jihad he should have gone to Saudi Arabia and done jihad there [against their Monarch], rather than wrecking our country. We have already paid a high price for [our earlier] association with al-Qaeda.*'

The analysis of the above quoted interview confirmed that the AfghaniTaliban and Afghanistan's allies had opposing views; the former viewed the Karzai regime as a puppet of the United States. But the west had invested much in the Karzai regime and was not ready to ditch it; the US wanted Taliban to negotiate with Karzai whereas *they were serious to subvert the Karzai government; their old enemy of the 1990s, the non-Pashtun Northern Alliance was placed next'*

Scenario 59

PAK-ARMY ON 'WAR ON TERROR'-II:

TALIBAN BACKED BY ISI OR NOT:

Then the situation croped up that the US & its Western allies and Karzai government in Afghanistan considered that the Afghan Taliban were supported by Pakistan and its ISI. Pakistan kept the convincing record that the casualties of about 40,000 innocent citizens & about 4500 army troops coupled with loss of infrastructure worth $70 billion were caused to them by the US, NATO and Afghan fighters merely on the basis of baseless assumptions.

A very cogent question at this stage that while there is customary to keep guns and Kalashnikov weapons by each male in the tribal areas then why the local tribesmen did not fight Al Qaeda or Afghani Taliban intruders themselves at the initial stage, a decade earlier.

The reply comes that there was enough potential for such awakening in FATA but the hurdle was the tribal-man's mistrust in Pakistani military leadership, especially the intelligence agencies deployed or working in proxy there. The Taliban and Al Qaeda had targeted many tribal leaders and killed about 120 of them labelling them 'spying for ISI & America'. The deployed military contingents did nothing to pursue the killers and failed to protect the tribal leaders.

However, a little different version came up from a research worker affiliated with the University of Oslo named Farhat Taj:

> *'The target killing of the tribal leaders started in South Waziristan almost at the same time when the US was bombing Taliban and Al Qaeda hideouts in Afghanistan in 2001 and the militants ran towards Waziristan. They were not welcomed by the tribal leaders. In order to have a strong foothold in Waziristan, the militants killed more than 120 tribal leaders.*

> *Clearly the then government of Gen Musharraf was playing a double game. On one hand it joined the US led war on terror, on the other hand it allowed the militants to kill the tribal leaders and replace the tribal order with the Taliban order.*

Next the killing spree was taken to other tribal areas including Khyber, Orakzai and Bajaur agencies. There is a strong perception among many Pashtuns that this killing was carried out with tacit consent of the intelligence agencies of Pakistan to create full leadership space for Taliban in the Pakhtun tribal society.'

Coming back and re-asserting that the remaining tribal leaders and young people in FATA hesitated from taking up arms against the Taliban and Al Qaeda due to non-cooperating rather humiliating strategy of one faction of officers within ISI though a strong potential was always available to place a challenge for them.

One more citation from Farhat Taj's version: *'that in tehsil Pranghar of Momand Agency, the people rose against the Taliban as soon as the Taliban first assaulted Momand Agency. Consequently, Tangi in district Charsadda is safe because of this event. Since 2004, we find sporadic uprisings against the Taliban but due to the inability of the Pakistani security forces, the leaders of Qaumi Lashkars (national force) were mostly target killed by the Taliban.'*

In nut shell, the problem remained that measures had never been taken by Army's high command to remove rift between officers of two schools of thought within the ISI. The policy should have been uni-directional. If for some professional reasons it was not possible then, instead of becoming target of Taliban on one hand and of American drones on the other, the government should have called back army from the front line in Tribal areas to relatively 2nd position till re-defining of goals in the national interest. Unluckily Pakistan's decision makers mostly deployed their troops as per American strategy and not considering 'Pakistan first'.

The American, British or European governments never believed that Pakistani ISI did not know the names and hideouts of Taliban or gangsters using the title of Al Qaeda who had brought Pakistan to this stage of ruins and wreckage.

It became more difficult when Pakistan Army slogans of **'the best and thorough professional network of strategic intelligence in the world'** were continuously and constantly preached all around. Pakistan could not convince the world that their ISI and MI did not know the figures behind this rampage and wilderness. May be some mid-order army officers knew it but the high command was kept in dark.

The fact remains that fragrance of 'Rule on Afghanistan' had not faded away from minds of some of the military commanders as they used to do in Taliban's era before Karzai's appointment. Pakistan lived in hope of dictating 'ruling techniques' to Afghanistan through possible comeback of Taliban's government there.

Pakistan's leadership did not accept the reality of changing circumstances in Afghanistan through a decade's American occupation but pushed the innocent children and women into fire of greedy gangsters in pursuits of certain disillusioned ambitions.

The political rulers of Pakistan in post Musharraf era, the President and PM of an elected government, could not pull strings of that faction of ISI and other intelligence network to make them believe that Pakistan's own interest should be FIRST. A handful of officers played with innocent lives of the people just pursuing a hope of changing government in Afghanistan for their own interests and the PPP government remained mum or at least non-interfering.

Pakistan Army kept on nurturing a wishful thinking that, sooner or later, the US and NATO forces would leave Afghan soils because of rising financial crunch in America and other European countries. After they leave, these Taliban would definitely take over the government in Afghanistan.

On the other hand NATO's Secretary General De Hoop Scheffer, while speaking on the **'Security and Defence Agenda'**, showered more fuel on fire on 29th January 2009 that:

> 'Urgent attention needed to be paid to South Asia as a victory for the Taliban in Pakistan and Afghanistan would be a disaster for international security thus a legacy we cannot leave for our children. NATO members should do more to help new US President Barack Obama tackle the growing threats of terrorism, weapons of mass destruction and failed states. NATO must engage with Iran to secure regional support for the escalating war in neighbouring Afghanistan.
>
> We need to stop looking at Afghanistan as if it were an island, as Afghanistan's problems cannot be solved by or within Afghanistan alone. There is a regional network of extremists which respects borders no more than they respect human rights or the rule of law.'

SHIFT IN US POLICY:

There prevailed a common myth amongst Pakistani Generals in this respect that Karzai's government was virtually limited to the outskirts of

Kabul whereas most of Afghanistan, especially the South and East, were in the hands of Taliban. Then what to Pakistan; it might be true at times, but till you wait for accomplishment of that wishful thinking again, Pakistan would be ruined to pebbles. Pakistan lost its security system of Tribal areas which was running successfully since 58 years based on mutual trust; now impossible to be re-constructed again.

If Pakistan's civil and military leadership would have taken stock of the situation at an appropriate hour, peace and prosperity all around could be seen and Pakistan would have surfaced again with the same old glamour, reverence, and respect on the globe. In the past, some local tribal groups had resisted Taliban but were mostly besieged till they were massacred because the Taliban were armed with much more sophisticated weapons than the tribesmen.

It is on record that once the Afghan government had announced their next general elections for 20th August 2009 hoping that security situation would be improved there due to increase in US troops. Mr Obama had already directed his military commanders to withdraw US troops from Iraq within 16 months. 30,000 men were to be additionally deployed in Afghanistan making a total presence of US military as 66,000 which were 36,000 troops previously.

Mr Obama's wish and decision was immediately implemented and the strength of American troops was raised to 68,000 in March 2009 and 98,000 in March 2010 (*At that moment Afghanistan had 70,000 foreign troops; 36,000 Americans, 8000 British and the remaining from other NATO member states*) Pakistan should have raised their voice against such huge deployment near its borders.

Hamid Karzai contested for his re-election saying that he had '*a job to complete*', but his popularity was contaminated and tainted both among Afghans and his Western masters due to alleged rampant corruption and weak governing outside Afghan capital. The fact remains that, due to shift in US policy interpreting Obama's new vision, Afghanistan was going to get more financial aid as per new formula of 'significant non-military component' meaning thereby more development aid.

However, Taliban insurgency had gone stronger in the ethnic *Pashtun* concentrated areas of the South and East of Afghanistan and they had also encroached into areas in the outskirts of the capital, the Kabul City.

[*It may be remembered that Hamid Karzai himself is an ethnic Pashtun from the southern part of Afghanistan. Since 2001, he is head of the state when US-led and Afghan forces had toppled the Taliban's government in the backdrop of 9 / 11 attacks on world towers. He was first saddled there as a head of interim administrative setup and then he got himself settled after winning an election held in 2004.*

Mr Obama held an opinion for Karzai before elections that: **'Karzai has not gotten out of the bunker and helped to organize Afghanistan, and the government, the judiciary, police forces in ways that would give people confidence'.]**

History tells us that military actions in any country never lasted longer; the set-up in Afghanistan was also bound to change. An opinion, cited in the **'Daily Times' dated 30ᵗʰ January 2009**, under head: *'Thinking afresh on Afghanistan'* said that:

'Perhaps Gates [US Secretary Defence then], and thinkers like him at the Pentagon and the White House, have realised that neither a military solution, nor leaving Afghanistan in the lurch is possible, as they did on attaining mean objectives after defeating the Soviet Union. The region and the world cannot afford to withstand another such blunder.

Thus, rather than pursuing a mindless policy of staying in Afghanistan or dragging on with unattainable military objectives, it's time for Washington to usher in an era of peace and political stability in the war-ravaged country, and plan an exit strategy at the earliest. Gates, fortunately enough, will have the added impetus of a similar thinking from Generals in the battlefield and Pentagon, such as Gen Petraeus who advocated the option of talking it out with the Taliban.

It is another promising sign that the new administration is working on a strategy in Iraq and Afghanistan by drawing lessons from experiences and reality on the ground. This is what makes President Obama's agenda of change achievable and realistic to the core.'

Since 2009 to 2012, the said objective had been followed by the White House though not so vigorously while trying to shift the whole emphasis on the weak shoulders of Pakistan through repeated slogans of *'do more'*. It was also a reality that, in such changing scenario, blaming ISI and asking Pakistan's army to 'do more' was an uphill task.

This time the people of Pakistan also comprehended fully the alarming situation on Pak – Afghan borders created by the presence of American

& NATO troops and retaliations launched by Taliban. Inside Pakistan, Swat was nearly lost. A particular faction in ISI was blamed for doing it deliberately because they were ideologically against the PPP theme.

In such lurking dark, Gen Kayani was taken in confidence and he stood by the PPP. This move was carefully designed and accomplished by Mr Zardari otherwise the PPP might have lost the game on two counts:

Firstly, giving next Army Generals to plan another take over by spreading news through their stooge media men that PPP had failed to deliver good governance; consequently PPP would have lost respect and power both. OR

Secondly, Swat might be lost or could be the whole Khyber PK province dismembered; God helped Pakistan. Had this event occurred, Benazir Bhutto's whole family and Z A Bhutto's name would have been negatively remembered in the history like Gen Yahya Khan who had lost the then East Pakistan.

BRITONS vs AMERICANS IN WOT:

In the 3rd week of September 2006, the British Prime Minister Tony Blair had paid flying visits to Pakistan and Afghanistan. The agreement announced on 19th September in Pakistan was a case in point. Mr Blair announced doubling of aid, to £480m, in part to help fund the reform of Islamic schools or *madrassas*. Some of these schools, attended often by the children of poor families, were blamed for the spread of extremist thinking.

The former US president Bill Clinton's speech at the Labour Party conference in UK during the last week of September 2006 had also carried his genuine regrets that:

'While he was in office, he should have focused on eradicating school fees [in Pakistan]. That would have stopped poorer parents sending their children to free religious madrassahs for their education, where many are radicalized.

It's much cheaper to help the economy in a poor country than to fight a war. The tragedy is that such a subtle approach is apparently anathema to the architects of the present calamitous war on terror'.

Through this exercise, indirectly the *madrassas* in tribal areas of Pakistan were blamed for radicalizing a section of Muslim youth in Britain. The much trumpeted Pakistan connection, however, was overplayed because this was not where Islamic militancy in Britain originated. Those extremists who visited *madrassas* in Pakistan were already committed to their path.

But Tony Blair's philosophy could not be given shape by world powers; years passed by.

A report had appeared in **the 'Daily Mail' [UK] of 18th July 2008**, titled as **'Journey inside the Taliban: Briton's dangerous secret meeting with the warlords who will never surrender'** written by **James Fergusson** told that the higher command of Taliban, attack planners and die hard commanders were called 'Tier 1 of Taliban's - warriors driven by ideology, the fanatical ones who would probably never surrender.

They hardly ever met together at one place for fear of a laser-guided bomb through the roof, wiping out the entire command. Even separately, they rarely slept in the same room for two consecutive nights. They were differentiated from Tier 2 - embittered poppy farmers and opium dealers dispossessed by the NATO presence - and the adventurers, impoverished peasants and other hired guns who made up Tier 3. Of course they held no match for the professionals of the British Army or NATO soldiers whatsoever but they were mission-full.

Major Dan Rex, the Gurkha's commander posted in Afghanistan had given a vivid account of just how tough and resourceful Taliban they were up against:

> *'They used cover well and they moved about very fast. They had sections of eight or 12 men, and a pyramid command structure just like ours. They don't wear badges of rank on their shoulders but that doesn't mean they aren't a proper army.*
>
> *Once his garrison came under small-arms fire at night; his men shot back. With hindsight, obviously they were testing us out. They were examining our arcs of fire, our fire-times, how soon before air support would arrive. It was professionally done.'*

The commander then explained how the Taliban launched an attack on his contingent and the fight continued for the whole night. The periodic attacks were initiated with most modern weapons from the nearby village where they had used living homes as bunkers. The Taliban's bravery had astonished the British Commander as he conceded openly afterwards during an interview. They only went back when our forces put them on targets of air attack.

Taliban's case was placed before *James Fergusson*, who was once treated as the British distinguished guest media man, emphasizing that **they were fighting because it was their religious duty to resist the infidel invaders - just as they had fought the Russians, and as their fathers and grandfathers in earlier times had fought against the British**. At that particular post there were 700 armed men, all in a state of constant readiness to attack a police station or an American convoy, or take over the entire province if ordered. They sleep during the day and did everything, including live-firing exercises, by night. 'Night-time is Taliban time there', the media representative had observed. They only need missiles to shoot the air strikers down without which they go helpless sometimes.

In Helmand at one time, the [Afghan] Taliban had 10,000 fighters and a further 2,000 suicide bombers standing by. They once hoped to 'break the back' of the British. Taliban knew that the British were not bad soldiers. They knew that:

> *'They are not cowards. They do not cry, or shout "Oh my God" in the front line as the Americans do. But still, they don't stand and fight like us. The British were defeated at Musa Qala, everyone knows this. We were going to slaughter them or capture them, but we [the Taliban] let them [the English soldiers] go out of respect for the elders.'*

In their eyes, defeating the English Army in 2006 was merely a revenge of history because the British had beaten them before, back in the 1840s. Taliban still believe that *'fighting the British feels like unfinished business for many of us.'*

The above lines confirmed the notion that: *'sending Army to win hearts and minds in Afghanistan, where the past was still so very alive, was a bad mistake,'* but in fact the Taliban hate Americans more than the British - and even more than the Russians who had brutalised their country 20 years earlier. The Russians fought man to man, but when one American soldier got hit, a whole village was razed by bombs in response.

It was easier to respect the Russians, the Taliban believed. Taliban's attitude to war was seen as out-dated or traditional because still they keep faith in mythical past when battles were won through courage and faith and not superior weaponry; but they won again & again.

Even now; fighting Americans is a holy duty for Taliban and they are winning. The Americans never hoped for victory but they had to resist because they knew the ground realities; and that the war would leave nothing for them except widows and destruction.

For Taliban war and jihad are two different things. **It is their moral obligation to resist foreigners on their land. One year, a hundred years, a million years, - it is not important but they will never stop fighting**. Most of them consider that on Judgment Day, Allah would ask them: *"Did you fight for your religion?"*

The normal Taliban members are astonished on the theme that:

> *'Why the Britons allow themselves to be the puppets of America. The British are clever people, it makes no sense. You were beaten here before, and you will lose this time, too. Why do you think it is any different now?'*

Might be the Americans in Kabul and the British in south of Afghanistan (and other NATO forces there) believe in the superiority of their technology but Taliban, equipped with Kalashnikovs and rocket-propelled grenades only, still aim to beat them all. The Taliban believe this known Islamic phrase that a Muslim does not get bitten from the same hole twice. The British commanders there tried to make them realize that this time the hole was different but Taliban were not convinced.

The allied forces told the Taliban that they had not come to occupy Afghanistan but to help them to secure economic development; but very simple question the Taliban made: *'Then why do you come here with guns and bombs?'*

Taliban believe that had the Americans and British come here un-armed they would have been Afghan people's guests. To a common question that why Taliban or Osama Bin Laden had caused 9/11 episode killing thousands of people, the Taliban reply that:

> *'..... Osama was a good Muslim, an honourable man and 9/11 was not an honourable event. There is no evidence that 9/11 was planned in Afghanistan. Those martyrs didn't learn to fly here. They were not*

Afghan nationals, they had no connections with Afghanistan; and they have never been here.'

A very common perception about the Taliban's denial of education to women; they maintain with force that it is not true. There are girls schools set up under the Taliban's regime in the past. Some girls schools had been burnt down *'but only those with Western curricula, where girls were being taught ....'.*

Taliban's this contention had been totally discarded by the western media in the light of available facts on record which speak that more than 1,100 girls schools were attacked or burnt where they prevailed power; thus lost thousands of their admirers. However, *James Fergusson,* (cited above) had to conclude that:

'Most of all, it is hard to imagine that they can ever be defeated; something genuinely moving about their fervour, however naive or wrong-headed it might be.'

The western social setups cannot reconcile with Taliban's way of life. For Taliban, faith comes even before love of family and children. They deliberately do not give enough time and fatherly love to their babies due to obvious reasons. When Taliban are questioned that how they feel they would be killed; very simple logic is forwarded by them that:

'Our fathers, grandfathers and great-grandfathers all died by the bullet. We all will die in the same way, and no doubt my sons, too. It is not so sad. It is glorious to be martyred. To die in the service of jihad is the ambition of all of us here.'

Hell of distance between the two cultures. For the western people, love of family is their most cherished value, the hall-mark of their civilisation. Contrarily the Taliban say that **'Allah gives us children, so it is our duty to give to Allah before we give to our family.'**

The Taliban often tell the coalition forces: *'You may have the watches, but we have the time.'* That is what they believe and that is what they deliver. This is the main theme of a book named: **A Million Bullets: The Real Story of the British Army in Afghanistan** *by James Fergusson,* published by Bantam Press UK in 2008.

These words should have emphatically apprised the Americans about Taliban's behaviour and thinking about on-going fights on their Afghan lands. What can you expect from the people who are always ready to give their lives as martyrs taking it as a noble cause and then feel proud of their deaths. No repents; no accusations on companions for a possible mistake; no obligation for the families left alone and no future plans like us, like western people.

The US pentagon, CIA and the western rulers keep a complete knowledge of the fighting factions in Afghanistan. They fully know who the Taliban are. They know that who are chasing and killing their troops in the rough mountains of Afghanistan. Thus it is evident that the western allied and NATO forces cannot win war in Afghanistan. It is history in making.

The Americans had thought and planned wrongly to bring Afghanistan under their thumb. Though the Britain and the US are allies in this war but from inside the Americans wanted to show their supremacy over the Britons also by occupying Afghanistan.

The US agencies wished to knock down the British intelligence and military planning divisions by proving that the dream of colonizing Afghanistan is fulfilled by the Americans while the British Crown could not occupy it during their 90 years of English Rule over India.

WAR ON TERROR FIZZLES OUT:

Up till now the Americans have learnt enough lessons during their militarised stay in Afghanistan. They have now believed the reasons that why the Britain could not occupy even a single inch of the Afghan lands during their rule on Indo-Pak territory from 1857 till 1947. This was the reason that most of the British intelligentsia had opposed the very idea of sending the English Army to Afghanistan by the then PM Tony Blair in 2001 though this time using another trap: War on Terror (WOT).

Pakistan landed in problems when Gen Musharraf opted to become a party in WOT game after American episode of 9 / 11. The General wanted dollars on which no audit or check from any corner would be applicable. After 3 / 4 years the Americans started feeling that they were not getting through their plans and, on the other hand, the allied countries were also showing reluctance in sending their troops to Afghanistan.

[*Referring to the press conference of 27th March 2013 at Karachi, Gen Musharraf was asked to explain that why he had opted to say yes to the American call in the aftermath of 9/11 2001 without consulting even his own commanders what to speak of the general populace of Pakistan.*

Gen Musharraf confidently replied that 'at that time it was in the best interest of Pakistan to say so'; a typical two edged political answer it was. Subsequent times proved it blatantly wrong.]

Throughout the whole journey of attacks & lies, it remained difficult for the US to admit their failure openly because it would have tarnished their image of number one super power on the globe. Till July 2008 Gen Musharraf had taken a handsome amount of about eight billion (out of total settled & negotiated deal of 10.67 billion) dollars from them.

As a face saving Mr Bush, with the help of his cronies in Pentagon, CIA, and Senate worked out a policy to shift the burden of their failure on Pakistan propagating that:

- there is Al Qaeda in Pakistani borders areas;

- bomb making factories are there on Pakistani border-regional belt;

- Pakistan is deliberately avoiding to help the US;

- Taliban are being controlled by the ISI of Pakistan;

- some Islamic minded Generals in Pak Army are helping Taliban;

- Gen Musharraf has not spent dollar-money on projects specified for;

- Pakistan is using his atomic deterrence to shelter Taliban.

Many more allegations could be added to this list. Then Mr Bush started sending his team members and policy framers like Richard Boucher, Mike Mullin and K L Rice to Pakistan frequently to meet Gen Musharraf. Immediate before change of the regime in Washington (in 2008), the White House held meetings with Mr Zardari and Gen Kayani just to give deceitful and erroneous impressions to the Americans and to the rulers of Allied countries. Mr Bush wanted to convince their people that:

'His policies in Afghanistan are correct (were the same correct in Iraq?) but Pakistan does not allow to register any progress on WOT. Pakistan's army is helping Taliban otherwise he would have conquered Afghanistan much earlier.'

All lies. Mr Bush and his friends were fully aware that it was a war of Taliban with US sponsored ruler Hamid Karzai on the soils of Afghanistan. *The Taliban wanted that no foreign power, including Pakistan, should interfere in their internal battles.*

Pakistan had also suffered a lot and is still suffering at the hands of Taliban because they consider Pakistan as a cogent ally to the US. On one hand Pakistan army is being targeted by the Taliban because of compromises with the US, whereas, the innocent tribes are also being attacked by the American drones on the charge that Taliban roam about in Pakistani border areas.

Neither Taliban understand Pakistan's viewpoint (rather they do not want to comprehend due to their die-hard thinking over the point that US & Pak-Army are allies) nor was the US giving way to Pakistan because Gen Musharraf had taken price of implementing US's plans in Toto in the region; all without people's will.

New Pakistani regime of the PPP also expected America's financial aid & loans, but could only get peanuts in the shape of humiliating Kerry Lugar Aid. The US till recently continued to frighten Pakistan because they had no other choice for face saving in an arena of their sustained defeats in Afghanistan at the hands of Taliban.

Both the governments of America and Pakistan avoided an open dialogue with Taliban, till at least mid 2012, not considering them a political party at par. Astonishingly, *Hamid Karzai then started accusing the US government with known popular Afghani demand that 'the US and their allies should leave our soils now'*

Lt Gen Asad Durrani, former DG ISI, had once said:

'Post 9/11 terrorism has become an instrument of state policy. Any of the Chechens, Uyghur, Hamas, Hezbollah, Kashmiris, and indeed the Taliban of all hues straddling the Durand Line - once labelled [as terrorist] is fair game. With Hiroshima, Nagasaki and Vietnam; and recently Fallujah in Iraq and Operation Balussa in Afghanistan, America leads the pack of states. The UK with its carpet-bombing of Dresden is not far behind.

No wonder, seeking a fatwa to exorcise suicide bombing does not work. It has nothing to do with religion, only with achieving a war aim. Though a myth of the 65 War; when it went around that some of our soldiers tied to explosives would jump in front of the Indian tanks, we did not invoke any religious injunction.

However today, the state is forced to compromise and thus the terrorists of yesterday become patriots of today and leaders of tomorrow. For that reason alone, it was prudent to keep a window open for some of those whom we had lumped under the Taliban.'

Let us wait for better days when the Americans and the Britons would comprehend facts on the ground.

WOT GIMMICKS IN PAKISTAN:

On 19th September 2011, a suicide bomber rammed his vehicle into the residence of one Chaudhry Aslam, a senior police official [*heading the anti-extremist cell of the Criminal Investigation Department (CID) and then leading a special campaign against the miscreants*] in DHA area of Karachi. Karachi had been considered the biggest source of funding through all viable means; Taliban immediately claimed the responsibility because the said police officer had picked up some of their activists in a campaign then going on.

The government named the *Tehreek e Taliban Pakistan* [TTP] for that rampage whereas the media had held those [about] 4000 Americans responsible who had managed to intrude in Pakistan through Hussain Haqqani & Rehman Malik's special visas in 2010.

Karachi was not used to intake such suicide bombings as other major cities, but it remained the home to thousands of the militants, criminals and foreign saboteurs. Taliban had also used the overgrown metropolis to avoid army operations in the tribal areas; no new phenomenon as it happens all over the world.

The first vehicle-borne suicide bombing in Pakistan was carried out in Karachi on 8th May 2002, when a suicide bomber had driven his car into a bus outside the Sheraton Hotel, killing 14 people including 11 French naval technicians. [*Subsequently that episode was linked to the Zardari's Agosta Submarine Deal with France and Admiral Mansoorul Haq's NAE case*]

This attack had come less than two weeks after another similar attack on 7th September 2002 in which a suicide bomber had rammed his explosive-laden vehicle into the residence of the DIG Baluchistan Frontier Corps of Quetta, killing his wife and 24 others in a high-security zone of the city.

The said DIG was involved in an operation capturing Younis al-Mauritani and his two aides named Abdul Ghaffar Al-Shami and Messara al-Shami [allegedly belonging to al-Qaeda]. The three operatives were arrested in a suburb of Quetta during a joint operation between the Baluchistan Frontier Corps and the ISI allegedly on American stance.

Coming back; it was on record that SSP Ch Aslam was once targeted earlier by a suicide bomber who had pushed his vehicle, loaded with explosives, into the CID HQ building in Karachi on 11th November 2010. Ch Aslam had escaped unhurt but it took lives of about 20 people injuring over 100 others. No clue could be found for its source.

The CID building was attacked a day after six activists from the Pak-Afghan border areas were arrested by the CID police Karachi. The officer and his team had allegedly arrested three successive *ameers* of the Karachi Taliban named Akhtar Zaman Mehsud, Bahadur Khan Momand and Maulvi Saeed Anwer; thus that event of 19th September was expected any time.

A leaflet was widely distributed in various outskirts of Karachi in the first week of July, carrying a "hit list" of *anti-jihadi* personalities and saying that *'previously, the word criminal was used for robbers and dacoits, but after 9/11 the Americans used this term for those who are sincere with Islam and want to wage jihad against the forces of the infidel; so be aware.'*

Those declared 'liable to be killed' in that pamphlet, along with the CID's Aslam Khan, included: DIG Saud Mirza; CID's SP Fayyaz Khan; Unit Chiefs Farooq Awan & Raja Omar Khattab; Sunni Deobandi scholar Mufti Naeem, Shia scholar Mirza Yousuf Baig; and MQM's Haider Abbas Rizvi; however, all personalities are alive till today.

Referring to 'The Assassination of bin Laden: Its Use and Abuse' written by *James Petras in Axis of Logic on 5th May 2011*, one can understand that Pakistani Taliban [TTP] has nothing to do with Afghan Taliban, no connection or no information sharing of any kind. In Afghanistan, the major forces resisting America and NATO are the Taliban and various other independent nationalist movements.

The Swati Taliban were totally independent of Al Qaeda in its origin, structure, leadership, tactics, strategy and social composition; whereas the Afghani Taliban is a mass organization with roots and sympathizers throughout Afghanistan. The later has thousands of trained Afghan fighters deeply penetrated in the Afghani government and military and once [on 1st May 2011 they had even planned a major 'spring offensive' against NATO forces.

Referring to *'the Friday Times' of 30th Dec 2011 - 6th Jan 2012* issue:

'Daily Jang quoted Taliban Commander Dadullah as saying that the Taliban will not talk peace with Pakistan Army before the enforcement of Taliban's Sharia in Pakistan. He said Maulvi Faqir of Bajaur - vice chief of the Taliban movement - was talking to the Pak army in his private capacity but Dadullah as commander of Taliban was not in favour of talking before the imposition of Sharia in Pakistan.

Maulvi Faqir of Bajaur was removed from the Deputy-Amir's slot of Taliban Faction of Pakistan in the last week of February 2012. One commander said in media that during peace talks the Army had released 154 Taliban members. He said he was very happy that Pakistan had quarrelled with America.'

In short; the **Afghani Taliban are overwhelmingly Afghan 'nationals'** in its composition, leadership and ideology; while Al Qaeda is 'international' (mostly Arab) in its membership and leadership. The Taliban might have tactically collaborated with Al Qaeda at some occasions but never had orders from Osama's leadership. The devastating majority of US and NATO casualties in Afghanistan were inflicted by Afghani Taliban. Limited operation and support in Pakistan could be linked to Afghani Taliban but not to the Al Qaeda's leadership; not to the Pakistani Taliban even.

The subsequent events proved that the Osama drama of Obama dated 2nd May 2011 had zero impact on Taliban activities in Afghanistan; it inflicted zero impact on the capacity of the Taliban to carry-out its prolonged war against the US occupation and the casualties of US lead forces kept on rising each week.

Contrarily, there are very strong beliefs and evidences that the Taliban in both the countries, Pakistan & Afghanistan, are one and the same; or at least there command level is interlinked; if at all Al Qaeda still exists.

Once CIA Centre at Khost in Afghanistan was stormed by a suicide bomber in which at least six CIA officers were killed. The suicide bomber was later identified as one Abu Dijana of Jordan who was trained, instructed, and sent by Hakimullah Mahsood. [Referring to *daily 'Jang' of 20th October 2012*, Saleem Saafi, the veteran columnist himself claimed to have seen the related video in person.]

This school of thought also quoted that:

- Nek Mohammad was once the Incharge Kargha Camp in Afghanistan when the country used to be under Mulla Umar's Taliban government.

- Baitullah Mahsood, before being head of the Pakistani Taliban, was the 2nd in Command with Mulla Dadullah, the known Afghan Taliban leader.

- Abdulla Mahsood, another Pakistani Taliban leader, was actually arrested in Afghanistan while fighting Americans there and was taken to Guantanomo Bay from where he was released after years to be welcome by Pakistani Taliban as their *Amir*.

- Most of the Taliban in Swat, who were later handled by the Pak-Army in 2007-08, were the same persons who had accompanied Maulana Soofi Mohammad to Afghanistan after Nine-Eleven episodes.

- Still Molvi Fazalullah of Swat [son in law of Maulana Soofi Mohammad] is in Afghanistan with his comrades.

The above spills indicate that the Taliban on both sides of Pak-Afghan border are inter-related; their targets are chosen by one command and their activities are controlled by one centralised body whether the operations are launched in Afghanistan or Pakistan. In Afghanistan, the US and NATO forces are attacked because they are considered as foreign intruders and in Pakistan the security personnel are targeted because the Pakistani government is considered America's ally.

However, so many reports have surfaced in the American media that most of the stuff like videos are 'manufactured' in the under ground laboratories of CIA and Pentagon; videos of Osama BL's speeches made public in 2001-02 & of *'Weapons of Mass Destruction'* [WMD] made on Iraq and released in early days of 2003 are especially referred to.

In between the two philosophies, the poor people of both the countries are being crushed; human blood is so cheap here.

The whole debate is being summed up with a script from an essay of Gen Asad Durrani, former Chief of the ISI, who once wrote that:

'....... *John Esposito* (Professor of International Affairs and Islamic Studies at Georgetown University) *associate it [the Islamic Funda-mentalism] with political activism, extremism, fanaticism, terrorism, and anti-Americanism. Any Islamic movement that makes them [the Western Powers] uncomfortable can thus be conveniently reviled as "fundamentalist".*

Jihad was a concept that expressed fortitude to fight ills in society - ignorance, illiteracy, bigotry, and all the rest. The use of arms indeed had its place - especially & exclusively - in self defence; no more. The mere mention of the word can now send chill up our spines.

The UN may sanction armed resistance against foreign occupation, but if waged in the name of jihad it must be condemned, and a jihadi prosecuted as a "terrorist". There were times one could sensibly discuss this phenomenon; but now - no longer. Post 9/11, terrorism has become an instrument of state policy.'

Thus, repeating again that the terrorists of yesterday may become patriots of today and at times leaders of tomorrow; so keep a window open for them.

Scenario 60

PAKISTAN ITSELF ATTACKED BY W O T:

Since about six years successively, the al Qaeda and militants supported by Afghani Taliban had hit several military and police bases near Pakistani nuclear facilities in northern Punjab and the Khyber PK province [previously known as NWFP]. These attacks had taken start soon after Nine Eleven of 2001 but had gradually gained momentum when on 8th November 2006 a suicide bomber attacked an Army base in Dargai near Malakand Division; mechanized infantry, armour and artillery were stationed in the garrison.

Over 45 Pakistani Army trainees were killed and 20 got seriously injured when the bomber, wrapped in a *chadar* around his body, came running into the training area and exploded him where recruits had gathered for exercise.

Dargai village otherwise was stronghold of militant group *Tehrik-e-Nifaz-e-Shariat-e-Mohammadi* [TNSM] so al Qaeda and TNSM were the primary suspects. The attack was considered a likely retaliation for the air-strike on Maulvi Faqir Mohammed's *madrassa* in Chingai, Bajaur in which about 84 children were killed.

In fact that air-strike on Faqir Mohammad's religious school was [perhaps] the first American drone attack on Pakistan considering that *Madrassa* as the 'terrorist's training camp' which was not a correct assessment. Gen Musharraf's military government had declared that air-strike was done by the Pakistan Air Force [PAF]; as per secret deal done by the General with the Americans.

On the same day, Governor NWFP [now Khyber PK] Ali Jan Orkazi [*himself a retired Lt General and Pashtun*] became target of a rocket attack in Wana, South Waziristan; three rockets were fired at him during his *jirga* [meeting] with tribal leaders The governor was there to seek peace deals in the tribal regions to fetch support for the Pakistani military and Gen Musharraf.

The fact remained that attacks against al Qaeda and Afghani Taliban infrastructure, designed to 'prove' Pakistan an ally in the war, only served to enrage the pro-Islamist elements within the military, increasing the likelihood of more attacks and coup attempts.

ATTACKS IN LAST YEARS OF MILITARY RULE:

In **March 2007,** the Kharian Cantonment [*House of 17th Infantry Division of the Pak-Army*] was attacked by a suicide bomber killing two recruits while eight were injured as they were on their training exercises. In July 2007, a suicide bomber attacked the Police Recruitment Centre in D I Khan killing 20 recruits and leaving about 50 wounded. Another similar suicidal attack during the same day was launched at Police Training College Hangu killing eight recruits there.

During December 2007, the militants went more aggressive, perhaps, due to Gen Musharraf's proclamation of Emergency of 3rd November a month earlier. The militants thought that due to 'Constitution held in abeyance'; the army would go more offensive. Thus **on 10th December 2007** they launched a stern attack on Kamra Air Base in Khyber PK province.

Those were the days when the Pakistani military was consolidating to regain control of the settled district of Swat. Though during the same days a suicide bomber had hit a police checkpoint at Matta [*near Swat's capital Mingora, where the Pakistani Army had just marked their presence*] killing ten people including two children and three policemen, but the area remained under control.

However, the attack at PAF base in Kamra, though only injuring seven people, had far more serious implications being a likely location for Pakistan's nuclear missiles and weapons. The suicide bomber had targeted a school bus carrying 35 children of PAF officers; the driver, a conductor, and five children were wounded in the strike.

While al Qaeda suicide bombers were targeting secure military facilities since 2006, the nuclear arsenals remained their focal points. For instance, two suicide bombing events in R A Bazaar Rawalpindi **on 4th September 2007** killing 25 and leaving 48 seriously injured, including military and intelligence officers as the direct target, were noted by the Pakistan Army very seriously.

Then on **30th October 2007** another suicide bomber launched attack in the same garrison town [outside GHQ's main gate] killing eight persons including two police officers and leaving about fourteen injured; it was a loud alarming signal.

On **1st November 2007,** a suicide bomber killed eight and injured 27 at Sargodha Airbase too; the bomber had driven his motorcycle into a bus carrying military and intelligence officers to the airbase for duty. [*The Sargodha PAF Base serves as the HQ of the PAF's Central Air Command and home of F-16 fighters and ballistic missiles.*]

On 23rd November 2007, two suicide bombers targeted the military and intelligence personnel in Islamabad and in Rawalpindi; one at a check post near GHQ Rawalpindi and the other was on a bus carrying ISI officers near Faizabad. Both these suicidal attacks were apparently aimed to erode the Pak-Army's capacity to defend nuclear installations if al Qaeda could aspire to seize nuclear weapons.

The intelligentsia had a strong view that attacks on military and PAF installations were aided and sponsored by the covert NATO intelligence officials posted around; they were testing the grounds in fact and miserably failed. Though there was a colossal loss to Pakistan but, with such failures of enemy attacks, the poisonous propaganda against *'Pakistan's ability to save their nuclear arsenal from Taliban & Al Qaeda'* went slow and ultimately died.

Since the first day of 2008, the security situation in Pakistan's Tribal Areas [FATA] had deteriorated as the militants had taken control of certain key points. In mid January, a militant group had taken away Pak-Army's supply convoy into hostage in Orakzai Agency. The Pakistani military launched an operation after two *jirgas* had failed to get the foreign and internal militant forces surrender the army vehicles; however, the soldiers were got freed.

Earlier, besides the references given above, on 6th July 2007 an un-identified group had attempted to shoot down Gen Musharraf's airplane as it left the PAF Base at Rawalpindi; he was travelling with senior military and political leaders.

The militants had conducted attacks on numerous mosques of the Khyber PK Province as well. The most high-profile attack occurred on 20th December 2007 in Charsadda, where a suicide bomber detonated in the mosque in an attempt to kill former Interior Minister Aftab Ahmed Sherpao while attending the Eid prayers. More than 50 were killed and about a hundred wounded.

The most drastic attack in that series was of 27th December 2007 in which PPP's leader and former Prime Minister Benazir Bhutto was eliminated along with 23 of her security guards including some members of the regular police. Taliban Commander Baitullah Mehsud had claimed credit for the assassination.

[*Details of this episode has been given in earlier Volumes of this book*]

ATTACKS IN 1ST YEAR OF PPP REGIME:

On 10th **January 2008**, a suicide bomber targeted the police contingent posted on duty outside the Lahore High Court Lahore killing 22 policemen and civilians; more than 70 were wounded.

On 16th **January 2008**, the militants attacked a check post at a fort in Northern Pakistan manned by the Frontier Corps [FC] in the town of Sararogha; more than 20 troops were captured.

On 17th **January 2008**, the same group of fighters took control of another check post at Saklatoi fort; about 40 paramilitary soldiers were on duty but they had to leave the post and fled to avoid clash.

On 25th **January 2008**, in the same Orakzai agency of Tribal Areas at Pak-Afghan border, near Darra Adam Khel village [*a well known bazaar for open sale of illegal hand-crafted firearms*], the radicals hijacked a military convoy carrying supplies and ammunition for Pakistani troops deployed near the border posts; at least six soldiers were captured during the hijacking.

34 militants and two Pakistani soldiers were killed after the Pakistani military cordoned the Darra Adam Khel region and launched an assault to take back their vehicles and ammunition and clear the area of fighter forces mostly belonging to the Central Asian States. Heavy shelling took place with artillery and gunship helicopters while militants claimed to have taken control of Zarghoon-khel check post.

The militants, in another parallel move, had abducted 14 Frontier Corps [FC] troops from a checkpoint in Kohat. The locals informed the media secretly that the militants had paraded the whole contingent of 14 hostages through the main bazaar of Darra Adam Khel.

In the same evening perhaps, eight FC men were slaughtered by that aggressive group; their bodies were dragged through the same main bazaar to expose the heads of the beheaded personnel. The militants were wearing Army and Frontier Corps uniforms while conducting that task to make the residents believe that more FC and military troops had been beheaded in their back yard.

During that siege, the militants took over the Kohat Tunnel Mountain also, a strategic link along the Indus Highway that connects Peshawar to the southern tribal agencies. The Pak-military declared a cease-fire in Darra Adam Khel next day while the local religious leaders formed a peace *jirga* to resolve the situation.

Maulvi Omar of the Baitullah Mehsud faction though formally denied the claim; but urged that 25 Pakistani soldiers and seven fighters were killed in the said encounter. The fact remained that the fighters loyal to Baitullah Mehsud were bravely resisting the military across the whole belt. Also that entrance to Waziristan was easy but maintaining writ there was a difficult task for any enforcement agency or army; whether from Pakistan or America or NATO.

A day after, **on 27th January 2008**, the military recaptured the Japanese built Kohat Tunnel after fierce fighting. As reported by the military media channels, 24 miscreants were killed; many had fled leaving behind huge quantity of arms and ammunition. However, the fighters had damaged the tunnel and attempted to demolish it to make the areas independent of Pakistan's control.

On 4th February 2008, the city of Rawalpindi was hit with another suicide attack after a bomber on a motorcycle rammed into a bus carrying military personnel, killing ten security personnel at least. The blast took place during rush hour on a road passing through much crowded market in Rawalpindi. The bus was carrying personnel from the Army Medical Corps; six soldiers and four civilians were killed and 25 more were wounded.

On 9th February 2008, a suicide bomber launched an attack in the settled district of Charsadda at an election rally held by the Awami National Party [ANP], a Pahstun political party; 25 civilians were reportedly killed and more than 35 were left wounded.

This was the third major suicide bombing in Charsadda since April 2007. The prior two attacks were directed at former Interior Minister Aftab Sherpao [*who was targeted while he was addressing his party workers on 28th April 2007*]; killing more than 28 and leaving tens wounded, including Sherpao's son who was a minister in the NWFP assembly, and several other lawmakers and security officials.

Taliban commander Abdullah Mehsud had claimed that assassination attempt; later Abdullah was reportedly killed by Pakistani security forces in July 2007, however, doubt prevailed.

On 11th February 2005, the militants struck another office of the ANP but this time in North Waziristan. Eight Pakistanis were killed, including two senior party leaders, and 13 were critically wounded after a car bomb slammed into the party office near Miranshah.

On the same day, Pakistan Army had arrested Mullah Mansoor Dadullah [*Taliban's former military commander in southern Afghanistan*] along with five other non-Pakistani fighters in Zhob district of Baluchistan province. Mullah Mansoor was fired after he was alleged for some activities which were against the rules of Islamic Emirate of Afghanistan; as per later statement from Mullah Omar.

Next day on 12th February 2008, the group retaliated by kidnapping Pakistan's Ambassador to Afghanistan Tariq Azizuddin; local Taliban immediately claimed responsibility for Azizuddin's kidnapping and demanded the release of Mansoor Dadullah as a pre-condition to set the ambassador free.

Ambassador Azizuddin was kidnapped near Jamrud in the Khyber Tribal Agency while travelling from Peshawar to Kabul without taking a security escort. The evnt was a troubling development as the Afridi tribe, which had control over the region, was considered friendly to the Pakistani government.

It was a disturbing situation for the Pakistan Army too, as the Taliban had negotiated with Pak-Army a cease-fire in the tribal regions and the settled district of Swat just a few days earlier and formal negotiations with Taliban were on the way through a *Jirga*.

On 24th February 2008, a prominent Taliban leader Mullah Obaidullah Akhund was arrested in Lahore. He was in Lahore in connection with raising money to fund their operations in Pak-Afghan border areas.

Next day On 25th February 2008, taking revenge for their arrested leader, the Taliban launched a suicidal attack on Lt Gen Mushtaq Ahmed Baig, the Surgeon General of Army Medical Corps [*by ramming an explosive loaded car into the General's staff car*] on the busy Mall Road at the GPO square in Rawalpindi. He was the senior-most officer killed since the Nine Eleven 2001's War on Terror. Eight others, including the driver and the accompanying guard, were also killed in the attack and 20 wounded.

On 28th **February 2008,** in a drone attack near village Azam Warzak of South Waziristan, over 13 Arabs and fighters from Central Asia [*Daily Dawn reported four Arabs, two Turkmen, and two Pakistanis from Punjab province*] were killed, reportedly including an al Qaeda fugitive from Egypt, but NOT Ayman al Zawahiri as was widely rumoured in the media.

[*Several senior Egyptian members of al Qaeda were known to operate in Pakistan's tribal areas. These included Abu Khabab al Masri, Abu Ubaidah al Masri, Abdul Rahman al Masri al Maghribi, Abu Ikhlas al Masri, and Sheikh Essa. Abu Khabab, Abu Ubaidah, and Maghribi were once believed to be killed in the January 2006 Damadola air strike, but the reports were false.*]

The militants belonged to the Abu Hamza group whose leader was said to be a follower of local commander Mulla Nazir, often characterized as a pro-government Taliban leader. The attack occurred at residential premises of Shero Wazir, a follower of Mulla Nazir who had rented it out to an Arab. Local Taliban cordoned the area and immediately buried those badly burnt and mutilated.

Many media reports indicated that a large number of Arabs and other foreigners had been living and doing business on Pak-Afghan border for years with local tribal names. Mulla Nazir, however, denied al Qaeda's presence in his territory, and instead claimed 'peace loving' Afghans were living there.

[*An Egyptian cleric named* **Sheikh Essa** *was their ideologue, based in North Waziristan, who used to advocate expanding the Taliban's jihad in Pakistan. Former members of jihadi outfits such as Jaish-e-Mohammed (JeM), Laskhar-e-Taiba (LeT) and Lashkar-e-Jhangvi (LeJ) had reportedly gathered in North Waziristan under his command and guidance.*]

Next day **on 29th February 2008,** just to take revenge for their humiliation and loss, a suicide bomber struck in the neighbouring settled district of Lakki Marwat in the Khyber PK Province. More than 40 Pakistanis were killed and scores more were wounded, many of them critically, in a suicide bombing at a policeman's funeral.

The suicide truck bomb was detonated at the funeral of a policeman who was killed a day earlier along with two other officers in an explosive attack. The attack was designed to inflict a large number of casualties as well as insult the service by teaching them a lesson. The blast occurred when police contingent were presenting the last salute of honour to their martyred fellow police officers.

The then media reports indicated that the Pakistan's military was chasing Baitullah Mehsud, the commander of the Movement of the Taliban in Pakistan but not to defeat Baitullah or necessarily capture or kill him; not at all. It was no easy The military only wanted to influence his policy of killing innocent people for no fault of them; thus essentially to marginalize him as a player.

On 1st March 2008, a suicide bomber attacked a vehicle of the Bajaur Levies; two paramilitary soldiers were killed and 24 wounded.

On 2nd March 2008, the militants executed [another] major suicide attack, fourth one in one week, in Kohat killing more than 40 persons and leaving behind about 40 wounded when a suicide bomber detonated his vest during a tribal meeting in a small town named Zargoan. A tribal *jirga* was being attended by over 1,500 members of five local tribes.

The *jirga,* mainly attended by Mehsuds, Orakzais and Wazirs was called to discuss the security situation in troubled Darra Adam Khel on instance of the government of Khyber PK and the military agencies. It was being held to suggest ways and means to flush out the foreigner militants from Kohat and its adjacent areas. The suicide bomber struck as the tribal leaders were leaving the meeting and most of the victims were local tribesmen and tribal elders; the father of one Pakistani senator was also killed amongst others.

On 3rd March 2008, Admiral Mike Mullen, Chairman of the US Joint Chiefs of Staff, landed in Islamabad to talk with embattled Gen Musharraf and Pakistan's military leadership in a changed political scenario after general elections of 18th February. The 2nd trip in one month's time to Pakistan reflected the US concern that a growing insurgency by Al Qaeda militants in the tribal areas, near the border with Afghanistan had posed an increasing threat.

Evidently, the threat of religious extremism was growing in Pakistan and the country's leadership was aware of the challenge facing the nation. Admiral Mullen met with Gen Musharraf, Chief of the Army Staff Gen

Kayani and Gen Tariq Majid, Chairman of the Joint Chiefs of Staff Committee.

Admiral Mullen discussed US plans to send 22 American personnel to train elements of the Pakistani military and the Frontier Corps to be expert in counter-insurgency and intelligence gathering techniques later that year. The plan called for the US training to last two years and to be passed on to about 8,500 Frontier Corps troops. The said American offer was kept in waiting for the time being as the new PPP government was just finding space to stand upon.

On 4th March 2008, the militants targeted the Pakistan Navy War College in Lahore killing seven military and Navy personnel whereas 21 were wounded. The suicide bomber entered the college by following a minibus, and detonated his vest shortly afterward. Some media reports indicated that there were four explosions with short intervals; meaning thereby there might be more militants around.

On 10th March 2008, two suicide bombers hit two buildings almost simultaneously in Lahore, killing at least 28 and wounding over 160 Pakistanis. One of the suicide car bombers struck an office building housing Pakistan's Federal Investigation Agency [FIA] headquarters and a US counter-terrorism team.

FIA Lahore office mainly used to deal with immigration and people smuggling but the building also housed the offices of a special US-trained unit created to counter terrorism; however, no death of any US citizen was reported in the blast that tore apart the 8-story office building.

The second bombing occurred outside an advertising firm, but the motive for this attack was not clear. At least six Pakistanis were killed and scores wounded in the bombing. That day's dual suicide bombing in Lahore was the sixth major strike inside Pakistan since the general elections held on 18th February 2008.

On 15th March 2008, the al Qaeda militants attacked an Italian restaurant in Islamabad killing one civilian and leaving 15 wounded. The said premises, known as Luna Caprese restaurant, used to be frequently visited by foreigners where the bomb was planted and detonated remotely.

The dying person was identified as a female Turkish nurse who worked at the US Embassy whereas seven US citizens, one Chinese national, one Briton, one Canadian citizen, two Japanese journalists and three Pakistanis were wounded.

On 1st June 2008, a bombing near the Danish embassy, situated in a secured region of Islamabad, killed eight people and wounded more than 30, some seriously; an al Qaeda affiliate group was suspected. The bomber had driven a car with diplomatic license plates through security, and parked it in a parking lot next to the Danish embassy. The car bomb, containing about 35 kg of explosives, was then either detonated remotely or by timer.

The blast left a crater about four feet deep and nine feet wide, and damaged the wall of the Danish embassy as well as the nearby offices of the United Nations Development Program. Later reports indicated that a foreign national was also killed in the blast.

In nut shell, till the end of 2008, suicide bombings in 2008 surpassed the last year's figures, with 61 attacks till then killing at least 889 people and injuring 2072 others, a source in the investigation agencies disclosed.

The total number of suicide blasts in Pakistan since 2002 had risen to 140 till June 2008 while 56 bombers had struck the previous year [2007]. At least, for 29 times, suicide bombers struck in Khyber PK while 16 others hit their targets in FATA. Swat topped the list of districts where 11 suicide bombers hit targets, killing 101 people and injuring 294 others.

ANP Chief, Asfandyar Wali Khan, had survived a suicide attack at his Hujra on 2nd October 2008, where three of his guests and a guard were killed. The Koocha Risaldar blast in Peshawar in December 2008 was considered the worst terrorist attack in the provincial capital of Khyber PK wherein 34 people were killed and around 120 wounded. A loss to private buildings had reached millions of rupees. Four suicide bombers struck in Peshawar city in 2008, killing 99 and wounding 226 others.

Punjab witnessed 10 suicide blasts in 2008 with five in Lahore city alone.

Three suicide bombers hit their targets in the federal capital Islamabad during that year including one of these targeting the Danish embassy. The Marriott Hotel blast at Islamabad was considered as Pakistan's worst-ever act of terrorism, occurred during the year when on 22nd September 2008, about sixty people were killed and over 200 wounded.

Leaving aside Karachi where three bomber attacks were reported, no suicide attack took place in other part of the Sindh province. One incident was reported in Balochistan [on 23rd September 2008] when a suicide bomber had blown himself up, killing one girl student and injuring 22 persons in Quetta.

During the year 2008, only twelve people could be caught by the security agencies before hitting their targets; nothing was heard about their fate.

In fact not even a single case had been investigated during the whole decade of War on Terror. Or if worked out by some investigation agency, police or FIA, the respective judiciary could not punish even a single culprit or accused through the whole decade; they were released Scot free on one pretext or the other.

ATTACK ON SRI LANKAN TEAM:

On 3rd March 2009, the Sri Lankan cricket team was attacked when a bus carrying their cricketers was fired upon by about 12 gunmen, hiding around at the Liberty Square near the Gaddafi Stadium in Lahore. The cricketers were on their way to play their third day of the second test against the Pakistani cricket team.

When the bus was crossing the Liberty rounabout the militants started firing, targeting the cricketer's bus. The police contingent escorting the team returned fire. In the ensuing fighting, six policemen, and two civilians died. After about 20 minute's operation, the militants fled, leaving behind rocket launchers and grenades. Six members of the Sri Lanka national cricket team were also injured.

Player Samaraweera sustained shrapnel wounds to his thigh, and Paranavitana to his chest and were hospitalised following the incident; the others had sustained minor injuries. The team's Assistant Coach Paul Farbrace was also injured.

The gunmen had first targeted the wheels of the bus, and then fired at the bus and its occupants. A rocket was also fired at the bus, which missed and hit a nearby electric pole. The bus driver, Khalil, told later that a white car had swerved in front of the bus, forcing him to slow. Television images showed gunmen emerging from the large grassy traffic circle and shooting at the bus from crouched positions. The players ducked to the floor of the bus and driver Khalil drove through the gunshots and whisked them to the stadium.

Later, the Lahore police found weapons stashes near the scene including 10 rifles, two rocket launchers, a 9-millimeter pistol, and detonator cable. The militants had also thrown a grenade under the bus, which exploded after the bus had passed over it smoothly.

A minivan following the team bus carrying the match referee and umpires was also fired upon; its driver was killed and an umpire Ahsan Raza got serious bullet wound on his chest.

Security cameras captured footage of several gunmen carrying automatic weapons and backpacks, firing on the convoy from the Liberty Square roundabout; later seen escaping on motorcycles. The attackers were armed with AK-47 assault rifles, hand grenades, RPG launchers, claymores, and explosives.

The Sri Lankan team were then taken to the stadium and airlifted from the pitch via Pakistan Air Force MI-17 helicopters, and immediate arrangements were made for the team to return to Colombo on the next available flight. The second Test, which was the last scheduled fixture of the tour, was abandoned as a draw. Earlier, in May 2002, New Zealand had abandoned their Test series in Pakistan after a suicide bomb attack outside their hotel. However, they returned in the 2003-04 season to fulfil their commitments.

The Sri Lankan team was particularly welcomed because it had agreed to play in Pakistan after other major world teams had refused to come, citing Pakistan's poor security. A year earlier, the Australian, British, and South African cricket teams said they would not take part in the Champions Trophy, a major world cricket event then scheduled in Pakistan. After the Mumbai attack, the Indian team had refused to come for matches planned in 2009.

In order to persuade the Sri Lankan team to visit, the Pakistan government offered to arrange "presidential-style security" but it was all the sham arrangements.

In 2004, a religious faction of Pakistan had issued a fatwa against playing Cricket calling it against Islam. The attack on Sri Lankan team was believed to have been carried out by *Lashkar e Jhangvi* [LeJ] or some other militant group close to Al-Qaeda. Contrarily Interior Minister Rehman Malik, told the NA Standing Committee that *'sufficient evidence has been surfaced pointing to involvement of a foreign hand'*; making Pakistan a laughing stock for the whole world.

The series was the first test tour of Pakistan since South Africa's visit in October 2007. It was the first attack on a national sports team since the Munich massacre of Israeli athletes by Palestinian militants in 1972. Most major cricket teams had refused to risk playing in Pakistan, making the country more isolated from the rest of the world.

The most alarming aspect was that the event took place in the heart of Lahore, the cultural capital of the country. None of the attackers were shot or caught while they were seen coming to the scene with big bags; that was ridiculous and it was a total security lapse.

The foreign press propagated that militant's attack on Sri Lankan team had some similarity to the attack of November 2008 in Mumbai, in which 10 militants attacked hotels and other targets over three days, killing 163 people. The attackers appeared to be in their 20s; wearing sneakers and loose pants; walking casually as they fired; carrying backpacks loaded with weapons and high-energy snacks of dried fruit and chocolates; like the Mumbai gunmen.

On 5th March 2009, Salman Taseer, the then governor of Punjab province [as CM Shahbaz Sharif's government was suspended for a month or so], offered a reward of 10 million rupees ($125,000 USD) for information leading to the capture of the militants responsible for the attack.

The Punjab Police arrested over 250 suspects, including 4 'prime suspects' and declared one Muhammad Adil [*who was running a sports bikes business in Islampura*] as the mastermind behind the attack. Reportedly he had received a call from one of the militants at 9:05 am on the morning of the attacks asking for instructions. One Shahzad Babar of Rahim Yar Khan and Aqeel of Kahuta were also arrested later.

Further investigations revealed that the attack was planned at a house rented for this purpose in Madina Colony, Walton Road Lahore. The auto rickshaws used in the attack were purchased by one Samiullah. As often happens with high profile militant attacks in Pakistan, a number of suspects were arrested but released later due to lack of evidence.

Imran Khan had criticised the security arrangements and said that '*the security provided was 10 times less than what was being provided to government officials like Rehman Malik*'.

After that bad occurrence, the Sri Lankan team was despatched to Colombo same evening. The New Zealand team cancelled its

December 2009 tour of Pakistan. Bangladesh also put off a scheduled tour for Pakistan due to security concerns after this attack. T20 league matches with India, due to be held over 45 days from 10th April to 24th May 2009 in 9 Indian cities were re-considered. Former Indian captain Sourav Ganguly said 'after these attacks Pakistan is not a safe country to play cricket'.

The 2011 Cricket World Cup was to be co-hosted by Pakistan, Sri Lanka, Bangladesh and India, but in the wake of this attack the International Cricket Council (ICC) were forced to strip Pakistan of its hosting rights. The headquarters of the organising committee were originally situated in Lahore, but were then shifted to Mumbai. Pakistan was supposed to hold fourteen matches, including one semi-final. Eight of Pakistan's matches were awarded to India, four to Sri Lanka and two to Bangladesh.

ATTACK ON MOSQUE IN JAMRUD:

On 27th March 2009, more than 70 people were killed and over 120 injured as a suicide bomber blew himself up inside a mosque during the Friday prayers in Jamrud town of Peshawar, situated near the main route to Kabul, starting point of the Khyber Pass. Such was the impact of the blast that the mosque was almost decimated. The congregation was attended by around 250 persons, including many security personnel from a nearby security check post, and truckers carrying NATO supplies.

In February 2009, a bridge at 15 miles northwest of Peshawar was blown up by radicals presumably sympathetic to or sponsored by the militants from across the border. This attack came a day after when at least 11 people were killed at a restaurant in the same northwest region in the Jandola district of South Waziristan. The next day a supply base for NATO troops was attacked and 12 containers were damaged.

The attack occurred just after the muezzin's call to prayer. As a result of the attack the upper floor of the mosque collapsed on the worshippers below; three columns supporting a beam connected to the Mosque's Minarets at either side of the structure were all that remained left with the Mosque.

The bombing of the Jamrud mosque came at a time of increased uncertainty in Pakistan following a high-profile attack on the Sri Lankan cricket team. There was also talk of an increased American drone bombing campaign into other areas of Pakistan.

Though there was no immediate claim of responsibility, but other details had pointed towards raised speculations for the local Taliban. Commander Nazir Afridi of TTP's Khyber Agency chapter had warned of attacks if the security forces did not vacate the FC's check posts in Jamrud and Landikotal by 20th February. They were not allowing the Peshawar-Torkham route to be used by vehicles carrying supplies for NATO forces in Afghanistan.

Asfandyar Wali Khan, Chief of the ruling party ANP commented that:

> *"The bomber and his operatives have once again demonstrated that this is not a war for Islam and Shariah. This is not jihad, but war against humanity....... If foreigners are allowed to live in tribal areas without passport and proper documentation, it will only lead to this kind of consequences."*

The bombing took place hours before US President Barack Obama had unfolded a new strategy for the Afghan war, which recognised Pakistan as key to eliminating Al-Qaeda and Taliban havens along the Pak-Afghan border.

ATTACK ON POLICE ACADEMY LAHORE:

On 30th March 2009, at 7.30am local time, a terrorist assault on Police Training School in Manawan, the eastern part of Lahore was launched by about 14 militants in which 34 police recruits [*official figures stayed at 9 policemen & 3 civilians*] were reportedly killed and more than 90 were seriously wounded during the fighting. The attack was the latest in a series of military-styled terrorist attack on civilian and government installations in Pakistan.

The school had more than 750 trainees on campus, plus scores of police officers as the teaching and support staff. The attackers were well armed with automatic rifles, hand grenades, and rocket-propelled grenades. They carried packs loaded with ammunition and other supplies on their backs. Some of the attackers were dressed in police uniforms, while others were in civilian clothes.

The armed militants entered the compound after killing the security guards at the back entrance of the police academy. The team then fanned out into the compound mainly to strike at the parade grounds, where recruits had gathered for morning exercises. The attackers lobbed grenades from three sides, then entered the parade grounds and opened fire on the survivors. The attackers then moved into a building and took more than 35 recruits and officers hostage.

Pakistani police cordoned the police academy and aimed for a counter-assault to dislodge the terrorists. Commandos from the Punjab Police as well as the Pakistan Rangers, backed by Army helicopters, launched an attack on the compound. Armoured personnel carrier was sent into the compound, the terrorists dealt with the forces but were overwhelmed after commandos air-assaulted the academy.

Police captured six [out of 14] of the attackers; one was carrying an Afghan passport in the name of Hijratullah from Paktika but was surprisingly speaking in Punjabi accent. Out of the remaining eight attackers, five were killed during the fighting whereas three had killed themselves by detonating suicide vests. One of them arrested from just outside the building when he tried to blow up an Army helicopter. That was the end: the terrorist blew themselves after wrecking hell upon the policemen and sending the whole nation once again into the awful feeling of helplessness, anger, and frustration.

Next day, *Fedayeen-e-Islam*, a little-known group, claimed responsibility; the same group had claimed responsibility for the bombing at the Marriott Islamabad on 20th September 2008. The same day, Baitullah Mehsud, the leader of TTP called the Associated Press [APP] and Reuters to claim responsibility.

The attack on police training facility was the latest in a series of military-styled terror assaults that were launched by the al Qaeda and their allied terror groups. These groups had conducted similar strikes in India, Afghanistan, Pakistan, and Yemen. Reportedly, Al Qaeda had revived its paramilitary army, formerly known as the 055 Brigade and then renamed as the *Lashkar al Zil*, or Shadow Army.

Those days al Qaeda and their allied terror groups had stepped up their attacks on Pakistani security forces nationwide, despite a peace agreement that had surrendered more than 1/3 of the Khyber PK province to the Taliban; the media had urged.

On the same day, in Bannu a suicide car bomber rammed into a military convoy, killing four soldiers and wounding several others. The suicide attack marked the ninth this month [of March 2009] as a day earlier, on 29th March 2009, Taliban surrounded a police outpost in Khyber Agency and had taken 12 policemen hostage who were reportedly beheaded later. On 28th March, a large Taliban force had attacked a trucking terminal outside Peshawar and had destroyed NATO vehicles and equipment while setting them on fire.

Going further back, on 27th March, the Taliban had destroyed a bridge in Khyber PK. That same day, a suicide bomber killed more than 70 people after detonating in the middle of a mosque in Jamrud [*details have been mentioned above*] The al Qaeda leadership had openly urged the Pakistani public and military to turn on the government and join the jihad.

Three scenarios were built on the basis of the then available information:

Was there any chance of Indian involvement?

Bahukutumbi Raman – the former head of the counter-terrorism division of the Research & Analysis Wing (RAW) and also a former member of the Special Task Force [India] for the Revamping of the Intelligence Apparatus – within hours of the Mumbai tragedy (on 26th November 2008) presented his recommendations to the Government of India. B Raman had proposed that:

> '*When Ashok Chaturvedi [then Director RAW] retires on 31st January 2009, he must be replaced by someone from outside RAW preferably a top-notch covert operator to re-energize RAW's covert capabilities to undertake operations inside Pakistan.*'

On 25th January 2009, K C Verma, a career officer of the Intelligence Bureau of India, was named as the new chief of the Research & Analysis Wing. K C Verma's appointment came as a surprise to India's bulging intelligence bureaucracy because P V Kumar was the senior-most RAW officer after Ashok Chaturvedi's retirement.

B Raman, who enjoyed a trusted association with India's official security and intelligence apparatus, in an earlier paper, had raised the question of **"how to make Pakistan pay a price..."** and recommended:

> '*Through covert action, which is deniable para-political and para-military action meant to make Pakistan's sponsorship prohibitively costly to it. Such a covert action would be directed against the Pakistan State and society and not against terrorists.*' [Paper no; 1893 at www.saag.org is referred]

Dr C Raj Mohan, widely acknowledged as one of *'India's leading foreign policy analyst'*, had argued that: *'If Pakistan is not willing or is unable to deliver an end to cross-border terrorism then perhaps India ought to execute alternatives.'*

Earlier, on *10ᵗʰ December 2008*, the *Hindustan Times* carried a column by Gurmeet Kanwal, head of the Centre for Land Warfare Studies, recommending that:

> *"To achieve a lasting impact and ensure that the actual perpetrators of terrorism are targeted, it is necessary to employ covert capabilities against Pakistan."*

Moreover, Christine Fair, Senior Political Scientist, RAND Corporation, suspected that the Indian involvement in Balochistan increased with encouragement from Kabul [*'the News' dated 6ᵗʰ April 2009* is referred]. It was an awful assessment as most of the militant organizations operating in Pakistan had their ideological and financial bases operating from Afghanistan.

ATTACK ON PAK ARMY's GHQ:

Before Pakistan could recover from a suicide bombing at a UN office in Islamabad and a massive bomb blast in a Peshawar market a week earlier, the brazen attack targeting Pakistan's most secure military complex – the Army Headquarters [GHQ] — jolted it further.

On 10ᵗʰ October 2009, a deadly terrorist attack was launched on Pakistan army headquarters [GHQ] in Rawalpindi. During the operation four terrorists who launched the assault with sophisticated weapons were killed whereas six soldiers including two senior army officials were martyred at the spot.

GHQ attack, the biggest terrorist attack on army in the history of Pakistan, was planned in Miranshah, North Wazirstan, by those militants who were encouraged after a broad daylight attack on the Sri Lankan team in Lahore.

Later the confessional statements of Aqeel alias Dr Usman [also alias Kamran alias Nazir Ahmed] to the military court revealed that *'they were planning to make hostage the high officers like army Brigadiers and Generals in order to get their detained militants released.'* The heads of

TTP Amjad Farooqui Group, Ustad Aslam Yasin and Ilyas Kashmiri had tasked him to launch an attack on GHQ.

The deadly weapon for the attack was brought by [another] Usman alias Ishfaq alias Gul Khan hiding them in a CNG cylinder of a Suzuki vehicle number FDV 3530. The total ammunition to be used here was comprising nine rifles, one rocket-launcher, around 50 loaded magazines ammunition pouches, fly liver-grenades, six AP Claymore mines, six rockets, six expelling charges, eight hand-grenades, eight detonators, and nineteen 40mm grenades of Gp-25 for the said attack on GHQ.

As per details published in *'PULSE' Weekly of 30th September 2011*, all the weapons mentioned above were brought from Dera Ismail Khan, Jhang, and Toba Tek Singh; stored in a house in Faisalabad, owned by Babar Shabbir and transferred it to Rawalpindi in four time consignments.

The idea of GHQ attack was floated by Ustad Yasin in the Miranshah meeting. Dr Usman claimed that he was reluctant to attack the army but the other two men argued and convinced him that the Pakistan Army, as an ally of the United States, was a legitimate target.

In that meeting, Ilyas Kashmiri said the plan was to hold army Generals hostage at the GHQ till they could get detained militants released in exchange. Yasin gave Dr Usman a list with 115 names on it; these were the men whose release was to be demanded. He also assured Dr Usman that he would be accompanied by a team of trained warriors.

Dr Usman and his accomplices used Google Earth to download the maps of GHQ on the basis of which they planned their attacks. The team, *according to the court documents,* took months for arranging and transporting the weapons to Rawalpindi and Dr Usman made multiple exploration trips to the GHQ during the summer of 2009. However, it was Wajid Mehmood, another accused from a non-military background, who pointed out the locations where high-ranking army officials like Brigadiers and Generals could be found.

Aqeel @ Dr Usman had been involved in a number of high-profile attacks, including those on Gen Musharraf, had joined Harkatul Jihad Al Islami [HJI] in 1999 after completing his studies and went to Afghanistan twice. After 9/11, he returned to Pakistan after being injured, and joined the Army Medical Corps (AMC) as a nursing assistant and was posted to the CMH in Rawalpindi. He was still in touch with *Jihadi* 'friends' then.

It was here that he developed friendship with another accused, Imran Siddique, who was then a soldier in the army.

Aqeel @ Dr Usman deserted the army in 2005 and became involved with the Amjad Farooqui group. By August 2009, the GHQ Attack plan was in full swing. Aqeel rented a room at Bilal Boys Hostel, Rawalpindi, and started surveillance of GHQ's surroundings. In September, he rented a house near Defence Housing Rawalpindi Cantt phase II. He also acquired a van which he got fitted with army number plates and spent Rs: 30,000 for buying Pak-Army uniforms for eight of his accomplices.

From October 1st to 9th of 2009, Aqeel, along with his accomplice Ali, carried out surveillance of the area and also briefed others on the attack by using "distance measuring tool" on Google Earth. Initially, the attack was planned for 6th October, but this was delayed to 10th October as one of the participants fell ill.

At the time of attack, the 10 attackers reached the GHQ via Murree Road and dispersed in different directions. The audacious attack as the men broke past the check post resulted in the death of four of them. The rest were able to make it in. However, on the court record, there is little information on what happened at the check post because the real guards who had faced the initial moments were also martyred at the spot.

It was on the court record that the militants made hostage five officers and 20 civilians. Before they took the men hostage, Aqeel shot dead the driver of a jeep who had refused to tell the locations of the Generals. Aqeel had claimed before the court that 'by 11am [mistakenly he wrote 11 Am; it was not correct], they had taken over the GHQ and the entire area was within their firing range', though admitting that they were surrounded by the army.

The negotiations continued all night; at six in the morning, the SSG attacked and entered the building. They killed the four other militants who were watching over the hostages. Aqeel @ Dr Usman survived this attack as he was holed up in a separate room from where he was carrying out negotiations over the phone. He then hid in an office, coming out only to join the men carrying out the rescue work; a building had collapsed and men were trying to rescue those trapped beneath the rubble.

Aqeel nearly escaped scot-free, but a security officer identified him; perhaps he was injured too. One Maj Akhtar Qamar, Security Officer

[Technical] at GHQ, who witnessed the whole episode on CCTV, identified him. Maj Qamar stated before the court that:

"I saw the whole incident on CCTV and observed that 10 terrorists had dismounted from a Suzuki van near the Tank Chowk picket. Here they attacked the picket as well as some security staff and five of them were hit, whereas other five managed to enter into the GHQ premises. I reported this whole incident to my superiors.

Later I assisted SSG persons and troops in planning the counterattack and recognition of the attackers since features & figures of accused number 1 [Aqeel @ Dr Usman] were very clear in the footage."

Major Gen Athar Abbas DG ISPR gave the official version that some terrorists, wearing fake army uniform, equipped with automatic heavy weapons, riding in a white coloured Suzuki carry-van and bearing army number plate reached a check post near GHQ where the army personnel on duty engaged them when they tried to enter the gate No 1 at 11:30am. They tried to move to another check post when security guards intercepted them and security forces retaliated effectively and killed four terrorists during an hour long exchange of fire.

Simultaneously, at second check post near Hilal Road square, the vehicle was stopped for identification by security officials. The terrorists left the vehicle and took their positions within a moment and opened firing on army personnel. They also threw some hand grenades on the check post due to which six army personnel including Brig Anwar-ul-Haq and Lt Col Waseem were martyred.

Soon after the attack, security personnel cordoned off the whole area and search operation started while air surveillance, with a view to locate the fleeing militants, was also commenced in the surroundings of GHQ. It took about 22 hours to end the operation because five terrorists had taken positions to squeeze and corner the hostages inside the GHQ.

Eye witnesses told that the militants hurled hand-grenades; five explosions rang out amid the gunfire. The situation went tenser while the firing was still going on; continued till next day morning. After the attack on GHQ, soldiers sealed off roads leading to the GHQ and an army helicopter remained hovering over the area to locate the escaped terrorists.

Albiet; effective military operations in Swat had taught the army that *'a stitch in time saves nine and that without public support no military campaign can succeed*. The army and police commandos cordoned off the whole area and traffic was diverted from Mall Road to other routes in Rawalpindi city. The educational institutions were closed; security of all sensitive places in the city was beefed up and extra contingents of police were deployed at places.

The government knew that the Taliban [Amjad Farooqi Group of the TTP], had made this move to avenge the death of their leader Baitullah Mehsud in a US drone missile attack in August 2009. The links between Amjad Farooqi, the old Harkatul Mujahideen fighter, and Al Qaeda were well known to the establishment till then.

In a telephone call made to a private TV channel, a member of TTP Group demanded halt to operation in northern areas, accountability of former President Gen Musharraf, sending off the '*Black-water*' back and closure of Western NGOs.

Later it was revealed that the Crime Investigation Department of Punjab had once shared its information with relevant government departments that *"terrorists belonging to the Tehrik-e-Taliban Pakistan (TTP), in collaboration with Lashkar-e-Jhangvi (LeJ) and Jaish-e-Mohammad (JeM), were planning to attack the GHQ."*

It even warned the local army intelligence on 5th October that the terrorists could be clad in military uniforms and while riding a military vehicle or a vehicle designed to pass as one belonging to the military; but their report was simply thrown in the bin being '*bloody civilian's bull**** paper*'.

GHQ is the nerve centre of the Pakistani military and is guarded by an Infantry battalion, along with a similar number of defence security guards (DSG). Over a thousand military officials work at the GHQ and they are responsible for running Pakistan's military apparatus. Alarming thing was that ten terrorists created mayhem for around 22 hours, disrupting normal operations within GHQ. Then SSG commandos were brought in from 70 kilometres away to end the stand-off after the terrorists took hostages in a block within the GHQ.

Liaquat Baloch of Jamaat e Islami [JI] on a special debate, just next day, at a local TV channel stated that '*the jihadis killing Pakistani civilians and the military were misguided and were only doing so because the Americans were in Afghanistan*'.

The phrase *"if the Americans were not in Afghanistan..."* gave the impression that otherwise those militants were peace-loving people who were only killing and maiming Pakistani citizens because they were *misguided....,* attacking mosques and killing prayer attending Muslims because *the Americans were in Afghanistan...* What an innocence the Pakistani politicians used to express.

Those *'misguided'* cold-blooded killers had executed four high-impact attacks in the earlier ten days, which had taken a total of 140 lives. This was not the work of **"misguided"** people. The symbolism of the attacks had not been lost on anyone either. See the details:

- The UN Food Programme was targeted to let the *'goras'* know that they're not safe.

- The suicide bombing in Swat was launched to let everyone know that it was still vulnerable.

- There were attacks on Peshawar, to let everyone know who the boss was.

- And then, of course, one of the most heavily-guarded installations in the country, the GHQ, to let the army know that even their headquarters wasn't safe.

Ordinary Pakistani were helpless but to ask that if ten *'misguided'* civilians could tie up two battalions for 22 hours, then how safe were they?

The episode concluded with the arrest of the Operation Commander [Aqeel, alias Dr Usman] and the killing of his nine associates who had coordinated their attack on the GHQ from at least two directions. Dr Usman hailed from Kahuta near Rawalpindi; he was a nursing assistant with the Army Medical Corps before he joined local militant groups in 2005; later he became a member of the TTP and remained a close associate of Ilyas Kashmiri, Al Qaeda's Chief of paramilitary operations in Pakistan.

One Shakir Husain in *'the News' of 15th October 2009* had opined:

> *'Even if the TTP and its friends are being "handled" by the "foreign hand" as the nutters would have us believe on a regular basis, the bulk of the fighting is being done by Pakistani citizens. Sure we have*

*a smattering of Uzbeks and Arabs running around in the North;
but the bulk of the recruits are Pakistani kids recruited from all over
the country.*

*We have the intelligence assets and systems in place to find out who,
when and what – it's time to change our collective mindset and handle
the enemy seriously before they inflict more damage to an already
battered state.'*

On 11th August 2011; Aqeel @ Dr Usman along with his seven
accomplices was convicted by a military court. However, the news got
the media coverage on 14th August after the relatives of some of the
convicts visited them at Adiala jail. The military court had sentenced
Aqeel to death while his accomplice, former soldier Imran Siddique, was
sentenced to life in prison.

Three civilians — Khaliqur Rehman, Mohammad Usman and Wajid
Mehmood — were given life terms while two others, Mohammad Adnan
and Tahir Shafiq (both civilians), got eight and seven years jail sentence
respectively.

The trial by the military court, which was headed by a Brigadier,
lasted over five months at an undisclosed location. Colonel (R)
Inamur Rehman, a defence lawyer for Wajid — one of the convicts —
had challenged the military court's decision before the appellant
authority.

Under article 199 (3) of the Constitution, verdicts handed down by
military courts cannot be challenged in a high court. However, a
Supreme Court ruling provides that those convicted by a military court
can petition a high court within 40 days if they could prove that the
verdict was *malafide*.

On 7th December 2012; the military court of appeal, by rejecting appeals
of convicted ex-army men in the GHQ attack case, maintained the
punishments awarded on 11th August 2011. Eleven soldiers had lost
their lives.

Under the normal process, a mercy petition could be filed with the Chief
of Army Staff after the appeal rejected; the convicts could also approach
the President. However, nothing heard afterwards.

ATTACKS EVERY WHERE IN THE ROW:

List of significant attacks on Pakistani security forces was long but some of the mentionable events in the first half of 2009 were:

On 6th January 2009, four policemen were killed during an attack on a checkpoint in Hangu.

On 11th January 2009, thirty People were killed after a suicide truck bomber detonated at a checkpoint in Peshawar's outskirts.

On 7th February 2009, An estimated 600 Afghan and other Al Qaeda fighters crossed the border from Afghanistan and joined hands with local fighters in the Mohmand tribal agency to attack a military outpost killing ten Pak-Army soldiers.

On 7th March 2009, a car bomb exploded at a checkpoint in Peshawar killing seven policemen and one civilian.

On 9th March 2009, the militants either killed or captured 17 members of the FC personnel, a lightly armed paramilitary police unit, along with three government officials from a civil department.

On 29th March 2009, a large group of militants captured 12 policemen after surrounding their outpost in Khyber Agency near Peshawar; their fate was not known till the end of the year at least. Probably they were butchered later.

On 30th March 2009, a terror assault team stormed a police academy in Lahore; more than 30 recruits and officers were killed [*the details have been given separately*]. On the same day, four security personnel were killed in a suicide attack in Bannu.

On 4th April 2009, the militants targeted yet another security installation killing eight policemen in an attack on the Frontier Constabulary Camp in the F-7/3 Sector in Islamabad. Five other paramilitaries were also wounded in the attack. The bomber detonated his vest after entering the back of the camp situated in protected location, near the UN Human Rights Council. One suspect involved in the attack was caught from around.

On 18th April 2009, a suicide bomber killed 25 men in uniform and two civilians in an attack on military convoy in Hangu.

On 20th April 2009, a local militant group kidnapped six Frontier Constabulary personnel in Swat; they were later got released but two of them were seriously injured. A week later they again took hostage of 60 security personnel in Buner and five more in Swat.

On 4th May 2009, five security officials lost their lives in a suicide attack in Khyber Agency and one policeman was killed in a cross fire shooting in Hangu.

On 5th May 2009, fifteen militant fighters and 2 troops were reportedly killed in a cross fire ambush. On the same day six Pak-Army soldiers were captured by a militant group after an attack on an outpost in Mohmand Agency border area.

On 10th May 2009, the militants destroyed the Camp HQ of the Dir Levies, killed one officer from Malakand Unit and captured three others.

On 14th May 2009, three Pak-Army soldiers and five militant fighters were killed in a cross fire ambush in a border village of North Waziristan.

On 20th May 2009, a suicide truck bomber attacked a fort in Tank and killed nine people including five policemen.

On 25th May 2009, the militants killed three policemen in Kohat and in another event killed three more in Haripur.

On 27th May 2009, a terrorist assault team killed 16 policemen and seven intelligence officials [totalling 23] in a complex suicide and conventional attack in Lahore while more than 300 were wounded. A team armed with assault rifles, machine guns, and hand grenades crashed their van through security barriers near the Emergency Police HQ and of the ISI and opened fire on security guards.

When the security guards retaliated, the militants detonated their van which was rigged with hundreds of pounds of explosives. The blast levelled a building used by rescue units and damaged the other police and ISI buildings. One gunman had entered the ISI building and fire-fighting lasted for nearly one hour.

The assault took a heavy toll on the police and the ISI whereas three of the attackers were captured and the rest were killed.

On 31st May 2009, more than 25 militant fighters and seven Pak-Army soldiers were killed during fighting in a South Waziristan's village.

On 1ˢᵗ June 2009, near Bakka Khel in North Waziristan, the militants carried out a brazen daylight operation that resulted in the kidnapping of about 350 cadets, teachers, and college staff as they travelled from their college. The said area of North Waziristan was under the command of one Hafiz Gul Bahadar with overall control of Taliban leader Baitullah Mehsud.

While the militants were escorting the hostaged cadets to an undisclosed location, one bus driver and more than 40 students had escaped hijacking. The militants were armed with rocket-propelled grenades, machine guns, and assault rifles. They halted the convoy of 29 minibuses travelling from the Ramzak Cadet College to the settled district of Bannu.

Just a day before, the police had detained one Asmatullah, a deputy of Baitullah Mehsud, along with 39 other group fighters in Mianwali district; they were to mine the region to slow any potential military offensive around. That capture of the cadets was an effort to secure the release of those 39 fighters then in custody. Then it was a prevailing practice to get exchanged the militant prisoners for captive soldiers, policemen, and government officials.

After getting confirmed the hijacking and kidnapping, negotiations went underway to secure the release of the captive cadets and teachers. Later, the cadets and staff left the college after being threatened by the militants, the reports confirmed.

Earlier, in August of 2007, Baitullah's forces were able to pull off the brazen capture of an entire company of regular Army troops as they moved through the same area; more than 300 soldiers had reportedly surrendered.

After that serious blow, the militant fighters continued their attacks on the security personnel and especially the police members who remained target for the whole month of June 2009. A brief detail is given here.

On 4ᵗʰ June 2009, six policemen and a paramilitary trooper were killed in Mardan city of Khyber PK.

On 5ᵗʰ June 2009, five soldiers were killed in attacks in South Waziristan.

On 6ᵗʰ June 2009, two policemen were killed, while four were injured in a suicide attack on a Rescue 15 Office in Sector G-8 Islamabad. The attacker attempted to enter the office by scaling a wall behind the building bordering a residential area, but was spotted by a guard who opened fire on him. Next moment he exploded himself.

On 9th June 2009, eleven troops were wounded in Mohmand Agency and eight policemen were seriously hurt in Dera Ismail Khan.

On 12th June 2009, four policemen were killed in an attack in Hangu and another in Kohat.

On 22nd June 2009: a suicide bomber killed two policemen in Shangla.

On 23rd June 2009, three policemen were killed in Peshawar city while an FC *jawan* lost his life in Khyber.

On 26th June 2009, three army troops and a civilian were killed in an attack in North Waziristan village area.

On 28th June 2009, eighteen militant fighters and 10 soldiers were killed during an ambush in North Waziristan; two soldiers were also killed in another ambush in South Waziristan terrains.

On 3rd July 2009, a Pakistani Army helicopter crashed in north-western tribal area; a known Taliban stronghold, killing at least 26 Pakistani soldiers and paramilitary fighters. The military held that the helicopter had technical problems and moreover it was carrying too many people, but the media had confirmed that the insurgents had shot it down. Information to be kept on record was that although the official number of those killed was 26, but in fact 41 people had died.

The crash — which the authorities said killed three officers too — was grim news for the army, whether militants were involved or not. The event occurred when the military was locked in renewed struggle with the militants; going full-scale offensive in South Waziristan.

The shooting down of the military chopper was perhaps an immediate response of the Taliban as in the earlier hours of that day; a drone attack on a militant training camp had killed at least 13 insurgents. The official note of the Pakistan army had confirmed the attack in Mazarai Nara but said that eight people had died.

Much of South Waziristan, as well as the area of the helicopter crash, in Chapri Ferozkhel, near the border of the Orakzai and Khyber tribal regions, was being controlled by forces loyal to Baitullah Mehsud, a mastermind of suicidal attack series of that time. The helicopter was being used for transportation purposes since a few weeks and on that fateful day it was flying low in an area of high mountains.

The crash could either be due to bad weather or because of excess weight; nothing was definite. As per manual, the MI-17 helicopter could carry 24 troops while there were 41 people aboard. The flying low could have made the helicopter vulnerable to being hit by militant fire.

On 9th July 2009, five security personnel were killed in Jaccobabab of Sindh province and wounded six.

On 27th August 2009, a suicide bomber entered a barrack of Pak-Afghan Border Guards at the Torkham crossing in Khyber Agency and detonated him, killing 22 guards as they gathered for an *iftari* meal at sunset in the month of holy Ramadan. The Taliban took credit for the attack saying that it was conducted to avenge Baitullah Mehsud's death at the hands of the US.

Just a day earlier, on 26th August 2009, the Pakistani military had taken notice of a militant camp in Swat that was responsible for three other smaller-scale suicide attacks in Swat over the past several weeks. Pakistan army helicopters attacked that training camp near Mingora claiming that 12 fighters, including six teenage suicide bombers, were killed in the attack.

After their retreat in January 2008, the Swati Taliban were attempting to reassert control in the valley; the military sources told that the Taliban strength in Swat had been estimated at between 5,000 to 7,000 fighters.

On 30th August 2009, a suicide bomber killed 15 policemen during an attack on the cadets when they were exercising at Parade Grounds of Special Police Training Centre in Mingora, capital town of Swat.

The militants had been targeting security forces since after Nine Eleven 2001 but during those years of ending Gen Musharraf's rule and beginning of PPP's government in 2008, they conducted scores of significant attacks against the police, the Army, the Frontier Corps, and other Pakistani security and intelligence services since July 2007 when Gen Musharraf's government had launched the operation to clear out radicals from the Lal Masjid [Red Mosque] in the heart of Islamabad city.

Referring to the book '<u>The Fall of North Western Pakistan</u>' compiled by
Bill Roggio appeared on line at '<u>The Long War Journal</u>' site:

> '*There were hundreds of smaller attacks in Pakistan that occurred on a
> daily basis. These attacks included suicide strikes and military assaults
> against checkpoints, training centres, and bases; ambushes against
> convoys; beheadings and executions of captured security personnel; and
> targeted assassinations against military leaders.*
>
> *No region of Pakistan had been spared. These attacks had taken place
> in Pakistan's major cities, including Islamabad, Karachi, Lahore, and
> Rawalpindi, as well as in the rural areas and Pakistan's lawless tribal
> areas.*'

On 18th September 2009, a suicide bomber killed 33 persons after
detonating a jeep laden with explosives at main market in a large town
of Ustarzai in district Kohat where the people from surrounding villages
had come to purchase supplies for the upcoming religious festival of *Eid
al Fitr*. More than 300 pounds of explosives were packed into a jeep,
which was then driven into the bazaar and detonated.

The blast had levelled nearby buildings and more than 50 civilians were
wounded. The militant group named *Fedayeen-e-Islam* had claimed its
responsibility. The same group had already claimed credit for the
deadly 22nd September 2008 suicide attack on the Islamabad Marriott
Hotel and the 30th March 2009 storming of a police Training School in
Lahore.

On 26th September 2009, a suicide bomber detonated vehicles packed
with explosives in the cities of Peshawar and Bannu simultaneously
killing 20 people and causing serious hurts to more than 100.

In Bannu, a settled town and gateway to the tribal agency of North
Waziristan, a suicide bomber rammed his truck into a police station,
killing 10 people and wounding about 75 citizen. A senior Taliban
commander, Qari Hussain Mehsud, who used to run a religious school
for children there, had claimed credit for the Bannu attack.

Two days earlier, the militants had killed seven pro-government tribal
leaders in village Jani Khel who had raised a militia force to oppose the
extremists. Al Qaeda's executive Shura, the decision making Council,
was also based in Jani Khel and their bank transactions were managed
in the same sub-town.

[The Taliban had announced that they would launch attacks in Pakistan if military operations in the tribal areas were not halted. Hakeemullah Mehsud, the leader of the TTP, conducted a press conference on 4th October 2009 to dismiss reports of his death and Taliban infighting, and said the attacks would begin again.

Over the past three years, the Taliban have conducted major suicide attacks and assaults in the cities of Islamabad, Karachi, Lahore, Rawalpindi, and Peshawar, as well as FATA and other settled districts of Khyber PK province like Kohat & Bannu.]

On 5th October 2009, a suicide bomber killed five United Nations workers in an attack at the UN office in Islamabad. The bomber penetrated the security barricade at the World Food Program offices and detonated him inside the building, killing four Pakistanis and an Iraqi national; six were wounded also. Astonishing was that how the bomber was able to get through strict security arrangements.

On 9th October 2009, a Taliban suicide bomber detonated a car packed with explosives in a busiest place named Khyber Bazaar in Peshawar, the capital of the Khyber PK Province, killing 49 people and causing more than 100 wounded. In this attack about 100 kilograms of explosive was used. Uniquely, the device was planted in the door panels of the vehicle and included machine gun ammunition, designed to cause maximum casualties. It was the second terrorist attack after Mehsud's press conference of 4th October.

On 12th October 2009, a suicide bomber had detonated his car packed with explosives when a military convoy passed through a checkpoint in a market town of Alpuri in Shangla [Swat]. Forty-one people, including six security personnel, were killed in the attack; twelve of the persons were injured seriously.

Earlier this year, the Pak-Army had launched an offensive against militant forces led by Mullah Fazlullah, the radical leader of Swat and the surrounding districts of Dir, Buner, and Shangla. Six of the 21 top fighter leaders wanted by the government had been killed or captured, but Fazlullah and some key military commanders had fled to Afghanistan in early 2008.

Since April 2009, the Swati militants had established their bases again nearly in all the districts of Swat and surrounding Mardan, Mansehra and Swabi; because of poor ANP government's control over Swat. Pak-Army did not take interest because action in civil areas was not its responsibility nor were they mandated for that.

Three days later, **on 15ᵗ October 2009**, a suicide bomber rammed a car into a police station in Kohat, killing eight people, including policemen and children.

On 15ᵗʰ October 2009 again, four unidentified gunmen fired gunshots on FIA building situated on Temple Road in Lahore; four government workers, four terrorists, and one civilian were reportedly killed during the fighting.

Militant assault teams launched simultaneous attacks against three police buildings in the eastern city of Lahore. Twenty-six people were killed in the attacks; a follow up of the assault on the Army GHQ in Rawalpindi. Different groups had attacked and tried to enter three police facilities simultaneously

A large blast was also heard at the Elite Force Headquarters [*the Punjab police's specialized unit assigned to counterterrorism and VIP protection missions*] at Bedyan Road Lahore; one policeman and one terrorist were reportedly killed in the attack.

The attacks on FIA offices in Lahore had attracted special attention of the militants; perhaps on two counts. Firstly that the American team of interrogators had their camping seats here and secondly, the detained militants from Punjab were kept in the FIA lock-ups of Lahore whereas in all over Pakistan they used to be kept in respective police stations.

That was why the attacks on FIA Offices of Lahore continued even after. **On 7ᵗʰ March 2010**, a suicide bomber killed 11 people and wounded 37 more in an attack on FIA Punjab's HQ in Model Town Lahore.

The suicide bomber rammed his car packed with more than 1,300 pounds of explosives into an FIA Office premises used as a safe house and Interrogation Centre by the Pakistan military's Special Interrogation Unit. The blast had leveled the FIA building which had more than 70 people working there at the time of the attack; many were believed to be trapped in the rubble.

Scenario 61

PAKISTAN: ISI IN POLITICS – I:

ISI SINCE 1948 & AFTER:

[*Gen (Rtd) Aslam Beg in his statement made in 1997 before the Supreme Court of Pakistan in Asghar Khan Case deposed that PM Z A Bhutto had dragged the ISI in politics. It is widely perceived that it was Bhutto who had first time assigned political tasks to the ISI in Pakistan. It was not the whole truth; see the following:*]

The Directorate for Inter-Services Intelligence [ISI] was founded in 1948 by an Australian-born British army officer, Maj Gen R Cawthorne, then Deputy Chief of Staff in Pakistan Army. Gen Ayub Khan expanded the role of ISI in 1950s, to safeguard Pakistan's interests, monitoring opposition politicians, and sustaining military rule in Pakistan.

Paying a tribute to **Altaf Gauhar's** article titled as **'*How Intelligence Agencies Run Our Politics*'** available on media record, one can trace out that in Pakistan's early days, despite odds, ISI and the Military Intelligence [MI] confined themselves to the matters of direct military interest and the Intelligence Bureau [IB] concentrated on domestic political activities. This arrangement continued fairly smoothly until the imposition of Martial Law in 1958.

[*Details of history about Pakistan's intelligence agencies have already been given in Chapters 14-15 of Volume-I.*]

In 1965 the ISI was headed by Brig Riaz, MI was under Brig M Irshad and A B Awan was the Director of the Intelligence Bureau (DIB). A B Awan was made member of Gen Yahya's Committee as the GHQ tried to put all the blame on IB for their incompetence. Gen Yahya wanted the committee to recommend that officers of ISI and the MI should be posted at district level but A B Awan strongly opposed the idea. When the meeting concluded, A B Awan had whispered that '*they are planning to impose another martial law.*'

During Gen Yahya Khan's rule [started in March 1969] the ISI jumped into the Political crisis in East Pakistan un-warranted. A National

Security Council was created by Gen Yahya Khan [headed by himself] with Major Gen Ghulam Umar as 2nd in command to control the intelligence operation in both wings of Pakistan to ensure that no political party should get an overall majority in the general elections of 1970.

An amount of Rs:2.9 million was put at the disposal of Gen Umar for the purpose. Before the army action Gen Akbar, then heading the ISI, had tried to infiltrate into the inner circles of the Awami League, but miserably failed. ISI's name was kept away but the operation proved another disaster though the NSC had aimed to get 'desired & suitable results' by distributing colossal amounts of money amongst his favourite parties and persons.

However, the fact remains that in those elections, the IB [then headed by Gen Yahya Khan's brother] was far more active than ISI or Gen Umar's Election Cell or NSC whatsoever it was named. *Dr Safdar Mahmood's 'Pakistan Kyun Toota'* is referred for more details.

Also referring to Lawrence Ziring: ['*The Tragedy of East Pakistan' Oxford Press 1997*]

'New efforts at a political solution might have been attempted later, but army intelligence failed time and again to correctly assess the situation, and the demeanour of the Generals was hardly conducive to rational decision-making.'

PM Mr Bhutto can, however, be named for strengthening the ISI's political role in mid 1970s in the backdrop of uprising in Balochistan and North-West Frontier Province [NWFP now Khyber PK]. Thus ISI's political cells were created in these areas in 1975 but it got bad name during general elections of 1977.

PM Bhutto had used both ISI and the IB to 'monitor' the elections though he was in a position to win majority seats in the Parliament. Both the institutions went overactive and intimidated many politicians to get Mr Bhutto, all the four Chief Ministers and key PPP members elected as 'unopposed'. Some Deputy Commissioners had played pivotal role to make the whole election process dubious & doubtful.

Despite the fact that PM Bhutto had patronized ISI above board but the army's loyalty always remained with the GHQ more than the PM House [and it should have been]. As a result during the 5th July 1977 coup, the

IB's Chief was arrested whereas the ISI's Chief, Gen Jilani, was first made Secretary Defence and then elevated to the Governor's slot in Punjab. Gen Ziaul Haq used the ISI giving those full perks and privileges as is being seen now; making them the most powerful.

One more reference to the ISI is available in **Stanley Wolpert's book 'Zulfi Bhutto of Pakistan: His Life and Times'**. The author states how the ISI and the IB cooperated with each other to interfere in domestic politics during the late Prime Minister Z A Bhutto's regime.

According to the book, the Director of the IB, M Akram Sheikh and the Joint Director (IB) Muhammad Isa were busy with the compilation of dossiers, analyses and detailed reports on National Assembly candidates and their respective election prospects. It is mentioned therein that on 9th February 1977 the ISI headed by its DG Gen Jillani Khan along with the IB jointly compiled an assessment of the PPP's election prospects. Brig (retd) Syed Tirmazi, a former ISI officer states:

> "It may be noteworthy that we hardly carried out any surveillance of politicians. The activities of some were, however, kept under discreet, decent, unobtrusive, and invisible 'watch'. At times, we were also ordered to bug the telephones of some individuals.

> Such orders came in writing from the Prime Minister himself. This authority he had not delegated to anyone else. We compiled the reports and sent it to the PM with appropriate recommendations to continue or discontinue the watch. In most cases it was discontinued".

Academically analysing such historical events, the rationale for the ISI involvement in domestic politics could be attributed to three reasons:

- The need for the military to manipulate politics and indirectly rule the country.

- To marginalise the civilian intelligence agency; this could become powerful with patronage from an elected government.

- The absence of a genuine external threat to national security.

Theoretically the ISI would fall under the category of an independent security agency with the characteristics that its goals are determined by the army bosses and are most likely to differ from that of the political governments.

Former Prime Minister Nawaz Sharif used the ISI in another way; to collect evidence of corruption by rival bureaucrats and politicians involved in major contracts with foreign companies [*kickbacks in Agosta Submarine deals and Zardari's Swiss accounts info are referred*].

The intelligence agencies have played a frontline role in the struggle for power between the PPP and the PML(N). So much so, the political leadership in the 1990s has not really used these intelligence agencies for promoting good governance; instead both used them in their hidden warfare leading to instability and a crisis in Pakistan. The Indian governments of the past always contended that

'*The ISI keeps close connections with the Harkat ul Ansar and the Lashkar e Toiba which are extremely active in waging terrorist operations against the Indian state and its people in Jammu and Kashmir for the past decade. This relationship between the ISI and fundamentalists, fostered among other objectives on anti-India interests, clearly characterises a close-minded approach of the ISI to any improvement in relations with India.*'

The Pakistan Army always and the political governments in succession vehemently denied the Indian stance terming it as 'poisonous propaganda' in the absence of any cogent proof in that respect. However, the fact remains that Lt Gen Hamid Gul, the former ISI Chief, have openly reiterated in all of his interviews that it was done so for the security of Pakistan and was our priority at times.

Concluding the above debate: for Gen (retd) Aslam Beg to claim on solemn oath before the Supreme Court of Pakistan that the ISI got involved in the internal politics of the country only after a special cell was created by Prime Minister Bhutto in 1975 is a culpable attempt at concealing the truth and distorting the record of the operations of the military intelligence agencies since independence.

Much after, an analysis made by M B Naqvi over 2001's scenario, then published in '*The News International*' said:

'...... *so far as Army high command (of Pakistan) is concerned, its pretensions rest on the undeniable fact of 'occupation'. It has been in the business of ruling the country continuously since 1958 except for two breaks: the first from 1972 to 1977 and the second time from 1988 to 1999.*'

But it has to be recognized by the Generals that it is a wrongful occupation of a house that clearly belongs to the citizens of Pakistan who pay their salaries and perks at great cost to themselves. If they do not vacate and begin obeying laws—made by, or on the authority of, the people — there might be unacceptable damage to the country through internal convulsions. Simply because of their brute force their right to rule cannot be accepted'.

POLITICIANS SPOILED ISI (?):

The ISI always had the cream of officers amongst the available lot in the Pakistan Army but the political masters always tried to spoil the atmosphere by sending retired or redundant faces like Shamsur Rehman Kallue (in Benazir Bhutto's 1st tenure in 1990s), Javed Nasir (in Nawaz Sharif's 1st tenure in 1990s) and Engr Ziauddin Butt (in Nawaz Sharif's 2nd tenure in 1990s) to manage the ISI. What could they deliver; nothing because all the three were declared PNG by their respective army chiefs making GHQ a 'No Entry' region for them. One episode is here for change of taste.

The International tribunal of Hague had once demanded the custody of Lt Gen (Rtd) Javed Nasir, former ISI Chief, for his alleged support to Muslim fighters of Bosnia against the Serbian army in the 1990s, despite an embargo by the United Nations. Islamabad had refused to send him; officially informing the court that **the former General had 'lost his memory'** following a recent road incident and was, therefore, unable to face any investigation into the matter.

[*However, his son Omer Javed had claimed,* **vide Express Tribune dated 20th September 2011** *that his father was not in army service during the Bosnia war in 1993-95.*] {Also see pages 430-431 of Vol-II of this book for some more background}

The summons were served on Government of Pakistan when Serbian army officials were put on trial by The Hague Tribunal for War Crimes and Crimes Against Humanity in Bosnia, during which it was revealed that Gen Javed Nasir was actively involved in the war and had supported and provided arms to the Bosnian resistance. The case was built on the 'confessional statement' that the General had made in a petition filed through his legal counsel against an English daily after the newspaper published a report of his alleged involvement in a case of embezzlement.

The Pakistan government had to avoid any untoward situation and save the General also. There was no alternative available except that the army doctors had to send a medical certificate in that respect saying: *'the General was not mentally fit then'* as stated above.

Gen Javed Nasir had himself admitted that over 300 articles were circulated on the internet by the western media containing references against him saying that he was the *'only radical Islamist head of the ISI who was an active member of the Tableeghi Jama'at'.*

The fact remained that in April 1993, the US once finally warned Pakistan in writing to remove Lt Gen Javed Nasir from his post of ISI Chief, after which he was prematurely retired from service by the caretaker government of Mir Balkh Sher Mazari on 13th May 1993.

[*The demand for Nasir's custody came when the International Criminal Tribunal put on trial the former Chief of the Yugoslavian Army Gen Momcilo Perisic and his Deputy Gen Ratko Mladic for war crimes and crimes against humanity during the war in Bosnia and Croatia in the 1990s.*

Perisic and Ratko had reportedly told the court that the military help to the Bosnian Muslims by Gen Nasir had forced them to retaliate against Bosnian Muslims, who were fighting against the Serb army for their national independence.

More than 100,000 people were butchered in about three years of conflict. The war saw a level of barbarism more marked by mass rape, torture and indiscriminate murder until the Dayton Peace Agreement paved the way for a settlement.]

To be remembered also that whenever the ISI was controlled by a civilian government the MI reoriented itself to political intelligence activity to keep the generals informed about the relevant developments in the country. In the process the IB by design and not by default was always relegated to a 'runners up' or second slot in the intelligence community with the first place reserved for the ISI.

In the past, the MI got itself involved with an internal role, in the name of combating counter-insurgency in Sindh, linking itself in provincial politics; not liked by many even within the army high ups; MI's role in the interior Sindh in Gen Ziaul Haq times of 1983-84, during PM Nawaz Sharif's tenure of 1992 in Karachi against MQM and its killing role during Gen Musharraf's rule in the alleged horrific events of 12ᵗʰ May 2007 and 18ᵗʰ October 2007 are referred by many insiders.

DANIEL PEARL'S KILLING (2002):

On an event of kidnapping and killing of Daniel Pearl of Wall Street Journal [*he was kidnapped in Karachi on 23ʳᵈ January 2002 in mysterious circumstances*], Dr Imran Farooq of the *Muttehida Qaumi Movement* (MQM) was bold enough to raise his voice high even up to the United Nation forum. Following is the full text of a letter sent to the then Secretary General of the United Nations by him:

26ᵗʰ February 2002

Mr Kofi Annan
Secretary General
The United Nations
U N Plaza, New York 10017
USA

Dear Secretary-General

RE: ISI IS BEHIND THE MURDER OF DANIEL PEARL

I hope that you are in good health and spirit. I know that you are one of the busiest person in the world and, therefore, I will try and keep this letter short, as much as possible which is about the subject mentioned above.

After the horrific terrorist acts against the United States of America on 11ᵗʰ September 2001, the United Nations, United States of America and the entire sovereign nations, peace loving political leaders including Mr Altaf Hussain, Founder and Leader of *Muttahida Quami Movement* (MQM), the third largest political party in Pakistan and the second largest in the province of Sindh, strongly condemned the cowardly acts of terrorism in the United States of America. MQM held the biggest rally on 26ᵗʰ September 2001 in Karachi (port city of Pakistan) to demonstrate its solidarity that it stands shoulder to shoulder with the international community against all sorts of terrorists' acts and terrorism throughout the world. MQM also offered its unconditional support to the international community against all sorts of terrorism.

As you would know that one of the journalists of the Wall Street Journal, Mr Daniel Pearl was kidnapped on 23rd January 2002 in Karachi. The kidnappers put certain demands for the release of Mr Daniel Pearl. The present Military Government of Pakistan and its high officials were assuring the entire world that the Authorities and police will recover Mr Daniel Pearl alive within two or three days but failed.

Pakistan's Interior Minister on Friday predicted a
"major breakthrough" and more arrests within 48 hours
in the search for Daniel Pearl. The official rejected a claim
from Pearl's self-confessed kidnapper that the
Wall Street Journal reporter is dead.
(Los Angeles Times, Breakthrough Expected in Kidnap Case,
Pakistan Says, February 16, 2002)

No one has explained why Sheikh Omar was held in ISI custody
for a week before civilian authorities were informed
of his arrest. Two former ISI officers have been
questioned about Pearl's murder.
(The Observer, Vicious Web of Intrigue that Trapped Daniel Pearl,
February 24, 2002)

Mr Daniel Pearl was decapitated ruthlessly. What plans had been made by the ISI in collusion with Ahmed Omar Sheikh while he was in its custody only God knows! The Interior Minister of Pakistan and even President General Pervez Musharraf were not aware of this plan.

Not only in Pakistan but also throughout the world, the educated and politically aware people know that the ISI is above all the institutions and even above the law in Pakistan. ISI is a State within a State. ISI is not answerable to the Presidents, Prime Ministers or anyone else.

'They are a state within a state... 'The ISI is the only institution
powerful enough to dare to disobey the President.'
(The Guardian, Torture, treachery and spies - cover war in
Afghanistan, November 4, 2001)

The ISI is responsible for harbouring the terrorists' not only in Pakistan but also throughout the world under the pretext of *"Jihad"*. The ISI is not at all happy with the decisions taken by the present Government for eradicating religious fanatics, as they are its own creation.

The ISI and only the ISI is behind this barbaric killing of Mr Daniel Pearl because the ISI wanted to give the message to the USA that by supporting the present Government the USA will not be able to achieve its goals and the United States of America must deal with the ISI and not with anybody else; and if the United States of America would continue to support the present Government then they have to face and see many more barbaric acts.

> *From early on in the Pearl investigation,*
> *ISI's involvement was evident.*
> *(The Observer, Vicious Web of Intrigue that*
> *Trapped Daniel Pearl, February 24, 2002)*

Dear Secretary-General,

The ISI has become a monster and until and unless the ISI is disbanded or dismantled, my apprehensions are that the ISI will continue to form, fertilize, harbour, train and provide financial support to create more and more religious fanatical groups like *Jesh-e-Mohammad* and others.

> *The intelligence agency's past actions indicate that its*
> *interests - or, at a minimum, those of former agency*
> *officials - have often dovetailed with the interests of*
> *Mr. Pearl's kidnappers, as reflected in their original*
> *demands. New disclosures of links between Mr. Sheikh*
> *and two recently dismissed agency officials only*
> *intensify suspicions about its role in this case.*

> *(The New York Times, Death of Reporter Puts Focus on*
> *Pakistan's Intelligence Unit, February 25, 2002)*

Dear Secretary-General,

I request you to convey my apprehensions to the International Community including the United States of America and its allies and to use your good office to ask the Government of Pakistan to dismantle the ISI. I would also request you that for the dismantling of the ISI, full support and active involvement of the United Nations, USA and the International Community would be required otherwise the present Government or any other Government in Pakistan would not be able to dismantle the ISI.

I also request you that if the United Nations Organizations and international community seriously and sincerely want to see the entire world free from any source of terrorism, they must take serious and practical steps and actions for completely wiping out the ISI otherwise, it would be too late for the world's sorrow and tears. The killings of innocent people would be the fate of the world.

Thank you for giving me your precious time.

Yours truly,

Dr Imran Farooq
Convener

This letter was sent from office of the MQM, by Dr Imran Farooq in his capacity of official spokesman of the aforementioned political party.

Another note from the history: During a formal meeting on *'terrorism in Pakistan'* amongst Republican Senators Don Nickles and Jeff Sessions during the days of Daniel Pearl's killing, it was a major question that: who is responsible? It was then unanimously opined that:

> *'President Musharraf was quite aware of the people who were involved in the conspiracy and murder of Daniel Pearl; they were members of extremist and terrorist groups which were known to be associated with various covert activities of the ISI.'*

But the point to ponder is that who brought Pakistan Army's name and character in question. The researchers trace it back to the Russian's movement in Afghanistan in 1980s, commonly known as *'Afghan jihad'* days when the CIA funded, armed and inspired the ISI to create a band of Afghan mercenaries to counter the Soviet invasion. The ISI not only set up training camps within Pakistan and in areas bordering Afghanistan but also acted as a conduit for arms and dollars flowing from Langley, Virginia, USA. To give this terrorist network a religious acceptance, the ISI called those fighters as *'jihadis'* the religious fighters.

The tragedy remained that since Daniel Pearl's abduction from Karachi on 23rd January 2002, all the concerned officials including the President of Pakistan were asserting that they see no reason to believe that Daniel Pearl was dead. Contrarily, the chief suspect and mastermind, Sheikh Ahmed Saeed Omar, himself had asserted before a court of law that Daniel was shot to death on 31st January 2002 by the abductors because he was trying to run away.

Sheikh Omar was one of the three Indian prisoners who were released to secure the discharge of passengers of the Indian airliner that was hijacked from Kathmandu (Nepal) and taken to Kandhar (Afghanistan) in 1999. He was alleged to be from *Jaish e Muhammad* (JeM) whereas the other two arrested persons in the case were identified as former ISI agents. Thus the footprints of JeM and *Harkatul Jihad e Islami* (HJI) were there to be seen. Gen Musharraf's government was still at an initial stage of dealing with alleged War on Terror spread on various grounds.

During the lengthy spills of interrogations since 5th February, Sheikh Omar was found changing his statements several times. The Karachi police was unable to get the trace to the Daniel Pearl or his abductor supposing he was still alive which was based on one fact that his dead body could not be found till then. Even it could not be ascertained that how Daniel was kidnapped, when, where and by whom; the most vital information the investigating agencies, including the intelligence agencies and the American FBI, needed at first hand.

The immediate funding for the operation was admitted by Sheikh Omar but where he got the money from was the really wanted information. In the meantime India got hold of a person who had funded Sheikh Omar; taken as a tip of an iceberg of a continental conspiracy at least. *'How nice it would be if Indian and Pakistani investigators could consult each other and collaborate directly rather than via Washington,'* the intelligentsia had observed.

Referring to one **Amir Mir's essay titled 'A scene from wreckage'** available in SAT Archives, a different scenario comes up. It says:

> *'Indeed, it was Ejaz Shah [former DIB] who had 'arranged' the surrender of Sheikh Ahmed Omar Saeed, the killer of American journalist Daniel Pearl, on February 5, 2005, in Lahore. Then, Shah was the home secretary of Punjab. Shah knows Omar's family well as both of them belong to 'Nankana Sahib' area of Punjab. The relationship between Shah and Omar was really one of a handler and his agent.'*

In an **interview with *Daily Times*, [dated 13th August 2007]**, late Benazir Bhutto had said:

> *"Brig Shah and the ISI recruited Omar Sheikh, who killed Danny Pearl. So I would feel very uncomfortable to have the Intelligence Bureau, which has more than 100,000 people under it, run by a man who worked so closely with militants and extremists."*

American's whole approach had less to do with finding Daniel than getting at the abductors because Gen Musharraf was likely to be on the state visit to Washington soon. One of the reports had suggested that the economic aid package that US President George W Bush had prepared for Pakistan was scaled down largely due to this case. The quantum of financial relief and aid that had been promised was much less than what was originally expected; indeed earlier indicated by the Americans.

Pakistan was a strategic partner; this was said several times during the visit. Putting Daniel Pearl's case in focus, the Americans pushed Islamabad hard to co-operate more closely with American intelligence agencies in pursuing the fleeing Al-Qaeda men and Taliban and their supporters in Pakistan.

M B Naqvi's version in that regard, as appeared in the **Deccan Herald dated 21st February 2002** held that:

'.....The Americans then persuasively pointed at ISI for Daniel as they had identified revolutionary and rebel elements of ISI for defiance of the government. This was too simplistic.

The ISI is army's department, run by the military personnel and has been reporting to the government and the army chief. As a government department it is not in a position to directly disobey the government or the President or run a policy of its own.

The fact of the matter is that the Americans have been unable to identify the culprit by name. It is a mind set and not an organised disciplined force. To think that the ISI can plan anything against the wishes of the government is nonsense. The problem is in part ideological, part political and part general decay of state structures that sustain the rule of law.'

However, Pakistan-US relations were not at all hampered or compromised over Daniel Pearl's disappearance barring financial assistance. The relationship remained of much value to the Americans rather went stronger in an arena of cooperation against War on Terror because Gen Musharraf was the most valuable ally for Americans.

ISI ALLEGED BY THE BRITISH (2006):

Going into the recent past of ISI; an article appeared in UK's daily **the 'Independent' dated 28th September 2006** written by James Tapsfield and Tony Jones said that:

'ISI is supporting terrorism by secretly backing the coalition of religious parties in Pakistan known as the MMA. The Army's dual role in combating terrorism and at the same time promoting the MMA, and so indirectly supporting the Taliban through the ISI, is coming under closer and closer international scrutiny.

Indirectly Pakistan, through the ISI, has been supporting terrorism and extremism whether in London on 7/7 or in Afghanistan or Iraq.'

{Independent's reporters and column writers were well learned and knew that MMA (*Mutehida Majlis e Amal*) was a coalition of six authentic politico-religious parties in which *Jamat e Islami* (JI) and *Jamiat Ulema e Islam* (JUI) were also included which, in media at least, had openly and repeatedly denounced their connections with Taliban. The MMA used to condemn the terrorist activities done in the name of Taliban; as much as the general populace in Pakistan.}

That article basically proposed using military links between the British and Pakistan armies at senior level to persuade Gen Musharraf to step down, accept free elections and persuade the army to dismantle the ISI.

Gen Musharraf was in London those days and a meeting between UK's Prime Minister Tony Blair was proposed same evening. The allegations on Pakistan were likely to add extra tension to that meeting between the two giants.

Gen Musharraf reminded the English media that US had threatened to bomb Pakistan **"Back to the Stone Age"** if the later did not co-operate against the Taliban in the wake of the 9/11 attacks. He had also criticised British intelligence for delays in informing the Pakistan authorities that two of the bombers who carried out the 7th July attacks in London had visited Pakistan just months earlier. But Gen Musharraf had insisted then that he would not give in to pressure to disband the ISI saying loudly to the world:

'I reject it from anybody - MoD or anyone who tells me to dismantle ISI. ISI is a disciplined force, for 27 years they have been doing what the government has been telling them, they won the Cold War for the world. Breaking the back of al-Qaeda would not have been possible if ISI was not doing an excellent job. UK is also at fault for not doing enough to stop its own home-grown extremists.

There's no doubt that the London (bombers) have some way or other come to Pakistan but let us not absolve the United Kingdom from their responsibilities.

Youngsters who are 25, 30 years old and who happen to come to Pakistan for a month or two months and you put the entire blame on these two months of visit to Pakistan and don't talk about the 27 years or whatever they have been suffering in your country.'

The UK's government and the media had no answer to Gen Musharraf's ending narration and the British government had to announce that:

'Pakistan is a key ally in our efforts to combat international terrorism and her security force has made considerable sacrifices in tackling al-Qaeda and the Taliban. We are working closely with Pakistan to tackle the root causes of terrorism and extremism.'

Next day, the same paper came up with another stance that Gen Musharraf would curb the excesses of the *madrasas* (religious schools) to combat terrorism in an effective way. On a broader level, he would return Pakistan to full democratic rule without delay. The world knew the hidden dangers of supporting local 'strong men' like Gen Ziaul Haq or Gen Musharraf in the Muslim world who lack democratic legitimacy.

Bill Clinton's speech at the Labour Party conference in those days was instructive. The former US president regretted that while he was in office so much aid to Pakistan had been given in the form of military hardware. He should have focused on eradicating school fees in most of the areas of Pakistan. That would have stopped poorer parents sending their children to free religious *madrasahs* (schools) for their education, where they go easily radicalised. President Clinton had rightly argued that:

'It's much cheaper to help the economy in a poor country than to fight a war. The tragedy is that such a subtle approach is apparently anathema to the architects of the present calamitous 'war on terror'.

The British PM Tony Blair, during his tour to Pakistan in ending 2006, had announced an aid of £480 million, in part to help fund the reform of Islamic schools or *madrassas* in the country. Some of these schools, attended often by the children of poor families, have been blamed for the spread of extremist thinking.

Mr Karzai, at the same moment, did not waste a single moment to blame the ISI and Gen Musharraf, might be to extort more funds from the UK, that Taliban commanders were living on the Pakistani side of the border, and it was their forces that had been harassing the British troops in Helmand province.

The British policy makers were able to grasp that five years after the Taliban were toppled, the infrastructure in many parts of Afghanistan was still in ruins, the opium poppy was back and corruption was endemic.

The distressing truth was that helping Karzai to oust the Taliban amidst putting baseless allegations on the ISI, Britain did precisely what it had promised not to do. The British PM's speeches in the Parliament are referred. *The British had "walked away" from Afghanistan and chose to fight a war in Iraq in 2003 onwards.*

The situation in the region was much deteriorated than of six years ago for anyone's comfort including UK, the Americans and Pakistan. ISI had little role in it.

Until this truth is acknowledged by the British historians as has been done by the American warriors; and suitable steps are taken in positive direction to indemnify those faults, there is no use of playing blame games in the name of ISI's activism. It stayed there as such; political wing is only one part of the organization.

Scenario 62

ISI IN POLITICS - II:

This role of 'taking over' of civil and political affairs of the governments in Pakistan by the army intelligence agencies is not a new phenomenon. Since the first day of independence the people are undergoing an undue surveillance by them as has been enumerated in the previous chapter.

Let us step into the recent past.

Pakistan's chief spy Lt Gen Mahmud Ahmad was in Washington when the event of 9/11 attacks occurred in New York. He had arrived in US on the 4th of September, a full week before the attacks. He had meetings at the State Department 'after' the attacks on the WTC but he also had 'a regular visit of consultations' with his US counterpart at the CIA and the Pentagon offices during the week prior to 11th September 2001.

Michel Chossudovsky, Professor at University of Ottawa [referred to *'Global Research' of Canada dated 2nd November 2001*] had then raised very cogent questions that:

- What was the nature of these routine "pre-September 11 consultations"?

- Were they in any way related to the subsequent "post-September 11 consultations" pertaining to Pakistan's decision to cooperate with Washington?

- Was the *'planning of war'* discussed between Pakistani and US officials?

GEN MAHMUD'S ROLE IN WOT:

On the 9/11 day (2001) while Lt Gen Mahmud was in the US, the Afghanistan's Northern Alliance Commander Ahmad Shah Masood was assassinated. The Northern Alliance had informed the Bush Administration that the ISI was allegedly implicated in the assassination.

The President Bush had consciously opted to cooperate with the ISI during Lt Gen Mahmud's *'post September 11 consultations'* in Washington having known their alleged links to Osama and the Taliban. Meanwhile, senior Pentagon officials rushed to Islamabad to put the finishing touches on America's war plans. But even then, *the US admin had asked Gen Musharraf to sack Lt Gen Mahmud before its first formal attack on Afghanistan on 7th October 2001.*

Truth was that, as per *report published in the 'Times of India'*, the Indian government had sent a brief to the White House [based on a French Press report] revealing the links between Lt Gen Mahmud and the presumed 'ring leader' of the WTC attacks Mohammed Atta.

The Indian intelligence / French Press report had also suggested that the 9/11 attacks were not an act of 'individual terrorism' by Al Qaeda, but rather they were part of coordinated military-intelligence operation, emanating from Pakistan's ISI. The Indians went successful in convincing the Americans that Lt Gen Mahmud had been coordinating with the alleged terrorist M Atta during his week's stay in America before 9/11 attacks on WTC.

The Americans were not so fool that they believed that cooked story first coined by the French Press [not the French Intelligence] then picked up by Times of India press, again not sorted out by the Indian Intelligence; but even then Americans believed it: salute to a super power.

Could one believe that the CIA & the Pentagon had not kept Gen Mahmud, a spy Chief of a 'suspected' country, on their surveillance devices to know his visits to any person during his stay in America? Could one believe that Gen Mahmood's hotel room, his mobiles and the car he was using during the said tour were not bugged through remote control gadgets.

The Americans should have pondered that Lt Gen Mahmud was a 'US approved appointee' as the ISI's Chief, was in liaison with his US counterparts in CIA, the Defence Intelligence Agency (DIA) and the Pentagon since 1999. Americans also forgot that ISI remained the launching pad for CIA covert operations in the Caucasus, Central Asia and the Balkans since decades. The American decision makers should have identified the relationship between ISI & Osama's Taliban faction and also the links between the ISI and the CIA & Pentagon, too.

Thus the conclusion surfaced that the Americans were indirectly abetting international terrorism, using the Pakistani ISI as a 'go-between'. While Lt Gen Mahmud was talking to the CIA & Pentagon during 9/11 days, and if ISI officials were allegedly also in contact with the 9/11 terrorists there, what does it lead to: that there did exist a nexus between ISI, CIA, Pentagon and 9/11 terrorists.

Michel Chossudovsky had also opined to a similar finale by saying that:

'[In the backdrop of the Indian intelligence report] ..... The perpetrators of the September 11 attacks had links to Pakistan's ISI, which in turn has links to agencies of the US government. What this suggests is that key individuals within the US military-intelligence establishment might have known about the episode.

The least one can expect at this stage is an inquiry. What is crystal clear, however, is that this war is not a "campaign against international terrorism". It is a war of conquest with devastating consequences for the future of humanity. And the American people have been consciously and deliberately misled by their government.'

India's lobby in the American Congress always tried to paint a thorny picture of the Pakistan's ISI pleading in the last that it should be banned; how it could be. ISI belongs to a sovereign state and India or America has nothing to do with its scope of duties or sphere of intelligence.

ISI IN BB'S INVESTIGATION:

The role of Pakistan's extensive network of intelligence agencies had come under scrutiny once more in the aftermath of the assassination of Benazir Bhutto. Whereas Gen Musharraf had categorically denied any possibility of an agency hand in the killing, fingers continued to be pointed in their direction. One of the reasons for such suspicions was the fact that though they consumed enormous budgets, the public knew nothing about their assigned role.

The lack of information about this role added to apprehensions that intelligence agencies worked like a state within state, with no control by governments. That both the interior and defence ministries had been telling the courts that the intelligence agencies did not fall under them; meaning thereby that their functions were laid outside the government's structure.

That was why there have been allegations that the agencies were at work in creating confusion about the murder of Benazir Bhutto. One could recall about 600 'disappeared' people in the country that the intelligence agencies had gained most notoriety. The Supreme Court had in the recent past held the agencies responsible for whisking away hundreds of citizens and keeping them in secret jails.

Talking about the later things; the **UN Commission** for investigation of Benazir Bhutto's assassination in Rawalpindi had mentioned, with utter surprise and sorrow, in their final report that the PPP government itself was responsible for slowing the process of investigation. For instance, the Government, which has been in office since April 2008, only commenced the further investigation in October 2009. The Commission's effort to determine the facts and circumstances of Ms Bhutto's assassination was not a substitute for an effective, official criminal investigation which should have been carried out, controlled and pursued simultaneously.

Another gigantic disappointment for the UN Commission was the overwhelming interest of Pakistan's intelligence agencies in the said investigation. The role of military intelligence agencies like ISI or MI, in the case during first three months of 2008 could be tolerated because of Gen Musharraf's rule but after April 2008, their role was neither justifiable nor necessary because a democratic setup of Benazir Bhutto's own party [PPP] was in saddles. The intelligentsia and many investigative media reporters speak about the omnipresence and clandestine role of these agencies in Pakistani society also.

During the course of this enquiry, the UN Commission got confirmation of this fact not only in law enforcement matters particularly in criminal investigations like of Benazir Bhutto, but also in various aspects of the country's political life during 2007. In terrorism cases, it is rational and tenable that intelligence agencies should provide support to police investigative parties but in case of Ms Bhutto's assassination, the role of intelligence agencies far exceeded an assisting role.

> [*There is nothing on record to show that ISI and MI or even the civil intelligence agency IB, had ever provided any lead or assistance in solving high profile cases.*]

In routine practice, the agency personnel otherwise remain present there at all scenes of crime but only to take notes for their own bosses and not for help or assistance to the civil investigators and not even to share with each other within intelligence circles. In most cases the uniformed civil investigators are always found scared of ISI's being there because their reports for their supervisors mostly contain critical remarks and negative connotations. The civil investigators mostly face humiliations at the hands of military's intelligence people on the basis of 'fault-finding' caricatures prepared under the garb of 'event reports' for their own.

The same happened in Benazir Bhutto's case. The UN Commission categorically mentioned that the agencies, and in particular the ISI, carried out parallel investigations into both the Karachi event of 18th October 2007 and the assassination of Ms Bhutto on 27th December 2007. The ISI had conducted its own investigation of the Karachi attack and had successfully detained four men who had allegedly provided logistic support for the attack. None of the police or other civilian officials was having any knowledge of such detentions.

Similarly, the ISI personnel covering Ms Bhutto's meeting at Liaquat Bagh were the first to secure her vehicle and take photos of it after the attack, among other actions. Even the high level state officials believed that the ISI, in fact, was made responsible for the investigation of Ms Bhutto's assassination. The Intelligence Bureau had never played any significant role in the investigation. What use of them; the living parasites on poor people's money!

Hold on! How the ISI or some other intelligence agency would help the civil police in Ms Bhutto's investigation. See an article of *'the Guardian'* date *26th July 2010:*

'President Bush could have forced Pakistan to break the ISI-Taliban nexus but did not. He was dealing with Musharraf who was in control of ISI. President Obama had to deal with an elected civilian government ....where Mr Zardari had opted to make the war on terror the centrepiece of his administration.

Taliban-linked extremists murdered Zardari's wife, Benazir Bhutto. ...... after reading the UN report, it is hard to avoid the conclusion that there was some level of official complicity in her killing, possibly by ISI officials. But Zardari does not control the ISI.'

The British paper had directly pointed towards ISI's possible connivance in Ms Bhutto's killing.

Analysing the situation on merits; the intelligence agencies work better when they are formally invited to join or associated with civil investigators in specific joint ventures. Members of the Joint Investigation Team (JIT) that investigated Ms Bhutto's assassination had admitted that much important information came from the intelligence side but much had been kept hidden from the civil for unknown reasons; especially related with identification and arrest of the suspects.

High ranking police officers believe that resources to build investigative capacity, especially in terrorism cases, have virtually been shifted to the military intelligence agencies, while police resources and capacity are far behind. Indeed, in the aftermath of the attempts on Gen Musharraf's life, the capacity of the ISI was strengthened to allow it to engage more effectively in such investigations. This tendency developed a distortion and imbalance in the functions of these institutions and posed a challenge for the future in ensuring the democratic rule of law.

Another aspect of the issue: take an example of Baitullah Mehsood's audio-tape referred by Brig Cheema in his media briefing of 28th December 2007. To determine the authenticity of suspects or back ground criminals, the phone interceptions might have been successfully used by the ISI or IB to reach that conclusion but using the same techniques to bug the politicians, journalists and social activists are not authorized in a democratic society.

Further than their involvement in criminal investigations, the UN Commission had felt a deep-root presence of intelligence agencies in several key aspects of the chaotic events of 2007. This persistent presence of agencies often hampered the ability of other institutions to exercise their mandate in the fields where they had to function independently.

The electoral process was one such area. The involvement of the ISI in influencing electoral outcomes in past elections is a well-documented reality; Air Marshal Asghar Khan's case in the Supreme Court can be cited as a cogent instance. That is why Ms Bhutto had to ask Gen Musharraf that keeping away of ISI should be included in the guarantee of free and fair elections [*January 2007's backdoor diplomacy & July 2007's meeting between Benazir Bhutto and Gen Musharraf are referred*]. The UN Commission mentioned that:

> '*The day after Benazir Bhutto's July (2007) meeting in Abu Dhabi with Gen Musharraf, an aide to Ms Bhutto was sent secretly to Islamabad on her behalf to review the work of the firm hired to create the new electoral lists; his site visits for this purpose were facilitated directly by Gen Kayani and other ISI staff.*
>
> *In 2007 the ISI had guaranteed that there would be no rigging. While by all accounts, the 2008 elections were "the most fair" (really?) elections in recent Pakistani history, constitutionally, the task of safeguarding the electoral process is the role of the Pakistan's Election Commission.*'

The UN Commission's observations were based on facts because the top army brass had purposefully involved the ISI in political negotiations between Gen Musharraf and Benazir Bhutto in all of its stages. Gen Kayani was praised from all corners for keeping himself, his army and the military intelligence units away from elections that time [in 2008].

ISI IN 'OTHER NATIONAL' AFFAIRS:

History has also witnessed that on 9th March 2007, when Chief Justice Iftikhar M Chaudhry was called in the Army House to surrender before Gen Musharraf, the chiefs of both ISI and MI were there to influence slaughtering of Justice and manipulate the composition of the Courts subsequently. The UN Commission's report had justifiably concluded that:

'.... *continuing involvement of intelligence agencies in diverse civil spheres, which is an open secret, has undermined the rule of law, distorted civilian – military relations and weakened most political and law enforcement institutions. At the same time, it has contributed to wide-spread public distrust in those institutions and fed a generalized political culture that thrives on competing conspiracy theories.'*

Talking about rigged elections of 2002, one may recall an interview published on *24th February 2008 in The News*, a daily English newspaper of Pakistan, the Deputy Chief of the ISI during 2002 elections, Maj Gen (Rtd) Ehtesham Zamir had admitted his guilt of manipulating the said [2002] elections, and directly blamed Gen Musharraf for ordering so.

As has been referred in Chapter 14 of Volume-I, Maj Gen (retd) E Zamir termed the 2008 elections *'fairer than 2002'*; the reason behind their fairness that there was relatively less interference of intelligence agencies this time as compared to that in 2002. When asked if he ever felt that he was committing a crime by manipulating political business at the cost of public wishes, Gen Zamir said:

'*Who should I have told except myself. Could I have asked Musharraf about this? I was a serving officer and I did what I was told to do. I never felt this need during the service to question anyone senior to me.*

Yes! Corruption cases were used as pressure tactics on lawmakers; not only by the ISI, the NAB was also involved in this exercise.

It was for this reason that I have never tried to preach others what I did not practice. But I am of the view that the ISI's political cell should be closed for good by revoking executive orders issued in 1975.'

[General elections held on 10th October 2002 were stolen in favour of PML(Q) on the orders of Gen Musharraf. The history would remember that Gen Musharraf's Principal Secretary Tariq Aziz was given the assignment to deliver a pro-Musharraf parliament. To fulfil this assignment, Tariq Aziz made indiscriminate use of ISI and the NAB. Gen Musharraf's aides, as well as PML(Q) leaders, termed the opposition leaders' statements as baseless and a lame excuse not to admit their defeat.]

Maj Gen ® Ehtesham Zamir's confession could be treated as the last nail in ISI's coffin if democracy was to be saved and strengthened in Pakistan.

The question arises that was it appropriate for a democratic government [PPP] or a professional military organisation like Pakistan Army to allow continuing these intelligence agencies, consuming a sizable chunk of Force's budget, to waste their energy and resources in settling miniature political manoeuvrings and intrigues that too at the cost of their primary duty of running for Pakistan's security from external and internal threats.

Referring to '*the News*' of 21st April 2008:

'The man who has ruled Sindh as a de facto chief minister for many years finally lost his powers on Saturday. Brig Huda, who was an ISI commander in Sindh, was in fact the caretaker of the MQM - PML(Q) provincial coalition government. He was responsible for running the coalition in a smooth manner.

All major decisions were taken after consultation with Brig Huda. He resolved the differences between former CM Arbab Ghulam Rahim and the MQM many a times. Many provincial ministers even used to say "ooper Khuda aur neechay Huda".

The brigadier's name figured in the power circles of Islamabad in the evening of May 12, 2007. Brig Huda was given credit for the show of massive government power in Karachi on that day.

Initially, the MQM was reluctant to hold a rally in Karachi on May 12. The then ISI DG Gen Ashfaq Kayani also had the same opinion that the MQM should not come out on the streets when Justice Iftikhar Muhammad Chaudhry would visit Karachi.

It was [Brig] Huda who played an important role in convincing the MQM not to cancel its rally. He assured the MQM leadership that there will be no riots on that day though he was proved wrong. He was very close to the then Army Chief Gen Musharraf. However, no action was taken against him.'

The blasts in the rally of Benazir Bhutto on 18th October 2007 at Karsaz in Karachi were another failure of ISI or Brig Huda. He was responsible for the security of Benazir Bhutto on that day. However, he was not transferred despite his repeated failures. His downfall started on 9th April 2008, when many people including lawyers were killed in the Karachi violence. The PPP government in Sindh felt that Brig Huda was still having immense political influence and was in contact with the anti-PPP forces. The key bureaucrats reported to the provincial government that Brig Huda was interfering in their departmental functions.

Brig Huda was more interested in "political makings and breakings" than doing his security job. After the episode of 9th April 2008, PPP leaders asked DG ISI Lt Gen Nadeem Taj through the PM that Brig Huda must be taken out. **On that day, six lawyers were burnt alive and 62 vehicles were set on fire around the City Courts** and S M Law College campus. See what a senior government officer told the media:

'We reached ...... and some people were firing in the air and asked us to stop and come out. Then they asked us to remove our shoes, which we did. They pointed gun on me and I shouted that I belong to your community. Then they turned to my driver who is a Sindhi and started beating him in-humanly.

I appealed them that he is my driver and I take full responsibility of him, then they stop beating him and asked us to flee and set my car on fire. We ran away and searched for a hide nearby and remained in that hide until my car was completely burnt.' [19th April 2008: www.pakspectator.com]

It took just a few days and Brig Huda was transferred and got replaced by another brigadier.

MEDIA'S BLUFF ON ISI IN AFGHAN CONFLICT:

Now let us take the other front of the military strategy [*till the end of 2012 at least*], where again Pakistan has been loosing.

Public sources, analysis and documents confirmed that Afghanistan war was being lost badly, the Afghan Taliban went continuously aggressive, US forces were not able to attack the right targets and the Western press continued blaming that 'elements' in Pakistan were supporting the Taliban. They maintained that *'raw intelligence spread over 90,000 pages'* [referring to documents allegedly recovered from Osama BL's premises] had shown a continued relationship between the ISI and the Taliban.

Not surprising. In the post 1980s era, the ISI helped create the Taliban and Pakistani support was decisive to the Taliban's capture of Kabul in 1996. From inside; the US authorities continued to force down that Pakistan did not break its ties with the Taliban as Gen Musharraf had promised President Bush.

According to the American version Mullah Omar and his close associates were in Pakistan since 2001. False or true; he might be there and even Pakistan's intelligence agencies had not genuinely known but that was why they vowed to launch more direct attacks on Pakistan as was done on 2nd May 2011 for Osama.

In the past, the ISI has been co-operating with the US by arresting militants like Mullah Baradur, the Taliban number two and a key figure in its military operations but the Pentagon kept echoing that the ISI played double game with them. The American blame of 'double game' playing by Pakistan was not new. The fact remains that Pakistan had been telling the US authorities every now and then in very clear terms that '<u>Americans are loosing in Afghanistan</u>'.

The *New York Times of 22nd July 2009,* in an essay titled **"Pakistan Objects to US Plan for Afghan War"** had itself mentioned that:

> *'The country's perspective [on the US surge in Afghanistan] was given in nearly two-hour briefing [a day earlier] for The New York Times by senior analysts and officials of Pakistan's main spy service, the Directorate for Inter-Service Intelligence.*
>
> *One of the first briefing slides read, in part:* **'The surge in Afghanistan will further reinforce the perception of a foreign occupation of Afghanistan. It will result in more civilian casualties; further alienate local population; thus more local resistance to foreign troops.'*

It was a clear message which the ISI itself had conveyed openly to the world. But how ISI was subjected to pressure, only few people know.

Once *'The Sunday Times' of early April 2010* published allegedly a baseless story with reference to a 'source' linked with London School of Economics (LSE) saying that:

'President Zardari and a senior ISI official met 50 high-ranking Taliban members at a prison in Pakistan. Zardari spoke to them for half an hour; also met Mullah Abdul Ghani Baradar, the Taliban's former second in command; also Mullah Abdul Qayyum Zakir and Mullah Abdul Rauf; both were former Guantanamo inmates......

To retain its influence over the Taliban's leadership, the ISI has placed its own men on the Quetta Shura. Up to seven of the Afghan Taliban leaders who sit on the 15-men Shura are believed to be ISI agents......

The ISI pays 200,000 Pakistani rupees (then £1,600) in compensation to the families of suicide bombers who launch attacks on targets in Afghanistan...... Camps within Pakistan train Taliban fighters in three different sets of skills: suicide bombing, bomb-making and infantry tactics.....'

It was all pack of lies. In routine the Sunday Times published the Afghan War stories communicated by its own correspondents, responsible enough for reporting but this 'source report through LSE' brought much bad name from fellow media circles because not even a single phrase was corroborated by any other media report or independent evidence.

Major Gen Athar Abbas of the ISPR had called all the claims ridiculous and absolutely baseless. Farhatullah Babar, a spokesman from the presidency had vehemently denied the story about Mr Zardari saying that: *"President Zardari never met Taliban leaders. This never happened."*

Sunday Times should have known Mr Zardari who had never issued any statement on 'Army Affairs' what to speak of meeting Taliban Commanders. Otherwise he as President, and the PPP as ruling regime, never approved ISI's policies in Afghanistan.

'The Economic Times' of 14th June 2010 also gave version of ISI's denial with much considerable comments.

What the western block wanted to get out of such baseless stories; to hit the ISI. Sometimes the media associates of Pakistan joined them too. The media, Pakistani and Western, paper as well electronic, often orchestrated negatively since at least 2007 over the alleged role of ISI in politics.

Z A Bhutto is said to have assigned some political work [*then mostly related to Balochistan affairs, it is believed*] to ISI but it might not be a policy decision. Anyway, what one Prime Minister did, any of his successors could undo it if it was considered wrong but it never happened. The fact remained that every ruler, civilian & military, found it convenient to use ISI in political manipulations. So, the practice continued, despite a lot of noise over the years.

Who were the people in the media and politics who wanted ISI under political control, or even its abolishment; mainly India and US for obvious reasons. Zaid Hamid, a veteran reformer, filed a petition [*on 2nd April 2012*] in the Supreme Court for trial of certain media warlords like Imtiaz Alam, Executive Director SAFMA, Sirmed Manzoor, Najam Sethi, Beena Sarwar, Nusrat Javeed, Khaled Ahmed, Marvi Sirmed, Ali Chishti, Hamid Mir, Hassan Nisar, Asma Jahangir and some others under 'high treason' clauses of the Pakistan Constitution but no cogent response till today at least. The said petition was drafted by Ahmed Raza Khan Qasuri on behalf of Zaid Hamid.

ISI ON OSAMA'S KILLING:

Thus, it was difficult to pressurize the ISI indirectly, too. Threatening to withhold US assistance to Pakistan could not work effectively; so there was no other option left with the Americans to bring down the ISI through an operation like of Osama's killing which ultimately bought humiliation and dishonour not only for the Pak-Army and the ISI but for the whole nation.

Why America resolved to this way out. Amidst miss-understandings between ISI and CIA, the US believed that their hi-tech weapons were not hitting at specific locations because of unreliable intelligence provided by their ally Pakistan's ISI. Poor intelligence brought more civilian casualties thus causing more problems for the NATO planners coupled with roaring tide of general hatred against the Americans. Pak-Army and the ISI was continuously pressurised and Pakistan was often punished as a scapegoat in that failed war.

After 2nd May 2011's attacks on Abbotabad, a joint parliamentary session was called on 13th May in Islamabad. The details of the proceedings have been given in a separate chapter on 'Osama's Killing'. However, referring to '*The Friday Times*' of 20-26th May 2011;

*'The resolution passed by the joint parliamentary session marked
the beginning of a new chapter of civil-military relations. The army
leadership, embarrassed by the American raid on Osama's compound,
mostly remained defensive throughout the session, because it needed
the parliamentary cover for their failings and inadequacies.'*

For nationalist people, it was not a moment to rejoice but an occasion to
revisit their policies and priorities in an arena of on-going relations with
the US. The members unanimously agreed to appoint an independent
commission on the Abbottabad incident to fix responsibility.

The parliamentary resolution also proposed blocking NATO supplies if
such an incident happened in the future, but bad luck for poor Pakistani
populace, this step was never implemented [*Though it was done later
when the US air attack of 26th November 2011 on Pak army's post at
Mohmand border [Salala] killed 24 army men including six officers, but
lasted only for a few months and the NATO supplies resumed again*].

Earlier, the people and intelligentsia had been raising loud voices to block
the NATO cargo route through Pakistan to stop the drone attacks but it
was never given serious thought either by Gen Musharraf's regime or his
successors since five years in saddles.

Once in the past too, Pakistan was able to test the grounds for launching
a halt for American's cargo transport when NATO helicopters had killed
two Pakistani soldiers in the Kurram Agency on 30th September 2010.
Pakistan Army had called back the security cover to the American interests
in that region while asking for an apology. The then US ambassador Ann
W Patterson had to offer a public apology at last on 7th October instant
but till then NATO's 150 trucks carrying food, fuel and weapons for
coalition forces in Afghanistan had gone up in flames.

The Army Chief Gen Kayani had ordered an investigation into the
Abbotabad episode to be done by a team of senior military officers which
was unanimously rejected by all. During the joint parliamentary session,
ISI and the army had to agree on an open enquiry by a panel of judges
of higher courts or at least a joint civilian body; another blow to the
military's legitimacy in Pakistan.

More seriously; on 14th May 2011, PML(N) Leader Nawaz Sharif
demanded in a press conference that:

*'It should be the parliament's prerogative to determine the kind of
relationship we need to have with India, the US, Afghanistan or any*

other country. Intelligence agencies should stop playing games, including making new political alliances and dividing political parties. They should stop running parallel government and dictating to elected representatives.'

The former Prime Minister had availed an opportunity to recount his days in two notorious jails; one in the Mogul era's Attock Fort and the other in Landhi, Karachi to back his claim that intelligence agencies used to break laws to make or break governments. Thus while the American raid on Osama's hide out had unified the political forces in Pakistan, it also provided them with a whip to wave at the hitherto 'unaccountable, all-powerful' ISI, whom the burden of circumstances had humbled into modesty, might be for the time being.

The point remains that had the Pakistani politicians behaved more responsibly, shown personal integrity and demonstrable commitment to the interests of the people, the dependence on ISI would have been outdated much earlier. The American raid at Abbottabad and the ensuing parliamentary debate of 13th May 2011 indeed marked the first step towards turning the balance of the civil-military relationship in the favour of the former; but if they could handle it.

GEN HAMID GUL'S OPINION:

An interview of the former *Chief of ISI, Gen Hamid Gul, appeared in magazine 'Newsline' of June 2011* reflected a true picture of America's designs to take control of Pakistan's military affairs.

Q: Terrorists are increasingly turning more deadly and hitting targets at will. The PNS Mehran attack [May 2011] speaks of the gravity of the situation. There is an impression that Pakistani forces are incompetent or unwilling to take on the terrorists head-on. What do you think?

A: Pakistan's armed forces and security agencies are in deterioration and disorientation phase and the Abbottabad and Mehran attacks are examples of just such deterioration. Operation Osama and Mehran were meant to fix the Pakistan military and ISI, and set them up for criticism and ridicule.

The US has been involved in every attack on Pakistan's strategic assets, aimed at creating the feeling among Pakistanis that their armed forces and secret agencies are incompetent and cannot protect their country.

[Gen] Pervez Musharraf is solely responsible for creating this mess in Pakistan by allowing the US to use its bases and other facilities and establish its network through Raymond Davis-like agents to destabilize Pakistan. A US-India sponsored group is involved in the Mehran attacks and its sole purpose was to hit the Pakistan navy's navigation surveillance system and deprive Pakistan of its ability to detect any Abbottabad-like operation in its waters.

Q: Some senior officials in Washington are accusing the ISI and Pakistan's military for providing shelter to Osama in Pakistan. The military maintains that they, including the ISI, were ignorant of OBL's presence in Pakistan until the US forces' operation. What do you believe?

A: The US has been working on an anti-ISI agenda for a long time. However, in the past, such tactics failed because they did not get the support of the Pakistani leadership. But today, danger looms more visibly than ever before because Pakistani rulers themselves are a party to conspiracies hatched against the country…….

Q: The US and ISI installed the mujahideen in Afghanistan; it is widely believed that the ISI's policy of controlling Afghanistan through the Taliban brought terrorism and insurgency to Pakistan. What do you say?

A: Our western border has always been a shield for Pakistan since our decision to demilitarize the Pak-Afghan border in 1948. By defeating the Soviets, the ISI protected Pakistan's interests in Afghanistan and made our western border safer, but what we miscalculated is the US thinking on Pakistan……

Q: In the in-camera briefing to parliament [dated 13th May 2011] on OBL's killing, DG ISI Shuja Pasha stated that some Islamic countries were funding JUI and other religious parties to carry out their respective agendas. Is there any truth to this?

A: Yes we had information that some religious parties were getting dollars from an Islamic country. But the ISI also had evidence that some politicians loudly demanding democracy in Pakistan were also being funded by foreign countries. I have many secrets about popular political leaders.

Q: It has been tacitly recognized by successive political governments and the public that the ISI operates as a completely independent body answerable to no one, and Pakistan's foreign policy has long been held hostage by the agency in pursuit of its own agendas, which are often in conflict with the governments. Do you concede this?

A: It is Pakistan's great tragedy that the PPP has always aimed at bringing the ISI under its control; whether it was Zulfikar Ali Bhutto, Benazir Bhutto or now Zardari and his party.

The PPP actually has always seemed to believe that if the ISI is not directly responsible to it, it will weaken the government. So the current PPP leaders are once again trying to bring the ISI under civilian rule. Basically the PPP wants to weaken the ISI as an institution and in the process, serve others' aims.

CIVILIAN CONTROL OVER ISI?

Referring to the daily *'Dawn' of 5th December 2011*; the principal character in the memo-gate scandal, Mansoor Ijaz, openly deliberates that *'the ISI is under nobody's control [like CIA of America] and always keeps its hand in politics'*. In an interview with CNN host Fareed Zakaria, Mr Ijaz said:

'The ISI has two critical branches in it. One is called CT, for counter-terrorism, and the other one is called S Branch for strategic — it's sort of the arm of the ISI that does everything from political interventions in other countries [for example: Afghanistan] which is what they're doing through the Haqqani network and the Taliban right now.

It is essentially the organ of the state that the army and the intelligence wings are using to, shall we say, coordinate or obstruct what it is that the political side of the government, the civilian side of the governments do in Pakistan.'

As per Mansoor Ijaz's version the ISI does a lot of political interventions in its own country and that S Branch was involved in manipulating elections and remained involved in different operations in Pakistan since very long. However, he did not mention that what kind of operations these were.

By the way; **why should ISI be under the Prime Minister**, as has been pointed out by Gen Hamid Gul in above replies? It is a joint intelligence service of Army, Air Force and Navy, staffed by personnel from all three services. Its objective is to protect national security through intelligence and counter intelligence. Being a military agency, it should not be under a civilian but, instead, politicians could have asked the respective army chiefs to *abolish the 'Political Wing' in the ISI* leaving it behind a purely professional espionage agency.

In the Asghar Khan Case judgment of 2012, the Supreme Court has already declared that the Pak-Army or the ISI would no more be doing any political interference AND since then it stands implemented.

Civilian Prime Minister already keeps under him the Intelligence Bureau [IB], a civilian agency dealing with national security in non-military matters and staffed mostly by police or IB's own cadre officers. It should be enough; incidentally, CIA is also a civilian agency, like IB. That is why it is under civilian control. If the politicians could never activate the IB, could not get desired results from them, could not make them powerful; Pakistanis should be sure that ISI would also go toothless there and become another parasite on the public funds.

Who are the people in the media and politics that want ISI under political control, or even its abolishment? Well, ISI finds out about the persons working for our 'friendly' enemies, like India and US. Naturally, it keeps a watch on them and neutralizes them. That makes those politicians mad whose main interests [financial too] lie out of Pakistan or whose strings are controlled from Washington or Jeddah or Dubai.

Just a passing reference from *'the Friday Times' of 30th Dec 2011 to 6th Jan 2012 issue*:

'Ex-ISI Chief Gen (Retd) Ziauddin said in *Mashriq* [a daily newspaper from Lahore] that Gen Musharraf and Brig Ijaz Shah [once the IB Chief] had given shelter to Osama bin Laden but Memo-gate was an American sting operation to entrap Pakistan. He said America could not save any government in Pakistan from being toppled. When it considers democracy inadequate, the Army takes over.

Gen Ziauddin said that America had trained 90 commandos to capture Osama but the then ISI Chief Gen Mahmud had scrapped the scheme.'

Another script from the same above reference:

'*Columnist Nazeer Naji wrote in Jang that Dr Abdul Nabi Fai from Indian administered Kashmir was resident in Washington and was honestly agitating for the freedom of the Kashmiris from India but was destroyed by someone in the ISI who thought of giving him money for doing what was his national mission. He was not made a formal lobbyist for Pakistan and was therefore caught and punished for [allegedly] taking money from the ISI.'*

Travelling through the history of Pakistan since 1948, gradually and triumphantly, it remains a fact that the politicians had always proved to be a disaster while trying to seize control of the ISI. Benazir Bhutto replaced Gen Hamid Gul with Gen (retd) Kallue; Nawaz Sharif replaced Gen Asad Durrani and brought Gen Javed Nasir as DG-ISI but both failed miserably. In 1999, PM Nawaz Sharif brought Gen Ziauddin Butt [a General from Engineering Corp] as DG-ISI but the the the then COAS Gen Musharraf made him ineffective by packing the ISI with his loyalists; all the three were declared PNG [*persona non grata*] in their respective times.

In nut shell, the intelligence agencies like ISI and MI had brought more criticism and less appreciation from the populace in general. On the other hand, the Pakistan Army, as an institution, has always been praised and applauded. A **Working Paper [no: 122 dated 10th February 2011]** compiled by **Institute of South Asian Studies Singapore** had mentioned that:

'The [Pakistani] army's role in meeting the disaster once again revealed that it is the strongest and most effective state institution. Even before the floods, the army had recovered the prestige it had lost during the end of the Musharraf era.

A study has revealed growing approval ratings for the army with 84 per cent of those surveyed expressing positive views, compared with 68 per cent in 2007.....

On the eve of the floods, President Zardari's poll standing had already been declined dramatically from the 2008 high point. His absence from Pakistan as the floods took their grip and the Federal Government's inability to deal with the natural catastrophe made him appear still more aloof from the people, therefore, further weakening his standing with respect to the army.'

See the later news now.

Referring to *'the Jang' dated 5th March 2012* PML(Q)'s Ch Shuja'at Hussain and Ch Pervez Elahi once went to the Army Chief Gen

Kayani and lodged their complaint in a very docile and humble way saying that:

> 'One of the heads of your intelligence agency [Gen Pasha, DG ISI he was] is overtly and covertly interfering in our [political] affairs; we've always been with you [the army]; we had never caused you loss or let you down but your agency is bent upon breaking our party; our members are being forced by your agency to join another political faction.'

The Chaudhrys were perhaps pointing towards Imran Khan's *Sonamy* with special reference to Amir Muqam's shaky behaviour those days. Gen Kayani might know but had not taken it seriously till then that his officers had gone so deep into the political game. The meeting brought fruit and the '*Sonami slogan*' of Imran Khan was initially halted for some days then started moving in routine gear.

The general populace of Pakistan has to consider all the factors seriously.

ISI – 'A STATE WITHIN STATE:

It is also a fact that Air Marshal Zulfikar Commission [formed during Benazir Bhutto's first regime] had recommended that the political cell should be altogether abolished from the ISI. Then Gen Hamid Gul was the Chief of ISI who had immediately sent a written confirmation to the Commission that '*the Army itself do not want this political cell in ISI, therefore, should immediately be abolished*'.

Air Marshal Zulfikar forwarded this suggestion to the then Prime Minister Benazir Bhutto for approval. The news was also leaked out for the press and media but then suddenly the ISI Chief Gen Hamid Gul received a call from Gen Nasirullah Babar of PPP saying:

> '*General Sahib! There is news in the press that the government is going to abolish the Political Cell of ISI. Forget it; the government has no such plans.*'

It is also available on record that on 5th July 2012 a 19-page draft bill was submitted in the Senate by President Zardari's spokesman Senator Farhatullah Babar for discussion. It was legislation regarding the ISI which was brought up there after having discussed with coalition partners but was termed as a private member's bill submitted by a parliamentarian in his individual capacity. The preamble of the Bill said that:

'In the case of missing persons, the government had formally submitted before the Supreme Court on 27th April 2007 that the operations of the intelligence agencies were beyond the control of the federal government. ....

[Thus] the absence of appropriate legislation regulating the functioning, duties, powers and responsibilities of the agency is not consistent with the principles of natural justice and accountability of authority and power and has given rise to resentment against the premier national agency.'

The proposed Inter-Services Intelligence Agency (Functions, Powers and Regulation) Act, 2012 suggested that *'the ISI should be answerable to parliament and the prime minister'*. It recommended internal accountability and a better discipline within the agency to put an end to enforced disappearances and victimisation of political parties.

The bill provided that the Director General of the agency should be a serving or retired civil servant in BS-22 or of an equivalent rank in the armed forces to be appointed by the president on the recommendation of the prime minister and should hold the office for four years. *'The agency shall be directly under the prime minister and not under any ministry,'* it was mentioned therein.

The bill had also envisaged an Intelligence and Security Committee of the Parliament comprising nine members drawn from both houses of parliament, none of whom could be a minister or minister of state, to examine matters relating to expenditure, administration and policy of the agency. The proposed committee was not allowed to go into the intelligence sources of the agency. The prime minister was suggested to lay before both the houses of Parliament an annual report of the committee together with a statement as to whether any matter could be excluded from it and why.

There were other clauses controlling the issues of methodology of detention, period of custody for 30 days and beyond, powers of Review Board, accountability & discipline, employee's terms and duties and appointment of Ombudsman for intelligene matters, trials & appeals etc but the PPP's ruling regime could not find enough strength in its own rows & columns to take the bill through.

Just six days after, on 11ᵗʰ July 2012, the bill was withdrawn from the Senate because on this private bill no one else in the PPP had spoken in its favour. Other coalition partners like MQM, PML(Q), ANP or JUI and the so-called opposition [PML(N)] all maintained silence on it. The fact was that most parliamentarians preferred to studiously ignore any attempts to take on the military.

Editorial of *'the Express Tribune' of 11ᵗʰ July 2012* commented that:

'*Intelligence agencies have seemingly always operated with impunity. The ISI and other military agencies came into being through executive orders but there was never any attempt by parliament to control their actions by passing legislation that laid out their functions. .....*

This PPP government's track record in that regard has been particularly poor. Soon after coming into power, in July 2008, the government tried [through Rehman Malik] to bring the ISI under the purview of the interior ministry, but took back the notification barely three hours later after the military vociferously and angrily objected.'

The ISI, IB and other intelligence agencies still operate through Standard Operating Procedures (SOPs) having no legal sanctity hence all actions carried out by them do not stand the scrutiny of law. Thus it may not be out of place to mention here that all such proposals regarding control of ISI and other intelligence agencies were elaborately discussed by late Benazir Bhutto and Nawaz Sharif in 2006 and later made part of their renowned and celebrated *'Meesaq e Jamhooriat'*. It is still available in their sacred document that:

- All intelligence agencies will work under the civilian government.

- ISI and the MI will be attached with Ministry of Defence whereas all other intelligence agencies will be attached with the Cabinet Division.

- The budget of these agencies will be provided through 'Cabinet Committee on Defence'.

- The political cells of all the intelligence agencies will be abolished.

- The appointments of senior officers in all agencies will be done by the civilian government.

However, when the so-called democracy prevailed in early 2008, both parties belonging to Benazir Bhutto and Nawaz Sharif never bothered to look back on their 'manifesto' which had been trumpeted in high volume ever since.

For ISI, a peculiar phrase [*of State within a State*] was beaten loud in Pakistan in the third week of December 2011 by PM Gilani while pointing towards the alleged anti-PPP activities of the then DG ISI Gen Pasha; soon after it became talk of the town; a spicy [and spiky too] subject for live TV shows, editorials, and columns in media.

As has been mentioned above, in July 2008, Asif Zardari and Rehman Malik tried to seize control of the political wing of the ISI by proposing its control with the interior ministry but the notification could survive only for three hours. Under Gen Pasha, the ISI caught hold of dictating foreign policy; allegedly disobeying, embarrassing and even destabilising the Zardari government on some occasions, until PM Gillani [once himself a beneficiary of the ISI and GHQ] was provoked to bitterly label the ISI as '*state within a state*'.

The fact remains that the able Senator Farhatullah Babar had taken the whole set of wording from the draft IB bill proposed in early days of PPP government in 2008; only the word IB was replaced with ISI. It was a replica of the same old draft of law which could not be placed before the Parliament due to unknown reasons. The bill was not even able to get approval of the PPP's own Federal Minister for Law and Justice Farook H Naek.

Though the proposed bill also aimed to empower the ISI to deal with terrorism, separatism and other anti-state activities in a legally effective manner but the PPP leadership, then besieged by the superior courts, could not find enough courage to encroach upon the powerful military, and avoided possible kick out. The proposed bill could, in one way, truly strengthen the ISI to defend the national interest especially in dealing with terrorism and missing persons affairs etc but the problem remained that '*who would bell the cat*'

Scenario 63

HATS OFF TO A CJP (JUSTICE DOGAR)

On 16ᵗʰ January 2009 during the final hearing of an issue before the Islamabad High Court (IHC), a petitioner Azam Khan Sultanpuri, who was one of the challengers of extra 21 marks awarded to one Farah Hameed Dogar, argued that the Chairman, Federal Board of Intermediate and Secondary Education (FBISE) acted in gross violation of the rules while awarding extra marks to the daughter of Justice Abdul Hameed Dogar, Chief Justice of Pakistan (CJP). The Court held that:

> 'There is nothing wrong in the marks increased in re-evaluation by the experts in the field and no exception can be taken by this court to the procedure adopted by the Chairman (Federal Board of Intermediate and Secondary Education) and the re-evaluation made by examiners.
>
> In order to foster the principle of justice a wrong had to be remedied. In the absence of a statutory provision, residuary power rests with the authority to undo manifest case of victimization by the examiners.
>
> An examinee may not suffer in his career on account of incorrect marks awarded by a sub - or head-examiner, in the absence of supervisory power with the board or the university directing re-evaluation.'

Chief Justice Sardar Mohammad Aslam of IHC observed as above while rejecting the two petitions for being without merit. The petitions were moved by Iftikhar Hussain Rajput and M Azam Khan Sultanpuri of the *Tehreek Falah e Pakistan*. The 14-page court order also asked the Secretary of the Ministry of Education (MoE), the controlling authority of the FBISE, to consider the possibility of bringing an amendment to the board rules to provide a procedure for re-evaluation of papers.

Going into details of the judgment; two samples of Miss Farah Hameed Dogar's answer sheets were made part of the Islamabad High Court's judgment to prove 'irregularities' that were cited as the reason for re-assessment of her papers. In one case pertaining to the paper of Physics II, despite her answer being incorrect, Miss Farah was given two marks while that part carried only one mark. In case of Urdu paper, despite making four mistakes in a two-line answer, she was given two marks out of three.

Ansar Abbasi, an Islamabad based correspondent, (Ref: *'the News' dated 19th January 2009*) after announcement of the judgment, obtained question papers of Physics II and Urdu for the FBISE Examinations 2008 and compared the same with the two samples reproduced in the IHC judgment. The comparison revealed that the judgment pointed out a wrong answer for the Physics II answer reproduced in the verdict.

On page 13, the judgment said:

> *'On visual examination of Physics-II paper, answer to question No 5(b) is given below: "No, the plates of capacitor are not of different sizes; however to decrease the electrostatic factor a dielectric medium is put in between them.'* **Then the judge wrote:** *'The examiner crossed the question and awarded zero mark. Later on, he gave one mark. On re-evaluation (re-assessment), another mark was added.'*

Meaning thereby that in this particular question of the paper, the candidate got two marks.

The question paper, however, had shown that the above answer pertained to XIV (b) of Q.2, which reads as: "A capacitor is connected across a battery: (b) Is this true even if the plates are of different sizes?"

It carried total one mark as part XIV, having three sub-parts — a, b and c — had total three marks. Against the answer reproduced above, the candidate, when reassessed, got two marks against the part that carried only one mark. It means even if Miss Farah's answer was 100 per cent correct, she would not have got more than one mark, but she got two.

The Chairman Department of Physics, Quaid e Azam University Islamabad, Dr Hoodbhoy, when contacted for opinion, said that in the above given sample in which Miss Farah was given two marks after the controversial reassessment, she actually deserved zero.

In Urdu paper, according to the judgment, one mark was awarded in answer to a question, reproduced in the judgment, while after re-assessment; the candidate was given an additional mark. The question paper of Urdu had shown that the question — 2(i) [asking about Babar's toughness] carried total three marks, out of which Miss Farah got two marks despite making two spelling mistakes and two mistakes of idioms. In a language paper, spelling and grammatical mistakes are taken seriously, but in Miss Farah's case, after one mark, she was given two marks.

After reproducing the two samples and details of marks originally given and revised, the IHC's judge said:

'I do find some of the irregularities in other papers too. In such a situation, when the chairman examined the answer books of the papers in dispute, he made a decision, rightly so to direct re-assessment. ......

There is nothing wrong in the marks increased in re-evaluation by the experts in the field and no exception can be taken by this court to the procedure adopted by (the) Chairman and the re-evaluation made by examiners.'

Overlooking such scandalous flaws, the above ruling of the judge left many questions to ponder upon our Pakistani system of extending personal benefits and favours to brother judges flouting the prevailing norms and taking camn care of the judiciary's reputation.

Going into more details of the IHC's verdict in this case, the law knowing people and educationists had declared it as full of flaws, discrepancies, inconsistencies and inaccuracies. A careful reading of the 14-page decision shows; on page 7 for instance, that the judge, perhaps confusing re-checking with re-assessment, gave a misplaced ruling:

'Bare reading shows that an embargo has been placed on re-assessment of any answer book until publication of the result.'

Rule 1.5 (a), quoted in the FBISE's rules and copied in the verdict, reads:

'The answer book of a candidate in any examination shall not be re-assessed under any circumstances. However, after the publication of the results of the board's examination, if a candidate, whether passed or failed, has strong grounds and belief that some mistake has been made in connection with his results, he / she may apply to the Controller of Examination (Secrecy) on prescribed application form along with attested photocopies of marks sheet for re-checking of his answer book, in one paper or more as the case may be, on payment of prescribed fee.'

This rule speaks of 're-checking,' not about 're-assessment' and only after the publication of the result, but the IHC judge's observation suggests as if re-assessment is allowed after declaration of result. The judgment simply omits Rule 1.5 (e), which, while explaining Rule 1.5 (a), reads that:

'Whereas the re-checking does not mean re-assessment or re-evaluation of the answer book, the chairman or any officer of the re-checking committee appointed by him shall see that:

1) There is no mistake in the grand total on the title page of the answer book;

2) The totals of various parts of question have been correctly made at the end of each question;

3) All totals have been correctly brought forward on the title page of the answer book;

4) No portion of any answer has been left unmarked;

5) Total marks in the answer book tally with the marks sheet;

6) The answer book or any part thereof has not been changed / detached;

7) The hand writing of the candidate tallies in the questions / answer books.'

Now the **second main issue**; IHC's judgment noted on page 5-6:

'The sole question requiring examination is whether the Chairman [FBISE] possessed any authority to direct re-assessment.

The board was created under the Federal Board of Intermediate and Secondary Education Act 1975. Section 11(4) confers absolute jurisdiction upon the chairman to see that provisions of this Act are faithfully observed and he shall exercise all powers necessary for this purpose.

Under Section 17, the board has been empowered to make regulations carrying out the purposes of this Act.'

But on page 7, the same judgment says:

'Regulations do not confer any power on the chairman to direct re-assessment / re-evaluation of any answer book but such a power does reside in him being the chief executive of the board.'

Moreover, the judgment seems to have omitted to ponder upon Clause 8 of Chapter 4 of the First Regulation of the Schedule of the Act titled **'Chairman's power in cases of hardship'** which says:

' .... *The orders of the chairman, passed under this regulation,*
shall be reported to the board for information; provided that such
orders of the chairman shall not alter the award of marks, obtained by
a candidate or his result determined on the basis of that award.'

It is therefore, clear that the Board's Chairman had no authority to pass
any order that could change the result of a candidate. Interestingly, while
the judgment ruled that the chairman had such powers, the case file of
Farah Dogar clearly said that: *'the chairman had passed the order for re-*
assessment in relaxation of the rules'.

The Act, however, does not give such power at all and there was also no
provision either in the Act or the rules allowing such a relaxation. It was
a cogent fact that the Federal Board had favoured Farah Hameed, may
be obliging government's instructions, during proceedings in the IHC by
twisting and wrongly interpreting their own rules.

It is commonly known that in all universities and boards, the answer books
of examinations are checked by examiners and then minimum 10% are
rechecked by Head Examiners. When the checking procedure is complete,
all lots of the papers are sealed in 'secrecy branch' from where it could only
be taken out under orders of the chairman when required for re-checking
(and not re-assessing). Each Head Examiner has to submit a certificate to
the board under Rule 7.6L(4) that *'at least 10% papers have been re-*
checked'. Under this rule this re-marking, re-checking or re-assessment by
the head examiner can only be done before the results are announced.

While explaining this rule in the IHC the Chairman and his counsel
produced this rule in a derogatory way conveying that perhaps this rule
could also be applied after announcement of results. This rule was
applicable as such in all the boards and university examination
directorates across Pakistan and everywhere its sanctity was always kept
in tact. So many times the higher courts were moved in some cases but
the courts especially the Supreme Court always avoided to issue such
decisions declaring all as 'technical matters'.

FACTORS BEHIND WRONG JUDGMENT:

In the said judgment dated 16th January 2009, the IHC had written that:

'*On 21-08-2008, answer scripts of Farah Dogar were submitted to the*
chairman, who ordered on 10-09-2008: "Please have the answer book
of this candidate re-assessed.'

The legal procedures first; the citing of judgments in all higher courts are substantiated on previous references of laws explained or rulings passed in similar or nearly similar cases. The analysis of the rulings used as basis of IHC's this decision comes up as; firstly, *PLD 1992 SC 263* (which does not issue any re-assessment order); the second case law - *1995 MLD 899* - points out flaws in the system and called for an elaborate mechanism against possible lapses of examiners, etc, but does not pass any direction to carry out re-assessment in any particular case.

The third case law pertains to a higher court seeking suitable amendments in the rules of a university so that "re-checking" of answer books in very genuine cases could be undertaken. Therefore, the case laws relied on in the IHC judgment either talk of the university system or of high court's decisions containing directions to make appropriate rules, none of them directly dealing with the re-assessment.

Thus most of the cited laws went irrelevant either because they pertained to universities or for the embargo laid down in the latest Supreme Court decisions. The Supreme Court, at numerous occasions, has categorically declared that re-assessment could result in the collapse of the whole education and examination systems. None of these Supreme Court rulings was cited in the IHC judgment. These SC rulings were **1996 SCMR 676, 1996 SCMR 1872,** and **2002 SCMR 504.** None of these case laws have directly ordered re-assessment but speak in general terms about framing of such rules.

The latest SC ruling (**CP No. 248 / 2002 written in 2004**), cited in the said Farah Hameed's case of the IHC basically restores powers of a vice-chancellor to direct re-evaluation which was taken back earlier from him by deletion of rule. It was done to keep a check and balance system in the university affairs. It seeks the reversal of the deleted power of the vice-chancellor to order re-evaluation and nothing to do with a question of re-assessment in a board's examination.

The intelligentsia believed that this derogatory decision was probably given by Justice Sardar Aslam khan of the IHC, because he was otherwise retiring in March that year and was hoping to be elevated to the Supreme Court as a reward for according a judicial certificate to a blatantly wrong action. His three-year extension in service was expected to be considered as a present for handing down the ruling in the said case of enhancing 21 marks of Farah Dogar in her intermediate papers through unprecedented re-assessment and re-marking.

The bar members in all chambers of Islamabad were comparing it with the past appointment of a CJP Irshad Hasan Khan as Chief Election Commissioner (CEC) after his retirement.

> '*As Chief Justice, while heading an enlarged Supreme Court bench, he had not only validated Gen Musharraf's October 1999 military coup but had also given him three years to rule, and in return got three years as Chief Election Commissioner.*'

There was more criticism on this decision of the IHC from all corners. The former **Acting CJ BhagwanDas** had opined that this decision of the IHC was against the basic principles of justice and prevailing legal provisions. In his opinion the Board (FBISE) had acted against the constitution of Pakistan because in this way the rights of equality for all was twisted and used to favour only one candidate because she was a daughter of the sitting CJ.

Acting CJ BhagwanDas especially quoted an example that if today son of a farmer gets top of the examination, tomorrow a feudal lord may use his influence and wealth and by means of this law he would get his son at the top.

CJ (Rtd) Saeeduzzaman Siddiqui told the pressmen that this decision must be challenged in the SC otherwise all the universities and boards would be under obligation to exercise and make use of it as law and it would become extremely hard and complicated for the education departments to survive with floods of applications after every exam.

Justice (Rtd) Wajihuddin Ahmed opined that this decision would be very detrimental for noble cause of education as a whole; if not fought against. He opined that:

> '*We've been receiving applications against the boards and authorities but in this Farah's case the applicant and the board were on the same side; very astonishing.*
>
> *This decision has not been drafted by a court, it seems. Only the courts acting under PCO or Martial Law provisions can announce such judgments; media should keep on pointing such flaws for the public so that the justice should find its natural way.*'

Barrister Akram Sheikh, Justice (Rtd) Tariq Mehmood, Senator S M Zafar, and Justice (Rtd) Fakhrudin G Ahmed had also conveyed similar feelings rather in more bitter words.

To summarize opinions of the above legal minds: *'if the re-evaluation could serve as a check on arbitrariness, casualness and negligent attitude of the examiner, it would benefit only the dominant people, who would be in a position to twist the arms of the chairmen of the examining boards to favour their kith and kin. This ruling can open the floodgates of massive fraud, abuse, misuse, manipulation and exploitation of the system by the mighty, high-placed and well-connected people in future.'*

Quoting an opinion from *'the News' dated 20th January 2009*:

'One can disagree with the IHC Chief's observation that (to foster the principle of justice a wrong has to be remedied); *in fact, a wrong has been condoned and reinforced in the instant case.*

A bad judicial precedent has been set. The chiefs of the examining boards and universities have now been armed with extraordinary authority. Its exercise would benefit only the children of the privileged, rich and wealthy people. The ruling has paved the way for favouritism, nepotism and an open discrimination.'

JUSTICE ACCOMMODATED: FULL DETAILS:

Farah Hameed Dogar had appeared in Intermediate (pre-medical) Part II examination 2008 under Role No; 545207. The result of the said exam was announced on 4th August 2008. In the result Farah Dogar secured 640 marks out of 1100 and thus awarded 'Grade C'. Farah Dogar, on 20th August 2008 had tendered an application to the Board for re-checking of her four papers i.e. English II, Urdu II, Pakistan Studies and Physics II.

The office hands of the Board received orders of the Chairman, written on Farah's original application of 20th August 2008 that: *'I would like to see her answer books myself also.'*

On 21st August, 2008 the Assistant Controller Examinations had sent the earlier mentioned answer sheets to the Chairman through his Controller Examinations. On receiving claims of Farah Dogar complaining 'wrong marking' on her papers, the Chairman on 10th September 2008 ordered in writing that *'this candidate's (Farah Dogar) answer sheets be re-assessed'.*

On 29th August, Farah Dogar submitted another application to the Board requesting to re-check two more papers; Chemistry II & Biology II.

Under the rules, all the papers were placed before the Re-Checking Committee. On re-checking it was found that there is a mistake of only one mark of Question no: 4 of Biology II Paper whereas there was found no mistake in the rest of the five papers. Approval of the competent authority was sought on 3rd September 2008 for an increase on one mark in Biology II paper of Farah Dogar.

But it was not considered enough.

A special arrangement was made by the Chairman of the Board to get Farah Dogar's papers processed again by passing through an arranged conspiracy of 're-assessment'.

The experts in concerned subjects and the head examiners were pressurized to complete the whole process of re-assessment as per instructions of the chairman. The manoeuvred details then cropped up as:

- The head examiners of two papers, Pakistan Studies & Chemistry II, had declared that the marking on their answer sheets were as per 'marking scheme' and did not need change.

- The head examiner of Biology II made up an increase of one (1) mark in Question 4 which was left over in counting by mistake.

- The head examiner of English II paper changed his assessment from 58 marks to 67 & a half.

- The head examiner of Urdu II paper changed his assessment from 62 marks to 67 & a half.

- The head examiner of Physics II paper changed his assessment from 32 marks to 38.

Once the Chairman had also written on Farah's file 'perused the record.' However, it is worth mentioning here that the Chairman's orders for re-assessment *"in relaxation of rules;"* were not valid which were probably made under immense pressure from the Chief Justice's office.

It is also on record that the applicant Farah Dogar had requested to recheck her six papers in two applications but only four papers could be re-assessed. In fact the head examiners of Chemistry II and Pakistan Studies had flatly refused to obey Chairman's orders for this illegal re-assessment. Again when the Chairman was subjected to more pressure, he had to note the above mentioned words on the file that: *'I would like to see her answer books myself also.'*

In nut shell Farah Dogar got total addition of 21 marks in her score. 20 marks were awarded as a result of re-assessment whereas one mark was added up which was left over in counting by mistake. The chairman had accorded *approval of this increase of 21 marks for her on 15th September 2008.*

This addition in marks brought an improvement of Farah's overall grade from 'C' to 'B'. The same day of 15th September 2008, the Controller of Examination issued / prepared an amended Mark Sheet with amended figure of 661 marks & amended grade of 'B' and personally handed over to the Chairman.

Media got smell of the whole exercise in FBISE and the matter came out open in public. Immediately after, two petitions each from Iftikhar Hussain Rajput and M Azam Khan Sultanpuri of the *Tehreek Falah e Pakistan* were moved in the Islamabad High Court which were thrown away tagged with the aforementioned judgment.

The decision totally omitted the fact that a re-checking committee — as provided for under the rules — was formed, which gave only one additional mark because of the re-counting and unanimously concluded that except one mark in Biology all other five papers were *'Checked & Found Correct'* (CFC). Dissatisfied with the addition of just one mark, the chairman later sought re-evaluation.

Strange enough that the Federal Board (FBISE) itself positioned before the Islamabad High Court along with applicant Farah Dogar and appraised the court that the board had used its powers under the rules and Law and awarded additional marks to the applicant as per available provisions.

While submitting para-wise comments in the said court the Board maintained they had not committed any irregularity while awarding additional marks to the applicant and they had done so within their powers. It was also suggested to the court that under provisions of Rule 1.2(1), the Chairman of FBISE could not be questioned in an administrative or legal proceeding and that the Board has powers under section 4 of 1975's Law to get action and implementation by all available means.

There was no mention of the fact before the court that Farah Dogar was one of about 1000 candidates who had applied to the board for allowing re-checking but only Farah's case was taken up for re-evaluation despite a clear legal bar. There was no explanation or reason offered on file as to how Farah's case was different from the rest of the candidates.

Evidently, the chairman had exercised this authority in the case because she was the daughter of the sitting CJP. Sources in the FBISE had confirmed that Miss Farah's was the only case where the answer sheets were re-assessed. While doing so the Board's Chairman ignored the fact that in all similar cases, the board or university concerned had always refused re-assessment on applications from candidates.

Some people had approached the courts in the past but in none of the cases the board or university had ever been ordered to re-assess any paper as was uniquely done in the case of Farah Dogar.

Submitting para-wise comments on the petition of Muhammad Azam Sultanpuri, the Board (FBISE) did not reply paras 1 & 2. While replying para 3, the Board admitted that total 201 candidates / applicants of this examination, including Farah Hameed Dogar, had been given an increase in their marks and grades.

It was not purposefully made clear that out of these 201 candidates how many were re-assessed like Farah Dogar. In fact there was only ONE candidate named Farah Dogar who had been considered eligible for re-assessment. The rest of the 200 applicants were subjected to avail benefit of re-checking only.

While answering this paragraph the Board had also tried to justify by saying that:

> 'In 2005, the FBSIE received 740 applications for rechecking and 73 candidates were awarded more marks. In 2006, the Board received 884 applications for rechecking and 132 candidates were awarded more marks. In 2007, the Board received 1104 applications for rechecking and 136 candidates were awarded more marks.'

COE: THE NATION NEEDS YOU:

In this regard, interview of the **Controller of Examination**, Muzaffar ul Hassan, taken and recorded by one M Ahmed Noorani of *'Daily Jang'* dated 15th *January 2008* was worth consideration.

Mr Muzaffar, attached with the FBISE since its first day's launching at Islamabad and kept an optimum reputation of honesty and straight forwardness. He first time, after Farah Dogar's case in offing, opened his mouth when he realized that his ex-boss & ex-Chairman Air Commodore (R) Sharif Shamshad had spoken a blatant lie on oath before the IHC while giving his testimony in the judicial proceeding.

Mr Muzaffar stated that ex-Chairman Shamshad had misled the court. He disturbingly told the media that ex-chairman had told a lie in the court because *'Rule 7.6L(4) does not give permission for re-assessments by head examiners.'* Under this rule the re-checking and re-assessment by head examiners could only be made before announcement of the result. After announcement of result no officer has an authority to re-assess the papers. In the case of Farah, re-assessment was made after the result.

Mr Muzaffar also stated the fact that *throughout his career of about 33 years in FBISE he had never seen such an event in the board.* He had never taken part in such re-assessment exercise using this rule after announcement of result nor did he ever witness such glaring violation of this rule.

Mr Muzaffar confirmed that in total 201 candidates were given an increase in their marks. Out of 201 applicants, 200 candidates were given benefit of a mistake in their totals (generally called re-checking). During this exercise Farah had also got one mark as addition, making 641 from originally secured 640 marks, due to mistake of totals in her Biology II paper. Only one applicant Farah Dogar got the benefit of getting her papers re-assessed under specific orders of the Chairman.

The process of evaluating the correctness of the case was in the offing when suddenly the Chairman of the Parliamentary Standing Committee [MNA Abid Sher Ali] took serious turn announcing that:

'The Committee intends to summon the CJP Justice Dogar to explain his conduct in the capacity of Farah's father.'

Naturally it was taken as a revenge from PML(N) on their years old stance that PCO judges should be removed and the judiciary of 2nd November 2007 should be reinstated by the sitting PPP government.

The sitting judiciary in CJP Dogar's Supreme Court planned to block that move in a different way. Therefore, on 5th December 2008, the High

Court while taking up a petition, had stayed the probe by the standing committee into the matter, and later dismissed the petition.

{*It is a point to keep on record that the IHC Chief had initially refused to stay the on-going proceedings in the Parliamentary standing committee on education on Farah Dogar case.*

Tormented by the refusal, a stay was then managed from a single judge of the Supreme Court on 5th December. It was all done by the sitting government to save Chief Justice Dogar from being dragged in the controversy.}

On 13th December, Farah Hameed Dogar personally came out in her defence saying that her career had no grey area and her blotless performance in school and college could be verified. This issue agitated many minds. Federal Minister for Education Mir Hazar Khan Bijarani himself explained (on 19th January 2009) while commenting on the IHC's decision on Farah Dogar case that:

'*There is no rule or provision for reassessment / remarking of papers after announcement of examination results under any circumstances and, if allowed, it will open a Pandora's box which will damage the country's education system.*

We will take all possible measures against........ **but only after the record are returned to us.** *But it is again asserted that re-assessment is not allowed under any law and under any circumstances whatsoever.*'

It is interesting to mention that President Zardari's block of companions was bent upon to save CJP Dogar in this quagmire. Though at last Farook Naik, the Federal Minister for Law and Lateef Khosa, the Attorney General of Pakistan made their way through on the basis of blatant lies which brought worse name to their offices and the PPP.

The MoE and the Ministry of Law gave wrong impressions to the court that all the 201 applicants had got the facility of reassessment whereas the fact was that only one case was considered for re-assessment and the rest of 200 applicants got their marks increased through re-checking.

Lateef Khosa, later backed out saying that he was not involved in the game nor was he authorized to vet the comments submitted by Chairman FBISE. The PM Gilani was not in favour of interfering in this dirty game, neither in the Parliament nor outside. Contrarily the moment he came to know that his Press Secretary Mr Bashir had facilitated a private meeting between Ansar Abbasi and the CJ Dogar (in December 2008); he immediately fired the officer and sent him home.

GEN ZIAUL HAQ'S GIMMICKS:

PML(N) Information Secretary Ahsan Iqbal then said that the said decision had strengthened PML(N)'s fears on PCO judges that these judges lacked the courage to give decisions against the wishes of those in the power corridors.

Just for a change of taste here, their attention is invited towards an historical event of Gen Ziaul Haq era, when:

> '*A politician close to him had requested him for the favour of admitting his daughter in Army Medical College Rawalpindi which had then sixty seats. Gen Zia sent her application to Gen Mirza Aslam Beg – then Deputy COAS with the remarks to accommodate her, who forwarded it to Major Gen Waheed Kakar the then Adjutant General (AG) for 'necessary action'.*
>
> *Gen Kakar, however, returned the file with the remarks* **'Regrets, she doesn't come up to the merit.'** *On his next routine visit to the GHQ, Gen Ziaul Haq just walked unannounced into the office of the AG [Gen Kakar] and confronted him with the application saying,* **'I am sure, there must be a way out to admit her'**
>
> *Gen Kakar, true to his reputation, stood his ground saying, 'Sir, under the rules I cannot. However, if you order it, I will admit her'. General Zia, probably resigning to the inevitable, started moving slowly towards the door but before reaching it turned back and asked where she stood on the merit list. 'Sir, she is 79ᵗʰ and we have only 60 seats', answered the AG.*
>
> *With a flash rising to the occasion,* **Gen Ziaul Haq ordered,** *'increase the intake to 80 from this year' and walked out triumphantly.'*

In the words of Col (Rtd) Riaz Jafri, '*rules were not violated and yet the ego vindicated.*'

But rules were seen flouted about one year later when illegal migration of Maryam Nawaz Sharif from Army Medical College, Rawalpindi to the K E Medical College, Lahore was pre-arranged, managed, ordered and affected.

Scenario 64

JUDICIARY RESTORED 2009:

Prime Minister of Pakistan, Syed Yousaf Raza Gilani, in a televised address to the nation, in early morning hours of 16th March 2009, announced reinstatement of the deposed Chief Justice Iftikhar M Chaudhry and other judges saying:

> 'I restore the deposed chief justice and others according to the promise made by me and the President; a notification to this effect is being issued now. Chief Justice Chaudhry would replace Justice Abdul Hameed Dogar, who retires on 21st March.'

The deposed Chief Justice Iftikhar Chaudhry was removed from service by the former President Gen Musharraf on 9th March 2007, once re-instated on 20th July 2007 after Supreme Court's decision; then with another spill of removal of 60 judges after they refused to take fresh oath of allegiance on 3rd November 2007.

The saga ended with sparkling wave of protest against Gen Musharraf that led to his resignation from his office on 18th August 2008. The prime minister also announced reinstatement of other judges of the Supreme Court while the number of judges for the apex court had already been increased through legislation to accommodate the reinstated judges.

Let us trace out its historical back ground whatsoever.

CONST'L PACKAGE OF MAY 2008:

By denying Benazir Bhutto's words and pledges, her husband A A Zardari negated BB's whole mission and sacred assignment. Not only this, Zardari had forgotten his own 62-point constitutional package of 31st May 2008, which was approved under his signatures. As PPP's Co-Chairman, Zardari had suggested and got incorporated some changes in the constitutional package designed for country's political structure. Immediately after, PPP's Federal Law Minister Farooq H Naek had distributed copies of that package to all their coalition partners.

Some of the amendments proposed in the constitutional package — such as the removal of presidential power to dismiss government and

Parliament at will under the controversial article 58(2b), raising the age limit for retirement of Supreme Court judges by three years, and the revival of the Council of Common Interest (CCI) — were indeed long overdue.

However, the proposal to fix the tenure of office of the Supreme Court chief justice to three years was a major stumbling block in the passage of the constitutional amendment bill, which Asif Zardari and his PPP intended to bring before the Parliament after the budget session of 2008.

Some of the proposed amendments, such as withdrawal of the president's power to appoint army, navy or air force chiefs, and also provincial governors etc annoyed Gen Musharraf who was in saddles then. The principal campaigner for Justice Iftikhar M Chaudhry's restoration in office, Aitzaz Ahsan, who was also the President Supreme Court Bar Association then, had already registered his opposition.

"It is not acceptable to us," he told a cheering crowd at a lawyers' convention in Faisalabad on 25th May 2008. The procession taken out by the deposed CJ Iftikhar M Chaudhry and his supporters were determined to show their strength to the PPP, Zardari and the PM that they disliked the intention to reduce the tenure of the chief justice to three years, meaning thereby that even if restored, Justice Chaudhry would retire on 30th June 2008. A mockery of justice it was.

The issue of judges' reinstatement was tactfully evaded by Zardari. He knew that Nawaz Sharif, who had withdrawn his ministers from the federal Cabinet on the issue of the restoration of judges on 30th April, would not agree to limit the tenure of chief justice. At that moment, even the combined strength of PPP & PML(N)'s senators in the Senate were not able to get the bill through.

Even so, the JUI's Chief had congratulated the law minister, terming the constitutional package a great victory for democracy. PML(N) considered the package immediately in their party meeting at Raiwind. It was conveyed that changes could be made in the constitutional package as per suggestions from all the coalition partners and others.

Some of the *proposals, finally agreed* to be given in the constitutional package were:

- *Restoration of judges through a constitutional amendment, and not a parliamentary resolution, with retrospective effect.*

- *Withdrawal of presidential authority to appoint judges in the superior judiciary.*

- *Appointment of judges will be finalised by the prime minister on the recommendation of names by a parliamentary commission (headed by the PM) comprising six members of the National Assembly (three each from the government and the opposition) and two senators (one each from the government and the opposition).*

- *A Supreme Judicial Commission, not the Supreme Judicial Council, will decide the removal of judges. Any judge taking oath under any PCO shall stand removed.*

- *As proposed, the president will be bound to act upon the advice of prime minister in 15 days.*

- *The authority to declare war will be given to the prime minister.*

- *Tenure of the chief justice will be fixed in consultation with all coalition parties.*

- *Violators of the Constitution will be tried under treason charges.*

- *Removal of the concurrent list will take effect to strengthen the provinces.*

- *Distribution from the Federal Divisible Pool to provinces will be made on the basis of population and resources.*

- *Balochistan Levies will be revived.*

- *Equal representation of provinces will be made effective in the Supreme Court.*

- *Repeal of the 17th Amendment except seats of women and minorities will be ensured.*

- *Reserved seats for minorities in the Senate will be ensured.*

- *If any chief minister resigns, the provincial governor would invite senior provincial minister to take oath of the office of CM till the next is elected.*

- *Any no-trust move against the prime minister must give the name of the new prime minister.'*

The draft had some relief for bureaucracy and police as it proposed that only a five member bench of the Supreme Court would be able to hear a *suo motu* notice against them.

> *[It may be recalled that the suo motu notice hearings by the Supreme Court under the then chief justice Iftikhar M Chaudhry and the ensuing resentment in the officialdom had been cited by the Army Chief Gen Musharraf when he imposed his PCO by holding the Constitution in abeyance in November 2007.]*

But Mr Zardari again turned around pushing his own package in dustbin.

ASPIRATIONS OF INDEPENDENT JUDICIARY:

Had Mr Zardari obliged his promises of reinstating the judiciary as per Benazir Bhutto's vision and her announcement of October 2007 at his doorstep [**that J Iftikhar Ch would be our CJ**], the NRO issue could have been dealt with in a different way. The two petitions challenging the NRO, from Roedad Khan and Dr Mubashshir Hassan each, which were still pending in the Supreme Court were intentionally being ignored by the then CJ Abdul Hameed Dogar, perhaps to be taken up later as a part of 'deal' with the PPP or Mr Zardari in the wake of pressure from the public or the party.

The whole nation was sentimental for the re-instatement of defunct judiciary back to the day of 3rd November 2007, and the whole nation was suffering from the nostalgia of 'independent judiciary'.

Quote of facts from print media that *"To talk about independence [of judiciary] is a cruel joke on the people of Pakistan. Its rulers have reduced the country to the lowest form of slavery."* A writer named Zia Sarhadi of 'Muslim media' had commented on the situation in daily *'Dawn' of 2nd June 2008.*

SG Jilanee while casting his ideas on *'Myth of Judicial Independence'* said that:

> *'...... the ongoing agitation about an 'independent judiciary' would appear totally misleading. That Mr Chaudhry's reinstatement deserved unqualified support, but to treat it as synonymous with judicial independence is sheer hokum and a cruel joke.*

Mr Chaudhry may be an exemplar of judicial independence. But first, the attitude is personal to him. History is witness that not even the greatest leaders have been followed literally by their disciples.

Second, Mr Chaudhry's display of 'independence' has been Musharraf-specific. The big question is, will he, (indeed, can he) demonstrate the same 'independence' vis-à-vis Nawaz Sharif?

The plain truth, therefore, is that the current agitation is actually not so much for 'judicial independence' as it is a vent for the seething anger against Gen Musharraf. It is a fig leaf for vendetta. And it is not Nawaz Sharif only who is obsessed with settling scores.'

Keeping this hard and cogent reality in mind, the PML(N) had considered the package of the PPP dated 31st May 2008 in their executive meeting, and assured PPP of its support to indemnify the controversial NRO, much to the relief of Zardari's person but in return sought early reinstatement of the pre-Nov 3 judiciary, making it clear that PML(N) would not accept any link between the constitutional package and the issue of the judges.

The PPP under the guidance of Mr Zardari had not taken any risk because the non-operational CJ Mr Chaudhry's consent was not seen amongst this vague and blurred assurance. However, the PML(N) Chief, in a meeting with Law Minister Farooq H Naek at his Raiwind residence, had revived that his party would continue pressing for restoration of the deposed judges through a National Assembly resolution.

Nawaz Sharif had also resolved that the PML(N) would not only extend its moral support to the forthcoming 10th June 2008's long march of the lawyer's fraternity but would also be an enthusiastic part of that major event. However, one would be sorry for Pakistan's ancestral and inherited politics, the people of Pakistan were kept in dark on the *'hidden' proposals* made in the package on the three main issues of public concern:

- *The restoration of the deposed judges.*

- *The question as to whether Gen Musharraf would get indemnity for the unconstitutional steps he took on 3rd November 2007.*

- *The fate of the NRO, which completed its four-month life on 5th February 2008 and therefore stood repealed from that day under Article 89 of the Constitution.*

The PPP's lawyers, constitutional experts and CEC members had considered that the NRO was to be reshaped as permanent law making it beyond any judicial review. This could only be achieved if amendments made to the Constitution under the PCO and the judgments given by the PCO judges were to be validated. Additionally, the deposed CJ Mr Chaudhry would either be kept out or his powers and tenure were to be curtailed. This arrangement was unacceptable to the PML(N) as it would amount to giving legitimacy to Gen Musharraf's 3rd November's order and his election as president in October 2007.

Contrarily, there were plenty of reasons and common understandings on constitutional issues between the PPP leadership, the PML(Q), JUI(F), ANP and the MQM. They were all in favour of indemnity for Gen Musharraf [*for the PPP leadership it was a fair price for saving the NRO but if dealt with intelligently*) and against restoration of the pre-3rd November judiciary.

Asif Ezdi, in his article titled '*Make no mistake*' *appearing in The News of 3rd June 2008* referred to the same proposition saying that:

> '*There was no difficulty in mutually agreeing (amongst PPP, PML(Q) & MQM) on the text of a constitutional amendment under which Gen Musharraf gets indemnity, Zardari gets constitutional protection for the NRO and the PCO judges keep their jobs, while Iftikhar Chaudhry is kept out in the cold.*
>
> *With the support of the PML(Q), the MQM, the ANP and the JUI, such a bill would also be able to muster the two-thirds majority in both houses of Parliament that is needed for its passage.*'

But PPP's advisors did nothing concrete in that direction.

At that time, some members of intelligentsia held the opinion that after the PPP's acceptance of the Murree Declaration, the civil society increasingly demanded not only that the deposed judges be restored but also that the sitting CJ Mr Dogar and the other PCO judges must go and be made accountable for taking oath under the PCO and later upholding Gen Musharraf's second coup.

The deposed CJ Mr Chaudhry had publicly expressed his will & confidence that these judges would be punished. To protect them from the charge of high treason under Article 6, Law Minister Mr Farook H Naek's constitutional package of May 2008 included a clause that only future judges who validate an abrogation of the Constitution would be guilty of this crime, but the present violators of their oath would not be held answerable.

Astonishingly, article 6 of the Constitution since it was adopted, the country has gone through three military coups d'état but this article remained dead because twice the military dictators got their actions indemnified by the respective Parliaments. The Eighth Amendment (1985) gave indemnity to Gen Ziaul-Haq and the last Parliament did the same for Gen Musharraf's October 1999 coup through 2003's Seventeenth Amendment.

It was another story that on 2nd June 2008, the PML(N) parliamentary party came up with categorical rejection of certain parts of the PPP's constitutional package dealing with indemnification of Gen Musharraf's 3rd November 2007 act and reinstatement of the judges, particularly seniority of the deposed CJ Mr Chaudhry but it could have been resolved amicably while sitting on the table.

Mr Zardari had not chosen that way but at the same time, did not complete his home work to face the counter attack of worse form because CJ Mr Chaudhry vowed not to leave any stone unturned to drag the PPP in the saline mud of accusations, trials, intrigues and blames.

Mr Zardari and his colleagues themselves had chosen this way irrespective of possible consequences. Nobody took stand by him not even his Prime Minister because they all felt helpless over the issue.

GOVERNOR RULE IN PUNJAB (2009):

On 25th February 2009, a 3-member bench of the Dogar's Supreme Court decided that the Sharif brothers were not qualified to be members of the parliament. The petitions on their electoral eligibility were dismissed. Justice Moosa K Leghari, Justice Sakhi Hussain Bukhari and Justice Sh Hakim Ali also de-seated the sitting Chief Minister Punjab Shahbaz Sharif in a short order announced after the Attorney General Latif Khosa [who had assisted the court as amicus curie] completed his arguments.

The SC held that 'for the reasons to be recorded later on, all the petitions are dismissed and the June 23, 2008 order of the Lahore High Court (LHC) is upheld'.

[A full bench of the LHC had disqualified PML(N)'s Nawaz Sharif from contesting a by-election on 23rd June 2008, citing his conviction for conspiring to hijack the plane boarding the then Army Chief Gen Musharraf to Pakistan. Gen Musharraf was coming back from Sri Lanka after attending an official assignment. Initially he was not allowed to land in Pakistan.

The coup succeeded, and Nawaz Sharif was convicted on hijacking charges and opted to go into exile to Saudi Arabia after being confined in Attock Jail for some months where he allegedly kept on weeping & crying all the time unlike any mature politician.

The court had conditionally allowed Shahbaz Sharif to hold the Chief Minister's office until an election tribunal decided his case.]

Shahbaz Sharif vacated the Chief Minister's House after the SC verdict, and returned to his Raiwind residence without protocol. In the later hours of the same day, President Zardari imposed a 2-month Governor's Rule in Punjab and Governor Salmaan Taseer had taken over the affairs of the province. However, Sharif brothers declared war on the Presidency the moment the SC announced its verdict; a revolt was immediately seen in various parts of Lahore.

The intent of Nawaz Sharif was obvious in his open calls of anarchy and rebellion. He demanded the police and other civil servants to disobey the orders of the government. On at least one occasion, Nawaz Sharif even promised to restore these civil servants to their previous posts once he was in power and promised to give them "gifts" in addition to their salaries as a reward for disobedience at his call.

Referring to the Breaking News at all TV Channels dated 25th February 2009, Nawaz Sharif was quoted as saying:

'*We do not accept the decision of the court because it is fake. **I have ordered the police not to obey the government's orders and wage jehad against them, and today I raise Alam-e-Baghawat.** I urge you join me in the long march and we will bring revolution in the country.*

I have asked Shahbaz Sharif to go to Assembly and establish your government again. He is the Constitutional Chief Minister of Punjab province.'

Interior Minister Rehman Malik had declared Nawaz Sharif and Shahbaz Sharif accused of "**...committing sedition for giving a call of** revolt…" adding that Nawaz Sharif sunk so low that he disregarded the well-being of the nation in order to have things his way.

President Zardari had imposed Governor Rule in Punjab under Article 234 of the Constitution, following the Supreme Court decision disqualifying the Sharif Brothers. PPP's Central Executive Committee (CEC) told the media that they had been left with no other constitutional alternative and thus endorsed the proclamation of Governor Rule by adopting a unanimous resolution of support for Zardari.

Mr Zardari and PM Gilani had chaired the CEC meeting. The CEC had empowered the PPP leadership to name a new Chief Minister and also to establish contacts with the PML(Q) for power sharing in Punjab and the Centre. Qasim Zia, Tanvir Ashraf Kaira and Foreign Minister Shah Mehmood Qureshi jumped in the run for Punjab's top slot whereas Zardari had called another immediate meeting of the party's MNAs and MPAs from Punjab to share with them the new political developments.

On the same day of 25th February 2009, JUI's Chief Fazlur Rehman called on President Zardari to discuss future plans after the SC's decision to disqualify the Sharifs. On the other hand the crisis was more deepened by the fact that the Punjabi population resented Mr Zardari's imposition of 'Governor Rule' or a federal take-over of the Punjab province, which had an elected provincial legislature in which the PML(N) was the leading party. The Sharifs were not going to put up with being excluded from politics, which Mr Zardari and his Dogar court tried to do as per traditions in Pakistan.

> [*However, on the similar lines, Sharif family's pet Chief Justice of Lahore High Court, Khawaja Sharif, had immediately issued stay order for that Governor's Rule reinstating the PML(N)'s government back.*
>
> *That was another interesting aspect of our judicial partisanship that throughout their tenure till March 2013 the PML(N) continued to rule Punjab on the basis of the same 'stay order'; Pakistani justice hurray!*]

While comparing Nawaz Sharif's second stint of premiership with AA Zardari's presidential canon in the then prevailing scenario, the intelligentsia of the PML(N) believed that Nawaz Sharif's rule had two aspects:

- Much of the heavy-handedness in Sharif's premiership was actually his attempt to impose the prime minister's [so called] legitimate powers *vis a vis* the military and characterized as civil dictatorship by military media versions.

- Nawaz Sharif's crackdown against the press as well as his half-hearted imposition of Islamic laws was done under a certain context where, despite being 'dictatorial' and having a 2/3rd majority in the Parliament, he had to constantly appease and repress certain segments of society in order to confine civil agitation.

[*This was the same strategy which the PPP had adopted when they were in power; they did not remove Shariah laws from the legal system and acted in similar ways towards journalists & opposition.*]

The nutshell comes that if the political parties are confident about the length of their term and non-interference by the military; and if there is rule of law, they will not have the capacity to crackdown on opposition.

The fact remains that after his come-back from exile in the last quarter of 2007; Nawaz Sharif had done and said things that irrevocably changed the political landscape of this country. He might not sincerely believe in them but was seen inclined to inculcate the rule of law and the democratic process as norms of society, might be for the time being at least.

BLACK COAT REVOLUTION:

Resuming with the opening paragraphs of this chapter, the judiciary was in fact reinstated by continuous and concerted efforts of all the lawyers making it a '*Lawyer's Movement*' which had actually taken start on 9th March 2007, when the CJP Iftikhar M Chaudhry was called in the Army House and then was dethroned in the same evening.

The government arrested detained and tortured lawyers on different occasions. For the first time in the history of Pakistan, armoured police vehicles entered the premises of the Lahore High Court (LHC) to attack the protesting lawyers who had sought refuge within the high court building. Several lawyer leaders were kept under house arrest for several months.

In Karachi, anti-lawyers groups and allegedly the government's ally MQM torched a lawyer's office in which *seven lawyers were burnt alive.* In Sahiwal, police acting on the orders of Gen Musharraf regime attacked the lawyers with a petrol bomb, causing several lawyers to suffer major burns. Even then the movement continued with intervals and the processions of lawyers remained the order of the day even after Gen Musharraf's departure.

The last spill started on 21st January 2009 when the LHC Bar Association carried out a *'Million Signature Movement'*. As the name suggests, the purpose of the movement was to get millions of signatures on a large white cloth which was to be presented to the parliament at the end of long march. Political party workers, concerned citizens and lawyers participated and signed the petition.

On 15th March 2009 the Lawyers' Community had given a call for nationwide *'Long March'*. Many political parties like the PML(N), Pakistan Tehreek e Insaf (PTI), Jamaat e Islami (JI) and others supported and participated in the Long March. All the supporters of the 'restoration of judges' participated in the Long March despite a ban imposed on protests and rallies under Section 144 by the government. See a media report:

> *'It is very sad situation in my beloved country today. The roads have been blocked by placing containers all over. The families are stuck up in the way to their destinations and food has been exhausted. Gas stations are closed. Businesses are no more operative since the last four days.*
>
> *The ships are waiting in the Karachi harbour but the containers are either hauled up by the police or the same have been grounded by the owners or drivers. The lawyers and the political activists are being continuously harassed and arrested. Many details are available on the media channels and newspapers, I'll not repeat them.'*

CJP Iftikhar M Chaudhry assumed charge of his office on 24th March 2009 with a call for the lawyers that *'there is rampant corruption in this institution (judiciary) and this cannot be eliminated without your help.'* While addressing the lawyers after he arrived in the main courtroom amid thunderous clapping and standing prolonged applause by all those present in the room, he continued saying:

> *'You people (lawyers) should come forward to point out such cases right from the level of civil judges to the judges in the Supreme Court; if there is any complaint, lawyers can substantiate it with evidence.'*

As the CJP along with other top judges arrived in front of the Supreme Court gate, hundreds of lawyers and civil society members, who were lined up there since early morning, showered petals on his car and escorted all of them to the building where police guards presented the guard of honour for the re-joining Chief Justice.

Gen Musharraf declared emergency in the country on 3ʳᵈ November 2007 and had put all these deposed judges under house arrest until PM Mr Gilani, whose PPP came to power and formed a coalition government with Nawaz Sharif's PML(N) after 18ᵗʰ February 2008 elections, announced to release all the judges in his first address to the national assembly.

However, the PPP failed to restore judges throughout the year 2008 despite repeated reminders by the PML(N), which forced Nawaz Sharif to quit the coalition government afterwards. He also announced full support to the long march that the lawyers' fraternity had launched from 11ᵗʰ March 2009 till restoration of the judges.

As the pressure mounted on the government allegedly from the country's powerful military, Mr Gilani had to announce restoration of the judges on 16ᵗʰ March 2009 at last. Subsequent news indicated that the COAS, Gen Kayani, had played a decisive role in compelling PM Gilani and President Zardari to make that historical announcement on immediate basis.

Meanwhile, a Pakistani lawyer petitioned the Supreme Court on the first day of independence of judiciary, challenging appointment of the judges of superior judiciary under Provisional Constitutional Order (PCO) after declaration of emergency in the country in November 2007. Mr Nadeem Ahmad, an associate of Sheikh Akram Senior Advocate and the petitioner, asked the apex Court to stop PCO judges from working as they were appointed without consultation of the [lawful] Chief Justice.

Juan Cole, President of the Global Americana Institute, expressed that:

'Pakistan Muslim League (N) leader Nawaz Sharif had defied the attempt of the government of President Asaf Ali Zardari to confine him to house arrest and was leading a procession to the capital from Lahore when he heard the news at Gujranwala. He then called off the "Long March", which aimed at rallying for the reinstatement.

Sharif was himself an extremely high-handed and dictatorial prime minister who violated press freedom and tried to move the country toward more Islamic laws, and he wasn't exactly a friend to poor people, so I personally don't trust his pledge to help Pakistan achieve real democracy.'

(Ref: Juancole.com)

The intervention of US Secretary of State Hillary Clinton was important in moving the government toward this historical but false-hearted compromise. The most conspicuous and obvious was that the Punjab police and judicial authorities more or less mutinied against the Federal government on this occasion, allowing Nawaz Sharif to escape house arrest and to lead big protests and to set out for Islamabad gathering millions of people on his way. Historically that move should have been taken as a prelude to revolution as it was done in Iran in 1978 before fall of Shah's regime.

Juan Cole further opined that *'certainly the overturning of Musharraf's illegal dismissal of (Justice) Chaudhry has an up side if it begins to undermine the edifice of arbitrary military dictatorship from which Pakistan has so often suffered. It would be more promising if (Justice) Chaudhry had himself opposed that dictatorship before he was dismissed.'*

[How Justice Chaudhry could oppose that move?

Historically, mention may be made of the rising of Justice Iftikhar M Chaudhry to the Supreme Court making him senior to Justice Falak Sher, the former Chief justice of the Lahore High Court.

Justice Chaudhry was then given an out-of-turn edge [irrespective of the details that who actually deserved] to which he had reciprocated within one year of his office, by blindly okaying CJP Irshad Hasan Khan's decision that Gen Musharraf could at once hold the offices of the President of Pakistan and the Chief of the Army Staff under the Constitution. *Was that observation of any judge reasonable?*]

Critical analysts of Pakistani politics have always insisted that the restoration of CJP Iftikhar M Chaudhry and his colleagues such as Khalil Ramday, Khawaja Sharif etc in 2009 was not possible without judges' NRO (agreement) with Pakistan Army.

Myra MacDonald in one of her articles under **'Pakistan: Now or Never'** [see Reuters of early 2009] appeared in internet media, had given very candid opinion about the CJP Justice M Chaudhry saying:

"The quiet, patient man is on his third life, having been deposed twice previously by former President Pervez Musharraf. Let's hope he serves

*his term completely, without obstruction, and for the public good. The
lawyers' movement was in some ways a triumph for civil society.*

*(CJP) Mr Chaudhry himself was first appointed by Musharraf after he
launched a military coup in 1999, so he cannot say he has always been
a loyal servant of civilian democracy. And the deal to reinstate Chaudhry
may have been achieved as a result of prodding from the Pakistan Army,
which begs the question of how well civilian democracy can flourish in
Pakistan if it has to be underwritten by the country's powerful military.*

**His promised reinstatement — announced after days of negotiations —
may also carry with it a political deal whose outcome and required
allegiances we are yet to discover."**

Nevertheless, as a result of CJP Justice Chaudhry's reinstatement, many
people saw him as a savoir even though the lawyers' movement was
essentially aimed at upholding the rule of law. The fact remained that
such unrealistic hopes were bound to produce disappointments because
some expectations are always frustrated.

Analyst Ikram Sehgal had opined in ***The News of 26th March 2009*** that
great expectations were vested in Justice Chaudhry's person but could he
be able to assuage the people's aspirations? Rebuilding the stature of the
Supreme Court, he can either play to the gallery and follow the path of
retribution or take the high road of reconciliation. The writer further
elaborated that:

*'Mian Nawaz Sharif kept his party together after the dark period in
mid-2008 when he was outsmarted lock, stock and barrel by Asif
Zardari. He consolidated politically by converting the floundering
lawyers' movement into the most political hot potato in the town, then
courageously leading from the front when the chips were down.*

*The "breakout" from his Model Town home on March 15, 2009,
raised the political stakes to an extraordinary height, the media force-
multiplying the sheer effect in pulling the masses in their thousands out
from their homes and into the streets. The rest is political history.'*

In nutshell; the series of judgments announced by the SC during 2009 till
2011 are witness to it where most of them made in favour of PML(N)
and against PPP's politicians, against PCO judges, mysterious silence
over FATA killings because of strong local political factions etc made the
people believe that they got an 'independent judiciary' in a sense that

the judges should do what ever they like *to take revenge* not what was justified.

The *New York Times*, dated *28ᵗʰ March 2009*, had given details of would be problems for the reinstated Chief Justice; thorny legal issues awaiting Mr Chaudhry's concentration included many politically charged cases, like those regarding hundreds of people who got disappeared after they were detained without charges by Gen Musharraf's agencies on suspicion of terrorism. Allegedly these persons were picked up by the intelligence agencies of Pakistan; most of them were shifted to Bagram Air Base near Kabul in Afghanistan to be handled by American CIA without any diplomatic note of formality or anything on record for any.

On the next stage, two cases bear directly on the fortunes of the nation's most prominent political leaders, President Zardari and <u>Nawaz Sharif</u> of PML(N). In one, the Supreme Court was expected to review the amnesty from corruption charges [*referring to the* NRO] that Gen Musharraf gave to Benazir Bhutto and her husband Mr Zardari. The other case was a petition regarding Mr Sharif's ability to run for the public office as discussed through above paragraphs.

PM GILANI BRINGS BACK SHARIFS:

Sharif Brothers disqualification issue was solved by PM Mr Gilani himself, by making announcement on behalf of the PPP that the federal government would file a review petition in the Supreme Court seeking reversal of the order of disqualification of Nawaz Sharif and Shahbaz Sharif, and addressing all issues in the light of the Charter of Democracy. He also asked the provincial governments to lift Section 144 immediately and release the arrested persons. He declared that the PPP had made a lot of contribution to the lawyers' movement and rendered numerous sacrifices so the same should not go waste.

However, the reinstatement of judiciary was loaded with potential conflicts of interest because Nawaz Sharif had rightly decided to brew benefit out of the Lawyer's movement to bring back Justice Chaudhry to office. CJP Justice Chaudhry defused some of the controversy by appointing a five-member bench excluding him, to hear such cases. Sharif Brothers case was examined in the backdrop of political negotiations between Sharifs and the PM Gilani where it was resolved that Punjab government would be repatriated to PML(N) by finding out a mid way.

This resolve saved the Supreme Court from expected embarrassment as the Bench had accepted a petition from the Sharif brothers demanding a status quo, which was gladly granted. The Punjab government was immediately restored through a stay order pending full hearing at some later stage [which remained pending till 16th March 2013 at least].

Contrarily, the review of President Zardari's amnesty was another issue in which CJP Mr Chaudhry was manifestly seen going partial and interested. Mr Zardari had blocked Justice Chaudhry's reinstatement because he feared that the judge would repeal the amnesty. The constitutional lawyers held that Mr Zardari, as president, had immunity from prosecution. President Zardari and Ms Bhutto had maintained that the corruption charges were politically motivated. CJP Justice Chaudhry should not have heard the case but he opted to head that bench.

Other potential minefields included cases involving the judges appointed by Gen Musharraf and Mr Zardari to replace those judges of higher Courts which were recruited in contravention of Judges Appointment Rules framed by the Supreme Court in March 1996 (Judges Case). Petitions were filed with the apex court to remove them, the same were admitted, heard and decision released to send them home. [*Details are available on other pages separately*]

The most important issue for CJP Justice Chaudhry was that as he had taken an oath to uphold the law, he had to consider the legality of Gen Musharraf's actions. The first petition was filed in the first week of his reinstatement asking to hold Gen Musharraf guilty of high treason. The Court had to carefully decide where it should exercise restraint or not. The petition was either silently dismissed or was buried in the piles of pending cases; the General was allowed to leave for abroad and with an un-precedented guard of honour from the PPP's government.

On the 'missing persons' issue, the bench held some proceedings under the chair of Justice Javaid Iqbal; some persons recovered but then the file was sent to cold storage. The credit goes to a most deserving lady named Amina Masood Janjua, who led the campaign to locate the missing persons including her husband. But she recognized that justice so long awaited might not come instantly. Her lawyers kept on telling her to hold on, not to be impatient. Case still goes pending [in mid 2013 at least].

In this whole scenario the Army, particularly its Chief, came out smelling roses because Gen Kayani was the sole person in the whole crisis visible from distant. He gave no statement. Neither the ISI nor MI got involved in the political brawls as they usually did in the past. Their reports were informational and routed through proper channels. In Gen Ziaul Haq's era the media got access to the military hierarchy and Gen Aslam Beg provided them extraordinary access. This time army appeared graceful and calculated and did not spare even one moment to gain its old pride assuming a guiding role for power thirsty politicians.

Coming back & cutting the story short, the PM Gilani and Gen Kayani paid a last determined visit to the President House at 11 PM on 15th March 2009 and apprised Mr Zardari about the procession or long march of 2/3 hundred thousand people leaving *Shahdara* Bridge of Lahore under the lead of Nawaz Sharif.

The President was also told that from all cities at GT Road on the way to Islamabad, thousands of people were likely to join this long march and Islamabad would be flooded with people. The technique devised by the Interior Minister Rehman Malik, to block the roads and streets by placing heavy containers on them, was totally flop; the president was briefed.

This was the moment when President Zardari had to issue green signal for reinstatement of the Chief Justice Iftikhar M Chaudhry along with his team of judges.

Astonishingly, playing with the history on record (and as reported by a columnist *Rauf Klasra on 25th December 2009 in 'the News'*); in a meeting with anchor persons from all the leading media channels of Pakistan on 24th December 2009, PM Mr Gilani finally disclosed that, contrary to the general perception, it was he, and not the Army Chief, who had restored the defunct CJ Iftikhar M Chaudhry along with his team on 15th March 2009. The meeting of media persons was perhaps called for that disclosure!

PM Gilani had also asserted that neither he nor the President (Mr Asif A Zardari) had asked the Army Chief Gen Kayani to make late night telephone call to Aitzaz Ahsan to terminate the long march. The anchor persons had raised their eyebrows that how an Army Chief could send a call for a lawyer (Aitzaz Hassan) at his own on such a big issue if he was not authorized to speak by any. Whereas it was in the knowledge of those anchor persons that Aitzaz Ahsan also had a secret meeting with the Army Chief in that connection.

The PM Gilani was denying the whole scenario altogether. The PM had once again tried to convince the media that Mr Zardari had ever resisted CJ's restoration, arguing that without President's sweet discretion the restoration of judges was not possible. The PM was bent upon asserting that '*only he deserves credit; not any body else*'.

PM Mr Gilani, while trying to dismiss the general impression, that the judges were restored on the intervention of Gen Kayani, said that:

> '*The decision to restore the Chief Justice was taken by him at 11pm and then he met President Zardari. Gen Kayani was asked to meet him and Mr Zardari in the Presidency at 12am so that he could be informed about the decision of the chief executive.*'

However, no sane person believed the prime minister.

PM Mr Gilani had also admitted that the statement of Federation's lawyer Kamal Azfar (that the GHQ and the CIA were hatching conspiracy against the PPP's democratic government) had damaged the government case. The PM revealed that Kamal Azfar was sitting with Gen Kayani and the US General Petraeus when the said statement was made. The PM was also trying to convey that '*so far the judiciary has not interfered in his executive authority.*' However, the ground realities went altogether different since that day.

Let us hope some true historian would bless us with the actual facts.

PAKISTAN's NEW JUDICIAL POLICY:

In the **first week of May 2009,** the Registrar Supreme Court Dr Faqir Hussain told the media men that the apex court was hearing 19055 cases; 18700 in NWFP now Khyber PK, 7654 in Balochistan and in Sindh this number had reached 44924. Highlighting salient features of new Judicial Policy, Dr Faqir Hussain said that the people would experience a positive change; a special cell would be set up to eliminate corruption from the judiciary and the judges would neither serve as acting Governors nor accept any other positions in Executive.

The Registrar told all the judges deputed to various departments had been called back and no judge would be appointed in his / her native district; bail-able cases would be heard on preferential basis while murder and narcotics related cases would soon be settled.

Every citizen keeps fundamental and inherent right to seek speedy and affordable justice, the provision of which becomes a state's duty and responsibility. In this regard, the announcement of "New Judicial Policy of 2009" was welcomed by masses, among many of them were made waited into their pending cases in the courts for years. Since the higher rate of pendency of cases, uncertain time limit for courts' decisions, remote accessibility to courts and affordability of legal fees were the main reasons for the demand of judicial reforms in the form of **"Nizam-e-Adal Regulation" in Malakand Division.** The Supreme Court of Pakistan's realization for the need to bring reforms in the judiciary was opening the doors of justice to a common man.

Since Pakistan's judiciary had started a new journey towards independence just two months earlier, so the other associated areas also needed vibrant shake. The SC then aimed to add further extensions in the Judicial Policy which included:

- The appointment and dismissal of the judges of SC and those of High Courts would need clarity and should be acceptable to every stakeholder of the state. This would require suitable amendments in the constitution.

- The practical implementation of the reforms introduced in the new policy was the most important task as *'justice not only been done, but seemed to have been done.'*

- Code of ethics for judges would revisit and were to be brought to the level comparable to that of judiciary in the developed countries.

- Remuneration and benefits provided to all the judges should be sufficient for their living to minimize the chances of corruption. The establishment of anti-corruption cell was appreciated by the higher courts.

- There was a need to bring improvements in the administration to ensure due dispensation of justice by the courts.

- The problems of uncertain time limit and the pendency rate of cases would be appropriately addressed with following steps:

  (a). Establishment of new courts and increase in the number of specialized courts particularly in remote areas to make justice easily accessible to every citizen.

  (b). A reasonable maximum amount of legal fees were to be specified for specified cases to make justice affordable.

(c). There was a need for public awareness about courts legal system of the state to make dispensation of justice easily understandable for a common man.

• Alternative Dispute Resolution (ADR) Forums on each separate legal area were to be established to encourage settlement and resolution of disputes through alternative means.

• There was a need to respond to the complaints and timely feedback to redress the grievances of the masses quickly.

• Minimum numbers of jail inspections in a specified period by authorized judges were to be prescribed to stop human rights violations and mal-practices in jails.

The general populace of Pakistan and especially the media are being requested to raise their hands if any of the point mentioned in the aforementioned Judicial Policy of May 2009 has been implemented till mid 2013 at least.

Scenario 65

PCO JUDGES CASE (2009-11):

After promulgation of Emergency and PCO Order on 3rd November 2007, Justice Abdul Hameed Dogar, a judge at no: 4 in the seniority list then, immediately took oath as Chief Justice of Pakistan along with three other judges of the Supreme Court on the same evening.

On 23rd November 2007, CJ Hameed Dogar and the newly constituted bench consisting of J Ijaz-ul-Hassan Khan, J Qaim Jan Khan, J Musa K. Leghari, J Ch. Ijaz Yousaf, J Akhtar Shabbir and J Zia Pervez declared that all judges, including the defunct CJ Iftikhar M Chaudhry were deemed to have been removed from the bench. In a later development, on 3rd December 2007 the federal government issued notification of removal of three judges named CJ Iftikhar M Chaudhry, J Rana Bhagwandas and J Khalil ur Rehman Ramday without any retirement privileges.

On 21st March 2009 when Mr Justice Dogar retired as CJP, the Chief Justice Iftikhar Chaudhry was notified as restored to the bench as Chief Justice of Pakistan and Mr Dogar was considered as a De-facto Chief Justice rather than De-Jure.

In the whole scenario developed after '**Black Coat Long March**' of 15-16th March 2009, the Sharifs [who were once the mobilisers for attacking the same Supreme Court in November 1997] projected themselves as champions of independent judiciary because they had en-cashed the opportunity of joining the Lawyer's March from Lahore which went successful due to blatant blunders of the Federal government and Interior Minister Rehman Malik. The Sharifs were intelligent enough to brew their success to restore their reputation out of follies of the PPP's political elite running the state affairs who had managed to block the way of 14 judges aggrieved by Gen Musharraf.

On 31st July 2009, the Supreme Court of Pakistan declared the steps [*promulgating 'Emergency'*] taken on 3rd November 2007, by Gen Musharraf as illegal and unconstitutional under the Article 279 of the Constitution. The judgment came after the 14-judge larger bench headed by CJP Iftikhar Chaudhry completed hearing of the constitutional petitions regarding PCO judges and appointments of judges of higher judiciary after Emergency of November 2007.

The short judgment released also stated that the results of general elections held on 18th February 2008 would enjoy the judicial protection and that President Asif Ali Zardari would not take a fresh oath again. Lawyers and advocates celebrated the announcement made by the apex Court. Gen Musharraf was summoned by the court, but his lawyers did not appear on various pretexts.

Going into details: Article 62(f), inserted by the dictator Gen Ziaul Haq and Article 63(i)(p), inserted in the Constitution through the infamous LFO of Gen Musharraf, were considered the most disliked and undesirable provisions, which had defaced Pakistan's legislative history. However, these provisions could only be repealed by the parliament, and not by the courts.

The main theme of concluding paragraphs [**NOT VERBATIM**] of the short order penned down by the CJP Iftikhar M Chaudhry were:

Paragraph 18:

i)   Gen Musharraf, in the garb of Emergency plus and the Provisional Constitution Order (PCO) made amendments in the Constitution by self acquired powers which all are unconstitutional, unauthorized, without any legal basis, hence, without any legal consequences;

ii)   Mr Justice Abdul Hameed Dogar, took oath as CJP in violation of the order dated 3.11.2007 passed by a 7 member Bench headed by de-jure Chief Justice of Pakistan and in pursuance of unconstitutional instruments introduced by Gen Musharraf, additionally knowing well that the office of Chief Justice of Pakistan was not lying vacant;

iii) Also, the Judges who were either retired or were not holding any judicial office, beside those in High Courts took fresh oath on their appointment on and after 3.11.2007 till 15.12.2007 in Supreme Court where the full strength of Judges along with an Ad-hoc Judge appointed under the Constitution were already working and thus there was no vacancy. Similarly, many Judges took oath in Provincial High Courts. All of them did so in violation of order dated 3.11.2007 passed by 7 member Bench headed by de-jure CJP. Four incumbent Judges already functioning in the SC took fresh oath under unconstitutional steps of Gen Musharraf;

iv)   The Petition 73/2007 filed by Justice (Rtd) Wajihuddin Ahmad challenging the eligibility of Gen Musharraf to contest for the office of President in uniform was dismissed purportedly on merits although the record maintained in the Supreme Court revealed otherwise;

v) The decisions in the cases of Tikka Iqbal Muhammad Khan granting validity to the actions of Gen Musharraf were without any legal basis hence, of no legal consequences;

vi) The amendments in the Supreme Court (Number of Judges) Act 1997 by way of Finance Act 2008 raising the strength of Judges in Supreme Court from 17 to 30 was unconstitutional because the strength of Judges of Supreme Court could be increased by Parliament as defined in Article 50 to be read with Article 260 of the Constitution;

vii) Powers to amend the Constitution were acquired by Gen Musharraf himself through the PCO and brought a host of unconstitutional amendments for his own benefits; and

viii) The present restoration of the CJP and the higher judiciary with effect from 3rd November 2007 implied that the government has denied the validity of the actions of Gen Musharraf taken from 3.11.2007 to 15.12.2007 during which the Constitution remained suspended.

19. Considering the above in the light of submissions of learned counsels and of material placed before us, the petitions are disposed as follows.

20. The judgment purported to have been delivered in Constitutional Petitions No: 87 & 88 of 2007 in TIKA IQBAL MUHAMMAD KHAN Case and the judgment dated 15.2.2008, purported to have been passed in C.R.P.No.7 of 2008 in the same case and other orders, if any, passed on the strength of the said two judgments are hereby declared to be void *ab initio*.

21. The Proclamation of Emergency issued by Gen Musharraf as the COAS (as he then was) on 3rd November 2007; the PCO Order No.1 of 2007 issued on the same date; the Oath of Office (Judges) Order of 2007 dated same; the PCO (Amendment) Order 2007 issued on 15.11.2007; the Constitution (Amendment) Order 2007 [President's Order No.5] dated 20th November 2007; the Constitution (Second Amendment) Order 2007 [President's Order No.6] dated 14th December, 2007; the Islamabad High Court (Establishment) Order 2007 dated 14th December 2007

[President's Order No.7]; the High Court Judges (Pensionary Benefits) Order 2007 [Presidents Order No.8]; the Supreme Court Judges (Pensionary Benefits) Order 2007 [President's Order No.9] dated 14th December 2007 are hereby declared to be unconstitutional, *ultra-vires* of the Constitution and consequently being illegal and of no legal effect.

22. As a consequence thereof:

i)   The Chief Justice of Pakistan; the Judges of the Supreme Court; any Chief Justice of any of the High Courts and the Judges of the High Courts who were made dysfunctional in pursuance of above mentioned judgments or instruments mentioned in para 21, shall be deemed never to have ceased to be such Judges, irrespective of any notification issued regarding their reappointment or restoration;

ii) It is declared that the office of the Chief Justice of Pakistan never fell vacant on 3rd November 2007 thus the appointment of Justice Abdul Hameed Dogar as the CJP was un-constitutional; void *ab initio* and of no legal effect; Provided that the said unconstitutional appointment of Justice Abdul Hameed Dogar as the CJP shall not affect the validity of any administrative or financial acts performed by him or of any oath made before him;

iii) Since Justice Dogar was never a constitutional CJP, therefore, all appointments of Judges of the Supreme Court, of the Chief Justices of the High Courts and of the Judges of the High Courts made, in consultation with him, during the period from 3.11.2007 to 22.3.2009 are hereby declared to be unconstitutional, void *ab initio* and of no legal effect and such appointees shall cease to hold office forthwith; Provided that the Judges so unconstitutionally appointed to the SC while holding the offices as Judges of any of the High Courts shall revert back as Judges of the respective High Courts subject to their age of superannuation and likewise, the Judges of the High Courts, who were District and Sessions Judges before their said un-constitutional elevation to the High Courts shall revert back as District and Sessions Judge;

iv) The Judges of the Supreme Court, if any, the Chief Justices of the High Court, if any, and the Judges of any of the High Courts, if any, who stood appointed to the said offices prior to 3.11.2007 but who made oath or took oath of their respective offices in dis-obedience to the order passed by a 7-Member Bench of the

Supreme Court on 3.11.2007 in C.M.A.No.2869 of 2007 in Constitution Petition No.73 of 2007, shall be proceeded against under Article 209 of the Constitution.

The Secretary Law Division shall take steps in the matter accordingly; Provided that nothing hereinabove shall affect those Judges who though had been appointed as Judges / Chief Justices of any of the High Courts between 3.11.2007 to 22.3.2009 but had subsequently been appointed afresh to other offices in consultation with or with the approval of or with the consent of the Constitutional CJP;

v)   Any judgments delivered or orders made or any decrees passed by any Bench of the Supreme Court or of any of the High Courts which comprised of or which included the afore-described Judges whose appointments had been declared void *ab initio*, are protected on the principle laid down in MALIK ASAD ALI'S CASE (PLD 1958 SC 161);

vi)   Since the Constitution (Amendment) Order 2007 [President's Order No.5] and the Islamabad High Court (Establishment) Order [President's Order No.7] establishing IHC for the Federal Capital Territory, have been declared to be un-constitutional and of no legal effect, therefore, the said IHC shall cease to exist forthwith.

All judicial matters pending before the said High Court before the passing of this order shall revert / stand transferred to the courts which had jurisdiction in the said matters before the promulgation of said President's Orders No.5 & No: 7 of 14th December 2007.

The Judges, officers and employees of the said Court shall, as a consequence thereof, cease to be Judges, officers and employees except those who prior to their appointments in the IHC, were Judges, officers & employees of some other High Court who shall revert to the court of which they originally belonged. The officers and employees of the said Court shall, if they were freshly employed, also cease to hold their respective appointments, and shall become part of the Federal Government Surplus Pool for further appointments.

vii) The Ordinances promulgated by the President or a Governor of a Province before 3.11.2007 which were given permanence by the

PCO No.1 of 2007 as also the Ordinances issued by the President or a Governor between 3.11.2007 and 15.12.2008 and were validated by the afore-mentioned judgment delivered in TIKA IQBAL CASE, stand shorn of their purported permanence.

However, since on account of the said judgment in TIKA IQBAL CASE purporting to be a judgment of this Court, the presumption that the said Ordinances were valid laws not requiring approval of the Parliament or the respective Provincial Assemblies in terms of Article 89 or 128 of the Constitution and since it is today that this Court has attributed invalidity to the said legislative instruments, therefore, the period of 120 days and 90 days would be deemed to commence to run from today and steps may be taken to place the said Ordinances before the Parliament or the respective Provincial Assemblies in accordance with law;

viii) Since the Constitution, through its Article 176, authorises only the Parliament to determine the number of Judges of the Supreme Court of Pakistan, therefore, the number of Judges of the Supreme Court for purposes of the said Article 176 shall continue to remain sixteen.

ix) In the Code of Conduct prescribed for the Judges of the Superior Courts in terms of Article 209(8) of the Constitution, a new clause shall be added commanding that no such Judge shall, hereinafter, offer any support in whatever manner to any un-constitutional functionary who acquires power otherwise than through the modes envisaged by the Constitution;

x) In view of our findings above regarding Justice Abdul Hameed Dogar not being a constitutional and a valid consultee, the notifications dated 26.8.2008 and 15.9.2008 extending the term of office of Justice Abdur Rashid Kalwar and of Justice Zafar Kalwar Khan Sherwani as Additional Judges of the High Court of Sindh are declared to be un-constitutional and of no legal effect.

xi) Any declaration made in this judgment shall not in any manner affect the General Elections held and the Government formed as a result thereof i.e. the President, the Prime Minister, the Parliament, the Provincial Governments, anything done by these institutions in the discharge of their functions. These acts are fully protected in terms of the age old of principle of *Salus Populi Est Suprema Lex* reflected in PLD 1972 SC 139.

xii) Before parting with the judgment, we would like to reiterate that to defend, protect, and uphold the Constitution is the sacred function of the Supreme Court. The principles of democracy, freedom, equality, tolerance, and social justice as enunciated by Islam shall be fully observed;..............Wherein the independence of judiciary shall be fully secured.

EFFECTS OF 31ST JULY JUDGMENT:

In nutshell this judgment of 31st July 2009, generally known as *Sindh High Court Bar Association Case* (**PLD 2009 SC 879**) was thus taken as a monumental judgment because:

(i)   It declared PCO oath immoral, illegal, and unconstitutional.

(ii) It had taken a stand in favour of the constitutional, democratic and civil set-up. None of the judges was in a position to take any PCO oath in case of a future military adventure. The entire court was made bound to resign in case of another PCO would be enforced.

(iii) The effect of the above declarations was that emergency of 3rd November 2007 and all actions pursuant thereto were held illegal and void *ab-initio*. Accordingly, all constitutional amendments, actions and appointments, including that of Justice Dogar as the CJP, were declared void with following two exceptions:

   a) Parliament could adopt all [the 34] affected ordinances after considering them afresh within 120 days from the date of that judgment.

   b) The oath of office, administered by the [illegal] Chief Justice Dogar to President Asif Ali Zardari, was validated.

Next day, CJ of the Lahore High Court (LHC) Kh Sharif referred the names of 12 judges who took oath under the PCO of Nov 2007 to the Supreme Judicial Council (SJC) for proceedings under Article 209 of the Constitution. The judges referred to the SJC were J Mian Najamuzzaman, J Maulvi Anwarul Haq, J Naseem Sikandar, J Abdul Shakoor Parracha, J Khalid Alvi, J Fazal-e-Miran Chohan, J Syed Shabbar Raza Rizvi, J Hamid Ali Shah, J Sajjad Hussain Shah, J Tariq Shamim, J Syed Asghar Haider and J Hasnat Ahmad Khan. J Rizvi, J Shamim, J Haider and J Hasnat opted not to do judicial work. J Kazim Ali Malik, J Ali Hassan

Rizvi and J Mazhar Hussain Minhas were reverted as Session Judges and were made officers on special duty (OSDs).

A deep legal crisis was seen in Baluchistan where all the five judges, including Chief Justice of the Balochistan High Court (BHC) had to resign. There was no one available to hear more than 5,000 cases and other legal issues. At that moment there were 11 vacancies of judges in the BHC but CJ Amanullah Yaseenzai, J Ahmad Khan Lashari, J Akhter Zaman Malghani, J Muhammad Nadir Khan and J Mehta Kailash Nath were serving since last several years.

All those judges of BHC were found guilty of taking their oaths on 4th November 2007 thus all of them resigned and left their seats on 4th of August 2009 with mutual consultation after Supreme Court's verdict of 31st July 2009.

More than 12 **review petitions** were filed with the Supreme Court on various counts mostly that the judges were punished unheard. A 14-members bench heard those petitions. This time the judgment was written by Justice Javed Iqbal; two judges, J Sardar Raza Khan and J Rehmat H Jaffri, had dissented. Sardar Raza Khan's dissenting note was not approved for reporting.

As the high stature judges were affected so the most learned and scholarly lawyers like Sheikh Akram, Naeem Bokhari, Dr Khalid Ranjha and Wasim Sajjad argued at length before the bench but were unable to seek relief for even a single petitioner.

On 13th October 2009, the judgment [short order] was announced declaring the review petitions non-maintainable but with the following added remarks:

> '*It is the first instance of the Supreme Court stating in a categoric, loud and abundantly clear manner* **that military interventions are illegal and will hardly find any colluder in future within the judiciary.**
>
> *The impugned judgment provides much needed redress as it will render considerable help in blocking the way of adventurers and dictators to creep in easily by taking* **supra Constitutional steps** *endorsed, supported and upheld* **under the garb of the principle of necessity in the past which will never happen again.**
>
> *The judgment impugned would encourage future justices to take the firm stand against usurpers........dated 13.10.2009.*'

UPROAR AGAINST SC's VERDICT:

At this moment one could recall another painting of 'doctrine of necessity' on validating the military coup [dated 12th October 1999] of Gen Musharraf for which Ayaz Amir had once written (*'the News' of 7th August 2009* is referred) that:

'Among this lot — *the* original lot, that is — was Justice Iftikhar M Chaudhry. And it was from this PCO crowd, which saw no evil in wearing the robes of the judiciary under [the same] usurping General.

Chief Justice Irshad Hasan Khan wrote the judgment and the other judges on the bench, including Justice Chaudhry, without adding a word of their own (which was slightly unusual) concurred with his sweeping validation. As PCO judges they were expected to toe the line dictated by the martial law masters and, in the museum dedicated to the doctrine of necessity this was another trophy.

Let him cast the first stone who hath not sinned, said Christ. Their lordships of the 'historic' judgment are no doubt made of sterner stuff, preferring to interpret the past as a closed and shut transaction.

The nation .... is being asked to believe; that Musharraf's rule was legitimate until Nov 3, 2007, and it was only his proclamation of emergency that evening which put him outside the pale of the Constitution. This is a very selective rendering with which most Pakistanis are not likely to agree.'

According to the above interpretation Gen Musharraf did nothing unconstitutional from 12th October 1999 to 2nd November 2007, and it was only the period of emergency [from 3rd November to 15th December] which was considered for judicial cognizance. In other words, as per SC's version, it was OK for nine years, which most people in Pakistan believed, but culpable for mere 40 days; astonishing judicial observation it was.

If Article Six is to be invoked against Gen Musharraf then what about Gen Yahya & Gen Ziaul Haq. In that case it is not he alone who should be brought into the dock but all his collaborators; the Generals who ordered troop movements on 12th October 1999 [*realistically speaking those Generals deserved more severe trials because Gen Musharraf was in the air then*], the judges who were effectively his collaborators later and all those who chose to serve under him in various capacities; in the judiciary, top bureaucracy and elsewhere.

Referring to '*the News*' of 1st *January 2010*:

> '*Talking of Musharraf's military rule; what was the role of Triple One Brigade on the take over day and few judges [barring Chief Justice Saiduzzaman Siddiqui and some more] who had taken oath under the PCO issued two months later. All of their present lordships took oath under the PCO.*
>
> *Not only were that some of them on the bench which validated Musharraf's takeover, a few, including the Chief Justice, were on the bench which approved him for the second time in another case (in April 2005).*
>
> *But then the principle should be for everyone. We should not be raising monuments to selective memory or selective condemnation. And if in this Turkish bath all are like the emperor without his clothes, the least this should inculcate is a sense of humility.*'

During the first week of August 2009, two Supreme Court judges J Faqir Muhammad Khokhar and J Javed Buttar had tendered their resignations because their cases were referred to the Supreme Judicial Council (SJC) for disciplinary action. The SJC meeting was to be convened three days after to review the matter.

During the same days Barrister Qazi Faiz Esa was appointed as the Chief Justice of Balochistan High Court, a notification for the purpose was issued on emergency basis and on the same evening the acting Balochistan Governor had administered oath on him.

For some from intelligentsia belonging to other school of thought, the SC's decision of 31st July 2009 was the biggest fraud in judicial history of Pakistan when it said that PCO judges would go home. In their opinion, **PCO Judges continued working and non PCO judges were sacked, packed and sent away.**

The beneficiaries of the said judgment were CJ Iftikhar M Chaudhry himself and seven of the member judges of the sitting bench. All the said judges had violated the constitutional oath and took oath under the PCO of 1999 coined by the same Gen Musharaf. That PCO of 1999 and decision subsequently made on the basis of that PCO, were given constitutional protection by 17th Amendment by another puppet Parliament of Pakistan of 2002-2007.

Justice Faqir M Khokhar and J Javed Buttar etc including other judges in High Courts who had taken oath under the PCO on 3rd November 1999 were sitting judges on that day of 31st July 2009. Interestingly, one lot of *42 judges who were sent home had never taken oath under any PCO*; most of them were not even appointed in Gen Musharaf's time; they were appointed after the restoration of democracy in the country.

In short, the fight between post 3rd November [2007] PCO judges and post 12th October [1999] PCO judges had resulted in ouster of judges who took oath only under the Constitution of Pakistan and never ever under the PCO. The media, PML(N), the lawyers and other political forces were mixed up and were rejoicing the ouster of constitutionally appointed judges and PPP went ignorant of this fact. Such things could only happen in Pakistan.

The confirmed judges who were sacked after the SC's decision of 31st July 2009 [because they were not recommended by CJ Iftikhar M Chaudhry] included J Mazhar Minhas, J Ashraf Bhatti, J Rana Zahid Mehmood, J Kazim Ali Malik, J Hafiz Tariq Nasim, J Khalil Ahmad, Justice M A Zafar, J Malik Saeed Ejaz, J Syed Shaheen Masud Rizvi, J Ali Akbar Qureshi and J Ahsan Bhoon.

In the 2nd week of December 2010, the Supreme Court continued the hearing of contempt of court notices to certain PCO judges in continuation of dismissing further objections filed against the bench hearing it. The apex court held that the matter relating to PCO judges was not personal in nature but relates to the sanctity of an institution. The SC bench heard contempt charges against former CJP Abdul Hameed Dogar and other judges for taking oath under the PCO in defiance of a restraining order issued by a seven-judge bench on the evening of 3rd November 2007.

The Supreme Court said that if needed, notices would be issued to army Generals and bureaucrats [*but it never materialized*] who did not comply with the apex court's judgement against the 'Emergency & 2007's PCO'.

A four-member bench, headed by Justice M A Shahid Siddiqui and comprising J Jawwad S Khawaja, J Tariq Pervaz and J Khilji Arif Hussain was made to hear the contempt of court cases against the PCO judges linked with Dogar court. Inclusion of certain judges on the bench was pointed out but dismissed. The court had also rejected the plea of two PCO judges' counsel to stop contempt of court cases until the decision of their intra-court appeal.

SC'S JUDGMENT NOT JUSTIFIED?

In fact, the decision of the apex court had summarily removed all those judges of higher judiciary who were not part of it as on 2nd November 2007. Their removal was ordered on ground that advice of *de-jure* (between the period of 3rd November 2007 and 22nd March 2009) Chief Justice of Pakistan Iftikhar M Chaudhry, was not obtained in those cases. There were three groups of those removed judges.

- Those who were elevated to higher courts and initially took oath on PCO of Nov 2007.

- Those who were elevated to higher courts after restoration of constitution [on 15th December 2007] but were appointed by President Gen Musharraf till August 2008.

- Those who were elevated to higher courts after restoration of constitution [on 15th December 2007] but were appointed by President Asif Ali Zardari after August 2008.

This decision of 31st July 2009 gave rise to an interesting situation where firstly the newly appointed judges who never took any sort of oath on PCO were removed. Secondly, the sitting judges who took oath on PCO 2007 were still acting as justices, though their cases were sent to Supreme Judicial Council. Thirdly, some of the sitting judges who accepted reappointments and took oath from Chief Justice Dogar were still acting as justices of court with no action. Lastly, the Judges who took oath on PCO of 1999 were still functioning as justices of higher judiciary.

A group of removed ad hoc judges of LHC filed several petitions in the Supreme Court for review of 31st July's unfair judgment, which had sent 76 judges of the Supreme Courts and High Courts home immediately.

They contained that they were qualified to be appointed as judges of the high court in accordance with the requirements of Article 193(2) of the 1973 Constitution and were offered to serve as ad hoc judges in consequence of consultation required under the Constitution. They accepted the offer and took oath after when emergency was lifted. They never took oath under any PCO and continued performing the functions as judges of the high court till the passing of the said judgment.

Further in LHC the selection of above petitioners judges was made by the Chief Justice (LHC) Zahid Hussain, who was till then serving judge of the Supreme Court and interestingly his case was also not referred to the Supreme Judicial Council. It was also contended in the petitions that neither the sacked judges were made party in the said proceedings nor had the court called for the comments of the sacked judges; concerned Judges were not even aware about the decision passed by the Supreme Court.

Moreover, no copy of the decision was either sent to the high court or to the judges concerned. The judges had taken oath according to the Article 189 of the Constitution. They argued that the said judgment had been passed in violation of the universally accepted principle of *audi altram paltrem* and they were condemned unheard.

In nut shell, the judgment of 31st July 2009 was being applied with retrospective effect from 3rd November 2007 and not from October 1999. The 14-member SC bench applied the sanction to all the judges who had taken oath under the PCO but excluding their own persons. By some it was considered contrary to the principles laid down in *Malik Asad Ali's case* wherein it had been held that the chief justice himself and the members of the bench as the case may be, were also bound by the said judgement thus Chief Justice Sajjad Ali Shah was removed from office and sent home in 1997 on the same principle.

In that way the members of the SC's bench themselves should have been affected too, because their holding of office was not constitutional and lawful. It was purely a *self-serving judgement.* J Abdul Hameed Dogar's holding of the CJP office was declared as unconstitutional till 24th March 2009 then how some of the SC judges, who performed their duties under Justice Dogar, were made members of the SC bench that gave the 31st July 2009's verdict.

Some pointed out that 31st July judgement had made exception by declaring the oath administered to President Zardari by Justice Dogar as an 'administrative act' of a CJP, but if it was so then how could such administration of oath to judges by him be treated unconstitutional?

Moreover, the CJ of LHC Syed Zahid Hussain had also taken oath under the PCO and was appointed as the CJ of LHC in consultation with Justice Dogar, who had continued to act as such even after assumption of the office by CJP Iftikhar M Chaudhry. He was elevated as the judge of the Supreme Court but the 31st July's judgement was not applied to him.

[J Syed Zahid Hussain was appointed as judge of the LHC on 21st May 1998 and was confirmed on 19th May 1999. J Hussain was made Chief Justice of the LHC on retirement of CJ Iftikhar Hussain Chaudhry, who retired on 31st December 2007. He was elevated to the Supreme Court on 12th April 2009. He had taken oath on the PCO of 1999 as a sitting judge of LHC like other judges including CJP Iftikhar M Chaudhry.

J Zahid Hussain also took oath on the PCO of 2007 (like Justice Dogar and some others) as a sitting judge of LHC again; being amongst 13 out of 31 sitting judges of LHC. Along with him justices Nasim Sikandar, M Khalid Alvi, Sakhi Hussain Bokhari, M Bilal Khan, M Muzammal Khan, Syed Shabbar Raza Rizvi, Hamid Ali Shah, Tariq Shamim, Syed Asghar Haider, Hasnat Ahmad Khan and Fazl-e-Miran Chohan as well as the then CJ of LHC Iftikhar Hussain Chaudhry took oath on PCO 2007.

The jurists would be able to opine if 31st July's judgement was to be implemented on him or not.]

Similar was the case of appointment of the then CJ of the Federal Shariat Court (FSC) as a judge of the Sindh High Court (SHC) in 2007. He, Agha Rafiq Ahmed Khan, was appointed as the Federal Law Secretary with the consent of Justice Dogar and later elevated as the CJ of FSC with the consent of CJP Iftikhar M Chaudhry.

[The logic behind his retention might be that J Agha Rafiq Ahmed Khan was coming up as District and Sessions Judge in various districts of Sindh from year 1997 to 2007. He was elevated as Additional Judge of the Sindh High Court on 14th December 2007.

After a few months, he was appointed as Federal Secretary Law and Justice Division in 2008. He was then confirmed as a permanent Judge of the SHC during December 2008 retaining his original seniority from 1995. On 8th June 2009, he was elevated as Chief Justice of the Federal Shariat Court of Pakistan.]

J Sardar M Raza Khan, J Tassadaq Hussain Jilani, J Shakirullah Jan, J Nasirul Mulk and J Sarmad Jalal Osmani, who were members of the 14-member Supreme Court Full Bench to give the 31st July 2009's judgement were also appointed with the consultation of Chief Justice Dogar.

Similarly, four LHC judges, eight Sindh High Court judges and three Peshawar High Court judges were appointed in consultation with 'unconstitutional' CJP Abdul Hameed Dogar but were given protection in the said judgement.

Leaving aside the criticism, let us move forward with actual proceedings.

JUDGES PRAYING FOR JUSTICE:

After the judgment of 31st July 2009, amidst disapprovals, appreciations and analysis, most of the affected judges preferred to put review petitions against their dismissals before the same Supreme Court. Objections raised in the review petitions against the 31st July's judgment and numerous miscellaneous applications in the same context were heard and decided by a four member Bench of SC.

In the last week of January 2011, the bench concluded the proceedings and reserved its verdict in the contempt charges against superior court judges for taking oath under the PCO of 2007 and for defying SC's [evening] order dated 3rd November 2007.

On 13th October 2009, while passing judgment against their own fellow judges on review petition no: 2745/2009 and in Constitutional Petition No: 08/2009, a bench of 14 judges of the Supreme Court of Pakistan had passed orders but the same were given finality *on 2nd February 2011* while observing that:

(1) The notices issued under Article 204 of the Constitution read with sections 3 and 4 of the Contempt of Court Act, 1976 or any other enabling provisions of the relevant law, to the Judges who have expressed their regrets and repentance; by tendering unconditional apologies and affirming their remorse through withdrawal of the petitions filed by them and tendering of resignations, are discharged.

(2) The Judges who have already retired and have tendered unconditional apologies and have expressed their repentance and remorse, the notices issued to them are discharged.

(3) The Judges, who are contesting notices, they shall be proceeded against separately along with the cases of those Judges, who have not filed replies and/or have prayed for grant of time.

(4) The Judges of the Supreme Court and the High Courts, who tendered resignations after pronouncement of the judgment

dated 31.7.2009 in deference thereto shall not be proceeded against.

(5) The Judges who have tendered resignations, but have not filed replies to the notices, the process shall be repeated to them so as to file the replies within two weeks.

(6) The Judges, who have neither tendered resignations nor have filed replies, are required to file replies within two weeks.

(7) Mr. Ahmed Raza Kasuri Advocate has prayed for grant of four weeks' time to submit reply on behalf of Justice (Retd) Abdul Hameed Dogar. Let the reply be filed within two weeks.

(8) Justice (Retd) Muhammad Nawaz Abbasi has filed reply, which is not unconditional apology; therefore, his matter shall be proceeded along with other cases.

(9) Syed Zulfiqar Ali Bokhari has tendered unconditional apology and has thrown himself at the mercy of the Court, the notice issued to him is also discharged.'

Justice Sardar Muhammad Raza, while giving a dissenting note to the main judgment had observed that the Supreme Court has unlimited powers under Article 188 of the Constitution, to review any matter relating to justice, through its own *suo moto* powers or on someone's application.

The words "the Supreme Court shall have power" or "the Court may review its Judgment or Order" makes it abundantly clear that the Supreme Court has wide; rather, *suo moto* powers to review its judgments or orders provided the grounds for such review are available. In order to do complete justice under Articles 4, 25, 187 and 188, the Supreme Court should rather assume jurisdiction instead of refusing to do justice [*as had been given in Malik Asad Ali's case* (**PLD 1998 SC 161**)].

Justice Rahmat H Jafferi had given a dissenting note disagreeing with the main review decision on the issue '*whether any person could file a review petition on behalf of other affected judge or only the interested / affected persons could do so*'.

Certain respondents from above and 61 others were issued notices to explain as to why proceedings should not be initiated against them for committing contempt of court. 72 persons either submitted their respective replies to the said notices or tendered unconditional apologies. Some of them resigned from office.

There were 10 respondents who had contested the notices issued to them. Mainly, the left over judges were J (retd) Abdul Hameed Dogar, the former CJP; Iftikhar Hussain Chaudhry, the former CJ of the LHC; and eight sitting judges named J Syed Zahid Hussain of the Supreme Court and Justices Khurshid Anwar Bhinder, Hamid Ali Shah, Zafar Iqbal Chaudhry, Hasnat Ahmed Khan, Syed Shabbar Raza Rizvi, Yasmin Abbasey and Jehanzeb Rahim hailing from various high courts.

The extensive arguments of learned counsels of the above named judges raised the following primary questions:

- *'Is it constitutionally permissible for the SC to proceed under Article 204 of the Constitution against Judges of the superior courts, for contempt charges?*

- *If yes; then as a matter of propriety, should the SC proceed against the said Judges or should it, bearing in mind the status of the respondents as Judges of the superior courts, discontinue these proceedings and discharge the notices issued to them?*

- *If it is decided that the Constitution does not place restrictions on contempt proceedings against Judges and if it is also found that questions of propriety do not stop the SC from proceeding against the respondents under Article 204 of the Constitution, then is there sufficient material available before the Court to charge the respondents for committing contempt of the SC on account of disobedience of its order dated 3rd November 2007?'*

The SC's four judge's bench, comprising Justice M A Shahid Siddiqui, J Jawwad S Khwaja, J Khilji Arif Hussain and J Tariq Parvez, considered the arguments of the counsels and came up with contentions that:

- *'In the given circumstances, the Constitution and law does not prohibit proceedings under its Article 204 against the respondents even though they may be Judges of the higher courts.*

- *Having considered the arguments as to the propriety of initiating contempt proceedings against the respondents and being fully conscious of the status of the respondents, the SC held that proceedings should be taken against them, with the exception of Mr Zafar Iqbal Chaudhry and Khurshid Anwar Bhindar.*

- *Having considered the record, facts, replies and the arguments advanced on behalf of respondents, the SC found sufficient material available to justify charging them, except the two mentioned above, for committing contempt of the apex court on account of disobeying an order dated 3rd November 2007 passed by a seven member Bench of the SC.*

- *Having considered the replies and submissions made by the two respondents, Mr Chaudhry and Mr Bhindar mentioned above, the apex court observed that as they took oath under the PCO on 14th December 2007 [and since they were not judges of the LHC on 3rd November 2007], they did not violate the said SC's order dated 3rd November 2007; though they may have violated its spirit. Thus their conduct in taking oath under the PCO is denounced in terms of Section 18 (2) of the Contempt of Court Ordinance 2003. The court held that they would not be charged to face trial.'*

KEEP THE SC RECORD STRAIGHT PL:

It is also available on Pakistan's contemporary history that once in May 2010 Barrister Jehanzeb Rahim [*a former Judge of the Peshawar High Court*] had asked the Supreme Court to recall contempt notices issued to various judges of the Supreme Court and high courts to avoid further damage to the institution of the superior judiciary.

Barrister Rahim had raised 28 questions challenging the validity of the orders passed on 3rd November 2007 by the 7-member bench of the SC, headed by the CJP Iftikhar M Chaudhry, against the proclamation of Emergency in the country.

Former Justice J Rahim raised questions in his reply in Cr Original Petition No 104/2009 submitted in the SC in compliance with orders of its 5-members bench dated 4th May 2010. He was also facing charges of contempt for taking oath on 3rd November 2007, along with many other judges under the 2nd PCO of Gen Musharraf.

Following were the questions raised in his reply:

1. Whether a 7-member bench of available judges was actually constituted in the evening of 3rd Nov 2007?

2. Whether this 7-member bench so constituted, actually assembled in the evening of 3rd Nov 2007 in the SC building?

3. Whether this bench actually passed an order in the evening of 3rd Nov 2007 and signed the same in the SC building?

4. Whether J Rana Bhagwandas was in Islamabad during the working week of 29th October till 2nd Nov 2007?

5. Whether J Rana Bhagwandas did not sign the order dated 3rd Nov 2007 on 5th Nov 2007?

6. Whether judges junior to J Rana Bhagwandas in seniority, signed the order dated 3rd Nov 2007 after 5th Nov 2007?

7. Whether J Rana Bhagwandas phoned Justice Sair Ali in Lahore on the evening of 3rd Nov 2007 from Karachi to inform him that an order had been passed by some judges in Islamabad and judges of the Lahore High Court [who had gathered at the residence of J Sair Ali] should refrain from passing any other order in respect of the Proclamation of Emergency issued by Gen Musharraf earlier that day?

8. Whether J Ghulam Rabbani was in Islamabad on 3rd Nov 2007?

9. Whether the signatures of J Ghulam Rabbani tally with his usual signatures on judicial orders?

10. Whether the order dated 3rd Nov 2007 was signed at one place in the SC on 3rd Nov 2007 or later by circulation?

11. Whether the names of J Rana Bhagwandas and J Javed Iqbal were written in Urdu to indicate the place where they were required to affix their signatures and what was the necessity of so indicating was their absence from the SC?

12. Whether the order dated 3rd Nov 2007 was actually faxed from the office of the registrar SC or from some other place and whether the order so faxed, contained the signatures of seven judges of the SC?

13. Whether the copy of order issued to press contained the signatures of any judge?

14. Whether J Javed Butter and J Nawaz Abbasi were part of the 7-member Bench constituted on 3rd Nov 2007 and are, therefore,

witnesses to the presence or absence of seven judges (members of the bench) and whether their evidence is not absolutely essential at this preliminary stage?

15. Whether the order dated 3rd Nov 2007 was faxed to the phone numbers of the registrars of the Sindh, Lahore and Peshawar High Courts or to some others?

16. Whether any of the judges who signed the order dated 3rd Nov 2007, ever examined the same in original after 3rd Nov 2007?

17. Whether eight judges namely J Sardar Mohammad Raza Khan, J Khalilur Rehman Ramday, J Tassadaq Hussain Jilani, J Ch Ijaz Ahmed, J Sarmad Jalal Osmany, J Mohammad Sair Ali, J Shahid Siddiqui and J Jawwad S Khawaja saw the order dated 3rd Nov 2007 in original before signing the judgment dated 31st July 2009 in the constitution petition No: 08 & 09 of 2009 or since then, to satisfy themselves individually that a 7-member bench was constituted, convened, passed and signed the order dated 3rd Nov 2007 on 3rd Nov 2007?

18. Whether the order dated 3rd Nov 2007 passed in the said constitution petition was available in original in the record of the SC from 3rd Nov 2007 till 22nd March 2009?

19. Whether J Abdul Hameed Dogar had taken oath as Chief Justice of Pakistan on 3rd Nov 2007 at 19:00 hours before the [above mentioned] order dated 3rd Nov 2007 was passed?

20. Whether copies of order dated 3rd Nov 2007 were or could be delivered to all judges of the SC at their residences "no sooner it was passed"?

21. Whether the CJP was not barred by Article IV of Code of Conduct to sit on any Bench to hear any application moved on 2nd November 2007 by Barrister Aitzaz Ahsan?

22. Whether the prohibition in Article IV of the Code of Conduct did not apply equally to the presence of the CJP with respect of Hamid Khan and Rasheed Rizvi, senior advocates of the SC, in that or any subsequent petition?

23. Whether the CJP Iftikhar M Chaudhry having decided on 17th October 2007 not to sit on any Bench hearing the petition filed by J Wajihuddin did not violate his own order on 3rd Nov 2007?

24. Whether the order of 3rd Nov 2007 can be said to be a judicial order on the touchstone of the findings, parameters and conclusions in Asad Ali's case?

25. Whether the undersigned [former J Jehanzeb Rahim], not having been heard in Review Petition No: Nil filed in the SC has not been condemned unheard and whether in the light of formulations No: 4.1 to 4.70 in that review petition, the judgment dated 31st July 2009 is to be recalled, varied and modified?

26. Whether the show cause notice issued and being responded to should also be issued to J Nasirul Mulk, J Shakir Ullah Jan (signatories to that order), J Tassaddaq Hussain Jillani and J Sarmad Jalal Osmany who took fresh oath from Abdul Hameed Dogar, 'the CJP' after 3rd Nov 2007 and before 22nd March 2009 in violation of the said order dated 3rd Nov 2007?

27. Whether J Nasirul Mulk should sit on a Bench in judgment over fellow judges in contempt proceeding for violating the order dated 3rd Nov 2007, when he himself had done the same and accepted Abdul Hameed Dogar as the Chief Justice of Pakistan?

28. Whether J Taric Pervez, having been re-appointed as Chief Justice of Peshawar High Court and taken fresh oath in violation of the order dated 3rd Nov 2007 on the recommendation of [CJP] A Hameed Dogar, can sit on a Bench constituted to look into the same violation by other judges and [CJP] A Hameed Dogar himself.

Former J Jehanzeb Rahim had requested the SC to decide the above propositions, some of which required evidence, in preliminary proceedings but the honourable Bench simply shelved them aside with sarcastic smiles. In fact the judicial minds were of the view that whether proceedings under contempt laws could be initiated against judges of the high courts and the Supreme Court of Pakistan under such circumstances.

However, the allegations of a former Justice [Jehanzeb Rahim] should have been probed and answered, especially if J Bhagwandas had signed the order on the 5th Nov 2007 instead of 3rd Nov 2007, to keep the pillars of justice upright.

The fact remains that after Barrister J Rahim's reply, next day two SC judges [J Nasirul Mulk and J Raja Fayyaz Ahmed] had disassociated themselves from that 5-member bench hearing contempt of court cases against PCO judges, and referred the matter to the Chief Justice Iftikhar M Chaudhry back for reconstitution of the bench.

Naeem Bukhari advocate was representing Barrister J Rahim. The three remaining members of the bench were J Jawwad S Khawaja, J Rahmat Hussain Jafferi and J Tariq Parvez.

[Justice Nasirul Mulk and Justice Raja Fayyaz Ahmed in the bench, were also members of the SC bench that ruled against the PCO and the emergency of November 2007. Justice Tariq Pervez had taken oath as a Peshawar High Court judge on former CJP Abdul Hameed Dogar's recommendation.

Some experts kept the view that, according to the code of conduct, the three judges could hear the contempt of court case against PCO judges. Former Justice Jehanzeb Rahim was one of 10 judges who had decided to contest the contempt of court charges.]

TEXT OF SC ORDER OF 3RD NOV 2007:

Going into the details of judgment of 31st July 2009, it was generally felt that most of the judges were shunted out on the *'charge'* of contempt that why they had taken PCO oath *'while defying Supreme Court's order of 3rd November 2007'*. The above 28 points of Barrister J Rahim basically pointed towards the same order of 3rd November 2007.

The said order of 3rd November 2007 was passed by the SC bench [*if it was so*] headed by CJ Iftikhar M Chaudhry on an informal petition of Barrister Aitzaz Ahsan. The SC bench hurriedly passed orders *'after knowing that the Emergency has been proclaimed'* by Gen Musharraf. See the text of the SC order **verbatim**:

This application was filed in court on 2nd November 2007 praying that respondent / Government may change the composition of bench by adopting extra Constitutional measures, which could mean either by placing Martial Law or bringing PCO or by imposing emergency.

Application could not be taken up as it was not numbered. However, now it has been marked to Bench. In the meantime, electronic and print media news appeared that PCO been promulgated to enable Government to administer fresh oath to the Chief Justice as well as to the judges of the Supreme Court so that favourable judges could be appointed.

Be that as it may, we feel that Government has no ground / reason to take extra Constitutional steps, particularly for the reasons being published in the news papers that high profile case is pending and is not likely to be decided in favour of the Government, although matter is still pending.

Therefore, a special Bench has been constituted and on considering present situation and news which have published in news papers, we direct as follows:

1. Government of Pakistan i.e. President and Prime Minister of Pakistan are restrained from undertaking any such action which is contrary to Independence of Judiciary.

2. No Judge of the Supreme Court or the High Courts Chief Justice(s) shall take oath. Under PCO or any other extra constitutional step.

3. Chief of Army Staff, Corps Commanders, Staff Officers and all concerned of the Civil and Military Authorities are hereby restrained from acting on PCO storming which has been issued or from administering fresh oath to Chief Justice of Pakistan or Judges of Supreme Court and Chief Justice or Judges of the Provincial High Courts. They are also restrained to undertake any such actions, which is contrary to independence of Judiciary. Any further appointment of the Chief Justice of Pakistan and Judges of Supreme Court and Chief Justices of High Court or Judges of Provinces under new development shall be unlawful and without jurisdiction.

Put up before full court on 5ᵗʰ November 2007

Islamabad
03.11.2007

The senior lawyers has cogent points to ponder that:

• If the petition was filed by Aitzaz Ahsan on 2ⁿᵈ November 2007, why it was not given importance to be numbered at least.

• Why the petition could not be heard during the whole day of 3ʳᵈ November 2007 when the '*Emergency was not there*'. [Emergency was announced in the evening hours]

917

- Who had written that order in haste; there were numerous grammatical errors in that half page order. Senior judges of the SC might not have written it.

- Why the SC order was not in usual order format.

- How the copies of that order were communicated to the concerned including GHQ, Presidency & PM House AND at what time.

There were many other questions about that order but who bothers in Pakistan – it was independent judiciary.

Astonishingly, media totally ignored the significance of those 28 points of former J Jehanzeb Rahim and the above BIG lapse except Najam Sethi. All the roaring live talk shows on TV and press conferences sponsored by the Federal Law Ministery went blank in that respect otherwise the whole judicial edifice could collapse and the moral authority of the then sitting justices would be shaken.

[*The judicial decisions announced since CJP Iftikhar M Chaudhry was restored would have gone void, including the 16th December 2009 & 12th January 2010 judgments invalidating the NRO for which the government had suffered later.*]

The order of the SC dated 3rd Nov 2007 was invoked about 20 times and made it a fundamental pillar of all major future judgements of the apex court.

In nut shell, the hearings to those review petitions had commenced on 3rd November 2009 and continued till 21st February 2011 when charges against the respondents were framed. Numerous eminent and senior Advocates including Mr Wasim Sajjad, Dr Khalid Ranjha, Mr Raza Kazim, Mr S.M. Zafar, Dr A Basit, Mr Ibrahim Satti, Mr Naeem Bokhari and Sh Zameer Hussain had addressed the apex court with exhaustive arguments on the arising issues.

The final verdict came on *18th May 2011* in that regard. A five judge's bench of the SC, comprising CJP Iftikhar M Chaudhry, J Mian Shakirullah Jan, J Tassaduq Hussain Jillani, J Sarmad Jalal Osmany and J Amir Hani Muslim, gave time to the government till 9th August 2011 to de-notify the judges. On that day, the apex court declared that seven high court judges, who had taken oaths under the PCO, were never validated as judges.

LAWYER'S & GOVERNMENT BOTH REACTED:

Referring to the '*Dawn* of 19*th* May 2011* Asma Jahangir, president of the Supreme Court Bar Association (SCBA), opined while referring to the SC's judgment on PCO judges that:

'*Police use third degree treatment but some people are doing it in the judiciary with their pen. This pen embodies the trust of the nation and it should not be used for settling personal scores and rivalries.*

I don't want to see justice stifled. Although he [referring to the CJP Iftikhar M Chaudhry] was a PCO judge, yet we supported him when he was sacked. We believed that if a dictator [Gen Musharraf] was allowed to ride roughshod over the judiciary this time, he [Gen Musharraf] would just bury the institution next time.

The decisions based on a feudal and 'panchayati' mindset would not work any more; strategy of 'jalao & gherao' (protests by burning) appeared to be working for induction of judges.'

Asma Jahangir commented on the SC's verdict of a day earlier in which intra-court appeals of judges who had taken oath under the PCO were rejected and the government was asked to issue a notification of their dismissal. She alleged that judges [of higher judiciary] were interested in 'big cases' that led to a '*mela*' (human crowd) in courtroom saying that '*we are not interested in fanfare. Lawyers have to take care of their clients, practice and offices.*'

On 5th August 2011, the Supreme Court granted two days more to the federation to issue de-notification of those former judges. A five member bench of the apex court, headed by the CJP Iftikhar M Chaudhry, expressed its displeasure in delay over issuance of required notification in pursuance of its 18th May order. Next day, PM Mr Gilani cancelled the appointments of Justice Syed Shabbar Raza Rizvi, Justice Syed Hamid Ali Shah, Justice Hasnat Ahmad Khan and Justice Syed Sajjad Hussain Shah as judges of the Lahore High Court (LHC) and Justice Yasmin Abbasey of the Sindh High Court (SHC). These judges were made entitled to service and pension benefits up to 10th April 2010, when the 18th Constitutional amendment was passed.

Meanwhile, legal experts and bar representatives once more termed the SC's orders unconstitutional and in violation of its own earlier orders; that in its 31st July 2009's judgment, the SC had declared that no judge would be removed or made dysfunctional through a notification by the executive and only the Supreme Judicial Council would initiate proceedings against judges under Article 209 of the Constitution.

A former law minister Khalid Ranjha and Azam Nazeer Tarar of SCBA told the media loudly that:

> *'The court's directive is confused. It [the apex court] has allowed for a way to get rid of any judge that it dislikes. I have no sympathies with PCO judges but only the SJC can remove judges through a reference. They cannot be removed through a Supreme Court judgment.*
>
> *Through this order, the court has made the executive abide by its judgment, but it has itself ignored legal provisions by penalizing judges by this act.*
>
> **The court's orders are based on personal likes and dislikes** and is *tantamount to subversion of the Constitution.'*

Ahsan Bhoon, President of Lahore High Court Bar Association (LHCBA) said that:

> *'The government has taken a constitutional step while **the Supreme Court's judgment was totally unconstitutional.***
>
> *It [the Supreme Court] had itself ruled that only the Supreme Judicial Council is the proper forum to decide the fate of judges. The government had no option but to act upon court orders.'*

The de-notification of the PCO judges took more than two years, a period during which a tussle between the two institutions of the state over their powers kept emerging off and on. On several occasions, the executive defied the implementation of the apex court's orders on one excuse or another. Not only the PCO judges' case, the famous Hajj arrangements corruption case and the National Insurance Company Limited (NICL) case intensified the tussle between the two institutions to an extent that threatened to derail democracy.

Due to the executive's invariable disregard towards the superior court's orders in numerous important cases, the CJP might have thought to call the army by invoking Article 190 of the constitution. Rightly it was not considered correct because:

'The judiciary is bound to demand army through the executive in case implementation on any of its orders is desired. The army in turn cannot act constitutionally without directions from the government'.

During CJP Sajjad Ali Shah's row with the PM Nawaz Sharif in November 1997, the CJP had asked the then Army Chief Gen Jehangir Karamat, to send army for SC's help and protection but was flatly refused in writing on the pretext that the permissions of both PM and President were required.

Many constitutional experts criticised the SC judgement on the PCO judge's appeals as discriminatory. Declaring the November 2007 PCO judges as unconstitutional while clearing those judges who took oath under previous PCOs, like twice taken by the sitting CJP Iftikhar M Chaudhry, could not find unanimous acceptance.

In this judicial cleansing process, about 104 judges were ousted, of whom 45 belonged to Punjab. The PPP government however tried to compensate some of them and assigned certain key posts in government institutions. One of those was Maluvi Anwarul Haq, who had not taken the oath under PCO but was ousted in 2009, served as Attorney General from April 2010 to April 2012, and later appointed by the government as an adviser to the president.

His successor, Irfan Qadir was appointed as the Prosecutor General of NAB by President Zardari. The SC found this illegal because Mr Qadir was the Prosecutor General during Gen Musharraf's era for three years and was ousted on SC's order. He was swiftly appointed as the Federal Secretary of the Law; later PM Yousaf Raza Gilani appointed him as the Attorney General of Pakistan during his trial in the infamous contempt case.

Known for his hard stance, Irfan Qadir often irked the SC by not lending legal assistance in many cases, most notably the contempt case. The apex court has expressed its displeasure over his conduct.

Yasmin Abbasi, was made Secretary of the Law Ministry and one Karim Khan Agha made NAB's Prosecutor General; both were amongst the ousted judges. In 2012, the government appointed Abdul Shakoor Paracha, who served as a Lahore High Court (LHC) and Islamabad High Court (IHC) judge, as its counsel in the pending Contempt of Court Act 2012 hearing in the SC. Similarly, the government selected Munir

Paracha, who was also a judge of the IHC, as its counsel in the case regarding the Balochistan law and order situation.

Ramzan Chaudhry, who is the chief legal adviser of Islamabad's Capital Development Authority [CDA], was also an IHC judge, and Shafqat Abbasi, an ex-PPP MPA, was given the slot of the Chairman of the Pakistan Press Council,

Unfortunately, it is Pakistan's judiciary where tens of pages can be written on 'selective justice'. Here the judicial norms develop on the whims and personal liking of the Chief Justices; see the history.

Scenario 66

PAKISTAN'S JUDICIARY IN 2009-10:

On 21st March 2009; Chief Justice of the Supreme Court of Pakistan, Justice Abdul Hameed Dogar, retired and Justice Iftikhar M Chaudhry took over his seat again. No 'Full Court Reference' was held in the honour of out-going CJP because he had assumed his office on 3rd November 2007, the Emergency day promulgated by Gen Musharraf.

JUSTICE DOGAR RETIRED WITHOUT REFERENCE:

Chief Justice Dogar was not the only CJP who had not been given the Full Court Reference [FCR] while departing, there were eight [out of total 19] other chief justices of Pakistan (CJP) also who had left that office unceremoniously on the completion of their tenure.

Traditionally, an FCR – a gathering of all judges of the Supreme Court – is held on the retirement of every judge of the court to honour the outgoing arbitrator. Papers are read out by a senior judge of the SC, the Attorney General, the Pakistan Bar Council and the Supreme Court Bar Association highlighting historic verdicts delivered by the outgoing judge. The details as collated by Masood Rehman of the *'Daily Times'* are given below.

Justice Sheikh Riaz Ahmad – who held the office of CJP from 1st February 2002 to 31st December 2003 –went without a 'full court reference', possibly because he had validated the controversial 'referendum' that gave a five-year term to Gen Musharraf as president and had accepted a three-year increase in the retirement age of judges of the SC and high courts, a decision that was later withdrawn.

Justice Bashir Jehangiri – who held office of CJP from 7th January 2002 to 31st January 2002 – could not get a full court reference, perhaps due to his short stay in the office.

Justice Irshad Hasan Khan – who remained the chief justice of Pakistan from 26th January 2000 to 6th January 2002 – could not get FCR possibly because he had validated the 12th October 1999's military takeover on the basis of the doctrine of necessity. He also gave Gen Musharraf the authority to amend the constitution and continue to rule the country un-interrupted for three years.

Justice Saeeduzzaman Siddiqui – who had declined to validate the 12th October 1999's military coup of Gen Musharraf – also went without an FCR because he was not allowed to come out of his residence when he had refused to take new oath under PCO. He remained the CJP from 1st July 1999 to 26th January 2000.

Justice Sajjad Ali Shah — who held the top SC office from 5th June 1994 to 2nd December 1997 – also went unceremoniously. His fellow judges had declared him 'inefficient and not fit to hold office of a judge' in the light of his own judgment of 20th March 1996 called 'Judges Case'.

Justice Muhammad Afzal Zullah – who was the CJP from 1st January 1990 to 18th April 1993 – also went without a reference in his honour.

Justice S Anwarul Haq: No reference was held in the his honour – who was the CJP from 23rd September 1977 to 25th March 1981 – possibly because he upheld the death sentence awarded to Zulfikar Ali Bhutto.

Justice Muhammad Yaqub Ali – who remained the CJP from 1st November 1975 to 22nd September 1977 – also did not get a full-court send off, possibly because he had accepted the bail application of Ms Nusrat Bhutto in respect of PPP's Mr Bhutto when he was arrested 2nd time on 13th September 1977.

CORRUPTION IN PAK JUDICIARY:

3rd July 2009: Chief Justice Iftikhar M Chaudhry directed the high courts to take action against those judges against whom complaints had been filed in the Supreme Court. Till then there were 10 complaints received by the Supreme Court office from high courts against the judges in the superior judiciary. Under the new Judicial Policy enforced from 1st June 2009 a cell was created for receiving complaints of misconduct and corruption in the judiciary.

Chief Justice of Pakistan was supposed to take appropriate action on such complaints in the capacity of Chairman of the National Judicial Policy Committee. Interalia, a complaint filed against the former chief justice of Islamabad High Court, Justice Muhammad Bilal Khan, was also pending before the Supreme Judicial Council (SJC), which was mandated to check misconduct, moral degradation and corruption in the higher echelon of the judiciary.

8ᵗʰ August 2009: In a meeting of the Supreme Judicial Council (SJC) presided over by the Chief Justice of Pakistan (CJP) Iftikhar M Chaudhry, a new clause was added to the code of conduct for superior court judges, forbidding any oath of office other than the one provided in the Constitution of Pakistan.

A 14-judges bench of the Supreme Court, earlier on 31ˢᵗ July 2009, had ordered the addition of a new clause to the code of conduct prescribed for the judges of superior courts in terms of Article 209 of the Constitution, decreeing that any such violation of the clause would be deemed to be misconduct. The new clause, approved by the SJC, said:

> *"No judge of the superior judiciary shall render support in any manner whatsoever, including taking or administering oath in violation of the oath of office prescribed in the Third Schedule to the Constitution to any authority that acquires power otherwise than through the modes envisaged by the Constitution of Pakistan."*

12ᵗʰ August 2009: Justice *Abdul Shakoor Paracha* of the Lahore High Court resigned in the second week of August 2009 to avoid facing references pending against him in the Supreme Judicial Council (SJC) for having taken oath under the 3ʳᵈ November 2007's PCO and for alleged corruption. The SJC issued him notice in the corruption reference in its meeting held on 8ᵗʰ August 2009. Justice Paracha was brought in the Lahore HC on 2ⁿᵈ May 2001. He was to retire on 30ᵗʰ June 2011.

The SJC, under the chairmanship of Chief Justice Iftikhar M Chaudhry, had also issued notices to another judge of the High Court on the charges of misconduct and corruption. It was Justice *Muhammad Afzal Soomro*, Judge of the Sindh High Court.

The SJC decided to constitute a two-member committee comprising Justice Sardar Muhammad Raza Khan, Judge Supreme Court (SC), and Justice Khawaja Sharif, CJ Lahore High Court (LHC), to further probe into the allegations levelled against the above mentioned judges. The committee visited Karachi in the third week of August 2009 for hearing and recording the statements of the complainants; they were also asked to submit affidavits and provide further material to substantiate their allegations.

The SJC, heard and examined complainants of S M Ismail and his son Dr Junaid Ismail against Justice A Shakoor Paracha and, after deliberations, decided to further inquire into the matter by issuing notices to parties including Justice Paracha.

The SJC in the same session had also considered the complaint filed by S M Ismail against Justice M Akhtar Shabbir, former judge of LHC / SC, and Justice Syed Qalb-e-Hassan, former judge of then defunct Islamabad High Court. It was decided that though these two judges had ceased to hold offices, there was a need of an appropriate action that would be recommended against them under the law.

What actions were taken or finalized against the said judges, not known till recent. Media investigators also never tried to lodge a probe into those issues. Pakistanis are part of a polarized society at one place or the other. When there are fingers raised against an army officer or a police inspector or a politician, or if there is any order passed by the Chief Justice, the Ansar and Kashif Abbasis write and speak in so high tone that all media activities are subdued and made passive to be seen or heard.

Uniforms are taken as symbols of authority and jealousy prevails every where; one has to be objective any way and ought to be. Many of the engineers, tax & revenue collectors, doctors, administrators, reformers, writers and speakers are corrupt, most of them are intellectually corrupt, so are the *khateebs* and judges; very little exceptions.

22nd December 2009: The Supreme Court of Pakistan gave a final warning to those who had managed to get their loans written off from financial institutions during the last 38 years and directed the State Bank to furnish a list of loan defaulters right from 1971 to date.

The Supreme Court had taken a *suo moto* notice on news reports appearing in media, about the huge Rs:54 billion loans write-off. The report had revealed that the previous government, in its five-year term, had written off the said amount of bank loans granted to big shots of Pakistan on the basis of a decision taken by the financial team of Gen Musharraf in December 2002. Chief Justice Iftikhar M Chaudhry observed, while hearing the *suo moto* case of written-off loans, that:

> '*Only one chance will be given to defaulters to return the loans and strict action will be taken against them without any discrimination, adding the court would look into the State Bank Circular 29 regarding writing off loans under Article 25 of the Constitution.*
>
> *The court directed the State Bank to ask the financial institutions in all the four provinces to prepare a list of loan defaulters right from 1971 to date and it should be placed on the record.*'

The State Bank submitted the list of the individuals and organisations that had got Rs:193 billion bank loans written off during the period 1997 to 2009. *The irony of fate was that the case was never heard and never chased.* No defaulter ever called, no reprimand, no further comments —- the superior court itself swallowed its own words ..... Hail the independent judiciary of Pakistan.

23rd December 2009: Chief justice Iftikhar M Chaudhry was reinstated to his original seat on 20th July 2007 by a full bench of the Supreme Court of Pakistan but the detailed judgment could not be written by the judges because on 3rd November 2007 most of the judges including the CJ were sent home after promulgation of an emergency by Gen Musharraf. On 23rd December 2009, the detailed judgment of the said proceedings was released.

The detailed judgment in the case of the restoration of the Chief Justice of Pakistan on 20th July 2007 revealed that not only Gen Musharraf but the then Director General ISI and the DG Military Intelligence (MI) had also insisted that the Chief Justice should resign during his illegal detention at the Army House Rawalpindi on 9th March 2007. The judgment, written by Justice Khalilur Rehman Ramday, said that:

> '*The petitioner CJP went on to depose that 'the respondent (the president) insisted that the deponent (the CJP) should resign'. He added that his refusal to oblige, 'ignited the fury of the respondent (the president); he (the president) stood up angrily and left the room along with his MS, COS, and the prime minister of Pakistan, saying that others would show evidence to the deponent' (about the allegations of misconduct against the CJP).*
>
> *As per the CJP, his meeting with the president lasted for about thirty minutes meaning thereby that the president and the prime minister would have left by about 12.15 / 12.30 pm and the CJP was then left behind in the company of the DG MI and the DG ISI allegedly to be shown the evidence in support of the above-noticed accusations.*'

The CJP had alleged in his petition that no evidence at all was shown to him and "in fact, no official except DG ISI had some documents with him but he also did not show anything to the deponent" (the CJP). He added that they only accused him of having secured a seat for his son in Bolan Medical College while he was serving as judge of Balochistan High Court.

The CJP had further alleged that the DG MI and the DG ISI kept insisting that he should resign from his office while he continued to assert strongly that the allegations were baseless and were being levelled only for a collateral purpose and that he would not resign at any cost and would rather face the said false charges before all the forums.

The judgment further stated that:

> 'While the CJP was still at the President's Camp Office in Rawalpindi during the said crucial 'FIVE HOURS' and when according to the CJP he was being detained there against his wishes after 12 noon and when according to the respondents he was sitting there, in the company of the intelligence chiefs examining the reference and the material available in support thereof, a notification dated March 9, 2007, was issued by the Government of Pakistan in the Law, Justice and Human Rights Division mentioning therein that since the President of Pakistan had been pleased to make a reference called a 'DIRECTION' by Article 209(5) of the Constitution to the SJC against the CJP, therefore, the President had restrained Mr Justice Iftikhar M Chaudhry from acting as the Chief Justice of Pakistan or even as a Judge of the Supreme Court of Pakistan.'

The judgment made clear that the case had nothing to do with army as an institution. The issue before the Court was an act of the President and it was just an accident or a coincidence that the said President also happened to be the Chief of Army Staff.

The judgment was appreciated because actually the involvement of junior military officers was minimal and was limited to the specific orders of Gen Musharraf only when needed. The emergency order was planned and ordered by Gen Musharraf and no other army or intelligence officer could be blamed for it. Therefore, Gen Musharraf alone must be held responsible for the treatment he meted out to the judiciary and the judges.

The senior army officers believed that Gen Musharraf tried to despatch the chief justice because he wanted extension in his tenure that was expiring; election results of his own desire and government of his own choice. He considered the chief justice as the only hurdle in the achievement of his objectives. Gen Musharraf used his senior colleagues to press the chief justice to quit. The DG MI was the strong man of Gen Musharraf being his relative too. Gen Musharraf acted on the advice of the DG MI, who was in fact responsible for spoiling Gen Musharraf's most matters related to judiciary.

Under Gen Musharraf's pressure the DG MI, DG IB and the then Secretary Interior and some others had submitted affidavits in the Supreme Court against the chief justice. He reminded that the DG ISI, Gen Ashfaq Kayani, did not submit an affidavit and despite Gen Musharraf's intensive efforts, the then DG ISI kept a reasonable distance from this issue in grace. The chief justice and all the members of the full court had praised Gen Kayani for showing such rare courage.

Signed by ten judges of the apex court, the 196-page detailed judgment in the Constitution Petition no: 21 / 2007 of the Chief Justice of Pakistan Iftikhar M Chaudhry against his illegal removal was issued after about thirty months because 13 out of 17 judges were sent home on 3rd November 2007 and returned back in the third week of March 2009. About the president's inherent powers, the judgment held that this Court had declared in *Nawaz Sharif Case* (**PLD 1993 SC 473**) that:

> "*Unfortunately, this belief that he enjoys some inherent or implied powers besides those specifically conferred in him is a mistaken one. In view of the express provisions of our written Constitution dealing with fullness, the powers and duties, there is no room of any residual or enabling powers inherent in any authority.*"

Justice Ramday had also observed that:

> "*it is, therefore, not possible for me to accept that in the constitutional, the legal and the legislative framework of our country, as noticed above, which did not recognise any inherent, ancillary or incidental powers with the competent authority to suspend or to restrain from working even a civil servant of the lowest grade who had no constitutional security, the Chief Justice of the country whose tenure in office stood guaranteed by the Constitution, could be suspended from office or could be restrained from exercising the judicial powers appertaining to his office.*"

The full court also declared the Acting Chief Justices' appointment of 9th & 22nd March 2007, without lawful authority. The verdict was announced with 10 judges in favour and three against. The three judges who opposed the verdict were not against the restoration of the chief justice; they differed on the constitutional point that the president was empowered to file a reference against the chief justice.

The three judges who dissented were Justice Faqir Muhammad Khokhar, Justice M Javed Buttar and Justice Saeed Ashhad. The ten judges who handed down the historic judgment were Justice Khalil-ur-Rahman Ramday, Justice M Nawaz Abbasi, Justice Mian Shakirullah Jan, Justice Tassadduq Hussain Jillani, Justice Nasirul Mulk, Justice Raja Fayyaz Ahmed, Justice Ch Ijaz Ahmed, Justice Syed Jamshed Ali, Justice Hamid Ali Mirza and Justice Ghulam Rabbani.

JUSTICE RAMDAY RE-EMPLOYED:

Justice Khalil ur Rehman Ramday of the Supreme Court of Pakistan was going to retire on 12th January 2010, the Chief Justice Iftikhar M Chaudhry had sent recommendations to the President that:

- Justice Saqib Nisar of the Lahore High Court, who was at no:2 in the seniority list, be elevated and be sent to the Supreme Court against a permanent vacancy caused by Justice Ramday's retirement.

- Justice Kh Sharif be left over in Punjab to continue as the Chief Justice of LHC.

- Services of Justice Ramday be hired again to continue as the judge of the Supreme Court for one year at least.

A threat of an imminent clash of the executive and judiciary surfaced because the President Asif Ali Zardari and the Governor of Punjab, late Salmaan Taseer, were resisting the appointment of judges recommended by the Chief Justice.

The president had refused CJ's recommendation for the elevation of Justice Saqib Nisar, the second senior-most judge of the LHC, arguing that instead the chief justice of the LHC, Justice Kh Sharif should be elevated to the Supreme Court.

Governor Taseer was also determined to freeze the appointment of judges against approximately 30 vacancies in the LHC on recommendations of Kh Sharif, Chief Justice of the LHC. The judgment of the Supreme Court in the Al-jihad Trust Case was being played from both sides.

[In 1994, the then President Farooq Leghari, acting on the advice of Prime Minister Benzair Bhutto, had appointed 20 judges to the LHC as well as acting chief justices to the LHC and the High Court of Sindh.]

Those appointments of pro-government judges were resented by all relevant stakeholders, including the Bar Councils of the country. The petitions were filed and finally the issue was resolved through a verdict of the Judges' Case (PLD 1996 SC 34)}

13th February 2010: Justice Khalil ur Rehman Ramday could have been ceased to function after completion of his service but the CJP Iftikhar M Chaudhry kept him working as he had sent his name to the Presidency to be an ad hoc judge. President Zardari had withheld Ramday's name because, as per Ministry of Law's advice, the appointment of a retired SC judge as an ad hoc judge was in violation of Article 182 of the Constitution as well as the principle laid down in the Judge's Case of 1996.

Here the Judges Case was interpreted that such appointments could be done only in extraordinary situations and the number of judges could be increased after the sanctioned strength of the SC is filled with permanently appointed judges. Lack of transparency was also visible in Lahore High Court's scenario encompassing CJ Khwaja Sharif & Justice Saqib Nisar's appointments divulging a popular impression that:

'The slogan of independence of the judiciary is orchestrated only when the PPP government is called in docks'.

The history will remember those hilarious moments when the SC's judgment of 16th December 2009 in NRO case was announced in which all the 17 SC judges reached the same decision in a matter that should have led to several differing opinions even if they agreed in essence to declare the NRO unconstitutional.

The same spirit was seen in early 2010 when an unprecedented unanimous resolution was passed by all the judges of the SC that Justice Ramday and Justice Rehmat H Jaffery be retained as ad hoc judges. Perhaps this was the reason that the sitting government immediately formulated a different way for appointment of judges and floated it on Parliament's floor which was passed as 18th Amendment just two months after that adventure of ad-hocism.

[Both J Jaffery and J Ramday, especially the later, were seen as close associates of the CJP Iftikhar M Chaudhry and were often seen on the same bench as he presided, along with another ad hoc judge J Ghulam Rabbani.

J Ramday was given preference for appointment as ad hoc judge over other recently retired judge Sardar Raza Khan because, perhaps, he had presided the 13 member bench of the SC in July 2007 which restored the CJP when the later was made dysfunctional by Gen Musharraf.

Justice Sardar M Raza Khan was not recommended for further appointment like Justice Ramday though he was also going on retirement on 9th February 2010.]

Coming back; the issues of seniority, suitability, and knowledge of law were to be judged by the chief justice whereas the Presidents and Prime Ministers could imagine the political suitability of a perspective judge. Amidst all the discussions till then, judicial appointments in Pakistan were not considered to be made upon the recommendation of an independent commission, as done in the UK, or after vetting by Parliament if the US model is followed.

[However, a process now stands evolved after April 2010's 18th & 19th Amendments in the Constitution]

The President and the Governor Punjab were under the impression that they could obstruct the appointments of judges to the LHC indefinitely. Since the refusal to appoint judges to the LHC was seriously undermining the capacity of that court and it was a matter of public importance, as envisaged in Article 199 of the Constitution, either the LHC or the Supreme Court could direct the president to comply with the Supreme Court's direction.

The government opted to proceed by the advices of their cronies. Here again, contrary to CJP Mr Iftikhar M Chaudhary's recommendation, President Asif Ali Zardari issued a notification on 13th February 2010 purporting to elevate Justice Khwaja Sharif (Chief Justice of the Lahore High Court) as a judge of the Supreme Court and appointing Justice Saqib Nisar as Acting Chief Justice of Lahore High Court.

However, both of the judges refused to accept the notification as valid. The then Federal Law Minister Babar Awan had met CJ Kh Sharif one Thursday evening at CJ's residence but Kh Sharif had refused to proceed for the Supreme Court.

CJP Iftikhar M Chaudhary, immediately took *suo moto* notice of the said step of the President and, in a rare nightly emergency session, constituted a 3-member bench that suspended the aforesaid notifications and declared the notifications issued by the Law and Justice Division as against the constitutional provisions.

The government initially defended its actions but relented in the face of rising public pressure and criticism from the bar, opposition political parties, and the media. The government withdrew the notifications on 17th February 2010 and the PM had to agree to make all judicial appointments in the Supreme Court and the High Courts according to the recommendations of the Chief Justice.

Amidst these developments, some constitutional experts, senior lawyers and former judges openly reflected their views, while quoting the judgment in the Judge's Case of 1996 (Al-Jehad Trust case) and criticizing the Chief Justice's recommendations that elevation of Justice Saqib Nisar of the Punjab High Court as a SC judge and appointment of recently retired Justice Khalilur Rehman Ramday on ad hoc basis was not valid.

Whereas some of the top lawyers also held that there was no mention in the 125-page Al-Jihad Trust case ruling that the chief justice of a high court must be elevated as a Supreme Court judge when needed and that a judge junior to the provincial chief justice could not be promoted. Similarly, the Judges Case did not bar the appointment of ad hoc judges.

Regarding appointments of the Chief Justices of the High Courts and the Supreme Court, it was held that the senior-most judge of that court would have a legitimate expectation to be appointed to that position once it becomes vacant. This issue was different from that taken up by the Supreme Court in the Judges' Case. Here the president's spokesmen were arguing that the senior-most judge of the High Court ought to be elevated to the Supreme Court.

It was generally opined that the Judges' Case laid down the principle of seniority for appointment of existing judges to the post of the chief justice, but it did not deal with the appointment of new judges to the Supreme Court, and it did not necessarily require the chief justices of the High Courts to be elevated when a vacancy occurs in the Supreme Court.

The top legal experts, including former CJP Justice (retd) Saeeduzzaman Siddiqui, Justice (retd) Wajihuddin Ahmad, Akram Sheikh and even the petitioner of the Al Jihad Trust case Wahabul Khairi advocate, in their views had said that:

'It is the CJP's discretion to promote any judge of the high court. It is not necessary to appoint the senior-most judge of a high court as a Supreme Court judge '

They agreed that the CJP's recommendations were in line with the Constitution as well as Al Jihad Trust case.

ELEVATING CJs IN HIGH COURTS:

Moeen Cheema, a lecturer of Law in an Australian University, interestingly observed that:

> "There was neither constitutional convention nor past practice to elevate the senior-most judges of a High Court to the Supreme Court. A comparison of Articles 177 & 180 of the Constitution of Pakistan made by the supreme Court held that the absence of the words 'most senior' in Article 177 for appointment of Judges of the Supreme Court would show that the seniority of a Judge in the High Court is not a sine qua non for his appointment as a Judge of the Supreme Court."

Moreover, this specific issue was also discussed in the case of Supreme Court Bar Association through its **_Hamid Khan vs. the Federation of Pakistan_** *(2002)* case where, once again, a 5-member bench examined the appointment of judges in the Supreme Court and the issue of seniority in the High Courts for such appointments. Explaining the spirit of the Judges' Case and subsequent precedents, the Supreme Court had held that:

> 'The contention that the chief justice of a High Court is entitled to be elevated to the Supreme Court due to seniority is misconceived and travels beyond the parameters indicated in the Judges' Case. In our considered view, the scope of seniority and legitimate expectancy enunciated in those cases is restricted to the appointments of the Chief Justice of a High Court and the Chief Justice of Pakistan, and these issues neither apply nor can be extended to the appointment of Judges of the Supreme Court.'

[**Mr Justice Khwaja M Sharif** was born on 9th December 1948 in Lahore. His father Kh Sadiq was one of the cloth merchants of Anarkali Bazar, Lahore. He was a close friend of Mian Muhammad Sharif (father of Nawaz Sharif and Shahbaz Sharif). Both of these families had joint interests in trading.

Khawaja Sharif was elected twice as President of Lahore Bar Association in the year 1989 and 1991. On both occasions, he is known to have used very strong [*and objectionable*] language against the Bhutto family.

In view of his loyalty to the Nawaz Sharif's family, Khawaja Sharif was appointed as Advocate General of Punjab by Shahbaz Sharif on 31st May 1997. On the recommendation of Shahbaz Sharif, he was appointed as judge in the Lahore High Court on 21st May 1998.

After the martial law of 1999, Justice Kh Sharif was one of those *'brave judges of Lahore High Court'* who took oath on PCO 1999, thus providing legitimacy to the military regime of Gen Musharraf but in emergency of 3rd Nov 2007, he remained deposed from the bench till 17th March 2009 when he was restored along with others. During deposition, Justice Kh Sharif used some of the worst kind of language against President Zardari and the PPP; the media record is there as witness. He was appointed Chief Justice of Lahore High Court on 12th April 2009.

In 2009, Justice Kh Sharif's LHC decided to adjourn elections in Rawalpindi and Lahore as per the wishes of his masters M/S Sharif brothers. Later the decision was quashed by the Supreme Court of Pakistan.

In December 2009, Chief Justice Iftikhar M Chaudhry's escort car met with an accident. Nothing happened to the car in which Justice Iftikhar was travelling but the then CJ LHC Kh Sharif said that the accident was in fact a conspiracy against the CJP Justice Chaudhry by the people who wanted him to give certain decision in their favour. *'Perhaps it was a warning because the CJP is tightening the noose around powerful mafias,'* he said, indirectly pointing towards President Zardari and the PPP's sitting government then.]

18th February 2010: Justice Ramday was appointed as ad hoc judge of SC, Justice Saqib Nisar and Justice Asif Saeed Khosa were elevated to the apex court while thirty-four new judges were appointed in the LHC and SHC. The outcome of the tussle between the Presidency and the Supreme Court came to an end when earlier on 16th February PM Mr Gilani reached the Supreme Court to attend a reception and invited the Chief Justice to the Prime Minister House. The next day the Chief Justice had a one-to-one meeting with the PM and the dust got settled.

However, the fact remains that the CJP Iftikhar M Chaudhry wanted to keep his team members at places where he wanted. Justice Ramday was the head of bench in 2007 which had brought the then defunct CJP Mr Chaudhry back to his seat. He was the judge heading the bench who made possible CJP Mr Chaudhry to sit on his seat again on 20th July 2007.

When Iftikhar M Chaudhry occupied the chair of CJP, Justice Ramday, being the senior most judge in the Supreme Court became his right-hand man. Among the bar it gave rise to an impression that because the CJP depends on him so *'he has [mostly] stepped out of his shoes'*.

Though the CJP Justice Chaudhry got his words and opinion approved in the appointments of three judges i.e. Justice Khawaja Sharif, Justice Saqib Nisar and Justice Ramday but the President House had taken it seriously; another cold war erupted between the two major institutions.

Media also played its role as usual. Ansar Abbasi of Islamabad Jang daily wrote many columns defending his Chief Justice; Nazir Naji of Lahore circle started series of threatening stories in Jang portraying Justice Kh Sharif because of his intimate relationships with Sharif Brothers of PML(N). Arif Nizami and Dr Shahid Masood also joined the orchestra against Mr Zardari.

On the other side the PPP had also done similar arrangements by winning people on ARY News through anchor Kashif Abbasi, Javed Malik and Dr Danish. In that whole scenario, there were fingers pointed out towards Judiciary's impartial behaviour while trying to settle the old scores. It was an obvious outcome.

SC GOT DENTED IT'S IMPARTIALITY:

The implications of this cold war surfaced when during March and April 2010, NAB and the Federal Ministry of Law did not bother to write a letter for re-opening of old Swiss cases against President Zardari and avoided on one pretext or the other. The Supreme Court had called all the concerned officers of NAB, Ministry of Law and Attorney General's Office in Court to explain that why the verdict of Supreme Court was not being implemented but all efforts went in vain.

Two Attorney Generals including Anwar Mansoor and one Federal Law Secretary, Justice ® Aaqil Mirza had also resigned but the issue of sending letter to Swiss authorities could not be solved. Ultimately the Court had to issue call notices for the Federal law Minister Babar Awan for appearance on 25th May 2010 which phenomenon was unparalleled, exceptional and extraordinary in Pakistan's contemporary history.

In this exercise too, the Supreme Court suffered on account of judicial wisdom and impartiality. The graph of judiciary's credibility was pulled down by the media live debates where more of the questions were related to the following points:

- Under the Constitutional provisions, Mr Zardari was enjoying immunity while he was holding the President's office, so should not be pressed.

- In 16th December 2009's judgment against NRO, there was a list of 8041 beneficiaries of NRO, then why Mr Zardari was singled out to be named out in derogatory sense.

- During hearing of NRO case, on 12th December 2009, the Chief Justice had mentioned to bring the list of people whose bank debts were condoned in billions. Next day the State Bank of Pakistan had placed an exhaustive list of defaulters since 1971, but the Supreme Court neither passed any order in that respect, nor the case was taken up further.

- The judiciary was blamed that because the list contained names of stalwarts from PML(N) and their family members as miss-users of loans, so the Chief Justice had purposefully ignored it.

- In the said NRO's judgment, the second named person was Justice ® Malik Qayyum. The Court had never bothered to chase him like President Zardari because the former was their old colleague.

The battle between the two big heads [of the Judiciary & Executive] entered a new phase when, in the third week of May 2010, a bench of Lahore High Court headed by Justice Kh Sharif in person, announced three years imprisonment for the Federal Interior Minister Rehman Malik under sec 31(A) of the NAB Ordinance on the charge of '**being absent from the Court**'.

Just after few moments, the President Zardari, while using his powers of Article 45 of the Constitution, condoned his Interior Minister's sentence; again causing another debate in the media. What the Lahore High Court & CJ Kh Sharif got out of balancing the personal scores to please their bosses in PML(N). What benefit for the higher judiciary as a whole.

A side effect: Justice Khalil ur Rehman Ramday, especially after his re-appointment in February 2010, had become so arrogant that many sober senior advocates of the bar started avoiding appearing before him in the Court. He had developed habit of bullying the bar members, particularly appearing on behalf of the ruling PPP, without reasons or cogent causes. One episode of 12th May 2010 may be taken as an example:

> 'The CJP and Justice Ramday were hearing petition (not regular but of a mercy type) of a lady teacher who was occupying a government house above her category in Islamabad and was asked by the Ministry of Housing to vacate it.
>
> During the hearing, Justice Ramday became furious when he was told about his own judgment which he had passed in a similar case just six months earlier, conveying a message that **'Government accommodations are not jagirs of civil servants so should not be kept held against the rules.'**
>
> The bench was told that till that day the High Courts had also decided eighteen (18) similar cases on the basis of Justice Ramday's above referred judgment.
>
> The judge threatened a young & new or under training lawyer (who had simply accompanied the fresh allottee officer and had handed over details of J Ramday's earlier judgments referred above) that he would be sent to jail straightaway for contempt of the Court.
>
> Ironically, that junior lawyer had immediately raised his hands for handcuffs saying:
>
> **'If the contempt comes on speaking truth before the apex court and especially while quoting the sitting judge's own judgment, then please go ahead'**
>
> The CJP Iftikhar M Chaudhry immediately intervened and handled the sentimental situation in a nice way but the panel went against their own earlier judgment. Justice Hurray!
>
> What a character of Pakistani judges occupying seats in higher judiciary.'

The media played at high pitch in this respect saying that the CJP and the PML(N) wanted to keep Khwaja Sharif in Punjab for greater political agendas of the ruling elite and other judicial favours in the High Court. President Zardari wanted all judicial appointments by following the principles of seniority.

On 22nd March 2010; In Faisalabad, Pakistani judiciary, engaged in a do-or-die battle for gaining independence from the executive, as both judges and lawyers took positions against each other to boycott the courts and staged protests after a lawyer slapped and manhandled a judge while he was holding the court. The menace spread all over the Punjab province next day.

Reacting to the aggressive attack, the judges belonging to subordinate judiciary stopped working demanding immediate and stern action against the lawyer Liaqat Javed who slapped the Civil Judge Tariq Mahmood, terming it extremely outrageous and devastating for the prestige of judiciary. All the judges wore black armbands as mark of protest till the cancellation of that lawyer's license.

With another day passed, about one hundred judges tendered their resignations in different cities of Punjab. This forced the Lahore High Court to take *suo moto* notice of the situation by ordering contempt of court case against the lawyer. However, the lawyer could not be arrested as he fled from home.

Then it was the turn of lawyers, who boycotted the courts and staged protests demanding the withdrawal of contempt of court case against the accused lawyer. The lawyers' defiant posture against the judges brought the institution of judiciary at crossroads again where it was faced with an enemy from within, the lawyer's community.

There had been reports of repeated attacks from lawyers on the media men, police officials, and their repeated attempts to pressure a court to release on bail a lawyer leader accused of torturing to death a minor-aged housemaid. Former vice chairman of Punjab Bar Council, Hamid Khan disturbingly opined:

> *"Such incidents not only brought bad name to legal fraternity but also posed a serious question mark on the future of judiciary's independence since these lawyers rise to become judges."*

The incident of slapping the judge was *"totally outrageous and uncalled for"* since the judge, hearing a loan default case, had refused to release the accused on bail as requested by the lawyer who insisted that the amount had already been deposited.

The judge ruled against the request observing that the case record had no mention of such payment. This flared the lawyer up and he started abusing the judge, and suddenly rushed to the rostrum and reportedly slapped the judge repeatedly. The judge was rescued by court officials and lawyers.

On 29th June 2010, addressing the Hafizabad Bar Association, LHC CJ Khwaja M Sharif asked *'the PPP to quit the Punjab coalition if it had objections to provincial Secretary Prosecution Rana Maqbool'*. Mr Maqbool, being IGP Sindh, was alleged of physically torturing President Zardari when he was in police custody during 1997-98 in the 2nd stint of Nawaz Sharif as prime minister.

Punjab PPP's leader Raja Riaz had even called the LHC CJ a *"PML-N spokesman"* and asked him to resign from his office to contest election on the PML(N) ticket if he was interested in politics. *"We will foil such designs of 'Kh Sharif Wish' against democracy,"* was the PPP's stance. The Punjab PPP roared with the words:

> *"We are going to file a reference in the Supreme Judicial Council against Khwaja Sharif for acting as a PML-N spokesman. Is a chief justice authorized to represent a proclaimed offender and can he advise a major political party to quit the government.*
>
> *Whether the statement of Khwaja Sharif was worthy of a high court chief justice?*
>
> *This is a conspiracy against the PPP government. CJ Kh Sharif is trying to corner the largest political party of the federation but we will not allow him to succeed. The PPP had defeated military dictatorships in the past and now it was capable of fighting against judicial dictatorship."*

PPP's Information Secretary MNA [late] Fauzia Wahab told the media that Khwaja Sharif's statement had "unveiled the mystery" as to why there had been "furors" over his elevation to the Supreme Court.

> *"He (Khwaja Sharif) is PML(N)'s trusted fellow and even he has admitted this in his last speech; that was why the Leaguers wanted to retain him in Lahore."*

Former SCBA president Aitzaz Ahsan had also criticized CJ Khwaja Sharif for 'giving a political statement'. *"A judge should resign from his / her office if he or she wants to do politics. Such statements bring a bad name to the judiciary and judges should refrain from doing so as they are supposed to speak only through their judgments,"* Mr Ahsan said.

Ahsan was on forefront in **'free judiciary movement'**, every one knew. He then added that:

"The people are raising fingers at the Supreme Court for laying so much emphasis on NRO cases as they think it was only because President Zardari was one of the beneficiaries.

Such a comment must not come from any member of the independent judiciary. These kinds of statements are bringing a bad name to the judiciary."

The rift between the PPP and the PML(N) developed posing serious questions on the superior judiciary. The whole conflict revolved around a single judge - Justice Khwaja Sharif - who had close ties with the PML(N). The media was of the view that the reaction displayed by the PML(N) to the political stand-off between the President and the CJP was of no surprise. Similar to calling Benazir Bhutto a 'threat to security', to undermine her governments in the 90s, PML had termed President Zardari as 'a threat to democracy' in 2010.

The intelligentsia pondered that what was so great about Chief Justice of the LHC, Khwaja Sharif, that he must at all costs stay in Punjab to oversee the judiciary there? Similar concerns were raised by many renowned names in the judicial community, including Ali Ahmad Kurd, once a very stringent supporter of CJ Iftikhar M Chaudhry, who expressed disappointment over the events and deplored that it appeared as Justice Khwaja had become the most important individual in the country.

[The history would be written as it was purely a political conflict with its core power politics in Punjab and the superior judiciary became a part of it. It was on record that Justice Khawaja Sharif had made 28 of his own politically motivated recommendations for the judges to be posted in Lahore High Court, only to be scrutinized by the Governor of Punjab.

The Governor, (late) Mr Taseer, once informed the President in his written summary that out of 28 persons recommended by CJ LHC, five persons Shahid Karim, Mamoon Rashid Sheikh, Waqar Hassan Mir, Ms Gulzar Butt; and Mian Mahmood advocate were directly or indirectly affiliated with the CJ [Kh Sharif]'s own Law Chamber.]

The rift between the Governor and the PML(N) widened when late Salman Taseer became a hurdle in the way of PML(N)'s politically motivated judicial appointments. The Punjab government used all its influence over the judiciary to get Justice Khwaja's recommended judges appointed at all cost. The Governor, however, ignoring all pressures, decided to accept 19 out of the 28 appointments. The Governor objected that the CJ LHC had evidently ignored certain judicious principles of seniority and legitimate expectancy. Pakistan was repeating the history as a senior lawyer Dr Khalid Ranjha said that:

> 'A vacuum is being deliberately created to pave the way for third party interference; an interference that Pakistan can't allow nor afford at this time'.

In the contemporary judicial history of Pakistan, some judges of higher judiciary could not prove themselves above board. Some were directly involved in financial corruption whereas one Chief Justice of a high court had openly sided with the ruling political party of the province, as detailed in above paragraphs.

Pakistan's judiciary under CJP Iftikhar M Chaudhry then had to prove it 'independent' as was anticipated.

> [That was why a poll conducted by Gallop Pakistan, referring to 'ARY News' dated 23rd June 2011, told that 'Pakistan's apex judiciary is assented by 51% people only'. Much alarming! It should have been rated 80%+ in the backdrop of lawyer's movement of 2007-09.]

SENIOR OFFICERS SENTENCED:

30th March 2010: Former Additional Director General of FIA Ahmed Riaz Sheikh, an NRO beneficiary, who was allegedly promoted despite being convicted in corruption cases, was arrested from courtroom on the orders of the Supreme Court and NAB was ordered to confiscate his property and submit a report to the court within three days.

Mr Shiekh was basically punished being a close aide of President Zardari and was sentenced to 14 years of imprisonment in 2001 on charges of corruption but got benefit from the NRO. While he was sent to jail by SC, not only important PPP personalities met him there but the president granted general pardon to Riaz Sheikh.

On the same day, NAB was given twenty-four hours to write a letter to the Swiss authorities regarding re-opening of corruption cases withdrawn under NRO, upon failure Chairman NAB was asked to face the winds of jail. NAB Chairman told the court that opinion of the Law Ministry was awaited regarding writing a letter to re-open cases against the president.

31st March 2010: Attorney General for Pakistan Anwar Mansoor informed the SC that the Federal Law Ministery was creating hurdles in reopening the Swiss cases. The court directed the Attorney General to assist Law Ministry in completing paper work on that issue. The court directed the government to send the letter to Swiss authorities by 1 pm that day after getting approval by the Prime Minister.

The PM Gilani was never so courageous thus the SC's all threats were simply ignored. The said letter was not written despite tall instructions of 24 hours or till 1 pm etc and the Supreme Court could never get the orders implemented though NAB had told the court earlier that a letter to the Swiss government against President Zardari was on the way. A blatant lie it was.

Next day, the Attorney General for Pakistan Anwar Mansoor Khan resigned from his post.

As per media versions, the Supreme Court was openly helping out the Punjab Government by getting them back their buddy CJ Khawaja Sharif but was adamantly going against the PPP in getting Mr Zardari hanged.

20th April 2010: 18th Constitutional Amendment was passed. The details are available in next pages.

On 29th April 2010; President Zardari, through a clandestine move, regularised the services of all federal law officers appointed during the period from October 1995 to October 2009 with hefty salary package besides other perks and privileges by promulgating an ordinance. The three-page ordinance was made part of gazette notification without making it public. The ordinance was named the **Central Law Officers (Amendment) Ordinance 2010** and it came into force with immediate effect. The said ordinance was promulgated with retrospective effect from 1st October 1995.

In clause 7 of this ordinance, it has been laid down in the sub clause A that *'all the appointments of federal counsels made by the federal government from 1st October 1995 to 30th October 2009 are regularized and the fees paid to them and other perks and privileges provided to them be deemed regularized'.*

In the sub section B it was said that *'any payment due to them if not made during this period be considered to be payable and this would be paid'.* The legal experts were of the view that the ordinance was aimed

943

at not only benefiting all the federal counsels appointed during Benazir Bhutto and Nawaz Sharif regimes of 1990s but also those who were enrolled during Gen Musharraf's rule for nine years.

These counsels appeared before the courts against Chief Justice of Pakistan (CJP) Iftikhar M Chaudhry during the hearing of reference filed against him. The beneficiaries of this ordinance were Sharif ud Din Pirzada, Waseem Sajjad, Khalid Ranjha, Ahmad Raza Kasuri, Hafeez Pirzada, Farooq Naik, Khalid Anwar and others.

The sub clause 3-A of clause 4 of the ordinance was amended that the Additional Attorney General, Deputy Attorney General, standing counsel and federal counsel would send their resignation to the president for acceptance.

7th May 2010: Federal Secretary Law Justice (R) Aqil Mirza resigned (though citing his poor health as reason but) because he was summoned by a five-member bench of the SC hearing the implementation of NRO verdict case.

J Aqil Mirza was the fourth senior official who had resigned since the SC started hearing the case regarding non-implementation of its judgment against the NRO. Others were NAB Chairman Nawid Ahsan, Attorney General Anwar Mansoor and Senior Joint Secretary Akbar Khan Achakzai. All these senior figures left their seats hailing Pakistan's independent judiciary who was ignoring its own words of 22nd December to get back the written off loans but was swiftly counting on scores against Mr Zardari; the only one of 8041 NRO beneficiaries.

17th May 2010: The Lahore High Court, under the able supervision of CJ Khawaja Sharif, restored the conviction of Federal Interior Minister Rehman Malik in two NAB references. President Zardari immediately granted pardon to Mr Malik to save his friendship and Mr Malik from more humiliation. Another NRO beneficiary, Sajjad Haider, Staff Officer of the Interior Minister Rehman Malik, probably a co-accused in Yellow Cab scam with the Interior Minister, was also granted pardon by the president.

Though it was termed as an unprecedented favour for those involved in corruption cases but the fact remained that the LHC had restored their convictions just to please their masters then holding reins of the Punjab government. The said cases were allegedly established by PML government in 1997 through a criminal minded pseudo-politician Mian

Saif ur Rehman of *Eotesab* Bureau when allocated special tasks of pushing all senior officers to jail who were on key posts in Benazir Bhutto's last tenure of 1994-96.

FACEBOOK BANNED:

On 21st May 2010: First time in the history of Pakistan, some superior court had taken notice of public protests and directed the federal government to lodge an official protest with the American authorities over the competition of drawing the blasphemous sketches of the Holy Prophet (PBUH) at a famous website [Facebook]. Justice Ijaz Ahmed Chaudhry had directed the Ministry of Foreign Affairs (MoFA) to submit the copy of official protest in the court.

The Court itself formulated the main body of the text as under:

> *"As per laws of commerce and business, Facebook is governed by legal jurisdiction of the United States of America and this global social networking has deliberately or recklessly been responsible for hurting feelings and causing discomfort to the majority of Muslim population of Pakistan.*
>
> *Facebook has deliberately or recklessly not taken effective measures for preventing, stopping or blocking blasphemous contest to which it has complete and autonomous authority and a built-in mechanism to block such profane misbehaviour or misconduct. These mechanisms have either been deliberately or recklessly not administered for preventing, stopping or blocking this blasphemous content taking place on Facebook.*
>
> *The announcement of this very blasphemous contest has caused an immense furore and enraged millions of majority Muslims of Pakistan and around the globe, who attach an immense sanctity to the holy status granted to prophet of Islam, Prophet Muhammad (Peace Be Upon Him)."*

Various countries including China, United Arab Emirates, Iran and Saudi Arabia had already imposed ban on it which had made easier for MoFA to raise the issue at international level.

It is a common understanding in law that a speech, an article written or read, any caricature or image designed to spread panic, incite violence and perpetuate hate is not protected by the principle of freedom of expression. Many statutes around the world forbid speech and written words which are intended to express hatred towards someone on account of that person's colour, race, nationality, ethnicity or religion.

The issue was that on 20th May 2010 a 'Draw Mohammad Day' was celebrated on the popular social networking site Facebook to 'avenge' the censorship of insulting remarks and images from a South Park episode by Comedy Central for fear of retribution from a 'radical' Muslim group. Facebook, rather than removing the page for reasons of hate speech and violation of its own Terms of Use, expressed disappointment at being banned in Pakistan and termed its website as:

'...... a place where people can openly discuss issues and express their views, while respecting the rights and feelings of others.'

It was the second time hit on the Muslim sentiments. Previously, in 2005, Jyllands-Posten, a Danish newspaper had published cartoons depicting the Prophet SAW (peace be upon him). Despite domestic and international outpour of rage from Muslims, no legal action was taken by the Danish authorities against the newspaper. In fact, the Danish public prosecutor had dropped the case declaring that he found 'no evidence' of insult or degradation in the publication.

Syed Umair Javed, in his article appeared on *22nd May 2010 in 'The News'* rightly pointed out that:

'The right to free speech has become a funny concept, at least for Muslims. While the Holocaust must not be denied – if you do so in Europe they will arrest and prosecute you – it is perfectly fine to ridicule Islam, the Prophet Mohammad (SAW) and Muslims – but not the holocaust.'

Such writings and caricatures are always deliberate and well-thought to incite religious and social tension in very peculiar circumstances. Thus for those, who think it is their right to taunt and insult a religion, it is to consume that basically they push some ones towards fundamentalism. There is no right without responsibility; and the principle should have been observed by the 'artists & actors' sponsoring that episode.

LATIF KHOSA SENT HOME AGAIN:

21st July 2010: Prime Minister's Adviser Sardar Latif Khosa, who had to quit office in disgrace for the second time during PPP's government, was trying to rewrite government rules and had he succeeded, present and future advisers to the premier would have become more powerful than their respective ministers. However, the PM Gilani stopped Mr Khosa before he could do any real damage. The fact remained that:

> "When Khosa phoned Gilani the other day, he was told that he was there just to advise the prime minister and was not to take decisions relating to the Information Technology Ministry independently."

The PM told Mr Khosa in unambiguous terms that since he himself presided over the IT Ministry and was competent to take decisions pertaining to it, it was his prerogative to allocate or not to allocate any powers to the adviser. Furthermore, that the IT Ministry would not directly send any file to the adviser for decisions but would continue to dispatch every summary to the Prime Minister's Office.

Mr Khosa insisted that being adviser with the status of a federal minister, it was his legal right to have all the powers concerning the IT Ministry and take decisions alone about its affairs. As a result, the PM Secretariat issued an order explaining the powers of the adviser and the authority of the minister in-charge [the PM himself in this case] of the IT Ministry.

This tangle led Khosa to his resignation, which he handed over but only after meeting President Zardari.

The source said the outgoing adviser was having a long running turf war with IT Secretary Najeebul Malik on the issue that who would run the IT Ministry. The Secretary did not send any file to the adviser pleading that this was not permitted under the Rules of Business, and instead used to submit all cases to the minister in-charge; whereas Mr Khosa repeatedly urged the Secretary to show him all the files and summaries. The Secretary stood ground and refused to oblige.

For quite some time ago, Mr Khosa had landed in a serious controversy over appointments and dismissals of directors in some organizations under the IT Ministry apart from his row with some segments of the telecom sector. However, he was a luckless diehard PPP leader, who earlier had to quit as Attorney General after he was accused of having taken Rs:3 million from a litigant but the major reason was some thing else behind his exit.

It was the attacking role of the People's Lawyers Forum (PLF) headed by Mr Khosa against the appointment of Masood Chishti, a junior legal mate of the Federal Law Minister Babar Awan, as the Federal Law Secretary. The Punjab chapter of the PLF, run by Khosa's son Khurram Khosa, had revolted to protest against Chishti's nomination.

At that time, the PM got his resignation but made him adviser due to the backing of Mr Zardari.

JUDGE's EXTENSION ISSUE & MISC:

On 4th December 2010, the Judicial Commission of Pakistan (JCP) proposed Justice Iqbal Hameed-ur-Rehman, judge of Lahore High Court, for his appointment as the Chief Justice of Islamabad High Court and Anwar Kansi and Riaz Khan as judges of the IHC, and also agreed to extend the tenure of four additional judges of the Balochistan High Court and six judges of Sindh High Court.

However, cases of Justice Bhajandas Dejwani and Justice Rukhsana Ahmed were deferred till the next meeting. The legal experts said that this was the beginning of tussle between judiciary and legal community.

The Supreme Court Bar Association termed those extensions to additional judges of the high courts as detrimental to the independence of judiciary. Moreover, that the extensions dropped by the JCP sent a poor message - a woman and member of the minority were made exceptions.

On the same day, the SCBA president in a written statement, given to media persons at the Supreme Court premises, had also expressed concern over the large number of enforced disappearances. It was noted that the disappearance of persons by the security forces had re-emerged after a short spell of reducing this practice dramatically.

The commission of missing persons had gone ineffective. Perhaps it had not comprehended the serious role that they were playing in recording evidence of those who were tortured during their period in arbitrary detention. The commission could not inspire the confidence of victims and was reduced to redundancy.

The SCBA also agitated that the Government had not fulfilled its promise on legal reforms. The jurisdiction of ordinary courts had neither been extended to FATA area nor the fundamental rights available to the people living there, who continued to suffer the rigors of the draconian Frontier Crimes Regulation.

The courts were not able to claim true independent character because they were not able to deliver justice to the victims and could not ensure that perpetrators were not granted impunity owning to gaps within the judicial system. The trial courts were overloaded with more than 1.3 million cases pending with them. Grant of bail was tough for an ordinary prisoner who did not have clout or nuisance value. There were about 2,800 people in illegal confinement in Swat alone who were not produced before the respective courts since more than a year; really alarming the situation was in Pakistan.

On 8th December 2010, the Supreme Court started hearing the infamous JAJJ CORRUPTION CASE; its details are given in separate Chapter.

On 11th December 2010; the Supreme Court issued notice to Member PAC and Chairman Earthquake Reconstruction & Rehabilitation Authority (ERRA) Hamid Yar Hiraj over allotment of a plot in the Diplomatic Enclave on cheap rates.

Chairman Capital Development Authority [CDA] was called for next day along with relevant record of the plot and to explain as to why a costly plot was allotted to Mr Hiraj in December 2007 on a meagre amount and against the rules and policy when he was holding the portfolio of minister of state in the regime of Shaukat Aziz.

Chief Justice of Pakistan Iftikhar M Chaudhry issued directive after taking notice on a telecast at a private TV channel on 9th December instant. The TV report had stated that CDA had allotted 19 kanals of plot to Mr Hiraj which was reserved for a school in the Diplomatic Enclave, in violation of rules / procedure. The Master Plan of Islamabad was altered without approval of the Cabinet due to which 37 kanals plot had been changed into 19 kanals plot.

The land worth billions of rupees had been allotted to Hamid Yar Hiraj at a cost of just Rs 7,16,03,200 whereas 18 kanals of land was left for the school though lying in the green belt.

The report alleged that Hiraj obtained the plot in the name of his relative who was running a private school at Multan. It was also claimed that initially a list of allotment was completed but he, using his influence, got the said plot allotted in the name of his relative in violation of rules.

(Part of this essay was published at www.pakspectator.com
on 23rd July 2011)

Scenario 67

KERRY-LUGAR BILL [2009]:

In the back drop of War on Terror on Pak – Afghan borders, the US government had pledged in September 2008 for economic assistance to Pakistan worth $2.3 billion for the year 2008-09 and a similar amount for fiscal year 2009-10, as both military and non-military aids.

On 30th September 2009, the US Congress approved another non-military aid to Pakistan to help fight extremism, and sent the draft to President Obama for signing into law. The legislation authorised **$1.5 billion a year for the next five years** as part of a bid to build a new relationship with Pakistan that no longer focused largely on military ties, but also on Pakistan's social and economic development.

The bill also stipulated that US military aid would cease if Pakistan would not help fight 'terrorists' including Taliban and Al Qaeda. The bill's sponsor, Howard Berman said that:

> '..... *Nor can we permit the Pakistani state – and its nuclear arsenal – to be taken over by the Taliban. To keep military aid flowing, Pakistan must also cooperate to dismantle nuclear supplier networks by offering relevant information from or direct access to Pakistani nationals associated with such networks*'.

Dana Rohrbacher, a Republican lawmaker, opined on the floor that '*the threat of radical Islam is real, but it's not going to be solved by us being irresponsible, with billions in taxpayer money*'. The bill passage process was followed by lengthy negotiations amongst lawmakers and the administration over what conditions to be placed on Pakistan.

The KL-Bill was introduced in the House on 24th September 2009 after the Senate had passed the measure and President Obama co-chaired Friends of Democratic Pakistan Summit with President Zardari's presence there to tell that the Taliban insurgency was expanding. The House Foreign Affairs Committee (HFAC) also authorized military assistance to help Pakistan disrupt and defeat al Qaeda and other insurgent elements requiring that such assistance be focused principally on counter-terrorism efforts. Congressman Howard Berman, Chairman of HFAC introduced that strategic legislation.

The bill had originally been under discussion in the Congress since 2008. That bill [no: S-3263], popularly known as '**Biden-Lugar Bill**' or '**Enhanced Partnership with Pakistan Act 2008**' was introduced in the Senate Foreign Relations Committee by its Chairman Senator Joseph Biden and Senator Richard Lugar and the Senate Committee had approved the bill unanimously in July 2008.

The bill recognized the role of Pakistan as US ally and the frontline state in combating terrorism and provided for $15 billion in economic assistance to Pakistan over the next 10 years beginning 2009. However, the bill died before it could be tabled before the Senate for debate following the upcoming presidential elections in December 2008. The bill was reintroduced in the 111th Congress session in 2009 as the Kerry-Lugar Bill.

It was told to the Congress that [till that moment] Pakistan had lost more than $ 35 billion in economic activity to fight against al-Qaeda and Taliban militants in its north-western areas since 11th September 2001 and more Pakistani soldiers and security personnel had laid down their lives than the combined losses of the US and Afghanistan together.

To support Pakistan's security needs to fight the on-going counterinsurgency and improve its border control etc; the bill authorized funds for the Foreign Military Financing (FMF) and International Military Education Training (IMET) for 5 years [*which was later put in suspension because of Pak-Army's objections*].

However, the fact remains that Pakistani aid bills even in the past have never been without strings; was tied even in the 1980's when the Reagan administration gave Pakistan $ 3.2 billion over a period of five years for helping Mujahideen to fight soviets with Pakistan's backing. But this time, a vast wrap of the Pakistani territory in FATA regions near Pak-Afghan border had become a conflict zone and the US drone attacks were also inflaming anti-American sentiments. A clear purpose of the KL-bill, with strong backing of the White House, was an effort to improve America's image in Pakistan which graph was wavering at 83% that time.

PAK-ARMY GOT ANGRY:

It is on record that the then US envoy to Pakistan, Anne Patterson, heard a hot criticism [over the Kerry-Lugar bill] from Gen Kayani and DG ISI

Gen Pasha in a two-hour meeting *on 6ᵗʰ October 2009*. Gen Kayani had made clear to the Ambassador and accompanying Gen McCrystal, during an urgent meeting at GHQ, about his concerns. Gen Crystal understood the viewpoint of Pak-Army and was not at all happy when he left the GHQ. Gen Kayani told them that there were elements in the bill that would set back the bilateral relationship, and critical provisions were almost entirely directed against the Army.

Gen Kayani was particularly irritated on clauses of civilian control of the military since he had no intention of taking over the government. '*Had I wanted to do this, I would have done it during the long march [of March 2009]*', Gen Kayani had told the US Ambassador clearly.

Getting hot blow from the GHQ side, the then Foreign Minister Shah Mahmood Qureshi was made to rush immediately to the United States even without providing input from his Parliament where the two houses were engaged in debate over the bill.

The reported remarks of the American envoy were that rejection of the bill would be taken as an insult and smack of arrogant attitude but, contrarily, some clauses of the bill could also be termed as insult to the entire Pakistani nation. If the objective of the bill was to assist Pakistani people and to create goodwill for the US then the KL-Bill in the given form was the quite opposite. Therefore, it was in the interest of the United States itself to drop those conditions by revising the bill.

At Washington a joint congressional explanatory statement was prepared which, according to FM Mr Qureshi, was placed before the US Senate along with supporting letters from US Secretary of State Hillary Clinton and Defence Secretary Robert Gates. The said statement was annexed to the act and would have 'the full force of law' dealing particularly with the misgivings over national sovereignty and security of Pakistan.

The '*TIME*' *magazine of 8ᵗʰ October 2009* told that:

> '*Unlike previous no-strings aid packages, Kerry-Lugar makes support conditional on Pakistan's military being subordinated to its elected government, and taking action against militants sheltering on its soil.*
>
> *[In Pakistan] the opposition parties unite against its "humiliating" conditions, with even the junior partners in Zardari's ruling coalition expressing misgivings.*

Public opinion ranges from suspicion to hostility. Following a meeting of its corps commanders, the army expressed "serious concern" over the "national security" implications of the aid package. It's a kind of political move on the part of the military.'

It was felt that the PML(N) leader Nawaz Sharif purposefully stayed away from the debate, and approached the US officials from London to register their his party's official stance so that the PML(N) could confront its opponents in power over the Kerry-Lugar Bill, while keeping its options open. The PPP, of course, could not defend the Bill properly because its second-echelon leaders were not convinced with the sincerity of their top while dealing with the said Bill.

Interestingly, contrary to his party's stance, PPP's PM Mr Gilani was often found contacting opposition leaders to inform them of *'the government's plan to pass a unanimous resolution in both Houses of Parliament, notifying the US that Pakistan would not accept any aid unless the US amended the controversial clauses'.*

The conditions attached with the bill had rubbed Pakistan the wrong way and produced negative reactions. The country's leading columnists rebuked the bill on the 'sovereignty' factor, abused it openly in print and electronic media whereas the legislators sitting on the opposition benches and political figures outside, displayed their hatred against America on the floor and outside.

Ayaz Amir, an opposition legislator, labelled the 'conditional ties' as grossly demeaning. In *'the News'* feature published in the first week of October 2009, under '<u>Kerry-Lugar: bill or document of surrender</u>', he opined that:

"*A convicted rapist out on parole would be required to give fewer assurances of good conduct.*"

Dr Muzaffar Iqbal wrote in the same daily on the same day that:

'*Turning Pakistan into a client state: ..... reduced to insignificant status with the acceptance of the aid bill, and the humiliation of Pakistan as it emerges as an <u>American satellite...puppet...neo-colony.</u>'*

Shafqat Mahmood opined in the same *'the News'* that:

'*Are perceptions of instability real?, there is an ideological difference within the power establishment regarding relations with the United*

States and India, and that the sniping on the Kerry-Lugar bill is an example of this'.

The Obama Administration was really caught in dilemma; firstly, that in Pakistan the military budget must be merged with the national budget, and secondly, that there should be no more military intervention in political and judicial matters. Constitutionally valid, the US stood committed to pursuing the democratic path while stipulating that *'it's either the Kerry-Lugar civilian aid, or no aid for the military.'*

But the million dollar question was: *whether to align with the powerful military to combat the militancy or take the principled stand in support of a weak democracy?* The later option was a long shot so the US authorities had to go mid-way though the Pakistan's Army Chief had openly conveyed to Gen Stanley McChrystal [when he met Pakistan's COAS at Pakistan's GHQ] that:

'The terms set in the Kerry-Lugar bill on the national security interests of Pakistan are insulting and are unacceptable in their present form.'

Even so, the final verdict had to come from parliament, where pertinently, a significant number of legislators subscribed to the military's viewpoint.

To keep the Pakistan Army on his right side, President Obama needed to remove the offending clauses of the legislation [*acknowledged by US ambassador Anne Patterson as badly drafted*] and to sign an amended bill which was already lying on his table. Reportedly, Senator Kerry had visited Pakistan three weeks later with that amended bill but for the Pakistan Army *'it was not suitably amended'*. Kerry had to conclude his trip to Pakistan saying *"take it or leave it."*

It was in this background that on *8th October 2009*, a serious argument between the Army and the government developed as the Presidency had straightaway dismissed the objections raised by the Armed Forces over the Kerry Lugar Bill. Farhatullah Babar, the spokesman of the Presidency told the media that the appropriate forum to express such views was the Defence Committee of the Cabinet (DCC) or the Ministry of Defence.

US SENATOR J KERRY EXPLAINED:

US Senator John Kerry, one of the co-authors had once [*10th October 2009*] issued a list of 'myths and facts' about the Kerry-Lugar bill himself. The myths contained that:

- The $7.5 billion authorised by the bill would come with strings attached for the people of Pakistan.

- The bill would intrude on Pakistan's sovereignty.

- The bill would interfere in Pakistan's internal affairs and imply that Pakistan supports terrorism and nuclear proliferation.

- The bill would require US oversight on internal operations of the Pakistani military.

- The bill would expand the Predator programme of drone attacks on targets within Pakistan.

- The bill would fund activities within Pakistan through private US security firms, such as Dyn-corp and Black-water or Xe.

- The bill would expand US military footprint in Pakistan.

- The US would use the bill as a justification for why the US Embassy in Islamabad needed more space and security.

The fact remained that these were actual anticipated results not myths. This was how this bill was sold to President Zardari and his cronies taking them stooges. Basically, it was a formal declaration of making Richard Butcher the un-official Viceroy of Pakistan. When objected that why US wanted to finance building mini pentagon in Pakistan, John Kerry tried to explain by saying that:

> 'There are no conditions on Pakistan attached to these funds except strict measures of financial accountability on these funds to make sure the money is being spent for the purposes intended.
>
> It was to ensure that 'the tripled] funds meant for schools, roads and clinics actually reach the Pakistani people. Nothing in the bill threatens Pakistani sovereignty and there is absolutely no US intention or desire whatsoever.

There is absolutely nothing in the bill related to drones. The issue of how American private security firms operate in Pakistan has nothing to do with this bill. The bill does not provide a single dollar for US military operations; the money authorised in this bill is for non-military, civilian purposes.'

The explanations forwarded by the American Senator were not bought by Pakistan's army on various counts. Primarily if the Kerry aid was for education, clinics and roads then why they had not mentioned about stopping the drone attacks. It was a strange strategy of helping the Pakistani people that:

'America would kill hundreds of innocent men, women and children in drone attacks and then provide them aid for hospitals to be treated in and for schooling of children if they survived.'

These hospitals, schools and roads would be made by Pakistani labour but would be supervised by crew from Black-water and XE. The $7.5 billion aid would be spent in five years apparently for the Pakistani people but personnel to spend and supervise them would come from America so the US Embassy in Islamabad would be expanded with another spending of a similar amount.

Referring to *Dr Ishtiaq Ahmed's* opinion appearing in the *'Weekly Pulse' of 2-8th October 2009* that the PML(N) stole a phrase from Gen Ziaul Haq's mouth when its spokesman Ahsan Iqbal termed the amount pledged under the Bill as 'peanuts'. The PML(Q) leadership called it an 'insult' to the nation; and allegedly the pro-alQaeda and pro-Taliban *Jama'at e Islami* (JI) declared it as 'death warrant' for the country.

However, the fact remained that John Kerry's explanations had completely ignored the main issues in the bill which had caused outrage in Pakistan. The main theme of the bill contained that:

• *'Pakistan must now cease terrorist activities against India...'*;

• *'US will conduct a review on terrorist activity figures every six months'*;

• *'If not satisfied Pakistan would be declared a terrorist state'*.

Kerry-Lugar Bill had also authorized the Secretary of State to establish an exchange programme between military and civilian personnel of

Pakistan and NATO member countries which was also held in abeyance later by the Pakistan government due to its army's reservations.

In the opinion of the foreign policy experts, the KL-Bill was a card for intervention in the purely internal policies of a sovereign state and this would turn Pakistan into a virtual client State. There were so much polarizations on this issue that even coalition partners of the PPP were either speaking against its intrusive clauses or had opted to keep mum for obvious reasons.

On 12th October instant; Pakistan and the US Congress agreed to issue a joint statement addressing all issues linked to the Kerry-Lugar-Berman bill. The decision to issue such a statement was taken after a series of meetings in Washington between the visiting Pakistani Foreign Minister Shah Mehmood Qureshi and senior US officials and lawmakers. Mr Qureshi had impressed that:

'We must address the concerns and fears expressed in Pakistan; we will not allow Pakistan's sovereignty to be compromised and will not allow anybody to micro-manage our affairs'.

Senator Kerry assured the Pakistani nation that the United States had no desire to manage its affairs; Washington had recognised the army's role in the war against the extremists.

Under this provision the US Secretary of State had to certify that Pakistan was making significant efforts to prevent al-Qaeda and associated terrorist groups, including *Lashkar e Taiba* [LeT] and *Jaish e Mohammad* [JeM] from using its territory to launch attacks against US or NATO forces in Afghanistan or cross border attacks into neighbouring countries, pointing out towards India.

The US Secretary was also required to certify that the Pakistan Army would not materially or substantially subvert the political or judicial processes of Pakistan. Many members of Pakistan's intelligentsia, however, endorsed this clause as the bill asked for a mechanism to keep army at bay or in barracks, to be exact. It was exactly what a proper democracy demands and so does country's constitution; any sane person even the professional army Generals had not raised objection to it.

[*Objectively speaking; had that humiliating clause stayed in the bill, even then the CIA's Director, or the US Joint Chiefs of Staff, or*

Secretary of State would never be calling Pakistan's army chief to tell him to desist from interfering in Pakistan's political affairs.

This was not to be considered diplomatic or polite. They usually convey their concerns with a carrot-and-stick approach. Defence equipment and security-related aids are always provided with certain conditions; take it or leave it.]

However, for Pakistani Generals, it was the most humiliating requirement that the US Secretary of State would certify, at six-month intervals, that the military remains under civilian oversight through control of senior command promotions.

Kerry-Lugar also required that the Pakistani military would act against militant networks on its soil, specifying those based in Quetta and Muridke. The US high command believed that both the Afghan Taliban and Hafiz Saeed's LeT had previously served as proxies of the Pakistan army which has never been a truth.

INDIA & HUSSAIN HAQQANI BLAMED:

Referring to *the 'Dawn' of 14th October 2009,* certain stinking clauses in the bill appeared to be the blessing of the Indian embassy in Washington and their lobbyists. These included the ones dealing with:

• the dismantling of alleged terrorist operational bases in Quetta and Muridke;

• preventing terrorist groups like LeT & JeM & others from operating in Pakistani territory;

• carrying out cross-border attacks on neighbouring countries;

• taking action when provided with intelligence on high-level terrorist targets including elements within the Pakistan military or its intelligence agency [ISI], particularly ones which conducted attacks against the territory or people of neighbouring countries [*referring to Mumbai attacks of Nov 2008*].

Point to ponder was that what details John Kerry or Richard Lugar knew about LeT or JeM or Muridke?

Media gurus and intelligentsia had also pointed out towards the same apprehension that on the strategic side, the uproar over the Kerry-Lugar bill had at least exposed continuing differences in both the US and Pakistani establishments. Quetta, Muridke and nuclear black-marketing crept into the Act because there was a significant camp in the US, including the Obama administration that believed Pakistan was first and foremost a part of the problem, and not necessarily part of a cooperative solution to regional problems.

However, some provisions were there in the bill which were apparently instigated by the Pakistani embassy in Washington; the details would come in next paragraphs with reference to Hussain Haqqani. Would the Americans, for instance, be interested in the security forces of Pakistan materially and substantially subverting the political or judicial processes in the country?

The irony of fate was that in Pakistan, the same legislators had been supporting the security forces, led by Gen Musharraf, until August 2008. Sudden change of mind was understandable; the ruling regime of PPP, in their infinite meetings with the Americans since early 2008, had repeatedly blamed the Pak-Army and ISI for the political mess expressing apprehensions that the political process could be subverted by the military any moment. They asked for help in the form of assurances from the Americans that they would be able to complete their tenure.

In Kerry-Lugar Bill, another humiliating condition was that '*Pakistan would grant US investigators direct access to Pakistani nationals associated with nuclear-proliferation networks*'. Of course, the Americans were referring it to Dr A Q Khan. To please their American counterparts, the Pakistani rulers in succession, Gen Musharraf & Mr Zardari, kept Dr Khan under house arrest but consistently refused to allow the foreign investigators to question him.

The people of Pakistan were angry over Dr Khan's maltreatment and more so because about 83% of Pakistanis had opposed both the rulers to be a part of war on terror (WoT); Zardari took it as politically motivated.

On 9ᵗʰ October 2009, during the parliamentary discussion on the said bill, the former Foreign Minister Sardar Assef Ahmad Ali passed very derogatory remarks against Dr A Q Khan for which there was seen a stern uproar on the assembly floor and in the media, too.

The Bill envisaged that the US Secretary of State must certify that *'Pakistan continued to cooperate with the United States to dismantle supplier network relating to the acquisition of nuclear weapons related material'*, such as providing relevant information from or direct access to Pakistani nationals. It was disgusting for every Pakistani because no one here wanted to hear any sort of derogatory compromise over country's nuclear programme.

True, that Mr Zardari or the PPP was in no position to reject the aid on offer but the people raised their voices saying that *'the dollars would never come in Pakistan; instead the same would fill the already bulky Swiss & Dubai bank accounts of their rulers'*.

HUSSAIN HAQQANI's DUBIOUS ROLE:

Astonishingly, Pakistan's Ambassador to the US, Hussain Haqqani told the media that the American policies could not be altered because:

> *'The US was the sole super power of the contemporary world and it was not possible for any country to influence its policies.*

> *The people who are criticising the recently passed Kerry-Luger bill have not studied the document in detail. Maintaining good relations with the US was in the larger interest of the nation.'*

Referring to <u>*Irfan Hussain's*</u> analysis, though much later, in the *'Dawn' of 31st March 2012*, the army's estimation was that the US needed Pakistan more so the later had a lot of margin in twisting the phrases and clauses. Though there was a bill that sought to transfer $1.5bn a year for five years to invest in Pakistan's economy and its neglected social sector then why so much uproar in Pakistan; general populace stood by the Generals at that moment because the super power was hinting at country's nuclear arsenals.

Moreover, behind the language of the bill, many in the army and the ISI saw the crumbling hand of Husain Haqqani; president Zardari's personal friend and policy agent in Washington.

Normally, no ambassador can dictate the contents of legislation specific to one's country to the host state but here Mr Haqqani did indeed manage to persuade US legislators to insert clauses aimed at keeping the army from staging another coup; hats off to the heavily paid PPP's lobbyists in US. It was a blessing in disguise for Haqqani as through the criticism on that KL bill he got succeeded in washing up his dirt of being an NRO beneficiary.

PPP's Minister of State, Afzal Sindhu, had brought forward a list of 8041 persons who were allegedly the beneficiaries of NRO including Benazir Bhutto and Hussain Haqqani but both were included in the list on different pretexts. An Entesab Case was registered against Haqqani for issuing a wrong 'FM Radio License' in 1997 and Senator Saifur Rehman was the kingpin behind it.

In 1999, when the Nawaz Sharif's government ended, Ehtesab Law was converted into NAB Ordinance and the said case was transferred to NAB HQ as such. Though Saifur Rehman was under custody then but he kept on helping the military government from 'inside' just to gain little favours during his 'detention' – a typical Pakistani style of leadership; as he had divulged false informations against his own chief Nawaz Sharif.

Gen Musharraf's government arrested Haqqani and was pressurized to become an approver which he had refused; later he was released on bail from Lahore High Court. Major Gen Rashid Qureshi of ISPR got that file of Haqqani closed and the later left for the States.

Haqqani wrote a book [titled *Between Mosque & Military*] while in America taking revenge from those Pak-Army people who had been exerting pressure on him for being an approver. This book whether succeeded in his peculiar objectives or not but the enemies of Pakistan brewed maximum benefits out of it.

In 2008, Hussain Haqqani was made Pakistan's envoy in Washington but in Pak-Army's record he was a 'grey' man. That was the reason; Haqqani was labelled as a dubious character in Kerry Lugar Bill.

There were so many others who were pushed into the NAB's record, thus labelled as beneficiaries of NRO, who could have approached the courts for getting clearance. They did not because Pakistani judiciary was known to all throughout its history, till 2009 at least; Zardari's nine years of record in jail could be cited as an example.

Zardari was allowed to be released on bail in some cases only when the judges of the superior courts [*perhaps including the incumbent CJP Iftikhar M Chaudhry too, as the PPP regime had continuously alleged*] used to get sure that the police were ready to arrest him from the court's door in some other case.

There were other such characters like Yusaf Talpur who were never called in any court but they were named in NRO; NAB was maintaining those lists only to keep their nuisance value and tyranny in tact.

Haqqani was a thorn for Pakistani Generals ever since his book [cited above] appeared in 2005. A study of poisonous nexus between the army and various extremist groups, the book did rounds in the American media and think tanks. So when Haqqani was named as Pakistan's Ambassador in Washington in 2008, the posting did not sit well with the Pak-military.

Pak-Army's suspicion that he was somehow serving American interests was reinforced when the draft of the Kerry-Lugar Bill became available.

Amid the growing discontent in Pakistan over the conditions attached with the said bill, Islamabad hired a new lobbyist, Robin Raphael of Cassidy and Associates, one of the biggest lobbying firms in Washington, for a whopping $700,000 a year plus 'other' expenses to push its cause in the aftermath of that historic blunder; clearly indicating at the same time that Pakistan was not satisfied with the work of the age-old lobbyist Mark Siegel, who was a close friend of former Prime Minister Benazir Bhutto.

> [*Previously Robin Raphael has been at the US Embassy in New Delhi (1991–1993). She has been the Ambassador to Tunisia and Assistant Secretary of State for South Asian Affairs during the Clinton administration. In this capacity she managed US relations with the newly formed Taliban government in Afghanistan.*
>
> *She retired from the state department in 2005 after 30 years of service. The Obama Administration appointed Robin Raphel as a member of the team of the late Richard Holbrooke, the Special Representative to the Af-Pak region – and the US coordinator of all aid to Pakistan.*]

KL-BILL: A POLITICAL FIASCO

Media reports and the official record indicate that initially, the PPP government had taken full credit of Kerry Lugar Bill and the Interior Minister Rehman Malik tried to get the federal cabinet adopt a resolution lauding it but could not succeed because of reservations of certain insiders.

The opponents of the bill, especially the army, took a different view. The army believed that some of its clauses posed a threat to Pakistan's security. President Zardari had also asked his ministers to go out and defend the bill with full force. At one point, the controversy became so intense that rumours emerged that Gen Kayani was being sacked. Then what was the politics behind this controversy?

The KL Bill required, in addition to all the gimmicks discussed above, from the Pakistan government to desist from using the American assistance for expansion of its nuclear programme, or reallocating Pakistan's own financial resources to its nuclear weapons programme. These provisions were apparently the same objectives that Pakistanis normally professed. However, the scrutiny told that through the KL Bill, the Americans wanted to advance its agenda against Pak-army because:

- As per US stance, the Pak-army was playing double role in Afghanistan; they had acted robustly against the Pakistani Taliban in Swat but failed to oblige their commitment against the Afghan Taliban having safe havens in Pakistan from where they attack the US & NATO troops.

- Allegedly, Afghan Taliban's leadership from Quetta used to control their operations. That was why the US Vice President Joe Biden had proposed the idea of 'Pakistan First'; targeting of the Taliban in Pakistan rather than those in Afghanistan.

- The US high Command believed that despite their ban on *jihadi* organisations like LeT and JeM, the ISI considered them strategic assets to be used against India [*for not arresting Hafiz Saeed in Mumbai terrorist attack*]. Through the Kerry-Lugar, the Americans wanted to pressurise the government to dismantle the Muridke base in particular.

- The US administration wanted Pak-Army to accept civilian supremacy in political matters, military budget, and the chain of command, promotion of seniors in military ranks and civilian control of the ISI.

- The US authorities wanted to keep a check on Pakistan's nuclear programme.

[During 2004, Senator Kerry as presidential election candidate, had declared that if he won, he would try to get control over Pakistani nukes]

Why were the PPP government & Mr Zardari so joyful over that Kerry-Lugar Bill; might be that some of the PPP stalwarts were thinking of riding a new gravy train but mainly they wanted to keep the army & ISI under their thumb. It was PPP's long standing wish; recall the ending July 2008's notification putting the ISI under the Ministry of Interior but had to withdraw the notification after three hours.

[At this moment, one can recall that the PML(N) in the post-Kargil scenario didn't act very differently, when Shahbaz Sharif flew to the US to obtain a statement from the then US administration to the effect that the US would not look favourably on a military intervention in Pakistan.]

Why the army did move public with its reservations on the bill; perhaps there was no option left for them. COAS Gen Kayani had informed the government about his reservations in writing and then had personally conveyed to the PM and President but of no avail. Fact remained that:

'The army contended that the last version of the KL-Bill they received on 15th September 2009 did not contain the 12 clauses which were added subsequently in the final version being most objectionable and derogatory.'

In nut shell, as per *'Daily Times' of 21st October 2009,* the army went successful by sending a loud and clear message to all that *'Zardari cannot hope to control the army by aligning himself with the US; nor the US by aligning itself with Zardari.'*

Later, referring to *'the Jang' of 26th July 2010,* the Kerry Lugar bill was the outcome of the conspiracy amongst the Americans [comprising of Gen Mike Mullen, Gen McCrystal, Hallbrook & Hilary Clinton as one party] and Zardari, Gilani & Haqqani being the second part in which the later group had come up with utmost irresponsibility as statesmen. The Pak Army had forwarded its reservations in writing through proper channel via Joint Chiefs of Staff Committee.

Perhaps the Americans had fair idea of such reprisal from the Pak Army but there was no harm in taking a chance. When the written retaliation came on record, the American government and Pentagon immediately issued an 'explanatory note' trying to absolve themselves of all possible fall outs.

'*A Pakistani person's discontent over the assistance, despite the fact that the aid focused on developmental sectors like health and education was understandable*', the US government was upset. But why US congress attached such conditions with the aid, was another question. US Embassy's Bryan Hunt had said:

> '*The Congress felt that the US should be dealing with civilian government; Pakistan also agrees that we should be dealing with civilians, and not the military.*
>
> *It is unfortunate as Washington wants to promote democracy in Pakistan, but the goal was being hampered by the wide-scale protests.*'

The American policy makers, however, had also lost sight that they were actually trying to reap their own interest in the garb of 'civilian aid'. Had they serious to serve the Pakistani civilian community they should not have included the conditions like:

> '*Civilian control of the army, no check on drone attacks, seeking allowance to investigate Dr A Q Khan directly, seeking permissions to expand the US Embassy premises and no check on the entry of security personnel for Black-water & XE*'.

These were all negative designs and the Pakistani Generals were no such goofs as the Americans, Rehmans & Rajas had originally thought of.

The press release stated; the military commanders' considered view was that "*it is parliament that represents the will of the people of Pakistan, which would deliberate on the issue, enabling the government to develop a national response.*"

SENATOR KERRY VISITS PAKISTAN:

On *20th October 2009*, when US Senator John Kerry was in Islamabad to celebrate the [miscalculated] American success, his body language was totally exhausted indicating his disappointment during his Islamabad visit where he was having '*so much difficulty in trying to give away 7.5 billion dollar aid.*'

Although he was careful not to express his distress after meeting Pakistani politicians and military leaders, a frustrated Kerry ended up saying:

'Take it or leave it; we should not play to cheap galleries here. If you don't want the money, say so. We're not forcing you to take it.

We are giving to Pakistan about 7.5 billion dollars aid and also listening its complaints; we can spend this amount in California where it is badly needed.'

Senator John Kerry had also made it clear that no change was possible in the Kerry-Lugar Bill. He had come to Pakistan because he was *'concerned that a straight forward effort was being misinterpreted'*. He was more upset because he was not expecting demands of 'further clarification' from PML(N)'s Nawaz Sharif at least.

Later, in mid May 2011, John Kerry again met Pakistan's Army Chief Gen Kayani who apprised him of the 'intense feelings' within the rank and file of his army on the US raid at Abbottabad to kill Osama bin Laden. Kerry was carrying a list of actions to ease tensions but contrarily the US government was trying to use the threat of Congressional cuts to the $3 billion [as leverage] in annual aid to Pakistan.

In Pakistan no one was actually bothered. Next day, Senator Kerry shunted out his frustration and humiliation by saying the media reporters in Mazar Sharif [Afghanistan] that:

'Terror attacks in the country are carried out by insurgents trained in Pakistan. It is really critical that we talk with the Pakistanis, as friends, in the best effort to try to achieve the most cooperation possible to make all of us safer.

We believe that Pakistan itself is challenged from these insurgents, extremists and terrorists.'

The gimmicks went on. Kerry-Lugar Bill remained in its place; however, the Pakistan Army's reservations were given serious considerations. The general populace could not know if any aid [$1.5 billion per year] was received by Pakistan nor Pakistan's 'vibrant' media ever brought any news in this regard till the 3rd week of November 2011 when the National Accountability Bureau (NAB) had decided to investigate reports of alleged corruption in the funds being disbursed to NGOs for development projects under the said KL-bill.

A 2-member delegation of the US AID had met the NAB Chairman Justice (retd) Deedar Hussain Shah and requested him to look into the matter to ensure transparency in the development schemes. As per Pak-US arrangement worked out later, much of this aid was to be spent through American NGOs for development projects at mass level in Pakistan.

[There have been reports that some local NGOs used US citizens as front men while some others pooled with the NGOs in US to squeeze funding. This was against the spirit of the funding agreement and prompted the US authorities to lodge complaints for a formal probe.]

A report by *Jane Perlez* in the '*New York Times*' **dated 1ˢᵗ May 2011** had earlier said that:

'The Kerry-Lugar aid plan for Pakistan is "floundering because Washington's fears of Pakistani corruption and incompetence have slowed disbursal of the money.

Quoting the US Government Accountability Office, only $179.5 million of the first $1.5 billion of the five-year programme had been disbursed by December 2010.'

The script speaks that how serious we were in using that $7.5bn aid.

On 18ᵗʰ April 2012, Pakistan's Federal Minister for Finance Dr Hafeez Shaikh along with Governor State Bank of Pakistan and Federal Secretary Finance landed at Washington to hold talks with the US and World Bank authorities about the restoration of aid to the country which was promised for Pakistan earlier in 2009 under KL-Bill. Federal Minister Dr Shaikh in his meetings with the US officials reiterated demand for payment of US grant under the Coalition Support Fund (CSF) to Pakistan which was projected at $ 800 million to be received during the previous year, while it did not get any funds since December 2010.

When the Kerry-Lugar bill was passed it was decided that Pakistan would receive an amount of US$ 7.5 billion in total over a period of five year (2009-14), however it was not decided that Pakistan would receive US$ 1.5 billion every year in the mathematical sense.

In 2011 Pakistan received US$1.2 billion while till the end of FY 2011-12 [June 2012] United States Agency for International Development (USAID) had disbursed an amount of US$ 2.6 billion for projects related to energy production, health, education and infrastructure, especially after Pakistan's floods.

[*USAID has provided assistance for the establishment of a new power project which can produce up to 400 megawatts of energy. They are also working on improvement of existing power projects so that their capacity can increase.*]

Now the ending words:

Taking light from Anees Jillani, referring to **the 'Dawn' of 14th October 2009,** the Kerry-Lugar Bill was passed by the US Congress and not by the *Majlis e Shoora*; it was not easy if not altogether impossible to get it modified. It became American law after President Obama's signature; we were not able to stop that process. However, we as a nation could at least do one thing; should have refused the aid.

Trying to be a democratic nation, Pakistan in its own entity, would not disagree with the '**lessons**' given in the bill through conditions. Pakistan should remain committed to eliminating terrorism, whether domestically or externally [stop thinking India or Afghanistan or China or Philippines].

There should not be any terrorist base in the country, whether in Muridke or Quetta or Southern Punjab or Karachi. The military should desist from interfering in the country's political process on all pretexts; but dictation from any quarter, any power or forum should not be accepted. This would hurt nation's ego, dignity and sovereignty, and would be an insult to millions of Pakistanis.

Don't accept American aids, military or civil, yes if possible borrow or buy their thinking: US President, Theodore Roosevelt, had once said: '*Speak softly and carry a big stick. You will go far.*'

[*Part of this essay was published at www.pakspectator.com as 'Lead Story' on 24th April 2012*]

Scenario 68

SC'S JUDGMENT ON NRO [2009]:

WITH REFERENCE TO SCENARIO 49 OF VOL-II:

Ms Benazir Bhutto, during her last days in exile, had agreed to negotiate a deal with the then military ruler of Pakistan, Gen Musharraf, under an umbrella of the American and British guarantors. It was a successful deal but then no body could imagine that the general populace of Pakistan would not fully agree with this discriminatory document. The reasons were obvious. It did not apply to all citizens of Pakistan equally; it was focused on some while ignoring others.

Pakistan Peoples Party [PPP]'s deal with Gen Musharraf, resulting with promulgation of *National Reconciliation Ordinance [NRO] of 5th October 2007* by Gen Musharraf, was generally termed as 'controversial'. It was rumoured that this deal had left PPP's supporters in shock ahead of BB's expected return on 18th October 2007 to Pakistan after eight years of self-exile. Till then the PPP affiliates were known as the liberal, moderate & secular bastion of resistance against military rule in Pakistan.

It was known to the media that Gen Musharraf had advised Benazir Bhutto to put the NRO off until his [General's own] election would be legitimized by the Supreme Court, but who cares such sermons in politics. From Benazir Bhutto's viewpoint, the said ordinance was coined, urged and justified in the name of *'smooth return to democracy'*. It was wrong; the final 'package of reforms' contained little more than the withdrawal of corruption cases against both of the PPP leaders; and that too as verbal assurances only.

Benazir Bhutto had to do it for her husband Mr Zardari. She had got finalized the deal after about a year of secret negotiations including two one to one meetings with Gen Musharraf in UAE; in January & July 2007 resulting as NRO signed in by Gen Musharraf only a day before his presidential election. In return for this amnesty, the PPP had legitimized Gen Musharraf's election by not resigning from Parliament and provincial assemblies; as the other opposition parties had done. The PPP abstained from the process to save face, a walkout by its parliamentarians from the National Assembly giving gloss to a token protest.

Replying criticism on the PPP on this count, Hussain Haqqani had once said in *'The Nation'*:

'That the cases against Ms. Bhutto had been hanging over her head for years without investigators unable to find the evidence to secure even a single conviction. It was now up to the people to decide if those charges were true; pointing to the inclusion of the words "politically motivated" in the ordinance as an admission by the regime that the cases were nothing but vendetta'.

The NRO withdrew all corruption charges filed against those in public office before the day Gen Musharraf seized power from Nawaz Sharif. This benefited Ms Bhutto, her family and friends, cases against whom were filed by the Sharif government. It also provided for withdrawal of criminal cases registered from 1986 to 1999 against political activists like MQM. The ordinance also included changes in election laws so that results, once declared, could not be tampered with.

More improvements in PPP's understanding with Gen Musharraf came after the presidential election and it brought more concessions, but the circumstances started changing with high velocity. Meanwhile, Benazir Bhutto had to defend PPP for approving an Anglo-American plan to keep Gen Musharraf in power. Ms Bhutto's main aim was then focused to keep PPP workers docile and satisfied. PPP's companions and supporters were not absolutely cheerful with this deal because the NRO had not included the cases against Sharif family, or some way out for the missing people allegedly taken away by Pakistani intelligence agencies.

On the other hand the PPP had to battle the ruling PML(Q) in coming elections. Backed by the establishment and Gen Musharraf himself, the PPP was expected to put up a fierce fight with Chaudhrys of Gujrat to make its way through. Though Gen Musharraf needed the PPP politically, he had felt threatened by its strength in the elections; one reason why he tried to discourage Benazir Bhutto from returning earlier. Contrarily even free and fair elections would not have guaranteed to keep PPP's seats intact which the PPP were having in the assembly then, had BB delayed her arrival in Pakistan obliging Musharraf's advice.

NRO CRITICIZED AT HOME:

It is on record that certain party rebels like Aitzaz Ahsan and Raza Rabbani, had openly questioned Benazir Bhutto's negotiations with Gen

Musharraf for extending PPP's favour in his election, but BB was really shocked when PPP's old friend, *Naseerullah Babar, quit PPP saying that 'Gen Zia hanged Zulfikar Ali Bhutto in 1979; Gen Musharraf killed the PPP on October 5, 2007.'*

Ms Bhutto felt more embarrassed when the hidden faces of both Muslim Leagues manoeuvred the media campaign against BB trying to convey an impression to the people that *'the military has once again managed to make politicians look ugly.'*

What happened afterwards? Only days after Benazir Bhutto's arrival in Pakistan, when a bench of the Supreme Court of Pakistan was to decide a petition challenging the constitutional validity of Gen Musharraf's re-election as president in the controversial elections of 6th October 2007, the General, as Chief of Army Staff, suspended the constitution, jailed several justices and lawyers of the Supreme Court including Chief Justice Iftikhar M Chaudhry, ordered arrest of political dissidents and human rights activists, and shut down all private television channels.

It was 3rd November 2007, when Gen Musharraf declared a state of Emergency in Pakistan which lasted until 15th December 2007. During this time, the constitution of the country remained suspended; a serious tragedy it was during which a new PCO was brought forward.

A day before departing for Pakistan, Benazir Bhutto had sent, from Dubai, an e-mail to PPP's friend Mark Seigal in United States. It was done so because Ms Bhutto was feeling insecure in Pakistan. Ms Bhutto had named Gen Musharaf, Ejaz Shah (Intelligence Bureau Chief then), Ch Pervaiz Elahi (Ex-CM of Punjab) and Hamid Gul (ex ISI Chief) responsible if she would be assassinated. With 18th October blasts in Karachi, a concerted effort to eliminate her, her apprehensions were proved correct. She had escaped in Karachi attack but the culprits took her life about two month later.

[*The above narration was kept on record as a piece of history. Zardari was not in Pakistan then and Benazir Bhutto was busy in her election campaign. The elections were announced for 8th January 2008 but the episode of 27th December 2007 removed her from Pakistan's political scene; great tragedy it was.*]

In nut shell the history witnessed that apart from some bureaucrats, the NRO pact was to favour the PPP and MQM leaders or workers. The NRO was a ploy to further the political interests of Pakistan Army's

Chief of Staff, Benazir Bhutto and the US, UK and NATO powers who had strived hard to promote that Musharraf - Benazir deal; in their own individual interests particularly.

MQM's deputy parliamentary leader in the National Assembly Syed Haider Abbas Rizvi told the Press on 16th October 2007 that the founder of the MQM, Altaf Hussain, might be among the top beneficiaries of the National Reconciliation Ordinance (NRO) if the law gets no objection certificate from the Supreme Court.

The historical joke is on record that among the **long list of 'cases' against Altaf Hussain,** one was that he had stolen a policeman's cap during a scuffle. Mr Rizvi secastically affirmed that *'Yes, it is true. An FIR was filed with the Liaquatabad Police Station several years back against our leader in this connection'.*

There were about eight thousand cases against the MQM workers; over 200 cases against its leadership. NRO was challenged in the Supreme Court immediately after its promulgation.

On **16th December 2009,** a full strength bench (of all 17 judges) of the Supreme Court of Pakistan, gave a unanimous verdict on constitutional petitions no: 76-80 of 2007 and seven miscellaneous ones, filed by twelve different persons including Dr Mobashir Hassan, PPP's former Federal Minister of Pakistan; Roedad Khan, a former Federal Secretary; Qazi Hussain Ahmed, then Secretary General *Jamaat e Islami* (JI) and Shahbaz Sharif, the Chief Minister of Punjab.

A few lines from *the 'Dawn' dated 19th December 2009:*

> *'Uncertainty, if not panic, is detectable in the ranks of the PPP brain trust......Sections of the media have gone into overdrive against NRO beneficiaries; panic, glee, consternation, joy amidst the welter of emotions; few have thought to step back.*

> *It is a process with no precedent in the country...... It is imperative that the judiciary should develop a road map to restore the pre-Oct 5, 2007 position of the NRO beneficiaries undoing an illegality, however blatant, must be done along legal principles, not political expediencies.*

> *The PPP-led government must resist the urge, if any, to respond to its detractors. Instead, it must demonstrate a genuine will to implement the SC's order.......'*

NRO'S PROCEDURAL WHEELS:

The background facts, as enumerated above, were that on 5th October 2007, a National Reconciliation Ordinance (Act of the Parliament No:LX) of 2007 (NRO) was promulgated by the then President of Pakistan, Gen Musharraf, apparently exercising his powers conferred by clause (1) of Article 89 of the Constitution. Through this Ordinance certain amendments were made in the Criminal Procedure Code (CrPC) of 1898, the Representation of the People Act of 1976 and the National Accountability Bureau Ordinance (NAB) of 1999.

By means of Section 2 of the NRO, Section 494 of CrPC was amended. Likewise, vide Section 3 of the NRO and Section 39 of the Representation of the People Act was amended; Sections 4, 5 & 6 of the NRO amended Sections 18, 24 and 31A of the NAB Ordinance respectively; whereas through Section 7 of the NRO, Section 33F was inserted in the NAB Ordinance. These petitions came up for hearing before the Supreme Court on 12th October 2007.

The Supreme Court had observed that:

' ..... however, we are inclined to observe in unambiguous terms that any benefit drawn or intended to be drawn by any of the public office holder shall be subject to the decision of the listed petitions and the beneficiary would not be entitled to claim any protection of the concluded action under Sections 6 and 7 of the impugned Ordinance, under any principle of law, if this Court concludes that the impugned Ordinance and particularly its these provisions are ultra vires the Constitution of Pakistan'.

The history took another turn when on 3rd November 2007 emergency was proclaimed in the country by Gen Musharraf (President & COAS at the same time) under the garb of Provisional Constitution Order (PCO). Provisional Constitution (Amendment) Order 2007 was also issued, whereby, Article 270AAA was inserted in the Constitution, which provided protection to all the laws including Ordinances in force on that day. The interest behind the insertion of Article 270AAA was that the NRO should stay and prevail for all times to come.

It remains a fact of the history that Mr Asif Ali Zardari was lucky on two more counts in addition to the sympathy vote for the PPP accumulated after Benazir Bhutto's untimely assassination. Firstly the NRO signed between Benazir Bhutto and Gen Musharraf and secondly the PCOed lot of judges in superior courts brought in after 3rd November 2007's Emergency. Mr Zardari was there to extract maximum benefits from both of those boons. He got all the criminal cases and enquiries against his person and his team finished within days from the courts comprising of judges who were highly insecure.

Very few people know that during negotiations between her and Gen Musharraf, Benazir Bhutto did bargain only over those cases in which the husband and wife both were involved and not those criminal [including murder of Shahnawaz Bhutto] cases in which Mr Zardari was otherwise named. Those criminal cases against him were got cleared by Mr Zardari at the first priority from that insecure PCOed judiciary which task was not otherwise possible without NRO in place.

MR ZARDARI BREWED MAXIMUM BENEFITS:

After February 2008 elections, Mr Zardari immediately went to Raiwind to see Nawaz Sharif and pledged that the judiciary of 3rd November 2007 would be reinstated as their first priority. Subsequently four more mutual meetings in Islamabad, Murree, Dubai and London [9-10th May 2008] were held on the same issue and two written agreements were also signed commonly known as Murree Declaration and Dubai Accord but Justice Iftikhar M Chaudhry and his judicial team were not reinstated.

The intelligentsia was aware that Mr Zardari had held those meetings in series just to linger on the PCOed judiciary of the then CJP Abdul Hameed Dogar which was in fact entrusted [*on 15th February 2008; three days before elections*] an agenda of clearing all pending cases against him and the PPP stalwarts. This Himalayan task could only be accomplished by the Dagar's insecure judiciary none else.

On that day of 15th February 2008, Mr Zardari had moved a Consti-tutional Petition no: 265 / 2008 in the Sindh High Court (SHC) praying that all pending cases against him in Pakistan and abroad, on the instance of NAB or otherwise, should immediately be withdrawn. The petition contained the following points:

- *Claim no: 156 of 2006 filed by NAB against them in the High Court (Queens Bench of Commercial Division) London [it was regarding Rockwood Estate Surrey commonly known as Surrey Mahal] should be withdrawn under the provisions of NRO 2007.*

- *Joint Petition preferred before the Swiss Government asking Investigating Magistrate Geneva to proceed should be withdrawn under the provisions of NRO 2007.*

- *References no: 14 / 2001 (Assets Case), no: 41 / 2001 (SBS Case), no: 23 / 2000 (ARY Gold Case), no: 1 / 2001 (Resource Tractor Case) and no: 6 / 2000 (Polo Ground Case) all the five lying pending before the Accountability Court II Rawalpindi should be withdrawn under the provisions of NRO 2007.*

- *References no: 59 / 2002 (BMW Case), no: 35 / 2000 (CoTechna Case), the two lying pending before the Accountability Court III Rawalpindi be withdrawn under the provisions of NRO 2007.*

Similar two Constitutional Petitions no: 76-77 / 2007 were already lying pending in the Supreme Court because both were challenged or objected by the opponents on the basis that NRO, under which the petitions were asking for relief, was not justifiable before the law.

When the then SC got known that the PPP had won enough seats to make out the government after general elections of 18th February, the SC's bench comprising of CJP Abdul Hameed Dogar, J Nawaz Abbasi, J Faqir M Khokhar, J Ijazul Hasan and J Ch Ijaz Yousaf issued orders for the subordinate judiciary on 27th February 2008 that the petitions filed by the PPP or Mr Zardari be dealt with priority.

For 27th February 2008, those petitions against NRO were fixed but kept pending except that the order dated 12th October 2007 was vacated by the court saying:

'These Constitution Petitions are adjourned to a date in office due to indisposition of the learned counsel for the petitioners.

Meanwhile, in view of the rule laid down in the case of Federation of Pakistan vs. Aitzaz Ahsan (PLD 1989 SC 61), the observations made by this Court in Para 8 of the order dated 12.10.2007 in Constitution Petitions No.76-80 of 2007 to the effect ('words of above paragraph reproduced here') are deleted.

Resultantly, the Ordinance shall hold the field and shall have its normal operation. The Courts and authorities concerned shall proceed further expeditiously in the light of the provisions of the Ordinance without being influenced by the pendency of these petitions.'

Going back for a while, the Proclamation of Emergency of 3rd November 2007 as well as other extra constitutional instruments were (managed to be) challenged before the Supreme Court through *Tikka Iqbal Muhammad Khan vs General Pervez Musharraf*. The then CJ Justice Hameed Dogar heard it in a bench and declared that announcement of Emergency, the PCO of 2007, Provisional Constitution (Amendment) Order 2007, the Oath of Office (Judges) Order 2007 and the President's Order No.5 of 2007 were validly enacted (**PLD 2008 SC 178**).

Consequently, on the very next day two judges bench of the Sindh High Court [SHC] named J Khawaja Naveed and J Allah Sain Dino took cognizance of Petition no 265 / 2008 mentioned above and issued instructions to the subordinate judiciary of Sindh, NAB Offices and the Accountability Courts of Rawalpindi to submit written reports that all the cases against Mr Zardari, criminal or of civil nature, had been withdrawn by the prosecution.

The above offices were also ordered that no further cooperation of any kind be extended to the foreign countries in any case if related with Mr Zardari or the PPP office bearers.

The 'compliance' reports were submitted to the Sindh High Court by all concerned on subsequent eight (8) dates till the whole lot of cases were sent into cold room; last being 16-17th September 2008 when the NAB authorities had placed that famous letter from the AG's Office telling the SHC that Swiss Magistrate had been told to end the investigations because the Pakistan government was not interested in its follow up.

Peeping into the political arena of those days, it remains a fact that while Nawaz Sharif and his colleagues were jumping with joy over the negotiations with Mr Zardari to reinstate CJ Iftikhar M Chaudhry's judiciary, Mr Zardari was gaining time to get his cases concluded from the Kangaroo courts keeping them under pressure. The Murree Declaration was signed on 9th March 2008 setting out a time limit of 30 days. Actually it was the 30-day's deadline for PCOed judges. Those PCO judges had in their minds that their future survival depended on Zardari's deep smiles and delight.

Thus just after four days, on 12th March 2008, CoTechna case was finished. On 14th March 2008, BMW reference was finished in the Accountability Court III of Rawalpindi presided by Judge Saghir Ahmed Qadri.

On 24th March 2008, another PCO Judge Sofia Latif acquitted Mr Zardari in the famous double murder case of Justice Nizam Ahmed and his son with the consent of the Special Prosecutor Ne'mat Randhawa.

On 7th April 2008, another PCO Judge of the SHC J Peer Ali Shah cleared Mr Zardari from the murder case of Mir Murtaza Bhutto; just one day before the 30-day's dead line. *The last three cases were declared as decided 'in routine' and not under the NRO provisions.*

The PPP leadership requested Nawaz Sharif to extend the deadline for reinstating the defunct judiciary by ten more days.

On 15th April 2008, the District & Sessions Judge Hyderabad was moved that Mr Zardari be acquitted in another famous murder case of Alam Baluch and astonishingly, next day the Sessions Judge issued orders of Zardari's acquittal in the said murder case.

On 13th May 2008, another PCO judge of the SHC Justice Binyamin signed acquittal orders of Mr Zardari and Wajid Shamsul Hassan [Pakistan's High Commissioner in London] in that case of smuggling eight (8) suitcases of antiques via PIA from Pakistan for Surrey Palace under the garb of diplomatic immunity. This court order was also issued out of the NRO's purview.

On 16th September 2008, the two members bench [again; J Khawaja Naveed and J Allah Sain Dino] of the SHC disposed off the said Petition no: 265 / 2008 dictating that the learned Deputy Attorney General (DAG) had confirmed in writing and assured otherwise that the Swiss Court's proceedings had been ended and the High Court (Commercial Division)'s proceedings at London had also been stopped. The petitioner's lawyers Abubakr Zardari and Mr Hyder Ali did not press for further action thus the petition stood disposed off.

NRO DIED DURING GIMMICKS:

All the above mentioned and other alike cases were mainly dealt with by Justice (Rtd) Malik Qayyum as Attorney General and his Deputy Salman Aslam Butt who had been assuming those offices since Gen Musharraf's days. When the entire task was successfully accomplished and all the cases and enquiries were made dead and the files got isolated from the respective courts, Malik Qayyum was once again removed from his office unceremoniously and Latif Khosa was made the new Attorney General.

Till then Gen Musharraf was there as the President. When Mr Zardari got the whole cleansing job finished, he at once contacted Nawaz Sharif again [on 7th August 2008] to negotiate another accord to expel Gen Musharraf from the presidency and made another false promise with him to rehabilitate J Iftikhar M Chaudhry and his team within 72 hours.

The innocent Nawaz Sharif again fell prey to Mr Zardari and agreed to stand besides the PPP in the Parliament for General's impeachment which drama ultimately ended [on 18th August 2008] with the resignation of Gen Musharraf from the presidential slot.

Mr Zardari again refused to oblige his accord, pushed aside the judge's case and started moving towards the presidency announcing that *'political accords are not Qura'an & Hadith'* to be followed so sacredly.

[**Keeping the record straight;** *those were the Americans who piled up the pressure on Gen Musharraf to quit as army chief, the corps commanders never opted to request Gen Musharraf that he should quit the power game. The judicial crisis and the lawyers' movement had weakened Gen Musharraf but only up to a point.*

External factors played a decisive role in determining the outcome. Moreover, Pakistan was wholly sovereign in its nuclear program; the rest were merely the cries to keep the general populace worried all the time.

American alliance! One can't get up a fine morning and say that no NATO containers will pass through Pakistani territory. Yes, one can negotiate better deals ...... with any of the paymasters.

Mr Zardari was part of this larger design. Gen Musharraf didn't quit the presidency just like that. The Americans wanted him out because by then he was of no use to them. The US has fine-tuned the art of getting rid of troublesome allies but Zardari ...... was tailor-made for American requirements.]

However, the Supreme Court's bench under CJP Iftikhar M Chaudhry, vide its judgment dated 31st July 2009 (**PLD 2009 SC 879**) declared all the aforesaid five instruments, including NRO, to be unconstitutional, illegal and void *ab initio* deleting Article 270AAA from the Constitution.

Consequently the NRO, as well as 37 other Ordinances, 'protected' under the umbrella of Article 270AAA and sanctified by the judgment passed in

Tikka Iqbal's above referred case by the SC during CJP Hameed Dogar's time were left open to be considered and validated by the Parliament.

For this purpose the life of the Ordinances stood extended for another 120 days in case of Federal Legislation and 90 days in case of Provincial Legislation. The Supreme Court gave an opportunity to the ruling Governments in Islamabad and Provinces to legitimize their acts, actions, proceedings and orders, initiated, taken or done under those Ordinances by placing them before the Parliament or Provincial Assemblies with retrospective effect.

The PPP's government had felt it an easy task and opted to handle this job amidst high hopes. The NRO was placed before the Standing Committee of the National Assembly on Law & Justice in its meeting held on 29th & 30th October 2009. During the discussions and deliberations, some of the members did not agree with the decision of the Committee and left the proceedings in protest.

However, on 2nd November 2009 the Committee recommended that, after the proposed amendments in the Bill for enacting the NRO, the same may be passed by the Assembly. It may not be out of place to mention here that despite finalization of the report of the Standing Committee on NRO and before its approval by the Chairperson of the Committee, the Presidency asked the Federal Minister of Law [Dr Babar Awan] to withdraw the Bill under Rule 139 of Procedure & Conduct of Business in the National Assembly; reasons were not declared.

The PPP's efforts to table the Ordinance in the National Assembly could not materialize because they were not able to cultivate favours of 51% members sitting on the treasury benches. Amongst the PPP's allied parties only Awami National Party (ANP) could extend them help whereas the MQM and the JUI had opposed it. This exercise brought no cogent results because some of the PPP's own members had refused to accept the NRO.

Contrarily, the PML(N) and PML(Q) openly contradicted the said law, terming it 'black law', in the house and JI conducted voluminous rallies on roads and in all cities to mould the public opinion against it. As a result, the NRO could not be passed by the Parliament within its extended life; therefore, it lapsed on 28th November 2009.

However, Mr Zardari's cases could not be reopened because his legal team, under the able guidance of J (Rtd) Malik Qayyum had timely

managed to get orders and judgments from the respective courts '*over &
above the NRO's purview*'.

When the PPP government failed to congregate parliamentary backing
for the NRO, the Supreme Court started hearings on that ordinance on
7th December 2009. Embarrassed by its failure to get the NRO passed
by the Parliament, *the PPP government refused to defend the ordinance*
before the Supreme Court.

Even this wasn't the end of the matter.

When the Supreme Court sought information concerning the details of
NRO beneficiaries, the government made futile attempts to mask such
information. The revelation of the nature and extent of the charges and
the names of the beneficiaries, many of whom were continuing to occupy
key positions within the government, had caused significant erosion of
political credibility of the PPP government in general, and of President
Zardari in particular.

At the very beginning of proceedings in the Supreme Court, the Attorney
General's Office submitted that the Federation or the PPP's government
had no intention to contest the petitions seeking NRO as void. Mr Shah
Khawar, Acting AG had submitted in writing that:

> '.... *The Federation believes in supremacy of the Constitution of 1973
> and the Parliament. That the National Reconciliation Ordinance 2007
> was promulgated by the previous regime and I am under instruction
> not to defend it.*'

Kamal Azfar, senior ASC had submitted on behalf of the Government
that:

> ' .... *those who have benefited under the NRO should be proceeded
> against under the appropriate laws before the courts having the
> competent jurisdiction; as factual matters need to be determined by the
> trial courts.*'

The Supreme Court, giving a short order on 16th December 2009,
announced and declared that promulgation of the NRO was found
against the national interest and the substance embodied therein was
contrary to its preamble. Thus, it violated various provisions of the
Constitution; therefore, the NRO was declared to be an instrument
void *ab initio* being ultra *vires* and violative of various constitutional

provisions including Article Nos. 4, 8, 25, 62(f), 63(i)(p), 89, 175 and 227 of the Constitution.

Furthermore, all steps taken, actions suffered, and all orders passed by whatever authority or courts of law including the orders of discharge and acquittals recorded in favour of the accused persons, were also declared void and of no legal effect. It was also declared that all cases in which the accused persons were either discharged or acquitted under Section 2 of the NRO or where proceedings pending against the holders of public office had got terminated in view of Section 7 thereof, would stand revived and relegated to the status of pre-5th October 2007 position.

Under this order of 16th December 2009 all the concerned courts including the trial, the appellate, and the revision courts were ordered to summon the persons accused in such cases and then to proceed in the respective matters in accordance with law from the stage from where such proceedings were terminated in pursuance of above provisions of the NRO. Respective governments and all relevant authorities were directed to offer all possible assistance required by the competent courts.

On the same lines, all cases which were under investigation or pending enquiries and which had either been withdrawn or where the investigations or enquiries had been terminated on account of the NRO were revived and the relevant competent authorities were ordered to proceed in the said matters in accordance with law.

Any judgment, conviction or sentence recorded under section 31-A of the NAB Ordinance or if any benefit derived by any person in pursuance of Section 6 of the NRO were also declared null and void and consequently of no legal effect; reverting the case to pre-5th October 2007 position.

The Supreme Court had also taken notice that the then Attorney General Malik Qayyum had acted at his own to contact the foreign authorities or courts contrary to the provisions of Article 100(3) of the Constitution. Therefore, such communications sent by him to the Swiss authorities to abandon the Government's claims of huge amounts of allegedly laundered moneys by Mr Asif Ali Zardari & others were declared to be unauthorized, unconstitutional and illegal.

The Federal Government and other concerned authorities were ordered to take immediate steps to seek revival of requests and status of GoP's claims and the competent authorities were directed to proceed against Justice (Rtd) Malik Qayyum in accordance with law for his illegal conduct. Prior to the NRO ruling, the *New York Times* had reported that:

> *'Indignant Supreme Court judges demanded to know why $600 million in the suspect gains of President Asif Ali Zardari had been given back to offshore companies in his name rather than returned to the national treasury; where they said it rightfully belonged.'*

In this case a displeasure was also placed on record for Mr Nawid Ahsan, Chairman of the NAB, the Prosecutor General of the NAB and his 2nd in command namely Mr Abdul Baseer Qureshi. The Apex Court had also ordered Government of Pakistan to change that whole team.

Through this decision, Secretary of the Law Division Government of Pakistan was also directed to increase the number of Accountability Courts to ensure expeditious disposal of cases.

No formal comments as it was a decision of the Apex Court, but find below a script from most media reports of the next day' dated 17th December 2009:

From Butterscotch: Completely understandable! A landmark victory, first of its nature in the history of Pakistan......those responsible for laundering money or accused of stashing billions must be brought to the court of justice. BUT PLEASE enlighten me:

> *'Will there ever like ever be any accountability process for the armed forces and the high civil bureaucrats. Military men and high bureaucracy who have made fortunes, men who are far richer than our politicians, Generals & Secretaries etc, would they ever be tried for their misdeeds.*

> *This is not the victory of masses or judiciary, simply put it, security establishment has done it again. Media has been constantly barking about corruption, Zardari 10%, 600 million $ kickbacks on Agosta submarines effectively highlighting Zardari's 4.3 m $ share yet deliberately ignoring 49 m$ for top Navy men.*

> *They accuse Zardari of amassing 1.7 billion $, I can name at least 5 retired / serving Generals with assets more than 2 billion$. What about Shaukat Aziz, what about Musharraf himself, what about Gen Akhtar Abdul Rehman and his clan, Gen Zia and family, the likes of Imtiaz Billa or the infamous Major Amir who back in late 90s had more than 500 million worth of assets!!*

Who's going to hold them accountable?

Is our establishment above SC judgement?'

- *Kindly help me understand.*

[*Ref: Internet Site 'Changing up Pakistan' dated 17th December 2009*]

From Kalsoom: Dear Butterscotch,

Again, I completely agree. You can't just single one person out in all of this. Frankly, I don't understand why the people who brokered the NRO are not vilified further – the ordinance was essentially promulgated not only to allow Benazir and her party members to run for elections, but also to preserve Musharraf's power at the time – shouldn't he be held more responsible in the aftermath of this mess?

What about the officials in the Bush administration or those from Britain who brought these parties to the table? These nations often call for "democracy" yet essentially legitimize corruption by allowing the NRO to pass in the first place.

NRO JUDGMENT - PPP's UPROAR:

At the end of the day, corruption is an entrenched feature in all societies; truer for Pakistan – it is ingrained not just in politics but in daily life – in police forces, engineering services, top bureaucracy and among the military etc. The lessons one could have taken after this court ruling was not just a witch hunt for the people on the beneficiary list, but question was why such ordinances were allowed to pass in the first place.

Why should one glorify corruption and graft and then hope for progress? Corruption remained as much as a hindrance as violence, sectarianism, terrorism etc to Pakistan's progress and prosperity.

To cut short on *21st January 2010,* the 287-page detailed judgmentt was penned down by the Chief Justice Iftikhar M Chaudhry. The judgment was signed by Justice Khalil Ramday on 12th January 2010 before his retirement. Citing the example of Philipino dictator Ferdinand Marcos, the ruling said that the Philippine government had also brought the looted money by the dictator back to the country from Switzerland, which could be taken as a reference.

While giving the detailed judgment on NRO case, the Supreme Court had divulged its clear intentions that the legislature should not trespass into the domain of the judiciary while making legislation. Such legislation would be against the independence of the judiciary as ensured by the Constitution. The intervention by the executive, contrary to the principles of independence of judiciary, would be taken as unconstitutional.

The 17-member bench of the apex court, in the judgment, stated that:

'The legislature is competent to legislate but without encroaching upon the jurisdiction of the judiciary. If, it is presumed that the insertion of clause (aa) in section 31A of the NAO 1999, by means of section 6 of the NRO 2007, [as it was apprehended then and vastly propagated in media] is constitutionally valid even then it would tantamount to allow the legislature to pronounce a judicial verdict against an order or judgment of a competent court of law, declaring the same to be void ab initio.

Therefore........the action of the legislative authority [inserting clause (aa) in section 31A of the NAO 1999], would be considered a step to substitute the judicial forum with an executive authority.

Thus, it would not be sustainable being contrary to the principle of independence of judiciary, as mentioned in Article 2A of the Constitution, which provides that independence of judiciary shall be fully secured read with Article 175 of the Constitution.'

The Supreme Court had observed that right from the case *Government of Sindh vs Sharaf Faridi* (**PLD 1994 SC 105**) to Mehram Ali's case (**PLD 1998 SC 1445**), followed by Liaquat Hussain's case (**PLD 1999 SC 504**), this court had always interpreted Article 175 of the Constitution read with the Objectives Resolution (Article 2A) of the Constitution, guaranteeing independence of judiciary.

The judgment also described the domain of the judiciary by saying that:

'That in view of Article 203 of the Constitution read with Article 175 thereof, the supervision and control over the subordinate judiciary vest in high courts, which is exclusive in nature, comprehensive in extent and effective in operation.

Thus order passed by any court or tribunal which is not subject to judicial review and administrative control of the High Court and / or the Supreme Court does not fit in within the judicial framework of the Constitution.'

Let us move forward with another bunch of roses.

The plus and minus points on the governance of Mr Zardari be kept aside for a moment. Think that why the issues related with NRO were trumpeted at so high tone; because the army and PML(N) wanted to equalize their own scores through CJ Iftikhar M Chaudhry; though the later had already got their price of favouring the CJ in March 2009 for his come back along with his team.

To mention a few which are available on record, allegedly Nawaz Sharif was given total relief in the criminal cases of conspiracy erected against him by Gen Musharraf in the backdrop of October 1999's army coup. He got his qualification back through the Court to contest election again. He got his brother's Punjab government back in early 2009 which was being snatched by Governor Salman Taseer. He successfully managed the Election Commission and the Higher Courts to keep pending elections on National Assembly seats from Rawalpindi constituencies for the time he considered appropriate.

Nawaz Sharif, as widely propagated by the media, was also one of the actual beneficiaries of NRO when he had agreed to join hands with Benazir Bhutto in 2007 after she had signed her come back to Pakistan. He should have raised his voice against the NRO when he and his associates were coming back to Pakistan under the umbrella of the same NRO.

Even afterwards, when the PML(N) knew it that Mr Zardari had not fulfilled his promises at Murree and Bhourbon in early 2008, they should have blocked his way to the Presidency. Why they remained silent and provided approval for his go-ahead. Joining hands with Zardari in August 2008 for cogent threat of impeachment of Gen Musharraf is referred here.

Very strange that when this NRO law was alive, all were silent and when it went dead, every body was bent upon to hit the Presidency on this pretext. All they tried their level best to fire **Hussain Haqqani** from NRO gun but when the columnist Saleem Saafi wrote an article in 'Jang daily' in March 2009 declaring him as '**US envoy in the US**' then no one was moved to follow the writer.

BRUTUS YOU, TOO; SAYS ZARDARI:

On 30th September 2010, President Zardari dropped a bombshell in the PPP parliamentary party meeting when he made the shocking confession that he was betrayed and trapped by top players of the NRO game.

He told the shocked members that he was given certain assurances in exchange for not defending it before the SC. Without identifying anyone, Zardari said in his firm style that:

'The "players of the game" did not execute their promise and the cases against him were reopened despite earlier secret assurances. .....

Though he was betrayed and trapped but he was not down and would not take any "dictation" from any one and would face the current hostile situation, as he had been doing in the past.'

That was the moment when Mr Zardari opened his heart before his party men first time and shared the top secrets pertaining to his government policy not to defend NRO in the SC a year earlier. But finally, a besieged Mr Zardari shared his secret as to why he had asked the law ministry not to take any position in the court during the hearing of NRO case, which had led to unanimous verdict of 17 judges on this controversial law.

The parliamentary party meeting was held in the Presidency with Mr Zardari in the chair; PM Gilani also attended the meeting. Senator Dr Safdar Abbasi had tempted Mr Zardari, amidst heated discussion, asking the PPP government to respect the judiciary as it had missed the bus for defending the NRO in the SC; but his voice was never given any importance in the PPP circles.

Dr Abbasi had also urged the parliamentary party meeting that it was too late to submit a review petition in the SC and challenge the unanimous verdict of the court, as the judges had already collected a lot of documentary and other relevant stuff from NAB against Mr Zardari and others. He argued that the SC had now gathered sufficient proofs to proceed further.

President Zardari had surprisingly admitted his mistake, saying the PPP government should have taken a position and defended the NRO in SC.

The fact remains that during the days of NRO case in the SC, a Karachi-based former judge had secretly met Asif Ali Zardari in Presidency.

In this meeting, the former judge had advised Mr Zardari not to worry about the Swiss cases, as they were closed transaction. That retired judge had assured him that the judges would not open the cases against him.

Mr Zardari later discussed that judge's advice with his top legal aides; Babar Awan, however, had strongly opposed the idea. Awan maintained that his government should strongly defend NRO in the court with all its documentary guns and arguments, instead of leaving the field open for the judges to give any kind of judgment against him and the PPP. Babar Awan was ignored this time.

President Zardari had the shock of his life when he learnt that SC had ordered reopening of cases against him including the Swiss cases, which were closed a year ago. Zardari was said to have commented after reading the explosive contents of NRO judgment that a former judge had clearly used his credibility to trap him.

On the other count, Mr Zardari was unlucky in a way that he did not have a team of 'sincere friends' around him who themselves would have resigned from their portfolios [*as Saeed Mehdi had done in Punjab for PML(N)*] saying that Mr Zardari should not suffer at least for their follies.

[*The National Accountability Bureau (NAB) had filed the polo corruption reference in the accountability court in 2000, and included the names of former PM Benazir Bhutto, CDA official Shafi Sehwani, Mr Zardari and Saeed Mehdi, the then Chairman CDA. Saeed Mehdi was alleged to have constructed a polo ground at the Prime Minister House during Benazir Bhutto's first term as PM.*

It was alleged in the reference that the construction of the polo ground was executed on the verbal orders of Asif Ali Zardari and Saeed Mehdi. The polo ground cost an estimated Rs:52.29 million to the national exchequer while Mehdi was alleged to have embezzled Rs:0.6million.

The case was closed in 2008 after promulgation of the National Reconciliation Ordinance (NRO) and it was re-opened on 16th December 2009 after the Supreme Court annulled the NRO.

On 1st April 2011, Accountability Court at Rawalpindi had absolved Saeed Mehdi because President Zardari, the main accused in this case, had immunity while CDA official Shafi Sehwani was dead.]

More strange that so many people, including both factions of PML [(N) & (Q)], were demanding or at least expecting resignations from the President and his friends like Rehman Malik on the basis of their alleged involvement in NRO. They forgot their own history that why Faisal Saleh Hayat and Aftab Sherpao were called from London by their masters and respected them for seven years as federal ministers despite the fact that they were wanted in the NAB cases. Their cases were also running in the courts then.

When Nawaz Sharif had taken oath of his second time premiership in 1997, there were so many cases against him in various courts running active. It is on record that in July 1997 only, the Lahore High Court had given him the green slips of acquittal when the three major references of corruption against him were got fixed before Justice Malik Qayyum who issued 17 pages alike 'judgments of honourable acquittal' in those cases; details are available elsewhere in this book.

Would the Supreme Court go back to open such cases of Malik Qayyum's vicious decisions again especially when the world knows that the former Judge was removed from judiciary in an un-ceremonial and disgraceful way in 2001 and on the basis of similar jokes on High Court forum related with Saif ur Rehman's whims.

A veteran columnist of **daily 'Jang' Salim Saafi** had analysed the two situations this way:

> '*Why we are not crying against Nawaz Sharif for an NRO similar to this. He was even sentenced in some cases, more severe and stern to think, and his cases were also finished in a deal with an army dictator. Recall his leaving to Saudi Arabia on 10th December 2000. Benazir had also done a similar deal with the same army dictator.*
>
> *The **difference lies that one PM signed a deal to go out of the country while the other PM negotiated a deal to come back;** and more honourably to come back along with his rival politician Nawaz Sharif.*
>
> *One PM Nawaz Sharif did a deal to keep himself out of politics whereas the other PM Benazir Bhutto had done the deal to come back in politics. Who was better? Now there are cries over one later NRO but there is silence on the previous NRO.... Why so?*'

Media was right to ask then if the Supreme Court was above law to make any order of his own choice.

NRO DECISION – FACTUAL UPSHOTS:

Now the other side of the picture!

The Supreme Court's short order dated 16th December 2009 gave birth to a constant tension for the ruling regime of the PPP thus starting a new era of confrontation between judiciary and the executive. NRO was universally condemned. None of the federal or provincial governments or any of the beneficiaries of the NRO had attempted to defend or support it before the Supreme Court rather they, including the president, had accepted and agreed to honour the judgment. Later, a review petition was preferred but half heartedly contested.

May be the PPP was not expecting such a 'harsh' decision on NRO from the Supreme Court of Pakistan. Just after two days Mr Zardari called an emergency meeting of its Central Executive Committee (CEC) and ordered to set a campaign after he had one-on-one sessions with different party leaders, who extended all possible cooperation to the NRO affected persons within the government and outside.

At the very outset, the then Punjab Governor Salmaan Taseer and Fauzia Wahab, the PPP Secretary Information, both spoke in a defiant tone, saying how a country could ask a foreign government to open corruption cases against its own president thus making a direct hint that the PPP would not bother about the Supreme Court's verdicts.

There was a general question, however, that why was the PPP being singled out for accusations and high blame game. Other PPP leaders, especially from rural Sindh, delivered sermons in hostile tones and the provincial assembly members held press conferences in favour of the president particularly focussing on their 'Sindh Card'. A senior Punjab Minister Raja Riaz's argumentative and aggressive statement that:

> *'Sindh had already received two dead bodies, and if there was another dead body it would come to Punjab.'*

It was disturbing for the media and the general populace of Pakistan.

The President Zardari had once tried to malign openly certain judges and some elements within the armed forces. While thinking to resign one time after the judgment he was loudly asking:

> *'If the NRO was bad then why nothing has been done about the person who issued the NRO.'*

The fact remained that the same Supreme Court had already declared Gen Musharraf a usurper on 31st July 2009. He was sure that some people within the judiciary and army got help from the media and hatched a conspiracy to overthrow him then. He informed some of his friends immediately after the court verdict:

> '*I know they are putting pressure on me to resign because they cannot impeach me but I will not resign, I will fight, and I am ready to die like my wife Benazir Bhutto.*'

Declaring the NRO unconstitutional, the Court ordered the government to restart cases against Mr Zardari in Swiss courts because in Pakistan he was enjoying constitutional immunity as president. The PPP was seen in a state of panic that was visible in its CEC meeting, in which its Federal Minister Khurshid Shah had made a profound statement saying that:

> '*We (Sindhis) have already sacrificed two prime ministers for the federation but will offer no more sacrifices for the federation in the future.*'

At the same time, Aitzaz Ahsan defended the Supreme Court decision and said the judgment provided strong protection to the system and democracy. Mian Raza Rabbani had demanded dissolution of the cabinet and exclusion of some tainted ministers but the committee decided that all the ministers facing NAB cases would appear in courts showing their complete confidence on the judiciary.

In fact the trio of Aitzaz Ahsan, Mian Raza Rabbani and Dr Safdar Abbasi had strongly argued for resignation of the NRO-tainted ministers on high moral grounds but their voices were subdued by majority of the CEC members of the PPP.

During those hard days Mr Zardari was disappointed when once PML(N)'s former accountability Czar Saifur Rehman broke his silence after many years and said that cases filed by him in Swiss Courts against Mr Zardari were based on solid evidence. Mr Zardari sent a message to Nawaz Sharif asking if this was his (NS) style of reconciliation in which Saifur Rehman had been unleashed. Nawaz Sharif responded through a messenger:

> '*Trust me, I am not part of any conspiracy against you, I am not in touch with Saifur Rehman for a long time.*'

In the meanwhile PML(N) MNA Shahid Khaqan Abbasi was given the task of making Saifur Rehman silent. To reciprocate, Mr Zardari had then called meetings of National Assembly and Senate on 4th January 2010 to implement the Charter of Democracy which had earlier been signed between Nawaz Sharif and Late Benazir Bhutto in London in 2006. But that fortunate moment never cropped up.

The political intelligentsia then held the view that had the parliament taken a strong position about corruption and corrupt people, the judiciary could maintain silence over subjects like NRO, which was pulled through in the standing committee of parliament in flip-flop manner by the PPP.

> [*NRO could have been approved by the parliament but the PPP's own Prime Minister Mr Gilani did not want so.*]

Apparently, the government 'high-ups', tried their level best to get it adopted in the two houses of the parliament, but the political polarisation came in its way. Some of the PPP members had gone hostile; on whose instigation, it was not clear then.

After the decision of the apex court on NRO, the National Accountability Bureau (NAB) suddenly became more active and its FIA-dealing wing even super active especially in connection with the Exit Control List (ECL). On the next day of the decision, the Federal Defence Minister Mr Ahmed Mukhtar was checked and held at Islamabad Airport and was not allowed to take flight for China. He was going there to sign some official documents on behalf of Government of Pakistan.

The Federal Minister came back from Airport and launched his disapproval before media whereas the Chinese Ambassador in Pakistan officially lodged his protest. When probed, the NAB authorities took back his words saying that they had not sent the list of persons to be placed on ECL till then. Resultantly, Federal Interior Secretary, one Additional DG FIA and some other officers on duty at Airport were immediately placed under suspension for being 'over-active'.

Astonishingly the NAB was to file fresh references in several high profile cases involving politicians, retired Generals, business tycoons and bureaucrats against whom the NAB was barred from proceeding by Gen Musharraf. A number of cases of alleged corruption, which were 'made out' by the Bureau but remained inconclusive because it was stopped midway by the military regime, were also brought in light by those super-active NAB officers who were 'properly greased' afresh by some to chase their political opponents or business rivals.

The said files were pertaining to top PML(Q) leadership including all the Chaudhry brothers (namely Ch Shujaat Hussain, Ch Pervez Elahi, Ch Moonus Elahi, Ch Wajahat Hussain, Ch Shifaat Hussain and others); JUI(F) leaders Maulana Fazlur Rehman and former NWFP Chief Minister Akram Khan Durrani and Awami National Party leader Azam Khan Hoti, who was father of the incumbent NWFP Chief Minister Amir Khan Hoti and many more.

A former Chairman NAB, Lt Gen (R) Shahid Aziz, told the media that there were certain complaints about the then exiled PML(N)'s associates but the Bureau was asked not to probe them. Insiders explained that it may not be in the notice of the Chairman NAB or Gen Musharraf but the game was being played from within.

Whenever a complaint against any member of the PML(N) came up for action, the former DG Hassan Waseem Afzal invariably intervened and approached the concerned officer to twist and turn around that complaint in opposite direction thus convincing the Chairman to shelve the same in the name of 'political victimization'.

Similarly, there were more allegations against former interior ministers Aftab Khan Sherpao and Faisal Saleh Hayat but were not followed. Ansar Abbasi in the *Jang daily of 21ˢᵗ December 2009* claimed:

> '....... *Gen Shahid Aziz said that besides others he also recalled the corruption scandals concerning Central Board of Revenue, Pakistan State Oil, Pakistan Security Printing Press, and stamp paper fraud case. Aziz [the then PM] said that certain leading business groups were also required by NAB but their cases were not formally probed.*
>
> *Some of the top business groups had confessed to have defrauded bank loans worth billions of rupees and consented to pay back the looted money in instalments, as a result of plea bargain but they, too, later did not pay the agreed amount after they had developed right political connections.*'

Before the next SC hearing of NRO implementation case **on 13ᵗʰ October 2010**, backdoor channels tried to defuse the otherwise dangerous tension between the judiciary and the government after PM Gilani had agreed to take drastic actions to appease the apex court. The government had taken a sigh of relief after the SC accepted its plea to start hearing of the review petition on the NRO judgment pending before the Supreme Court since six months earlier.

During those backdoor discussions, it was considered that the summary would not be tabled in the court and most importantly certain actions would be taken in the light of the SC decision to send a loud message to all that the government was implementing the verdict.

Possibility was there that the parliament could take up and decide the issue of immunity to the president under Article 248 to dump the whole issue, which was the only irritation between the government and the judiciary. PM Gilani had already given a statement that he was going to fire all those ministers and officers who were the beneficiaries of the NRO.

To a question as to why the government had filed review petition in the SC when in the first place it did not defend the NRO in the court last year. It was revealed that the PPP government was feeling betrayed at the hand of a Karachi-based retired judge; as detailed above.

That former judge was considered close to the judiciary; had taken a draft with him to the President to ask his legal team not to contest the NRO case in the Supreme Court. As the top gun of the government felt betrayed, a decision was taken to file a review petition in the court and get the judgment reversed.

Perhaps that judge was known as 'Fakhru Bhai' some people opined.

SC's USELESS MONITORING BODY:

The SC had announced in their decision of 16th December 2009 that a monitoring body would be set up to chase the Accountability Courts dealing with NRO cases. It sparked a controversy of its own kind. The PPP considered it as an interference in the executive functions whereas the PML(N) and their allies took it otherwise. The PML(N) succeeded in gaining sympathies of a former Chief Justice of the Supreme Court, Saeeduzzaman Siddiqui, who opined that:

'I don't see any constitutional or legal hurdle in the setting up of these monitoring cells by the apex court for keeping a check on the functioning of the executive.'

[The PPP media Cell came forward with high peak voices that it was being done to chase the cases of Mr Zardari to settle their old score of not re-instating the apex judiciary throughout 2008. As per their version, the judiciary had forgotten that the accused, Mr Zardari, had been unable to get justice from them for more than eight years.]

Another former SC judge Justice Wajihuddin Ahmad added that:

> *"These cells will monitor whether the accused persons are trying to delay the court process through wrong tactics or whether prosecution is playing its role according to the law. These monitoring cells will have nothing to do with the decisions to be made by subordinate courts.*
>
> *There were many examples of such monitoring cells even in the case of the Indian Supreme Court.*
>
> *Trying to mould the things to serve some vested interests is very unfortunate on the part of certain elements who argue **why the judiciary is not considering some other cases**."*

(Ref: The News dated 21st December 2009)

Pakistan as a country was so unlucky that both the above referred Chief Justices, one of the Supreme Court and one of the Sindh High Court, never opted to make any such 'monitoring committee' for any of their decisions and never bothered to take cognizance of any corruption case or corrupt practice at their own throughout their tenures in their respective offices; most of the NRO cases belonged to their terms though.

Under that monitoring scheme, Justice Javed Iqbal was serving as a monitor for anti-terrorism courts of Sindh; Justice Khalilur Rehman Ramday for Khyber PK province; Justice Nasirul Mulk for Balochistan ACs; and Justice Sardar Raza Khan was monitoring the performance of the Punjab ACs. Till today not even a single 'monitory report' has come on record; or if it is there, the same was not made public.

On SC's said judgment on NRO, Ali Ahmed Kurd, the firebrand leader of the lawyers' movement and former president of the SCBA, who initially kept quiet for quite some time, surprised many with his blunt criticism on NRO's judgment. *Judges should "behave like judges"*, he said.

Speaking during a talk show on "Challenges facing the judiciary", Mr Kurd said that people had reservations about the verdict handed down by the SC on petitions challenging the NRO; the judgment appeared to be based on newspaper headlines and talk shows of private TV channels.

The NAB was being condemned by the NRO beneficiaries while the Supreme Court also found NAB's incumbent Chairman, the Prosecutor General and the Deputy Prosecutor General incompetent, therefore, the apex court judgment had directed the Bureau to transmit periodical reports of the actions taken by them with regard to NAB cases to the Monitoring Cell of the apex court set up following the same order.

No such progress report was ever sent by the NAB while the apex court never considered it worth chasing its own order.

For instance, the appointment of one banker named Hussain Lawai as president Arif Habib Bank Limited (AHBL) was challenged in the Supreme Court in the third week of December 2009. A social worker Tahir Amin of Lahore had challenged this appointment under Article 184(3) of the Constitution pleading that a person of dubious character who had been an NRO beneficiary and faced NAB cases after committing fraud of nearly Rs:1.82 billion could not be appointed as president or CEO of a public bank. Hussain Lawai had committed this fraud being the president of the Muslim Commercial Bank (MCB) and remained fugitive for over a decade.

On the request of the government of Pakistan, Interpol had arrested him from Canberra on 4th March 1998. He was brought back to Pakistan where he faced NAB cases but later he was given benefit under the NRO.

The court had admitted the plea at once for hearing.

At the same time, a venomous but an eye opening analysis of the NRO decision and its later developments was offered by Messrs Rivkin and Casey, Washington D.C. based attorneys, who had served in the US Department of Justice during the Ronald Reagan and George HW Bush administration; let us go through it now:

> 'Chief Justice Chaudhry's decision to overturn the NRO, opening the door to prosecute President Zardari and all members of his cabinet, was bad enough. But the way he did it was even worse..... The decision's lengthy recitations of religious literature and poetry, rather than reliance on legal precedent, further pull the judiciary from its proper constitutional moorings.

The fact that Mr Chaudhry's conduct has led some of his erstwhile allies to criticize him and speak of the danger to democracy posted by judicial meddling in politics; the stakes are stark indeed.'

Rule by unaccountable judges is no better than a rule by the Generals.

Pakistan is going normal amidst the fiction & facts of corruption, as it used to be. People are yet to see the fate of 'others' [beyond Mr Zardari] especially how [about 7750 out of 8041] Karachites got themselves absolved through making out a 'special committee' to review the NRO cases pending in NAB and the NAB Courts whereas the rest of the lot sitting in Punjab, Baluchistan, Khyber PK and Islamabad were left to go through the mill of hatred and humiliation.

Let us hope equal treatment for all in Pakistan.

[Part of this essay was published at www.pakspectator.com
on 19th January 2012]

Scenario 69

INDEPENDENTCE OF PAK-JUDICIARY [2010]:

Abdul Hafeez Pirzada, while drafting the 1973's constitution, might have trusted innocently that Pakistani and Indian's living were similar and both countries had experienced the same legacy of English rule so the judicial systems of the two countries could go alike. Thus he had worked out correctly that in Pakistani constitution the method of appointment of judges be inserted cn the pattern as in Indian Constitution wherein the same or similar provisions were given in sections 124 & 217 though now stands much reformed through various stages.

It was OK then but the time has gone much fast. Our Pakistani politicians and military rulers have been using this way of appointments in a wrong way that is why Pakistani court verdicts [mostly] are not trusted at any world forum [till 2009 at least]. Our courts are not believed; our decisions are not quoted anywhere, not even in Indian courts, declaring worthless.

Basically Pakistan had got a force of political appointees in the courts having constitutional security of service up to a certain age. What happened; that when a seat occurred in some High Court, the sitting political government or military ruler used to forward names of some advocates, having the required period of bar membership and age. They used to be either relatives of known politicians, or staunch workers of that political party, or 'paid sources' of ISI in military regime or they might have 'invested' huge amount of money to get their names approved, or might be lawyers but not be good law knowing persons with crystal conscious. Good lawyers earn much more money than judges.

Contrarily, some very competent lawyers might be available in the same bar but because they were not having any 'connection' with a top politician or a serving military General so could not come forward. This had been the situation which multiplied our hard luck.

There was always a mixture of political appointees in all the High Courts; old & fresh judges but with multiple attitudes, variant orientations and diverse senses of direction. All the bar members and the media knew well that which judge usually favours which party or military executive, therefore, it could easily be ensured that the cases of political nature or cases in which government was party, would go to 'certain named' judges only.

Once in the PML(N) government, the then Chief of *Ehtesab* Bureau Mian Saifur Rehman made sure that all the corruption cases on Benazir Bhutto and Mr Zardari were not to be dealt with on merit. He managed to place them before Justice Malik Qayyum.

It is still on record that in 1997, when the *Ehtesab* slogan was initially trumpeted high by Mian Saif, a deputy secretary named Aftab Syed from Establishment Division was specially sent from Islamabad to Lahore to 'launch & chase' those cases of corruption against Ms Bhutto, Mr Zardari, PPP's nearby officers and politicians. He stayed there initially for 22 days in a 5 star hotel on government expenses till he was sure that all 'important' cases were fixed before Justice Malik Qayyum.

This officer and another 'so-called honest' Deputy Secretary Nusratullah were later on awarded for getting all pre-arrest bails rejected, temporary injunctions terminated and permissions of FIRs granted against PPP-connected persons and some senior officers, all jobs accomplished by J Malik Qayyum; a judge on Ehtesab Bench of the Lahore High Court and real brother of one MNA Pervez Malik of PML, who was given an unopposed seat of the National Assembly vacated by the Prime Minister Nawaz Sharif himself from Lahore.

There were 30-35 more judges in Lahore High Court then, why only J Malik Qayyum and J Ehsan Paracha were entrusted this sacred job; because they were close to PML and thus in contact with Saifur Rehman all the time. Benazir Bhutto thought that 'enough is enough'. She was in exile at London and was mostly encouraging her associates to come forward with suggestions for a better Pakistan. Most of their deliberations were incorporated in '*Meesaq e Jamhooriat*' finalized in May 2006.

PRESIDENT's POWERS TAKEN OFF:

In Pakistan, the standing practice was that the Chief Justice used to recommend a list of names of proposed judges to the President and the President selected Judges from the said list. The recommendations of the Chief Justice were binding on the President, except for sound reasons to be recorded by the President.

Similarly, the most senior judge [normally] used to be appointed as the Chief Justice, except for concrete and valid reasons to be recorded by the President. In February 2010 an issue cropped up between the CJP and

President Zardari on judges appointments. The rumours cropped up that Mr Zardari was being sent home by the SC; it could not happen but powers to select superior court's judges were, however, snatched by judiciary's smart moves.

The script of ousting Mr Zardari was being written and staged by many players. *The Wall Street Journal of 23rd February 2010* had once mentioned that:

'*It was Mr Chaudhry's dismissal by then President Pervez Musharraf in 2007 that triggered street protests by lawyers and judges under the twin banners of democracy and judicial independence.*

This effort eventually led to Mr. Musharraf's resignation in 2008. Yet ***it is now Mr Chaudhry himself who is violating those principles, having evidently embarked on a campaign to undermine and perhaps even oust President Asif Zardari.***

Any involvement in politics by a sitting judge, not to mention a chief justice, is utterly inconsistent with an independent judiciary's proper role. What is even worse, Chief Justice Chaudhry has been using the court to advance his anti-Zardari campaign. Two recent court actions are emblematic of this effort.'

David Rivikin Jr & Lee A Casey, while giving above opinion were in fact referring to two judgments of the SC; one of 16th December 2009 in NRO case and the other was related with blocking of appointments in the superior judiciary by the SC in February 2010; a 3-member bench of the SC had given the verdict that '*the president failed to consult with the CJP*'.

This constitutional excuse had never been used before. The paper concluded by saying:

'....... *The second anti-Zardari effort occurred just a few days ago. There were street protests [sponsored by Nawaz Sharif's panel of lawyers]. Former PM Nawaz Sharif is now a leading opponent of the regime. There is a strong sense among the Pakistani elites that Justice Chaudhry has become Mr Sharif's key ally.*'

The stakes are stark indeed. ***Rule by unaccountable judges is no better than rule by the Generals*'** [Ref: **Judicial Coup in Pakistan** by Rivikin & Casey]

Taking light from the *'TIME' magazine of 27th March 2010* the bill [of 18th Amendment] was actually meant to take superior judicial appointments out of the hands of the president and place them before a legal committee that also included several justices. Instead of President, judges were to be confirmed by a parliamentary vote.

The analysts held that in fact the Prime Minister Gilani had very shrewdly played the double role in deflowering his own party's leader, President Zardari. The TIME's article spelled out that:

> *'Chief Justice's hand in the eleventh-hour stalling of parliamentary debate on the package through Nawaz Sharif was visible who objected to proposals on the selection of judges. Sharif's opposition resulted from being pressured by Chaudhry [the CJP].*
>
> **The chief justice threatened. He said he'd open up all cases against him. The other faction keeps that the conflict is caused by the government wanting a chief justice and court which is compliant, not independent.'**

The fact remained that Pakistan historically lived with the military's whims; transitions had been disrupted, and the judiciary in the past had invariably supported every military intervention. Thus there were perceptions that the Generals might be colluding with the judges to limit the civilian powers, already groaning under the weight of the president's sagging popularity.

Amidst all conspiracy theories 18th **Constitutional Amendment** was passed **on 20th April 2010.**

In pursuance of the 18th & 19th Amendments, a Judicial Commission was proposed to be created to recommend the appointment of Judges of the Superior Courts in Pakistan. Following is the collective text of the Article 175 (A) which was inserted in the constitution of Pakistan through this amendment.

Article **175 A.** Appointment of Judges to the Supreme Court, High Courts and the Federal Shariat Court:

(1) There shall be a Judicial Commission of Pakistan, hereinafter in this Article referred to as the Commission, for appointment of Judges of the Supreme Court, High Courts and the Federal Shariat Court, as hereinafter provided.

(2) For appointment of Judges of the Supreme Court, the Commission shall consist of—

    (i)   Chief Justice of Pakistan; Chairman

    (ii) [four] most senior Judges of the Supreme Court as Members

    (iii) a former Chief Justice or a former Judge of the Supreme Court of Pakistan to be nominated by the Chief Justice of Pakistan, in consultation with the [four] member Judges, for a term of two years; Member

    (iv) Federal Minister for Law and Justice as Member

    (v)   Attorney-General for Pakistan as Member

    (vi) a Senior Advocate of the Supreme Court of Pakistan nominated by the Pakistan Bar Council for a term of two years as Member

(3) Notwithstanding anything contained in clause (1) or clause (2), the President shall appoint the most senior Judge of the Supreme Court as the Chief Justice of Pakistan.

(4) The Commission may make rules regulating its procedure.

(5) For appointment of Judges of a High Court, the Commission in clause 2 shall also include the following, namely:-

    (i)   Chief Justice of the High Court to which the appointment is being made; Member

    (ii) The most senior Judge of that High Court; Member

    (iii) Provincial Minister for Law; Member

    (iv) an advocate having not less than fifteen year practice in the High Court to be nominated by the concerned Bar Council for a term of two years; Member

    [Provided that for appointment of the Chief Justice of a High Court the most Senior Judge mentioned in paragraph (ii) shall not be member of the Commission:

    Provided further that if for any reason the Chief Justice of High Court is not available, he shall be substituted by a former Chief Justice or former Judge of that Court, to be nominated by the Chief Justice of Pakistan in consultation with the four member judges of the Commission mentioned in paragraph (ii) of clause (2)]

(6) For appointment of judges of the Islamabad High Court, the Commission in clause (2) shall also include the following, namely:-

(i) Chief Justice of the Islamabad High Court as Member
(ii) most senior Judge of that High Court; Member

Provided that for initial appointment of the [Chief Justice and the] Judges of the Islamabad High Court, the Chief Justices of the four Provincial High Courts shall also be members of the Commission.

Provided further that subject to the foregoing proviso, in case of appointment of Chief Justice of Islamabad High Court, the provisos to clause (5) shall, mutatis mutandis, apply.

(7) For appointment of Judges of the Federal Shariat Court, the Commission in clause (2) shall also include the Chief Justice of the Federal Shariat Court and the most senior Judge of that Court as its members:

Provided that for appointment of Chief Justice of Federal Shariat Court, the provisos to clause (5) shall, mutatis mutandis, apply.

(8) The Commission by majority of its total membership shall nominate to the Parliamentary Committee one person, for each vacancy of a Judge in the Supreme Court, a High Court or the Federal Shariat Court, as the case may be;

(9) The Parliamentary Committee, hereinafter in this Article referred to as the Committee, shall consist of the following eight members, namely:

(i) four members from the Senate; and
(ii) four members from the National Assembly.

Provided that when the National Assembly is dissolved, the total membership of the parliamentary Committee shall consist of the members from the Senate only mentioned in paragraph (i) and the provisions of this Article shall, mutatis mutandis, apply.

(10) Out of the eight members of the Committee, four shall be from the Treasury Benches, two from each House and four from the Opposition Benches, two from each House. The nomination of members from the Treasury Benches shall be made by the Leader of the House and from the Opposition Benches by the Leader of the Opposition.

(11) Secretary, Senate shall act as the Secretary of the Committee.

(12) The Committee on receipt of a nomination from the Commission may confirm the nominee by majority of its total membership within fourteen days, failing which the nomination shall be deemed to have been confirmed:

> Provided that the Committee for reasons to be recorded, may not confirm the nomination by three-fourth majority of its total membership within the said period.

> Provided further that if a nomination is not confirmed by the Committee it shall forward its decision with reasons so recorded to the Commission through the Prime Minister.

> Provided further that if a nomination is not confirmed, the Commission shall send another nomination.

(13) The Committee shall send the name of the nominee confirmed by it or deemed to have been confirmed to the Prime Minister who shall forward the same to the President for appointment.

(14) No action or decision taken by the Commission or a Committee shall be invalid or called in question only on the ground of the existence of a vacancy therein or of the absence of any member from any meeting thereof.

(15) The meetings of the Committee shall be held in camera and the record of its proceedings shall be maintained.

(16) The provisions of Article 68 shall not apply to the proceedings of the Committee.

(17) The Committee may make rules for regulating its procedure.

18TH CONSTITUTIONAL AMENDMENT:

Till 20th April 2010, the day the 18th Constitutional Amendment was passed in the Parliament, the power to appoint judges to the Supreme Court (SC) was enjoyed by the President & the CJP; a system perhaps contrary to what the Constitution had suggested.

Through 18th Amendment in 2010, Pakistan got two forums for appointment of judges to the superior judiciary: a Judicial Commission with representation from the judiciary, lawyers and the federal government, responsible for recommending names of perspective judges; and a parliamentary committee to approve or reject these names but with assigning reasons if some name is rejected.

This mechanism had in fact curtailed the powers of the President and the political executive, which was also objectionable in deed, but the propaganda in the media was made that *'CJP's powers have been curtailed'* in the name of 'meaningful consultation' [*the phrase devised and more emphasized by the CJP Sajjad Ali Shah, in fact*]; poor PPP workers.

It was after the <u>Al Jihad Trust Case</u> (**PLD 1996 SC 34**) that the Supreme Court elaborated the meaning of the word 'consultation' and held that *'the consultation should be effective, meaningful, purposive, consensus oriented, leaving no room for unfair play'*.

In fact, the 1973 constitution intended to give the executive a lot of discretion in the appointment of judges. That was the reason they used the word 'consultation' and not 'advice' in Article 177 as well as Article 193 of the Constitution.

The 18th amendment also provided (vide Para 3 of Article 175A) that the president shall appoint the senior most judge of the Supreme Court to the office of the CJP thus formally recognising the principle of seniority and legitimate expectancy enunciated by the apex court in the Al-Jihad case and subsequently reiterated in some other cases.

The above given text of article 175A was inserted in the Constitution as 18th Amendment which was specifically concerned with 'judges appointments' but was challenged [*or manoeuvred to be challenged*] in the apex court on the pretext of independence of judiciary, a basic feature of the Constitution.

13th May 2010: Chief Justice Iftikhar M Chaudhry constituted a full bench [comprising of 17 judges] to hear petitions against the 18th amendment to commence on 24th May; about 15 petitions were filed in that row. Article 175 of the 18th amendment, dealing with the appointment of judges, was also challenged by some of the petitioners.

On 28th May 2010, the federal government raised objections on presence of the CJ in the larger bench hearing those petitions as was directly involved in the appointment of judges. The government was of the view that *'the Supreme Court can interpret the constitution but can not nullify an amendment'*.

It was urged that the 18th Amendment was not going to affect the judiciary's independence, as the three pillars of state were being given representation for judges' appointment; thus the petitions were liable to be dismissed.

Contrarily, the petitioners had insisted that the JCP's part for the appointment of superior courts' judges was against the basic structure of the Constitution. Advocate Akram Sheikh argued that the procedure for appointing judges was not included in the mandate of the parliamentary committee. He also requested for Article 175, dealing with the procedure of appointing judges, to be declared as null and void.

The proceedings went on day to day basis. On 3rd June 2010, Justice Ramday asked rhetorically: *'who would be responsible if the system itself commits suicide.'* Akram Sheikh maintained that the independence of the judiciary had been undermined with the insertion of Article 175-A in the Constitution. Justice Asif Saeed Khosa asked Mr Sheikh to give arguments on the merit of Article 175-A.

There appeared to be a vivid division amongst the respectable judges of the bench and once the CJP had to observe that *'the judiciary never claimed to be above the Constitution and the points raised by the judges of this bench "including me", are their personal opinions. However, the case would be decided on merit.'*

Justice Saqib Nisar inquired from Sheikh Akram whether the right of judicial review has been weakened with the inclusion of Article 175-A in the 18th Amendment. Further, that with three judges of the SC, Attorney-General and law minister included in the JCP, how could the judiciary's independence be undermined; even if two members of the Commission were from the outside.

Mr Sheikh continued that, due to this legislation, the judiciary had been undermined as two members, essentially outsiders and uneducated about such matters, would be authorized to appoint judges of the superior courts. *'The parliament did not say so nor the right to judicial review had been taken away'*; the CJ had observed

Lawyer Hamid Khan had argued that the procedure detailed in article 175-A for appointing judges to the superior courts violated the Objectives Resolution and contrary to the basic structure of the constitution; he criticized the composition of the JCP but from different angle. He also addressed the scope of presidential discretion in making appointments saying that:

> "While making the 1973 constitution, Bhutto consulted the then chief justice of Pakistan regarding the appointment of judges and those consultations were made part of the legislation.
>
> Since the US has a presidential system of governance, the Senate is authorized to appoint judges."

Justice Tariq elaborated that 'not only does the US president appoint judges but also ministers and diplomats, in consultation with the Senate. It's just in Pakistan that the Parliamentary Committee [PC] has been established just to appoint judges.'

Mr Hamid Khan told the apex court that he had objections to the inclusion of the Law Minister and Attorney General in the Judicial Commission. 'As the offices of these two people are temporary, therefore, should be excluded from the commission; also that the chief justice of Pakistan should head the judicial commission for the appointment of judges,' Mr Khan maintained.

Meanwhile, Justice Khalil-ur-Rehman Ramday also objected to the inclusion of retired judges in the Judicial Commission.

PM GILANI WENT AGGRESSIVE:

On 18th October 2010, PM Gilani conveyed his legal team appearing before the SC that day, not to give anything in writing from his office to confirm or deny previous week's development as he was greatly hurt and humiliated. His words as the chief executive of Pakistan were not believed by judges on bench despite his loud denial about unconfirmed reports of withdrawal of notification of judges' restoration.

It was with reference to rumours in the capital that, to end the Judiciary – Executive row, the PM was going to issue a notification of withdrawing his order of 16th March 2009 so that the whole set of 'reinstated judges', including the CJ Iftikhar M Chaudhry, would once more go home.

PM's utterance was a sort of defiance because the 17 judges clearly wanted a written statement from PM Gilani to confirm or deny the news about withdrawal of judges' restoration notification in writing because the SC did not believe in his verbal assurance. It was the most difficult day of PM Gilani's political life, since after 16th March 2009, when he had to convince President Zardari to restore judges.

PM Gilani was otherwise upset on two more counts; firstly because the MQM had suddenly announced a day before court hearing to send resignation of the Sindh Governor to the President. Secondly; because of an unexpected press conference of Nawaz Sharif in London in which he first time sent a loud message to all that finally Mr Gilani's government might not last long.

PM Gilani was under strong impression that he had good working relationship with the CJP. On several occasions, during hearing of various cases, the CJ had been making positive comments about PM Gilani. Likewise, first it was an uninvited PM Gilani, who had landed in the Supreme Court some months back in the evening followed by CJ's visit to PM House. This meeting had helped both sides to resolve the issue of Lahore High Court judges' appointment.

In those days, the working relationship between the two institutions were so good that PM Gilani had even issued instructions to his Principal Secretary Nargis Sethi that every file or order sent from the CJ office should be implemented even without brining the file before him.

However, last week's dramatic development had greatly disappointed the PM and he openly reflected his disappointment in his speech to the nation. That unexpected hard-hitting speech, full of carrot and stick policy, was jointly authored allegedly by PM Gilani and his Law Ministery.

By keeping the three provincial chief ministers at his flanks while making the speech, PM Gilani had tried to send a loud message that if his government was sent home; it would mean coup as three smaller provinces had complete faith in his government. The CM Punjab Shahbaz Sharif was not invited to attend that important meeting.

19TH AMENDMENT IN CONSTITUTION:

On 21st October 2010, the Supreme Court resolved many objections in the original text and for procedural implementation it asked the Parliament to reconsider Article 175A, thus the *19th Amendment in the Constitution* was passed which gave effect to the Supreme Court's observations. The changes made were:

Firstly; the number of the judicial members of the commission was raised to four from two (excluding the CJP).

Secondly; in case the PC rejects a JC's nominee, it would give reasons for the same to the latter through prime minister [in original 18th amendment the PC could reject any name without assigning any reason].

Thirdly; the meetings of the PC would be held in camera, where it might discuss the conduct of superior court judges [in original 18th Amendment it was not so provided].

Fourthly; in the event of the dissolution of the National Assembly, the PC shall comprise the members drawn from the Senate only.

The Charter of Democracy signed in London by Benazir Bhutto and Nawaz Sharif in May 2006 had provided a similar mechanism, no doubt, but in fact the Chief Justice had prevailed upon the political set up then in vogue. In doing so, it is said, that the PM Gilani's secret hand or his incapacity [*to smell the intrigue being the Chief Executive*] played a vital role.

What intrigue; one can compare the formation of the SJC and the Parliamentary Committee [PC] with the JSC [Judges Selection Commission] proposed in the Charter of Democracy.

• In the Chief Justice's SJC the names of the judges to be considered would always come out of the pocket of the CJP; no recommendations from Executive, or Bar Councils or any other legal forum.

• Think! which names or list of judges would be considered in the SJC; nothing except the CJP's sweet wish.

• CJP got the veto power to bring his own team of judges through SJC & PC gimmicks.

• SJC has the majority of judges in it and PC cannot discard the selection made by SJC.

Whereas in the original plans of Benazir Bhutto, the list was to be prepared by the Judges Selection Committee from open applications, from all practising lawyers on merits and through vast advertisements as now prevails in the British Judicial System.

Thus the tussle between the PPP government and Chief Justice Iftikhar M Choudhry once reached a decisive point when the Supreme Court was about to give its decision on the 18th Amendment; both parties entered an end game phase apparently. Babar Awan put up a boasting performance in his press conference and pointedly warned:

'There is also the case of some judges who have challenged the validity of the contempt of court notices issued to them.'

His message adequately hit his target as the SC's judgement on the 18th Amendment turned out to be a non-event [though the poor guy paid a heavy price later for saying such facts].

The SC's decision of 18th May 2011 used the 18th Amendment as tool declaring that 'the PCO judges can not be regarded as judges from 20th April 2010 when the 18th Amendment was passed and their removal from office therefore does not need the Supreme Judicial Council (SJC) process which applies only for judges.'

The government had not accepted the SC verdict initially but had to de-notify the said judges under 'warnings & threats' from the apex court.

Referring to Sa'ad Rasool in *'Pakistan Today' of 2nd June 2012*:

'....and perhaps most disappointingly, a resurgent Supreme Court that prides itself on its independence, also seems to have fallen prey to the same ideology of demonstrating institutional solidarity – apparent from the fact that **over the past three years (since restoration of the honourable judges) there has been no voice of dissent from any judge, on any bench, in any case** (with the exception of a partial dissent from Justice Nasir-ul-Mulk in the Mukhtaran Mai's case).'

See the 18th Constitutional Amendment through which an Article 63A was included in the Constitution which expressly declared that any member of the Parliament who "*Votes or abstains from voting in the House contrary to any direction issued by the Parliamentary Party to which he belongs shall cease to be a member of the House*" upon the recommendation of the 'Party Head'.

In other words, no member of the parliament was able to exercise his or her own mind to independently support or oppose a prime ministerial candidate or the budget, or any change in the Constitution. Even then Article 63A was unanimously accepted and endorsed by all.

More disturbingly, when the 18th Amendment was challenged in the Supreme Court, no one (the lawyers or the judges) suggested that inclusion of Article 63A had affected the 'basic structure' of Pakistan's constitution. The character of this constitution is trumpeted high as democratic but it is not; it has never been so.

Every political party in Pakistan is headed by some one Zardari, Sharif, Chaudhry, Pir, Wali or a Religious leader who then transfers that party to their sons & daughters taking it as family property; no elections in any party have been held ever. All party tickets in national & provincial assemblies and even for senates are either sold or given to their family members. All nominations are sold in the name of 'party fund', which is in fact the pocket of that Party Chief because the parties have never submitted their accounts to the Election Commission [till ending 2012 at least].

Who was to bother about; the judges and the CJP remained worried defending an age-old process of their own appointments.

The tragedy with Pakistan is the greed and incompetence of mostly ruling politicians belonging to all sects and parties. Due to their incompetence there were 'martial laws' and behind all the four martial laws there was a nexus of Generals, judges and a section of the press having 'good relations' with ISI or GHQ. Once Justice Ramday of the Supreme Court of Pakistan had opined that:

> 'Whereas the higher judiciary gave a temporary reprieve to military rulers, parliaments gave them permanent relief'.

Ayaz Amir, in his column in *'the News' of 16th July 2010,* had not considered it as the whole truth. The fact remained that the parliaments which sanctified the actions of military dictators were the creatures of those dictators and shaped by them but the judges who legitimized military takeovers were not under such compulsion. They were on their benches before those takeovers.

It is generally argued that no constitution in the world says there should be elections in political parties; not even American which poses as champion of democracy. Yet the lordships of Pakistan's superior courts observed that:

> 'With the provision of party elections deleted from the constitution, the command of the constitution is affected'.

The picture should be seen from both sides. In Pakistan, the politicians got it inserted through the 18th Amendments in the Constitution, making it mandatory, that there would be no elections in the political parties. Like the outer world it was not left open as choice of time.

In the rest of the world, the democracy stands established since centuries; why not we argue that there is no constitution in United Kingdom so why in Pakistan. In Pakistan our big politicians got this clause inserted only to keep the rule in their families; consider the PPP, PML(N), PML(Q), JUI(F), PML(Functional), ANP in that perspective

JUDGES BEHAVIOUR IN ARMY & CIVIL RULE:

The flag bearers of **independence of the judiciary** soon started roaring in the name of *'flouting the Constitution'* and approached the SC. Some held the opinion that it was basically instigated by the custodians of the apex judiciary because the CJP's chair was loosing 'some powers' for all times to come; some held that it was the president who had lost all his powers.

The SC heard the case for five months and *'directed the Parliament'* to amend the mechanism [*many believed that the SC had no authority to issue directions to the Parliament requiring it to amend the Constitution*]. The Parliament, however, had incorporated the Court's directions through the 19th Amendment to assign a 'bit larger' role to the CJP; the Parliamentary Committee would state reasons for rejecting the Judicial Commission's nominations.

Going into details: the SC Bar Association and some senior lawyers had filed the above mentioned petitions challenging the 18th Amendment largely on the basis that:

(i) The apex court has the authority to consider amendments to the Constitution on their merit and strike them down if they are found inconsistent with the Constitution's 'basic structure.'

(ii) The new mechanism for appointment of judges undermines the independence of the judiciary and should thus be declared invalid.

Babar Sattar, in his analysis [*'the News' of 24th April 2010* is referred], opined that *'the court can change its mind on a matter involving constitutional interpretation but Hamid Khan, Qazi Anwar and Akram Sheikh should have acknowledged that they are once again asking the court to do what it has refused many times over the last 35 years; making*

India's structure theory a part of Pakistan's constitutional doctrine and strike down constitutional amendments on its basis.'

India's basic structure theory is that the parliament's amendment powers do not give it the right to alter the basic structure of the constitution as determined by the judiciary. This theory raises two fundamental questions:

(a) How is a written constitution to be amended, and can a parliament bind successor parliaments; and

(b) What are the limits of judicial review powers and whether judges make law or interpret it?

In Pakistan's case, Article 239 unequivocally states that (i) there is no limitation on the authority of parliament to amend the Constitution, and (ii) the court must not entertain legal challenges against constitutional amendments.

In the light of these phrases the court should not disregard unambiguous provisions of Article 239 under the garb of constitutional interpretation nor should it inject judicial assumptions into the Constitution. In fact Articles 238 and 239 were incorporated in the 1973's Constitution to specifically empower future parliaments to facilitate the evolution of our fundamental law in accordance with changing needs and wishes of the society.

In the past, Pakistan's Supreme Court has maintained through its earlier case laws that *'the court has no authority to strike down a constitutional amendment'*. However, the apex court's contention that 'the parliament has limited authority to amend the salient features of the Constitution' seems to be stepping out its limits because it is the domain of the people of Pakistan not of the court.

However, the lawyer's community went divided on the 'basic structure' doctrine. One thing which was felt missing from all this drama was the quotes of relevant jurisprudence. In *State v. Zia ur Rehman, PLD 1973 SC 49* the Supreme Court had held:

'So far, therefore, as this Court is concerned it has never claimed to be above the Constitution nor to have the right to strike down any provision of the Constitution ..... And that it will confine itself within the limits set by the Constitution'.

In the case of *Federation of Pakistan v. Saeed Ahmed Khan, PLD 1974 SC 151* the Court's response was:

'*In any event, it is not possible for us to declare that a provision of the Constitution is not law ...... We cannot strike it down. We can only interpret it, according to the accepted rules of interpretation and define its nature and scope*'.

In the case of *Islamic Republic of Pakistan v. Abdul Wali Khan, PLD 1976 SC 57*, the court had stated that:

'*This Court is committed to the view that the judiciary cannot declare any provision of the Constitution to be invalid or repugnant to the national aspirations of the people and the validity of a Constitutional amendment can only be challenged if it is adopted in a manner different to that prescribed by the Constitution*'.

In 1977, the Supreme Court again rejected the argument that it could strike down a constitutional amendment; this time in the case of *Federation of Pakistan v. United Sugar Mills Ltd., PLD 1977 SC 397*. This case is particularly significant because the challenge here was to the 4th Amendment which restricted the power of the courts to grant interim relief and thus directly affected judicial power. Here too, the Supreme Court upheld the amendment and rejected the basic structure argument.

However, in many subsequent judgments, the Supreme Court of Pakistan had noted that '*certain basic features of the Constitution cannot be altered by the Parliament*'. For example, in the case of *Mehmood Khan Achakzai v. Federation of Pakistan, PLD 1997 SC 426*, the then Chief Justice Sajjad Ali Shah identified these basic features as "federalism and Parliamentary Form of government blended with Islamic provisions." [However, two other judges (Justice Saleem Akhtar & Justice Raja Afrasiab) had differed with their CJ.]

Later, the whole issue of basic structure was re-examined by a seven member full bench in the case of *Wukala Mahaz Barai Tahaffuz Dastoor v. Federation of Pakistan, PLD 1998 SC 1263*. In his leading judgment, the Chief Justice Ajmal Mian had concluded that:

'*It is evident that in Pakistan the basic structure theory consistently had not been accepted. But if the Parliament by a Constitutional Amendment makes Pakistan as a secular State, though Pakistan is founded as an Islamic Ideological State, can it be argued that this Court will have no power to examine the vires of such an amendment.'*

[One can ponder into the saga of our judicial past that the three case laws relating to the 1970's had judgments declaring that Constitutional Amendments 'cannot be altered by the SC'.

The later three case laws which said that 'SC can take up petitions challenging Constitutional Amendments' belong to the 1990's, also an era of democratic rule in Pakistan.]

Finally, in the case of *Zafar Ali Shah v. Federation of Pakistan, PLD 2000 SC 869*, the Supreme Court held that while Gen Musharraf could amend the Constitution in his discretion, he could not alter the basic features of the Constitution (this time declared as 'independence of Judiciary, federalism and parliamentary system blended with Islamic provision.')

Let us move forward. In the case of *Pakistan Lawyers Forum v. Federation of Pakistan, reported as PLD 2005 SC 719*, a five-member bench of the Supreme Court again examined the whole basic structure controversy and noted that:

> '*It has repeatedly been held in numerous cases that this Court does not have the jurisdiction to strike down provisions of the Constitution on substantive grounds. The 1973 Constitution has certain "basic features" but this did not mean that it was the job of the judiciary to enforce those basic features.*
>
> *[Observed in Para 56 that] while there may be a basic structure to the Constitution, and while there may also be limitations on the power of Parliament to make amendments to such basic structure, such limitations are to be exercised and enforced not by the judiciary but by the body politic, i.e. the people of Pakistan.*'

The 2005's judgment in the Pakistan Lawyers Forum Case was signed by Justice Iftikhar M Chaudhary [CJP at the time of 18th Amendment and its challenging petitions] and Justice Javed Iqbal [later retired].

The judgment given by the SC in Al-Jehad Trust Case [in 1996] had provided opening for a new constitutional order by redefining the amended constitution in a manner conceived to promote a process of genuine democratization. Whereas some argued that the Supreme Court, in the 'Judges Case' had acted beyond its jurisdiction and had gone to the extent of enacting the law rather than interpreting it.

Several constitutional experts had disagreed with the CJ Sajjad Ali Shah's Court ruling on the binding recommendations of the Chief Justices for the appointment of judges because the President, not the Chief Justices concerned, was the appointing authority. In some countries the appointment of the judges of the superior courts is made by the Chief Executive.

The 1973 constitution, in force during the 3rd spill of PPP's political rule, still retained some features of the anti-democratic amendments which Gen Ziaul Haq had incorporated at the gun point. The apex court had struck down in those days Gen Zia's legacy of Article 203-C, (which provided for the transfer of judges to the Shariah Court) being in conflict with Article 209; though had entered an uncharted terrain but it was a healthy development.

DISCRIMINATION FOR LADY JUDGES:

The percentage of women judges in superior courts has been 2.91 % as against the 33 percent required by the UN Beijing Conference of 1996 to which Pakistan is a signatory. The reasons defined by the activists were:

- Firstly, that there is no culture in the superior courts for accepting women as being intelligent and capable of becoming a good judge.

- Secondly, that the female judges cannot provide justice because they are more concerned about their dress and covering their body parts rather to concentrate on the case law during a hearing.

The mindset is strong in the higher judiciary that the appointment of female judges should be resisted. Two senior women judges were 'convinced' to withdraw their names from the list for elevation to the Supreme Court; **Justice Mrs Fakhrunnisa** of the Lahore High Court had been very active in the Black Coat Movement but was dropped being a woman.

Justice Mrs Khalida Rasheed, former judge of Peshawar High Court [PHC] was qualified to become the chief justice of the PHC in 1997 but, to block her way to the Supreme Court, was given an international assignment. She was the only candidate qualified to fill that vacancy then. This was PML government which wanted to impose Shariah law though it was finally rejected by the Senate but Mrs Khalida was made a scapegoat in the name of Shariah implementation.

Instances are there where the women judges were not treated as equal partners. A former lady judge, **Justice Qaiser Iqbal** of Sindh provincial High Court, was terminated on the charges of taking the oath on the PCO of Gen Musharraf.

During her appeal in the Supreme Court, the judges at the bench, including the Chief Justice in person had insulted her and passed sarcastic remarks on many occasions. She was made to stand for the whole day before the bench and was not allowed to take a chair; an utter disgrace for a lady judge of the High Court. She became so dejected by the insults at the hands of SC's bench that *she once tried to commit suicide.*

Justice Mrs Yasmin Abbasi of the Sindh High Court was also terminated on the charges of taking oath under Gen Musharraf's PCO. She fought her case bravely but was assigned a government job instead. She was bold enough to tell the Supreme Court bench that she would not apologise at any cost; she never took the oath illegally. Later, she was transferred to the Ministry of Law as Secretary.

Justice Ms Rukhsana Ahmed, confirmed judge since 2010, was terminated on medical grounds, and accused by male judges of being mentally ill as she always decided cases on merit. She further angered them by not agreeing with the chief justice's opinions on politically motivated cases. It was hard to punish her on the charges of taking her oath under the PCO being a confirmed judge so was simply sent home on other grounds.

Justice Majida Rizvi, was the first woman judge in Pakistan, was also not given the position of senior judge when a dispute arose amongst justice Bhagwan Das, Justice Nazim Siddiqui and her. She was appointed as judge in Sindh High Court in 1994 when Benazir Bhutto became PM for the second time. If she was given the status of senior judge of the High Court she would have become the judge of the Supreme Court along with justice Bhagwan Das.

Fact remains that women judges have never been considered for the Supreme Court slots; a clear indication of gender discrimination. **There has been no woman judge in the SC since decades.** The Federal Shariah

Court has two judges neither of which are women. The Islamabad High Court has three judges once again none of them are women. It is generally felt that there is a mindset in the superior judiciary of Pakistan to neglect women or undermine their capabilities of doing justice.

A judicial policy was announced in 2009 by the Chief Justice Iftikhar M Chaudhry where there was no mention of seats for women judges nor there do any mention about the court's will to work against this discrimination. The Asian Development Bank has spent more than USD 350 Million for the reforms in Pakistan's judiciary and has mentioned that woman judges should be appointed; but no heeds.

LAST WORDS – NOT PERSONAL:

Black Coat Movement of March 2007-09 brought many other virtues in the superior judiciary in Pakistan; reinstatement of CJP Iftikhar M Chaudhry and his fellow judges was the initial benefit which had marked the history. But vendetta and revenge in Pakistan's judiciary and politics remained intact since decades and continuing till today even; one can see CJP Iftikhar M Chaudhry's numerous hearings after 2009.

In 1994, when Dr Nasim Hasan Shah retired as Chief Justice of the Supreme Court, Justice Sa'ad Saud Jan should have rightly taken his place; but was superseded by Justice Sajjad Ali Shah, who ranked third in the seniority.

The *US Human Rights Report on Pakistan [1995]* had termed Pakistan's judiciary as 'not independent in reality'. It stated that:

> 'The constitution provides for an independent judiciary but in reality the judiciary is not independent. Through the President's power to transfer high court justices and appoint temporary and ad hoc justices, the executive branch is able to influence the Supreme Court, the provincial high courts, and the lower levels of the judicial system.
>
> It has become a standard practice to appoint judges to the high courts and Supreme Court on temporary basis for a period of one year and later confirm or terminate their appointments after an evaluation of their performance. Those temporary judges, eager to be confirmed tend to favour the government's case in their deliberations. Judges in the Special Terrorism Courts are retired jurists, who are hired on renewable contracts.

The Supreme Court once denied bail to an MNA of opposition in case where bail would routinely have been granted by a lower court.

On 31st July 1994, Qurban Sadiq, a special judge for the Banking Court, was removed from the post a day after he granted interim bail to the father of opposition leader Nawaz Sharif.'

On 19th April 1999, the Chief Justice of the Sindh High Court (SHC), when elevated to the Supreme Court had admitted in a full court reference held in his honour that:

'Confidence of the people in the judiciary had been shaken. The concept of accountability of the superior judiciary [under Article 209] by the Supreme Judicial Council (SJC) has failed in checking and containing malpractice, corruption and misconduct within the judiciary.

The council, constituted under Article 209 of the constitution, performs its functions only at the whim and fancy of the president'.

Let us hope if the dreams come true.

[Part of this essay was published at www.Pkhope.com on 14th July 2011 under title 'More Reforms needed in Judiciary']

Scenario 70

ON NRO'S IMPLEMENTATION:

On 25th November 2011, the review petition in respect of National Reconciliation Ordnance of 2007 filed by the PPP regime in early 2010 was dismissed by the Supreme Court of Pakistan. The government was told in explicit terms that the decision of 16th December 2009 should be implemented in letter and spirit. The much debated question of the presidential immunity was once again answered by the apex Court when it clearly said that it did consider documents, pertaining to Swiss courts, but still dismissed the review petition.

The SC order, like the NRO's original judgment, did not talk of any immunity but fully endorsed its original ruling, asking for re-opening of all the corruption cases both within the country and abroad.

PPP'S OFFICIAL STANCE:

The Government of Pakistan maintained that the cases which had been mentioned in the NRO were politically motivated and amounted to victimization. This argument failed to find any favour with the judges. Then falling on the second line of defence according to which the president's office was enjoying immunity under the constitution.

It was for the legal minds to decide the immunity question. Outside the courts the ultimate public jury remained furious over mega scandals of corruption which were more visible in times when the rulers of PPP & PML(N) both were unable to provide relief to the people. The factor went as the biggest cause of concern for Mr Zardari and his set-up.

A little back; referring to *'the News' of 13th May 2008*, Farahnaz Ispahani, an MNA from the PPP, in her article titled 'Understanding Reconciliation', kept the view that:

'*The flip side of the argument is that Ms Bhutto "accepted a deal" to save herself and in return helped save General Musharraf. The fact being ignored in this debate relates to how the investigation, prosecution, and judicature system in Pakistan has consistently been a political exercise, susceptible to the influence of the state instead of being an independent process.*

Some people now want Pakistan's largest political party [PPP] and its leadership to remain hostage to court proceedings even after eleven years of non-stop vendetta.

None of them protested when Asif Zardari was kept in prison for eight-and-a-half years, without bail and without conviction in a single case. But they express outrage over a settlement that makes it possible for the country to move forward the process of democracy and to end the politics of vengeance and vendetta.'

On **1ˢᵗ December 2009, a live program of GEO** with video showing Wajid Shamsul Hasan carrying cartons of documents from the Swiss Solicitor's office was shown at world media channels and is still available on **Youtube.** The comments given therein were:

'This is a clear signal to Pakistani people to wake up. Your leaders and their appointees are only there to kill, rob and disgrace you in front of the other nations. What a bizarre ambassador who was appointed in last PPP (no offence plz) Government and stayed in the UK as asylum seeker (fake) for years.

How can he be sincere with Pakistan? Please all you who love Pakistan and want to help or come along, please join my voice....UNHCRO (United National Human Civil Rights Organization) coming soon.'

Referring to Amanda Hodge's essay published in *'The Australian' of 10ᵗʰ December 2009,* a week before the SC's judgment on NRO:

'President Asif Ali Zardari amassed a fortune of more than $US1.57 billion during his slain wife Benazir Bhutto's time as prime minister.

Mr Zardari was facing charges [before the SC] of amassing assets beyond his means, including six cases of kickbacks and misuse of power, when former president Pervez Musharraf introduced controversial amnesty legislation in 2007 [NRO].

The cases included the alleged misuse of authority to grant concessions to shipping companies and a gold importing firm and to purchase tractors for a government-run scheme, involving hundreds of millions of rupees (millions of dollars) in public funds.

Mr Zardari owned properties and bank accounts in several countries, including Britain, the US and Spain, and that in 1996 he purchased a $US 4 million, 144ha estate in Surrey, England.

Mr Zardari earned himself the unflattering moniker of "Mr Ten Per Cent" during his wife's time in power, because of his rumoured demands for kickbacks.'

[During the second week of December 2009, the NAB had submitted details of Zardari's assets, worth 1.5 billion dollars before the Supreme Court. The *Dawn quoted* the NAB, as alleging that Zardari had accumulated these assets through 'illegal means' which Mr Zardari had denied.

Mr Zardari's illegal assets were confiscated by NAB, but de-frozen within days of the promulgation of the NRO in 2007. Presidential spokesman Farhatullah Babar confirmed that Zardari had taken back all his frozen assets through courts after the NRO was implemented. Some details were:

• Around $13 million were frozen in bank accounts in Geneva; allegedly kickbacks from Swiss cargo inspection companies.

• Twenty-five bank accounts of Zardari were frozen—and then defrozen after NRO. These included accounts in the Union Bank of Switzerland (UBS), Citibank Private Limited and Citibank, Dubai.

• Among the confiscated properties belonging to the couple, or held in *benami*, were 150 acres of land in Sanghar, Nawabshah and Hyderabad; eight acres of land at Hawksbay and one-acre plots each in Clifton and Saddar, Karachi; six sugar mills, two textile units, one cement, two chemical and one ice factories.

• 365 acres of Rockwood Estate (Surrey Palace), apartments in the posh Queens Gate Terrace and Hammersmith of London, four shops in Brussels and two apartments in Brussels. The Surrey Palace later was sold to an English property developer.]

Fascinatingly, the prime minister, his cabinet members and the PPP leaders had been claiming blanket immunity for President Zardari after 16th December 2009's decision on NRO, but this very question was not raised by federation's any counsel or President Zardari's representative lawyer or the federal law ministery even once during the hearings of the petition.

The SC's judgment did not recognize any exception or immunity while declaring the NRO void *ab initio*. In its decision [dated 16th December

2009] on the NRO, the SC did not discuss President Zardari but had ruled:

> 'From the day of its (NRO) promulgation i.e. October 5, 2007, as a consequence whereof all steps taken, actions suffered, and all orders passed by whatever authority, any orders passed by the courts of law, including the orders of discharge and acquittals recorded in favour of accused persons, are also declared never to have existed in the eyes of law and resultantly of no legal effect.'

Similarly, without talking of any immunity, the SC had ruled that *all cases* which were under investigation and which had either been withdrawn or where the investigations or enquiries had been terminated on account of the NRO of 2007 shall also stand revived and the relevant and competent authorities shall proceed in the said matters in accordance with the law.

Contrarily, the NAB under Admiral (retd) Fasih Bukhari, was completely satisfied with the implementation of the NRO judgment; posing complete trust in the Bureau's prosecution [*in fact behaving as a friendly prosecution*] but disowned the standing and credibility of the corruption cases framed by the Ehtesab Bureau under Saifur Rehman.

NAB also maintained that all NRO cases had already been reopened while the question of writing to the Swiss government and other foreign authorities for reopening of corruption cases abroad did not pertain to NAB but related to the Attorney General's office. In fact NAB never went into review but started implementing the NRO decision of December 2009 with all zeal and fervour.

Though the NAB argued that the question of writing to the Swiss and other foreign authorities for reopening of corruption cases against President Zardari abroad did not pertain to their domain, the officials believed that writing to the Swiss authorities for reopening of corruption cases, as was directed by the apex court, was no more required because the ground realities had changed.

Interestingly, NAB, which had spent millions of rupees from the public pot during the last 13 years, disowned the NRO cases and started questioning the evidence collected. Moreover, NAB remained with the view that:

> 'Since the trial courts had acquitted all the accused here in Pakistan, some [pointing towards Benazir Bhutto] have already expired while

President Zardari enjoys constitutional immunity, therefore, writing to the Swiss authorities was no more required'.

ADNAN KHWAJA & BRIG IMTIAZ's CASES:

At an earlier hearing, the court was informed that one Adnan Khwaja was appointed as Managing Director of the Oil & Gas Development Corporation Limited (OGDCL) on the verbal orders of PM Mr Gilani.

'Is appointing a matriculate [an education level in Pakistan a year less than GCSE of UK] as head of the OGDCL not misuse of authority?'

Justice Khosa had asked; adding that NAB's silence over the misuse of official authority was criminal negligence. NAB's Prosecutor General, K K Agha, had told the court that NAB had not investigated the said case.

The apex court directed NAB to investigate the appointment of Khwaja as OGDCL's head and directed the NAB Chairman to personally appear at the next hearing along with records to explain the appointment of Khwaja and Ahmad Riaz Sheikh, an FIA officer but later convicted, who was then reappointed FIA Additional Director General at a later stage.

The Supreme Court noted that Ahmed Riaz Sheikh was a convict and thus an inquiry into his reappointment was necessary. The apex court also summoned the acting law secretary who had prepared the summary of Mr Sheikh's reappointment. A little more details here.

On 21st September 2010, the SC ordered the NAB to take into custody former spymaster Brig (retd) Imtiaz Ahmed and the recently appointed and removed Managing director [MD] of OGDCL, Adnan A Khwaja, who had been in appeal against their conviction on corruption charges. Both Mr Khwaja and Brig Imtiaz were taken into custody by Islamabad Police straightaway from the courtroom and were escorted to judicial lock-up in a police vehicle already parked in the SC premises. They were required to furnish fresh surety bonds within three days as their earlier surety bonds for bail stood discharged after their acquittal under the NRO.

Additional Prosecutor General NAB Raja Aamir Abbas had informed the bench that Brig Imtiaz had undergone a part of sentence till then and he still had to undergo the remaining period prison even if he paid the fine. Rawalpindi's Accountability Court had awarded Brig Imtiaz eight years rigorous imprisonment and a fine of Rs:7 million on 31st July 2001. He was released from jail on bail by the Lahore High Court on 8th June 2002.

Adnan Khwaja was sentenced to two years rigorous imprisonment and a fine of Rs:200,000. Till then he had already served one year, one month and eight days in jail, including remissions, but 10 months and 22 days were still remaining.

After the promulgation of NRO both the accused, Brig Imtiaz & Adnan A Khwaja had claimed benefit under it. After the acquittal under NRO, Mr Khwaja was appointed Chairman of the National Vocational and Technical Education Commission (Navtec) on 2nd June 2008; was not allowed to draw any salary, but entitled to all perks & and privileges. However, when the NRO was declared unconstitutional by the Supreme Court, the acquittal earned by them stood set aside.

The court felt surprising that despite Accountability Court's decision barring him from holding any public office for 10 years, Mr Khwaja continued to perform his functions as Chairman Navtec and even after 16th December 2009's verdict.

*[**Brig Imtiaz**, an ex-ISI officer of 1980s and then the Intelligence Bureau Chief in 1990s revealed in August 2009 on electronic media that the known politician from Muzaffargarh Mr Mustafa Khar [uncle of the then PPP's Foreign Ministar Hina Rabbani Khar] had once planned to blow GHQ with all the top officers in conspiracy with some officers of Pakistan Army, who had earlier been Court Martialled and thrown out of the Army.*

Mr Khar had links with RAW, the Indian counterpart of ISI, which had supplied the weapons and Bombs to these officers after his [Mr Khar's] visits to India.

*According to Brig Imtiaz, Mr Khar was also responsible for kicking out a serving **Army Chief Gen Gul Hassan**,* an honest & the only army General who never owned a house and could not afford his personal car.

On 3rd March 1972 Gul Hassan was summoned to the President House along with Air Marshal Rahim Khan and made to sign his resignation. Subsequently Governor Punjab Ghulam Mustafa Khar drove him in his car with Communications Minister Ghulam Mustafa Jatoi holding a gun on his head to the Punjab Governor House.

Meanwhile the post of Army C in C was abolished. Dr Mobashir Hasan, the Finance Minister, brought Gen Tikka Khan in a helicopter to Rawalpindi to take over as Chief of Army Staff. Gen Gul Hassan was forced under duress to resign from the service because he was poor and Pashtun.

Khan's alleged involvement and his controversial approvals of military operations [as DG Military Operations] during 1971 in East Pakistan was disliked by Mr Bhutto's team then but he was cleared by Hamoodur Rahman Commission.

ISI's famous Midnight Jackal Operation was done under Brig Imtiaz to topple Benezir Bhutto's elected government. In his opinion, pro-Establishment Jama'at Islami and other religious political parties were on pay-role of the ISI to eliminate PPP for ever; so Brig Imtiaz was the one who paved the way for cronies of Gen Ziaul Haq to take over once more.]

The apex court observed that not only did Adnan Khwaja continue the job, but was also appointed MD of OGDCL on 7th September 2010. However, the PM Secretariat and the Establishment Division rescinded the notification of his appointment when the case was taken up by the Supreme Court. In such circumstances it was an obligation of the NAB authorities to have taken the convict into custody and the properties *[restored in pursuance of the Islamabad High Court order]* should have been retrieved immediately.

[Much later; on **4th December 2012**, former PM Mr Gilani was issued a notice by the NAB to submit his stance on the matter in two weeks' time as Adnan Khawaja was known as his personal friend who had developed a close friendship with him during his days in jail about five years ago. However, Mr Gilani's counsel told the NAB on 11th December 2012 that:

'The former PM will not appear before the NAB for statement as it is unconstitutional. All appointments were made in good faith and like any other constitutional functionary he is not answerable for his decisions made in official capacity.

In addition, in absence of any direct and highly convincing evidence of any wrongful gain, it would be highly irrelevant in law to furnish any reply to allegation in question. As such any allegation of illegality or impropriety in these circumstances against the prime minister is based upon misconception of law and constitution.'

Khawaja was also said to be a close friend of Faisal Sakhi Butt, an Islamabad-based friend of President Zardari at that time.]

It was clear that the wrong-headedness and inflexibility towards the court orders had been coming straight from the high executives of the government in power. The people recalled that how the head investigator in the Hajj Scam was transferred after he summoned the son of the then PM Mr Gilani to record his statement before the FIA.

Arrest warrants of Adnan Khwaja, former illiterate Chairman of OGDC; Ahmed Riaz Sheikh, Additional DG of FIA who was once convicted by an Accountability Court but was pardoned by the President Zardari under his constitutional powers of Article 45 and one Raja Ahsan were issued while Tahir Shahbaz, Akhlaq Jillani, Razia and a number of other NRO beneficiaries were served with notices to appear before the bureau in connection with the cases pending against them. In short, except the corruption cases involving President Zardari, who enjoyed immunity under Article 148 of the Constitution, and three cases against Sharif family members pending in the Lahore High Court, rest of all the cases were re-opened.

According to the list provided by the NAB, out of total 8041 cases withdrawn under NRO some 233 NAB cases involving 248 people were withdrawn. Of these 248 people, 22 were politicians while the remaining 226 were government employees who had secured benefit of the ordinance within the initial period of 120 days.

Coming back; MNA Sherry Rehman, former FIA Director Ahmad Riaz Shaikh, Ch Tanveer, Faisal Sakhi Butt and Dr Qayyum Soomro tried to meet Brig Imtiaz and Mr Khwaja at a police station of Rawalpindi, but they were not allowed to do so. Both Brig Imtiaz Ahmad and Adnan Khwaja were shifted to Adiyala jail next day.

SWISS LETTER ISSUE DEEPENED:

Let us peep into the original events of those days.

On AG Justice ® Qayyum's widely discussed letter sent to Geneva, **Stephanie Nebehay's report dated 1st April 2008** [referring to Geneva Reuters] was an eye opening treat that:

'*Pakistan* has dropped out of a 60 million Swiss franc ($59.6 million) Swiss money-laundering case against the widower of assassinated PM Benazir Bhutto. He (Mr Zardari) has been charged with aggravated money laundering by a Swiss court and the Pakistani government had joined the case as a civil party.'

Swiss lawyers said the lack of a criminal prosecution against Mr Zardari in Pakistan and the government's withdrawal as a civil party in the Swiss case had greatly weakened the chances of convicting Zardari under Swiss law. The case against Bhutto ended with her assassination in December 2007 while campaigning in Pakistan's election. Dominique Henchoz, a lawyer for Pakistan, confirmed its withdrawal as a civil party in remarks to the '*daily Le Temps*':

"*Just because there has been an amnesty for the good of the country doesn't mean that no crime was committed.*

Pakistan remains a civil party in the Swiss case against a disbarred Geneva lawyer who was administrator of offshore accounts linked to the inspection kickbacks, Henchoz told the paper.

Benazir Bhutto, Mr Zardari and the lawyer were convicted by a Geneva court in 2003 of laundering $13 million linked to the kickbacks.

But that verdict was thrown out on appeal, sparking a wider probe by an investigating judge who indicted all three on charges of aggravated money laundering.

The case was then in the hands of Geneva's Chief Prosecutor Daniel Zappelli, who could close it or bring it to trial. Some 60 million Swiss francs remained frozen in Swiss accounts in connection with the case.

"*Pakistan has withdrawn as a civil party, which proves it does not feel that it suffered damages,*" Zardari's lawyer Saverio Lembo told Reuters.

In Pakistan, for President Zardari, the Supreme Court in its judgment remarked that why a one page summary was not sent to the prime minister despite a lapse of three months in accordance with paragraph 178 of the NRO judgment.

The paragraph 178 of the judgment in NRO had said that:

'*Since the NRO 2007 stands declared void ab initio, actions taken or suffered under the said law are also non est (unconstitutional) in law, and since the communications addressed by Malik Muhammad Qayyum to various foreign authorities / courts withdrawing the requests earlier made by the Government of Pakistan for mutual legal assistance; surrendering the status of civil party; abandoning the claims to the allegedly laundered moneys lying in foreign countries, including Switzerland, have also been declared by us to be unauthorised and illegal communications and consequently of no legal effect, therefore, it is declared that the initial requests for mutual legal assistance; securing the status of civil party and the claims lodged to the allegedly laundered moneys lying in foreign countries, including Switzerland, are declared never to have been withdrawn.*

Therefore, the Federal Government and other concerned authorities are ordered to take immediate steps to seek revival of the said requests, claims and status.'

The 3-judge bench comprising Chief Justice Iftikhar M Chaudhry, Justice Tariq Parvez and Justice Ghulam Rabbani also summoned Federal Law Secretary Masood Chishti and ordered him to complete within three days the task of writing a summary for a fresh executive decision by the prime minister on implementing the NRO verdict that required, among other matters, reopening of Swiss cases involving President Zardari.

Needless to say, as Ayaz Amir opines [*the 'News' of 21st May 2010* is referred] that powerful should be the first to be called to account but, **for the sake of credibility, the SC was expected to exhibit judicial enthusiasm, instead of appearing to be selective, '*by travelling also a bit left and right*'. The apex court wasted its time for un-achievables, might not be in line with constitutional commandments,** though the aims were commendable.

The higher courts could serve the people more if, while remaining within limits; it could stick to the meaningful & enforceable decisions. The SC during Gen Musharraf's days stopped the sale of the Steel Mills. What the people got out of it; average Rs:15-20 billion more input each year but still a bigger white elephant today; negative production since the six years at glance. The SC once tried fiddling with petroleum prices, not to much avail. The Chief Justice of the Lahore High Court once tried fixing the price of sugar, with less than happy results.

Price of sentimental reacting to newspaper headlines and attracting media attention kept on travelling high on the graph. The nation struggled for the restoration of an independent but the rightful judiciary; they wanted to see it on high echelons. Most elements were pointing towards Judges' own rampant enthusiasm and the judicial activism. Lack of implementation of NRO judgment, though proved the callous & uncaring nature of the ruling executive, but also added in the frustration and anger of the higher courts.

Some of the intelligentsia kept another viewpoint that after NRO proceedings, the singled out Zardari went more stronger later than was in 2009; some grey areas went bright and the GHQ more concrete. The presidency was benefiting from circumstances, hats off to the Afghan situation; the White House, the Pentagon, the CIA and NATO never wanted Zardari out. The Americans wanted our army to remain engaged in FATA; PPP government to continue playing a supporting role; and, of course, no tension on the Pak-India border. Therefore, no one bothered about judiciary's disturbing shouts.

When the historian would glance at the larger canvas, the collision theory of Presidency vis a vis the Supreme Court would surface as a small fry of harmless events.

On 25th May 2010 four legal brains under the lead of Federal Law Minister Babar Awan spelt out in the Supreme Court reasons for not writing letters to Switzerland to reopen the money-laundering cases against President Zardari. Attorney General [AG] Maulvi Anwaarul Haq was his nominee to advocate his opinion. Mr Awan had wholeheartedly supported Additional AG K K Agha's selection for the job by President Zardari. Irfan Qadir, the just appointed Prosecutor General of the NAB, was directed to stand by the law minister.

The government's four-member core legal line-up comprising Babar Awan, Anwaarul Haq, KK Agha and Qadir remained constantly in contact with Mr Zardari seeking fresh guidelines. Their prime task was to put hurdles in the way of implementation of the apex court's ruling on the NRO especially the revival of the cases against the president.

NAB officials said that the new prosecutor general did not approve the letters that NAB Chairman Nawid Ahsan had written to Swiss authorities for reinstatement of the graft cases against Zardari *as the president cannot be prosecuted at home or abroad*.

On 12th October 2010, a day before the hearing of the NRO implementation case in the Supreme Court, the PPP government decided to move a new petition before the judges to straightaway challenge the implementation process of the NRO judgment of 16th December 2009.

The new petition was a bid to ease the mounting pressure on PM Gilani to write a letter to the Swiss authorities against President Zardari. The president had issued fresh instructions to PPP's legal aides after he was briefed about the SC's unexpected ruling for not allowing the government to bring a new lawyer in place of Kamal Azfar after he was notified as the prime minister's adviser on disaster management.

The government's legal team also filed another petition challenging the decision of the SC to disallow it to bring a new lawyer to defend its review petition telling about circumstances which led to the removal of Kamal Azfar. A long list of arguments was prepared by the legal team in that regard too.

The main theme of the new petition challenging the implementation of the NRO judgment was focussed to justify as to why the letter to the Swiss authorities could not be written. The sources said the PPP government has made up its mind that it will be preferable to go down fighting instead of being seen as dictated by the court and then made to go home or collapse under the burden of the NRO judgment and more. It was generally felt in government circles that:

> *"PM Gilani was not ready to hand over his own president to Swiss authorities as he feared that if he wrote any letter to Swiss authorities, then it would amount to withdrawing the immunity and he would face charges of violation of Article 6, which is punishable with death penalty."*

It was also decided from the government side to ask the Supreme Court to form a larger bench to hear the review petition challenging the implementation of the NRO verdict; to gain more time obviously.

SC GONE HARD ON NRO's ORDER:

At last **on 25th November 2011** the PM was specifically directed again to write to the Swiss government to withdraw that objectionable letter written by the then Attorney General Justice ® Qayyum Malik in respect of Mr Zardari's hefty accounts there.

The Supreme Court **on 3rd January 2012** issued its last warning to the government and all concerned authorities to ensure implementation of its verdict against the National Reconciliation Ordinance (NRO), warning that beyond this date, the court would not pass any more orders but take direct action.

A five-member special bench headed by Justice Asif Saeed Khan Khosa heard a case pertaining to the non-implementation of the NRO verdict. The court inquired whether a letter was written to the Swiss authorities after the dismissal of a review petition against the NRO verdict.

Attorney General (AG) Maulvi Anwaarul Haq contended before the court that the letter to the Swiss authorities could not be sent so far and was postponed due to the hearing of the NRO review petition. The apex court noted that the court did not grant any stay on the implementation of the NRO verdict during the hearing of the review petition.

During the last hearing of the NRO implementation case, the court had directed PM Mr Gilani to dispatch a new summary to Swiss authorities, the law secretary had sought more time for a new summary, but the later did not turn up despite being summoned by the apex court.

On 10th January 2012, the five member bench of the Supreme Court decided to place six options relating to the NRO implementation case before the Chief Justice, also requesting for constitution of a larger bench for hearing of these options. Announcing the verdict on NRO implementation case, the bench headed by Justice Asif Saeed Khosa handed over those six options to the Attorney General (AG). The options were:

1. To initiate the contempt of court proceedings against the Chief Executive and the Secretary Law for not implementing the NRO verdict.

2. To declare the Chief Executive [the Prime Minister] ineligible from the membership of the Parliament.

3. The apex court may form a commission to get the verdict implemented.

4. The people themselves decide on the issue and the apex court exhibit patience.

5. Contempt proceedings against Chairman NAB may be initiated.

6. The action may be taken against the President for violating the Constitution.

The Supreme Court declared in its order that the government has failed to implement the verdict; not taking interest to observe the order for the last two years. The apex court, interalia, observed that:

- 'The president in an interview to Geo News said his government would not implement one part of NRO verdict.

- **Prima Facie the prime minister is not an honest man and violated his oath.'**

The SC bench in its order asked the AG to apprise as to why any of the options might not be exercised by the Court in this matter. The apex court held that:

> 'It goes without saying that any person likely to be affected by exercise of these options may appear before this Court on the next date of hearing and address this Court in the relevant regard so that he may not be able to complain in future that he had been condemned by this Court unheard.'

In non-implementation of the NRO [and several other verdicts of higher judiciary also], the SC behaved with unlimited care; cautious not to tilt the precarious balance. The SC never wanted matters to spin out of control but the government had other things on its mind; the result was obvious.

Following the strong reprimand by the Supreme Court, the NAB enforced its action on the re-opened cases after the scraping of NRO by the apex court. Soon after declaration of NRO as void *ab initio* by the court on 16th December 2009, all the cases once withdrawn were re-opened by the then Chairman NAB Nawid Ahsan, but later these cases could not be pursued as the department was incapacitated by the government both in terms of manpower and finances.

In the other cases the Supreme Court was constrained to observe that the Prime Minister Yousaf Raza Gilani had misused his authority by appointing convicted people, including NRO beneficiaries Adnan Khwaja and Ahmed Riaz Sheikh. In cases dealing with the appointments of Adnan Khwaja as the MD of OGDCL and of Sh Riaz as the ADG FIA, the NAB was trying to save the key respondents and thus the country's top officials were involved in corruption.

However, Prosecutor General NAB KK Agha informed the court that no reference had been filed against Mr Gilani though, in its NRO ruling, the

Supreme Court had directed NAB to take action against Mr Sheikh, Mr Khwaja and officials of the Establishment Division, Interior Ministry and FIA who were involved in the illegal contractual appointment of Khwaja and illegal reinstatement and promotion of Sh Riaz.

The NAB had argued that Adnan Khwaja remained OGDC MD only for seven days and caused no loss to the national exchequer. However, references were sent against Ismail Qureshi, former Principal Secretary to the PM, Saeed Gilani and Rang Zia, bureaucrats involved in the appointment of Adnan Khwaja.

[*Ismail Qureshi, the then Secretary to the PM had issued the notification of Adnan Khwaja's appointment as MD OGDCL on the orders of the then PM Mr Gilani so the NAB sent a reference against him on that count.*

Later Mr Qureshi had also issued appointment of one Zain Sukhaira, friend of Abdul Qadir Gilani (son of the PM) against the rules and regulations.

FIA team collected all evidence related to this process; despite the fact that it was in his knowledge that Sukhaira was facing a corruption case in an Anti Corruption court. The FIA held that Ismail Qureshi misused his powers and remained involved in this case of appointment deliberately.]

Former Federal Secretary Ismail Qureshi was arrested on 13th January 2012 by a NAB team in Lahore then shifted to Islamabad for interrogation in connection with another corruption case pending against him.

Mr Qureshi was given immediate relief by the apex court asking that how a reference could be filed against the people who followed the order but not against PM Gilani who ordered them. Justice Khosa remarked that the officials had carried out the orders of their political masters.

Justice Asif Saeed Khosa, during the hearing of the case, maintained that Malik Qayyum had misused his authority as the Attorney General. When asked whether a reference was filed against Justice (Rtd) Malik Qayyum, the NAB's Prosecutor General said that NAB wanted the inquiry against Malik Qayyum to be stopped.

[*On 4th December 2012, Waseem Sajjad, counsel for former AG Malik Qayyum told the apex court that NAB had completed inquiry against*

Malik Qayyum and in Executive Board's meeting the case had been discussed and closed.

Justice Tariq Parvez noted that the court would like to see whether the inquiry conducted by NAB was transparent or not; it would be seen in the light of Asghar Khan & Anita Turab Ali Cases.]

In the case of transfer and reinstatement of NICL's Zafar Qureshi also, it was clear that the authority to issue notifications in both regards was the prime minister himself. In NRO also, the PM Gilani being the Chief Executive, should have taken special interest in getting the verdict implemented but he did nothing.

CONDI REVEALS FACTS IN 2011:

Referring to the recent book ['*No Higher Honour': Crown; November 2011*] of the former US Secretary of State, *Condoleezza Rice*, on NRO deal; she does not seem to know how Gen Musharraf finally agreed to it. Her version was that:

Benazir Bhutto had two conditions for the said NRO deal:

• She be allowed to become the Prime Minister for the third term.

• The cases pending in courts against her and others be withdrawn.

President Musharraf believed that withdrawing the cases would not be appropriate and courts alone should deal with them. However, she could become the Prime Minister if her party won enough seats in elections.

On return from Dubai [in July 2007], Gen Musharraf gave his views in a meeting with top leaders of the Muslim League [PML(Q)], including Hamid Nasir Chattha, Farooq Laghari, Sh Rashid, Ch Shujaat, and Parvaiz Ellahi.

According to Shaikh Rashid; that BB should not be allowed to become the Prime Minister for the third time because that would jeopardize the prospects for the other leaders. (Ch Parvaiz Ellahi was very insistent on this point) As for the pending cases, they did not object to their withdrawal.

Gen Musharraf was not convinced. Then Ch Shuja'at Hussain met him and succeeded in changing his mind. He opposed the third term for BB but not the withdrawal of cases. He had an ingenious argument.

He argued that NRO would be obviously unconstitutional and the Supreme Court would strike it down within no time. Thus, the President could claim that he did what BB wanted but was helpless regarding unfavourable judgment of the court, if any. The argument made sense and Gen Musharraf went for the NRO.

The problem arose when the Supreme Court [of CJP Abdul Hameed Dogar] did not strike down the NRO; it merely suspended its operation. That did not solve the dilemma. NRO remained as a law until the Supreme Court [of CJP Iftikhar M Chaudhry] finally declared it unconstitutional in December 2009, long after Gen Musharraf had gone.

Had Chief Justice Hameed Dogar done the assignment complete, the cases would have been still there and Gen Musharraf would not have to face one of the greatest embarrassments of his life. Neither he nor Ch Shuja'at Hussain could tell his fellow Pakistanis later about their clever plans because it could embarrass both.

Astonishingly, regarding the NRO deal between Gen Musharraf & Benazir Bhutto, Condi admits everything and reveals how she toiled for many sleepless nights to bring the two 'moderates' together in 2007. According to her version:

> *'In the beginning of 2007 Gen Musharraf had asked [the US] for help in bridging his differences with Bhutto.*
>
> *[If the deal goes successful] It would shift the weight of politics towards the moderates and undermine the Islamists, as well as **Nawaz Sharif**, who ....was suspected of maintaining close ties to the militants.'*

As per details given in the book, Richard Boucher, the Assistant Secretary for South and Central Asian Affairs, became the point man for the US in exploring a deal. Shuttling back and forth between the parties — usually meeting Bhutto in London — Richard got them close enough to make a face-to-face meeting possible.

That encounter took place in the UAE in late July, but their discussion was inconclusive. By early October 2007, there were four outstanding issues:

- When would Gen Musharraf shed his military uniform (before or after the elections);

- Would Benazir Bhutto and her party colleagues be immunized in the multiple corruption cases against them (including those against her husband, Mr Zardari);

- Could she become prime minister despite a constitutional prohibition against a third term (she'd already had two terms);

- Would Gen Musharraf support her return to Pakistan before the elections?

Condi describes in her book that:

'I put those questions to Musharraf in a phone call on Oct 3 at 4:47 pm. At 5:47 pm I got back to Bhutto with his response. At 6:18 pm I talked to Musharraf again. At 6:53 pm I called Bhutto.

That continued every half hour until 11:28 pm, with nine more calls back and forth. Bhutto was suspicious of Musharraf's motives and he of hers. Benazir kept saying that she had to bring her party conference along because they didn't want a deal with Musharraf.

I argued that she had to do it for the good of the country — only an alliance between the two of them would allow elections to take place in a stable environment.

I was also concerned that we might be accused of interfering in the democratic process. Why not just let the elections happen and let the chips fall where they may?

I went to bed at about midnight, only to be awakened at 12:41 am by Musharraf. Well, I had said he could call anytime. I called Bhutto at 4:58 am and relayed the latest offer. The next morning, I talked to each of them one more time.

They had a tentative deal — not firm but detailed enough that Bhutto would be permitted to return to Pakistan to stand in the parliamentary elections that would be held by mid-January.'

As Gen Musharraf had made an announcement to take off his uniform only after being elected as President, a wave of distrust again surfaced and the whole exercise of US Secretary of State seemed to drown in doldrums but then Condi writes:

'Bhutto had told me that she didn't trust him to follow through with his pledge. "I'm taking this as a US guarantee that he will," she'd said.'

The deal was announced on 4th October and on 18th October 2007 Benazir Bhutto landed on Pakistani soils.

NRO was agreed upon between the two for their own mutual interests but in the name of democracy.

Scenario 71

THE FAKE DEGREES CASE [2010-13]:

On 25th March 2010, MNA Jamshaid Dasti of PPP, MNA Nazir Jatt of PML(Q) and MPA Muhammad Ajmal of PML(Q) from PP-63 (Faisalabad-XIII) had submitted their resignations before the Supreme Court. On 30th March 2010, Sardar Allah Wasaya alias Chunnu Leghari, an MPA of PPP also tendered his resignation for having fake degree. It was the same week the PPP had earned plaudits for shepherding the 18th Amendment bill through parliament.

In the 2nd week of April 2010, the PPP parliamentary board, headed by party leader President Zardari, had bizarrely seen it fit to nominate the very same members who humiliatingly had to submit their resignations before the apex Court. And in another sordid twist, the PPP had even given its party ticket to a PML(Q) legislator who had to resign his National Assembly seat from Vehari on similar grounds.

Several points to note here; while the Bachelor's degree requirement for assembly men and women had been dropped, the members were hauled up before the SC for submitting fake documents, taking the same as grounds for disqualifying an elected representative. So the point here wasn't about higher education but the moral and legal lapses by the elected representatives. Why was the PPP continuing to support members who, being liars or fraud, did not deserve to be the representatives of the people?

The government had preffered to send a terrible signal to the electorate and the political class.

On 12th April 2010, a 3-member bench of the Supreme Court comprising of Justice Mian Shakirullah Jan, Justice MA Shahid Siddiqui and Justice Mian Saqib Nisar reserved the judgement on two petitions challenging the degrees of MNA Rasheed Akbar Nawani from NA-74 and MPA Saeed Akbar Nawani from PP-49; both constituencies of Bhakkar District.

The Punjab University official filed the academic record of the two lawmakers and told that the degrees acquired by them in 2002 were fake though both the brothers had earned genuine BA degrees in 2004.

On 21st April 2010, another 3-member Supreme Court (SC) bench finalised the case of PML(N)'s MPA from PP-160 (Lahore-XXIV) constituency named Rana Mubashir Iqbal who had tendered his resignation over possessing a fake graduation degree.

The bench – comprising Chief Justice Iftikhar M Chaudhry, Justice Ch Ijaz Ahmed and Justice Ghulam Rabbani – disposed of the said case, observing: *"The petition is disposed of without any prejudice and the Election Commission of Pakistan is required to issue the notification for holding by-elections".*

JAMSHED DASTI's CASE:

The obvious message [that the PPP handed out tickets for the by-elections to the same alleged liars] conveyed was: the presidency could be thumbing its nose at the SC? Forgetting that it was a SC bench led by Chief Justice Iftikhar M Chaudhry that had shown great revulsion at the mischief of the politicians caught lying and left them to resign only. Was that a proper way to thank the judiciary for its mercy otherwise the members could have been sent to Adiala jail straightaway.

Ordinary citizens of Pakistan as well as sincere workers of the PPP were disappointed by such decisions by the party leadership. Could not President Zardari and the PPP identify a single person higher in integrity and commitment to the PPP's manifesto than Dastis, Jatts and Wasays in their respective constituencies?

On top of it, PM Gilani appointed that former MNA Jamshed Dasti as his adviser on livestock after he resigned from his National Assembly seat when his degree was found fake. Instead of sending him to jail, the prime minister elevated him to a position where he enjoyed even more perks and privileges at poor nation's expense. Irony of the nation was that on the same day his namesake, Nasir Jamshed, a poor cricketer, was sent to jail for allegedly cheating in his Class IX exams, about six years earlier.

Hurray! One cheat was instantly arrested and sent to jail while the other was made adviser to the prime minister of Pakistan? The prime minister should have appointed Nasir Jamshed as his adviser on cricket affairs too. Politics in Pakistan, and its version practised by the PPP, was devoid of ethics. PPP's own sane and sincere workers felt disgusted at the PPP's decision to appoint Jamshed Dasti as an adviser to the PM; an insult of the collective public opinion.

The general populace was not surprised that the two major parties, PPP and PML(N), had adopted the 'cheats' and fielded them again. Besides the PPP's cheats with party tickets named above, the PML(N) also picked Mian Asif Ajmal for PP-63. PML(N)'s Senator Pervez Rashid had responded to a media question that:

> "*I think the people of his (Ajmal)'s constituency will reject him if they think that he had done something wrong by becoming an MPA on the basis of a fake BA degree.*"

Such logics of 'democratic steps' could only prevail in Pakistan where Senator Rashid was replying the next question as "*let me clarify that the PML-N will not re-award a ticket to any such candidate of its party keeping in view the moral grounds.*"

> [*Later, during a fine evening after 15th May 2010, all those cheaters were again reading oath in their respective assemblies – a typical example of Pakistani Democracy. Where were the Articles of 62 & 63 or the ECP as the newly elected members were proven liars till then?*]

Re-election of **Jamshed Dasti** as MNA is a case study in the politico-judicial history of Pakistan and a permanent chapter of humiliation and torture for courts and judges to come.

In June 2010, the Supreme Court of Pakistan passed a judgment 'on fake degrees of parliamentarians' saying that FIRs should be registered against all of them who keep fake degrees while sitting in the Parliament. What happened at last?

Next, whether it was the lethargic procedures of the Election Commission or our 'parliamentarian supremacy' that since two years only 13 cases of fake degrees were reported to the police, though 37 degrees were declared fake within one month of judgment [till February 2013, 59 declared fake].

> '*So far, 37 have been confirmed fake and only 183 real, said a senior member of the HEC. The rest are still being verified. If the nearly one-fifth ratio holds, he added, "a government could lose its majority", referring to both the federal and Punjab governments. If the ratio rises, a political crisis could emerge, furnishing an opportunity for opponents of the government to push for mid-term elections,*' an analyst opined in UK's daily '**Independent**' dated 21st July 2010.

Even in those 13 cases no further investigation. No member, except only one in Balochistan, was dislodged from his seat in any Assembly or Senate. No arrest, no disqualification and no reprimand what so ever. Higher Education Commission (HEC) and Parliamentary Standing Committee had completed their tasks of verification quite in time but the members of Election Commission of Pakistan [ECP] were there to compromise with the wrong doers.

During the process of verification of degrees, it is on record, that the Chairman HEC Javed Leghari and his family members were persecuted, threatened, maltreated and victimized on various counts but the Supreme Court never bothered to offer him protection, not even once, as it has been providing to Zafar Qureshi of FIA every time and again. What a justice it was.

When a matter of torture in Sialkot appeared in press, the whole hierarchy of administration including IG, Home Secretary, Interior Secretary, DIG, SSP and SHO concerned were called to attend the Court at Islamabad and made to sit outside in corridors for hours. When NICL case appeared, the DG FIA was charged under Article 190 of the Constitution for not taking care of Zafar Qureshi but when the matter of legislators with fake degrees cropped up, the Articles 62 & 63 were altogether ignored and the file was dumped; both by the ECP & the judiciary.

No member of ECP was called to stand in apex court to be labelled as guilty of Article 190. Where one man's case was involved, the court spent months in shouting at poor servicemen [especially of police] and when a case of two hundred parliamentarians cropped up, the file was sent to the cold room.

For Pakistan judiciary, the historians would be calling them '**penny wise & pound foolish**'.

After the SC's judgment, the HEC had sent 376 degrees to the Punjab University for verification but till the first week of 2012 [in 27 months], the University could only tell that eight degrees were fake while the six were declared 'suspicious'.

Much later; referring to a live *TV program [60 minutes] at 'Samaa' Channel dated 26th March 2013*, in which Afzal Khan of the Election Commission of Pakistan [ECP] and Javed Leghari Chairman of HEC were also the participants, Jamshed Dasti told the viewers that:

'I had not attended any regular school. I belonged to such a poor family who was not able to meet the two times bread requirements. I had to attend an Islamic Madrassah from where I got a certificate equivalent to FA [intermediate exam] pass in Pakistan.

However, I was the only person who was picked up by the superior courts and punished because I was a poor MNA. There were 54 cases in the lot but I was singled out.'

Chairman HEC Mr Leghari told that in 2010, the ECP had sent 1095 degrees of the sitting Parliamentarians to the HEC for want of verification. In the first instalment, HEC told them that 58 degrees were found fake whereas the action on rest of the degrees was in progress. Mr Leghari alleged that the ECP issued orders for taking penal actions against 'picked & chosen' 27 persons and put the other names 'under further scrutiny' for which ECP had no right.

MNA ABID SHER ALI GOT UP:

The fake degrees issue, originally initiated by the Supreme Court, was taken over by PML(N), not as a matter of party policy but simply to target PPP on account of Jamshed Dasti. Soon after, the whole issue was handed over to Ch Abid Sher Ali MNA to stand by the media to change the wind against the ruling party. When the fire spread, some faces of PML(N) were also got burnt. PML(N) at first issued tall press statements against their own members but soon opted to tighten their lips due to party pressure from within.

A rift prevailed between members of the PML(N) and the Parliamentary Committee on the issue of fake degrees because the Higher Education Commission (HEC) had told the media that no record was found about the degrees of 56 law makers of the PML(N) and 41 of the PPP and PML(Q).

The Chairman Standing Committee on Education Abid Sher Ali MNA was facing severe criticism from the ranks of his own party and due to this issue the PML(N) lawmakers allegedly having fake degrees turned their backs during the budget session of the National Assembly saying that no other party had left their members without support like the PML(N) did over the issue.

PML(N) members quoted example of Jamshed Dasti and said the PPP stood behind Dasti when he was held ineligible by the Supreme Court over his fake degree and gave him ticket in the by-election and got him re-elected. The party members were not happy with Ch Nisar Ali as he was then hotly pursuing the verification matters in the HEC.

The PPP had earlier retaliated to the Supreme Court's move of degrading the party in public and got Jamshed Dasti re-elected again from the same constituency of Muzaffargarh District. On this move, there were disagreements within the PPP on the strategy of 'adopting' the wrongs but the party vowed.

In early June 2010, an election tribunal, comprising Justice Nasir Saeed Sheikh of the Lahore High Court had disqualified PML(N) MNA from NA-100 Gujranwala, Haji Mudassar Qayyum Nahra, for obtaining a graduation degree by concealing facts. Nahra had won the MNA seat in 2008 general election as an independent candidate but later he had joined the PML(N).

On 30th June 2010, Justice Khwaja Imtiaz Ahmed of LHC's Rawalpindi bench in a short order had declared Malik Yasir Raza disqualified on a petition filed by Ishtiaq Mirza, a PPP candidate. The petition had challenged the validity of Raza's Higher Secondary School Certificate (HSSC) obtained from the Federal Board of Intermediate and Secondary Education in 1995 and the subsequent graduation degree.

The HEC had submitted its report with the apex court over the *Sanad* obtained by Zahoor Hussain Khosa, MPA from Balochistan which was not recognized by it.

Above mentioned three appeals of Haji Mudassar Qayyum Nehra of PML(N) who was elected from NA-100 Gujranwala; of Malik Yasir Raza PML(N) MPA from PP-13 Rawalpindi and of Mir Zahoor Hussain Khan Khoso, MPA elect from PB-26 Jaffarabad-II Balochistan were dismissed by the Supreme Court later. A 3-member bench comprising Chief Justice Iftikhar M Chaudhry, Justice Ghulam Rabbani and Justice Khalil ur Rehman Ramday heard separate pleas filed by these ex-members against verdicts of election tribunals.

In nut shell, amidst differences amongst the party members, the PML(N) cooled down because the Supreme Court, on 29th July 2010, had upheld decisions against three legislators. The Election Commission of Pakistan (ECP) was directed to proceed against the disqualified legislators under the law laid down in its decision on Rizwan Gill and for violating Representation of Peoples Act 1976.

The intelligentsia went critic upon that judicial activism on part of the apex court because the matter was left at the mercy of ECP, a total failure and inefficient organization. The Election Commission and Higher Education Commission had both failed to check the authenticity of the educational degrees in time. The Supreme Court had failed to hold the ECP accountable for this grave act of negligence on which millions of the taxpayer's money went waste.

The ECP's attitude could be judged from its ill-intentions that the SC had ordered for FIRs to be lodged against the fake degree holders but, through various gimmicks, most of the fake parliamentarians kept seated there in assemblies. When asked, the ECP itself filed a petition in the SC for 'seeking further guidance'.

In the first week of November 2010, a 3-member bench of the apex court heard that petition filed by the Secretary ECP. The bench was chaired by the CJP Justice Iftikhar M Chaudhry [Justice Tariq Pervaiz and Justice Ghulam Rabbani were other two members]. Attorney General Maulvi Anwaar ul Haq said that the ECP was incomplete; a flimsy excuse it was. Any responsible officer of the ECP could send cases to the session courts but nothing moved. The SC could not get its own orders implemented.

The Attorney General had taken stand that the said law was inequitable because with adult literacy at only 55%, nearly half the country would be ineligible to run for elections. Nevertheless, the court wanted to know if the then sitting parliamentarians [*who had been elected for office while the law was in effect*] had abided by its rules.

The SC, on the same basis, ruled that any authorized officials including Chief Election Commissioner could challenge fake degrees, wrong details of assets and corrupt practices; according to the Section 80 of the relevant act.

What happened later, nothing? The cheaters again became legislators and the Supreme Court could do nothing but had to follow the acts and amendments passed by the same fake legislatures. What a mockery of justice for all times to come. However, ruthless media trials continued to change the minds of the youth at least.

Till after about a year even, the CEP was incomplete. It was being kept so with a specific purpose; fake members continued sitting in the assemblies till the completion of their 5 years term – democracy hurray.

WORLD PRESS LAUGHED AT PAKISTAN:

This peculiar situation made Pakistan a laughing stock in the whole world. All leading newspapers and magazines brewed spicy connotations out of that scenario; see daily *Al-jazira dated 30th June 2010*:

> '*Scores of Pakistani politicians could lose their seats in parliament after authorities opened an inquiry into claims 10 per cent of federal and provincial legislators had lied about their qualifications.*
>
> *Up to 160 elected officials have been accused of faking their degrees in order to meet a requirement for holding office. The supreme court has ordered the elections commission to vet the credentials of most of Pakistan's 1,100 federal and provincial politicians.*'

Al-Jazira mentioned that President Zardari had also faced questions about his qualifications. He claimed to hold a bachelor's degree from a business school in London but his party was unable to produce a certificate or establish what he studied. Mr Zardari, however, escaped the scandal because of the immunity available in the Constitution.

The fact however, was that [traditionally] feudal ties or business successes had more appeal in Pakistani politics than academic achievements.

TIME Magazine of 21st July 2010 held that:

> '*Zardari's ruling PPP tried to make that point with Jamshed Dasti, [MNA] of southern Punjab, whose complicated case came up for judgment shortly before the controversial ruling in June. Dasti had been hauled before the Supreme Court to be tested on claims that he completed a master's in Islamic studies.*
>
> *But when the judges asked Dasti to name the first 15 chapters of the Koran, no reply was forthcoming. "How about the first two?" one judge inquired. Dasti's silence endured. He was asked to resign and save himself the indignity of going to jail.*'

The TIME mentioned about PPP vs SC row, Jamshed Dasti was elevated to the post of special adviser to the Prime Minister on livestock affairs. Within days, he was renamed as the PPP's candidate in a special election for his vacated seat. Development funds were lavished on his constituency as politicians, including PM Gilani himself, were flown in to campaign for him. He won and has become even more popular in his constituency.

The PPP leaders especially made it a point because the Supreme Court itself had knocked out the PPP, though on correct footing.

The task of verifying the parliamentarians' degrees was handed to the Higher Education Commission [HEC], headed by Javaid Laghari, a former PPP Senator with a Ph.D from the State University of New York. When Laghari initiated the process, he was urged by the 'high executive' to bring it to halt or at least slow it down. Laghari refused. In mid-July 2010, his brother was picked up on corruption charges and kept in police custody. Three days later, for no stated reason, local police raided Laghari's own village farmhouse, breaking doors and taking eight servants into custody. Never mind, it is true Pakistani culture.

Once there was likelihood that a government could lose its majority, be it the Punjab government or the federal government, if the verifications would have done speedily. That was why HEC's Leghari was attacked with full force. Had the ratio gone up a little more as per HEC's original pace, there could be crisis showing the way for a new general election. At that moment no one was sure about SC's mood with the results of verifications: Jail the offenders or would throw them out of office.

The Higher Education Commission [HEC] and the Election Commission of Pakistan [ECP] had locked horns over the speed of moving forward plans.

The ECP once asked the HEC not to overstep its remit and stick to checking only bachelor degrees. Whereas the HEC believed that many members of parliament possessed though original bachelor degrees but some of this might have been obtained on the basis of fake school-leaving qualifications, which would make the degrees invalid.

Thus the HEC wrote a letter to the ECP asking it to provide copies of the intermediate and metric certificates of 428 lawmakers. The ECP officials denied receiving the letter. HEC later issued a press release asking the lawmakers to provide the certificates directly for onward verification. Till ending 2012, the HEC had received 1,084 degrees of provincial and federal legislators for verification; returned 603 degrees to the ECP after checking, declaring 545 to be genuine and 58 to be fake or invalid.

It was evident that the number of fake degrees could go up if verification of certificates below the bachelor's level was taken up by the HEC. Abid

Sher Ali, Chairman of the NA Standing Committee on Education, once told the media that:

"Many parliamentarians did not submit even copies of their educational certificates to the ECP at the time when they filed their nominations, and the ECP never bothered to check whether one of the prerequisites to contest election was fulfilled or not."

Abid Sher [*who holds a master's degree in business and finance*] had written to the Commission demanding that his Standing Committee would suspend the membership of parliamentarians who had not submitted their degrees to it; but no action was reported. Once he opined that:

'Nations have to sacrifice some individuals in the process of becoming great, so we should not be scared of the situation we're facing now.'

However, the membership of 148 MPs was suspended for not providing declarations of their assets to the ECP – also a legal requirement in Pakistan for members of parliament and other public office holders but the education side was ignored.

It was in January 2012, when the Supreme Court had to issue directions again to the ECP and police to register cases against fake degree-holding parliamentarians. It could not bring fruit as most of the disqualified parliamentarians were re-elected in by-elections held after a constitutional amendment that ended the requirement that those contesting an election be in possession of a degree.

A big crowd of politico-religious activists staged a sit-in outside Pakistan's parliament in January 2013 in protest against large numbers of parliamentarians having fake degrees. Dr Tahirul-Qadri, during his march and speeches, had slated the parliamentarians as liars, cheats and thieves. His words were:

"Shame on this parliament, which has most of the cheaters re-elected through the 18th amendment approved by political thugs of both opposition and treasury benches. You have changed the law to suit your own interests and the place for criminals like you is jail, not parliament."

Independent observers were of the view that the fake degrees issue had been buried and nothing further would happen, as all parties in parliament had got within their ranks members holding bogus degrees.

It is on record that when 59 parliamentarians were exposed as having forged degrees, government institutions, including the HEC and ECP, were directed not to disclose or answer media queries on the number of MPs holding fake degrees. However, independent sources had the exact numbers and their track records also for onward pass to the next generations.

Court orders against the offending Parliamentarians were not taken seriously by the government. Former minister and HEC Chairman Atta-ur-Rahman once opined before the media that: "*We suspect that the number of fake degree holders in parliament might go to 300 if it is probed honestly. They [the MPs] refused to provide their papers for verification in spite of the orders of the Supreme Court.*"

See an excerpt from the *daily 'Independent' dated 21ˢᵗ July 2010*:

> '*Scores of Pakistani parliamentarians who faked university quali-fications could be unseated in a growing political crisis with echoes of the British expenses furore that has raised the prospect of change in government and even a fresh general election.*
>
> *The crisis has unnerved senior members of the ruling Pakistan People's Party (PPP), headed by the President Asif Ali Zardari. Among those suspected of holding fake degrees are the sitting federal ministers including Faryal Talpur, the President's sister and top party operator.*'

Because of HEC's behaviour towards their dearest members of national and provincial assemblies, the PPP once thought that why not the whole HEC be dissolved by taking away its independent status. The government issued a notification saying that '*the HEC would be an attached department of the Ministry of Education and the Secretary Education would be its Executive Director*'. Its privileges and prerogatives were immediately withdrawn.

The matter was challenged in the superior court.

In the second week of April 2011, the Supreme Court (SC) ordered the government to restore all the privileges of HEC and to keep it operating until the new legislation promulgated. A 3-member bench, hearing the case regarding devolution of the HEC, observed that:

> '*The notification dated 31ˢᵗ March 2011, shall have no effect on the functioning of the HEC in view of the provisions of the Ordinance*

of 2002, and in case of any conflict between the notification and provisions of the ordinance, the ordinance shall prevail.'

Attorney General of Pakistan, Maulvi Anwarul Haq, appeared in the court and told that *'the commission still existed and after the consultation with educational experts and vice chancellors a new law would be constituted for HEC.'*

SUMAIRA MALIK & OTHERS:

MNA Jamshed Dasti was sent home on the charges of having a fake Master's degree in 'Islamiat [Islamic Studies]; as mentioned in earlier paragraphs, he was not able to recite some very basic verses before the apex court's bench. Mr Dasti resigned from the seat. The PPP took it to the heart very seriously and got him elected MNA again from the same constituency two months later.

This reaction of the ruling party PPP made the law and political ethics a mockery; a Pandora box opened all around. Even some seasoned parliamentarians like Gohar Ayub and Abida Hussain, who had obtained their degrees by appearing in regular examinations in their old ages of 50s, were also dragged in courts by their opponents.

Before general elections of 2002, one Parliamentarian named Sumaira Malik, an agriculturist by profession, was considered having FA certificate only because she had got married during her 3rd year in college. Later she graduated with an M A in Political Science [*daily 'Jang' of 29th July 2010 said that she had appeared in BA's exam then*] from University of the Punjab in 2002 after obtaining a diploma in Interior Design from Home Economics College, Lahore in 1987.

However, she had contested election from NA-69 Khushab and won after securing 71,500 votes. His opponent, who had got 58,500 votes, approached the court in 2003 challenging her degree. Lahore High Court [LHC] rejected the plea but that opponent took the case in the Supreme Court which also rejected the challenge in 2006.

When Sumaira Malik again contested from the same seat in general elections of 2008, his opponent did not challenge her nomination papers. When she got elected, her opponent again made her degree an issue. On 23rd February 2013 once more, an election tribunal of the LHC sought her computerised national identity card (CNIC) record from NADRA on a plea for her disqualification.

The tribunal, consisting of Justice Ijazul Ahsan, passed the order on a petition filed by Malik Umer Aslam Awan, seeking directions to disqualify the respondent MNA for having a fake degree. However, on 4th April 2013, the high court formally declared Sumaira Malik's credentials as genuine; she was qualified to contest elections of May 2013 and she won.

The Balochistan High Court had disqualified Syed Ehsan Shah from his post of Minister for Industries for possessing and using a forged degree. When media asked the Chief Minister Balochistan, **Aslam Raisani of the PPP,** to comment upon, he sarcastically placed his mind before the media by saying that

> *"My position is clear; a degree is a degree! Whether fake or genuine, it's a degree! It makes no difference!"*

The Chief Minister had himself claimed to have a master's degree in political science.

During the same days Sardar Assef Ahmed Ali, a cabinet member in PPP's government, placed his deliberations on **TV channel GEO** News:

> *"I am accountable to the parliament not to HEC. It is the education ministry, not the HEC, which is legally authorised to review the degrees of parliamentarians and we shall review the HEC decisions regarding fake degrees."*

Ultimately, the row between HEC and the education ministry had led to reduction in the HEC's powers and its funds curtailed [*later reinstated by the Supreme Court*]; HEC used to send its budget-related proposals on higher education directly to the prime minister or the federal cabinet.

One more episode; that after SC's judgment, the media immediately came out with the list [known till then] of suspected fake-degree holders which included two senior cabinet ministers and others close to President Zardari. In one of the cases, *a provincial lawmaker belonging to PML(N) claimed to have obtained a master's degree in 2002, graduated from college in 2006 and finished high school in 2007.*

He should be *"disqualified for stupidity, not fraud,"* Salmaan Taseer, the late Governor of Punjab had commented.

Another lawmaker claimed to have passed from high school at the age of 10, prompting local wits to dub him "Doogie Howser, MNA"; another claimed to hold three degrees, each with a different surname.

Marvi Memon, a prominent opposition lawmaker and a graduate of the London School of Economics, once commented that *'for the past two years, I had trouble believing that I was sitting in a parliament full of graduates.'* For others, however, this was all too much protest [and excitement] about a piece of paper.

Strange enough that Gen Musharraf's original law, though it appeared to put education on a pedestal, was also a disguised device used by the dictator to exclude some of his opponents. It accredited Gen Musharraf's allies in the religious parties, in MMA — where a stay in *madrasah* [religious school] for about five years was certified as being equivalent to master's degrees.

Gen Musharraf had included that condition of being 'graduate' through the Conduct of General Elections Order 2002. The Representation of people's Act [RPA] 1976 was then amended to include the said 2002 Order, which was later also included in the constitution by the Musharraf-led parliament. Parliament abolished this condition through an 18th amendment to the constitution, which was enacted in 2010. But a court ruling declared that the degree condition was applicable to legislators who contested 2008 election, when the law was still in force.

TWO ECP MEMBERS SOLD OUT?

To hold the fair general elections of 2013, the ECP, **on 7th February 2013,** issued a letter to the concerned office heads of the PPP government to procure degrees of 249 Members of National and Provincial Assemblies for verification within 15 days. The letter said:

> *"The Honourable Election Commission has taken a serious view for the delay in completion of verification process and has directed that it should be completed without further loss of time.*
>
> *It is, therefore, requested to produce original Secondary and Higher Secondary School Certificates or copies thereof (duly verified by the Board of Intermediate & Secondary Education concerned) before the Higher Education Commission, Islamabad, within 15 days of the*

issuance of this letter, failing which your degree / sanad will be treated
as fake and criminal proceedings will be initiated against you."

In the ECP's letter, the MPs were also told that the Supreme Court of
Pakistan, in its judgment dated 14th June 2010, passed in CP No 409/2010
[*Rizwan Gill vs Nadia Aziz*] reported as **PLD 2010 SC 828**, directed the
Election Commission to initiate action against all such persons who were
accused of commission of corrupt practices; of committing forgery of
using, as genuine, documents which they knew as forged. In compliance
copies of bachelor's degrees / sanads were sent to Higher Education
Commission for verification, but the process could not be completed even
in almost three years.

Interestingly, as enumerated in above lines, even before the intervention
of the apex court in 2010, it was the Chairman of the NA Committee
on Education Abid Sher Ali, PML(N) MNA, who had sought the
verification of degrees of all MPs after the publication of news reports in
that regard.

However, the ruling PPP in federation and the PML(N) in Punjab got
immediately furious and joined hands over this letter. The end reaction
was seen when the PML(N)'s leader Ch Nisar Ali Khan told the media
loudly that *'he'll prefer not to contest the election but will not submit*
his degree to the ECP'. [*Later, when the SC ordered on 29th March that*
all the 249 members should get their degrees verified from HEC before
5th April 2013, Ch Nisar Ali Khan was seen amongst the first ten persons
in the queue at HEC gate.]

The ECP was previously seen almost surrendered to the pressure from
parliamentarians on that issue of unverified degrees because highly
influential members belonging to both sides of the political factions were
included in the list of 249.

More disturbing development was that the Chief Election Commissioner
Fakhru Bhai personally called the leader of the opposition, Ch Nisar Ali
Khan, **on 21st February**, a day before the target date of 15 days, and tried
to pacify him. The fact remained that the letter of 7th February was
issued to the 249 MPs following the decision of the five-member Election
Commission. The '**independent ECP**' could have lost confidence to
implement the 2010's orders of the Supreme Court.

The intelligentsia knew that the ECP was doing this exercise of calling
the degrees of 249 representatives just to sort out the '**character**' of

would be candidates of the coming elections of 2013 otherwise neither it was a constitutional requirement nor mandatory under the Peoples Representaticn Act 1976.

Leader of the Opposition, Ch Nisar Ali Khan was actually indicating towards this aspect of **'character scrutiny'** and was demanding that *'this character analysis should also be done for those who had been members of assemblies in 2002 elections'.*

That was another issue that the MQM, **on 24th February 2013,** had formally demanded through a press conference in Karachi that *'Ch Nisar Ali Khan should display his degree before the media if he does not want to send it to the ECP'.* PML(N) had no answer perhaps.

However, the ECP took a firm stand and clarified next day that *"it has not withdrawn from the fake degrees' issue; that it is determined to implement the judgment of Supreme Court in letter and spirit; the process of verification of degrees would be completed so as to achieve the objective of Article 62 and 63 of the constitution."*

On 27th February 2013: the ECP got embarrassed by a mega scandal just two weeks before the announcement of the schedule of general elections 2013 as they had illegally 'cleared' 27 degrees [out of 59] of sitting MPs which were declared invalid by the Higher Education Commission [HEC]. It was clear floating of SC's orders and noble intentions.

Only 32 cases were sent to concerned police for initiation of criminal proceedings as per the apex court 2010 judgment; thus clean chit was given to 27 MPs in sheer and blatant violation of law and rules. As per definition:

> *"If a candidate has managed to take a bogus degree of any recognised institution, it is termed as 'fake' whereas if a candidate has managed to prepare or fake some document / degree in the name of some unknown institution, it will be termed as invalid. There is no difference between a 'fake' or an 'invalid' degree and an 'invalid' is also a 'fake' degree."*

The HEC was the only authority as law of the land to decide validity or invalidity of any education degree.

On 1st March 2013, Dr Atta ur rehman, a former minister, wrote to media that there was, in making, a strong group of allegedly fake degree-holders in the outgoing Parliament, who wished to contest the next elections of 2013. The group was gaining strength because of the failure of the ECP to properly verify their credentials.

The fake people were allowed to continue in power despite the SC decision that the ECP should check their documents. For three years ECP kept on sleeping over that order thus those fake degree-holders would again be contesting the upcoming elections.

The HEC has been rightly asking for the matriculation and HSC certificates for verification, according to its normal procedures, because some politically affiliated vice chancellors had refused to cooperate with HEC in verifying the nature of degrees. The ECP remained under pressure by politicians that *there should be no requirement to check school certificates.*

Had some older politicians genuinely lost their credentials they could ask the HEC to examine their annual attendance records in the respective institutions. HEC could be requested to check their mark sheets in various tests that appeared in.

The fact remained that four of the members of the ECP were nominated by political parties; so they were acting in the interests of their parties. In this scenario, how one could expect the ECP to be fair and unprejudiced? The ECP, therefore, needed to be revamped as per scheme trumpeted by Dr Tahirul Qadri by getting the four new members nominated by the Supreme Court.

'None of the persons involved in holding fake degrees should be allowed to contest the next elections; if they do not have genuine degrees, criminal cases must be initiated against them', Dr Rehman held in the end.

The gimmicks of the Pakistani system, however, prevailed and in general elections of 2013, all those fake degree holders were allowed to contest elections through one loophole or the other. Mostly it was the judiciary which helped them out in appeals.

Earlier, **on 5th March 2013**, the ECP had categorically stated that none of those MPs whose degrees had been found fake by the HEC and even endorsed by the ECP as such, would be barred from contesting the next election unless convicted by a court of law. Two members of the commission, Justice (retd) Riaz Kayani and Justice (retd) Shahzad Akbar Khan told the media that:

'The SC's order does not allow the commission to bar such MPs from contesting the polls or disqualify them without a conviction from a court of law.'

Till then, amongst dozens who had been found to be fake degree holders, only two MPs were convicted by the respective Sessions Courts but even in their cases they had got stay orders from high courts, thus were declared eligible to contest the elections.

This was strange to say the least. It was not a question of being a graduate or not, but it was matter of character failing. Any person who proffers any fake document for any office is committing an act of perjury and is a cheat. What else did the ECP want to have to disqualify a person under articles 62 and 63 of the constitution than such a proof?

It was Justice (retd) Riaz Kayani, a member of the ECP, who was openly flouting the apex court's orders with sarcastic smiles that *'...as of today, not even a single fake degree holder, whether found so by the HEC, or even convicted by the court of law, could be barred from contesting the next election.'*

Regarding the tax and loan defaulters, the two members of the ECP held that they would not allow any tax and loan defaulter to contest but only if the State Bank of Pakistan and Federal Bureau of Revenue would give their final verdicts respectively. About the ECP's decision not to touch six senators whose degrees were found fake, the two members said that *'Section 76 of the Senate (Election) Act 1975 does not allow them to look into such forgery or corruption cases after six months.'*

It was all Justice Riaz Kayani's ill intention or wilful wrong interpretation because the SC order in the fake degree issues had made such a legal provision irrelevant as the court itself took up the matter after the expiry of six months and had directed the ECP to initiate criminal proceedings against them.

In a way it made clear that Dr Tahirul Qadri's deliberations regarding ECP's ineptness was based on facts. It also embarrassed the Supreme Court who had directed the ECP at a number of times to go strong but on each step the ECP proved its wilful weakness. The SC was looking for an appropriate moment to put the things right.

On 8th March 2013; the HEC challenged the ECP's above contention for opening green gates for the fake degree holders to contest the upcoming elections. In a letter to the ECP, the HEC declared in categorical words that there were '*discrepancies*' in the ECP press release admitting that it had cleared cases of 27 fake degree-holder parliamentarians.

Four of these 27 did not exist in the HEC's list of fake degree-holders whereas according to this letter, only in three cases out of the remaining 23, the concerned universities confirmed to the HEC that degrees were found genuine after a later investigation. Thus 20 out of 23 MPs cleared by the ECP were given a clean chit wrongly. In many cases the ECP declared some one's degree fake but did not proceed against him on 'other' grounds such as that MP was re-elected or had resigned.

However, HEC admitted that only in three cases, the decision was reversed out of its list of 59 fake degree-holders. In a press release, ECP had given details of about 27 parliamentarians; declaring two parliamentarians who had resigned were given clean chit by the former CEC on 15th January 2011, whereas four members were re-elected and inducted in office by administering oath to them on 13th June 2011.

On 14th March 2013, annoyed and irritated MNA Jamshed Dasti vowed to file a petition in the Supreme Court saying that "*Why the ECP inquiring about him only while many of the other parliamentarians were given green signal despite having fake degrees.*" Jamshed Dasti was issued a fresh notice then and was summoned for 13th March.

On 26th March 2013, the Supreme Court of Pakistan once more ordered the ECP that action be taken against fake degree holders within two days; reiterating that elections would not be allowed to be delayed in any way.

A 3-member bench headed by Chief Justice Iftikhar M Chaudhry took up for hearing the *fake degree implementation case*. The CJP said:

> "*No one should remain under any delusion. Those contesting the election will be subjected to all types of scrutiny. Why action has not been taken against fake degree holders so far? No other matter can be of more public interest than this. Why are names of candidates not being published?*
>
> *Voters should have all information about their respective candidates. Enough is enough. No corrupt elements will be allowed to go to parliament. Fake degree holders have not only deceived the nation but also made a mockery of their mandate. Such elements don't deserve any leniency.*"

[The beauty of the Pakistani politics remains that despite repeated 'threats' from the SC, ALL fake degree holders contested the said election]

Till then the number of bogus degree cases had gone up from 58 [59-1] to 68 and 34 degrees were still pending. Cases of eight people were pending with respective District & Sessions judges. The bench ordered that voters should seek access to all information under Article 19. Nomination paper be posted at websites and mode of websites should be simple.

Contrarily, the general populace declared all such court exercises as *'topi drama'*. In their opinion *'the SC kept on sitting on all these cases for years and now that the govt's term is over they want to come out as heroes; shame on them for trying to fool the nation.'*

On 30th March 2013: the Chief Justice of Pakistan Iftikhar M Cahudhry took notice of the 189 Parliamentarians whose degrees were still pending verification even after a passage of two-and-a-half years and despite repeated reminders by the ECP. The parliamentarians had failed to provide their certificates to the ECP or the Higher Education Commission (HEC).

In a way it was a fresh *suo moto* notice on a press clipping of a daily Urdu newspaper of that day wherein it was reported that the HEC sent a list with regard to verification of fake degrees of 54 members of parliament. It also appended a list of 189 Parliamentarians whose cases were still pending verification since long and despite repeated reminders by the ECP; they had failed to provide their certificates to the ECP or the HEC.

According to the HEC letter sent to the ECP, Akhunzada Chataan, Samina Khawar Hayat, Ghulam Dastagir and Wasim Afzal Gondal had all been proven having fake degrees. Nasir Ali Shah, Mir Badshah Qaisarani, Seemal Kamran and Shumaila Rana also had fake degrees while the degrees of Israrullah Zehri, Imtiaz Safdar Warraich, Qasim Zia and Umar Gorgage were not recognised.

The HEC also submitted the names of 189 members who had not submitted their Matric and / or Intermediate certificates to the ECP. These politicians included Khurshid Shah, Chaudhary Nisar, Bushra Gauhar and Faisal Saleh Hayat. Afrasiyab Khattak, Javed Hashmi, Samsam Bukhari had also not submitted in their certificates till then. HEC had further stated that cases of 19 Parliamentarians were under litigation in various courts for verification of their degrees.

However, surprisingly, no prosecution was initiated against both the categories of the Parliamentarians in accordance with Para 18 of the judgment in the case of **Rizwan Gill v. Nadia Aziz (PLD 2010 SC 828)**, which had said that:

> *"The Election Commission is, therefore, directed to initiate action against all such persons who are accused of commission of corrupt practices; of committing forgery and of using, as genuine, documents which they knew or at least had reason to believe to be forged.*
>
> *The Election Commission shall ensure that the investigations in these matters are conducted honestly, efficiently and expeditiously and shall depute one of its senior officers to supervise the same.*
>
> *The learned Sessions Judges to whom these trials shall then be entrusted, are also directed to conclude the same without any delay, in consonance with the spirit of the Elections laws as displayed, inter-alia, by the Provisos newly-added to subsection (1-A) of section 67 of the said Act of 1976 through the Amending Act No.IV of 2009 promulgated on 2-11-2009.*
>
> *In any case, it should not take each learned Sessions Judge who gests seized of the matter, more than three months to conclude the same."*

In view of this order, the apex court sought explanation from the ECP for not implementing this judgment in letter and spirit. The SC issued notices to the concerned and directed the trial courts to dispose of all cases against fake degree holding parliamentarians **until 5th April 2013** by all means.

A 3-member bench headed by Chief Justice Iftikhar M Chaudhry had also directed the Registrars of the High Courts to place the names of Sessions Judges before the respective chief justices so that appropriate order could be issued against them for not disposing of the cases expeditiously. The court also directed the Sessions Judge Muzaffargarh to decide Jamshed Dasti case before 4th April 2013. The CJP asked Dasti to demonstrate his qualification to contest election in the forthcoming elections.

The first assembly elected with the graduation condition, was elected in 2002, and then the second in 2008, though Parliament passed the constitutional amendment that reverted to the previous situation where educational qualification was not a condition. However, members of these assemblies were liable for the degrees they submitted.

The Returning Officers were asked to carry out 'strict scrutiny', which they were supposed to, but the process was not supposed to defeat the purpose of the poll. The graduation condition was no longer a requirement for 2013 polls too.

The ECP, on the other side, did its best to facilitate candidates and parties, and did not use its powers to keep away the loan defaulters or utility bills eaters. Simple interpretation of the whole exercise was that people guilty of fraud and deception should not be allowed to stand for public office but the ECP ensured that SC's directions and the Constitutional requirements of Art 62-63 MUST not be met at all.

Due to such shady compromises within the Parliament and the ECP's conduct, Pakistan became a banana republic; self-respect lost and spirit of democracy both either crushed or lost.

The superior judiciary could not assert its authority due to certain restraints; could not punish even a single cheating parliamentarian and the people started loosing faith in justice and judicial set up.

Every profession has its rogues; why to confine up to [some] Generals & [some] judges; why not all who are wrong. No cheating – let the truthfulness prevail.

As an old Chinese saying goes, *"When small men begin to cast big shadows, it means that the sun is about to set."*

On 12th April 2013, following an order from the Supreme Court, lower courts started convicting former members of parliament who contested the 2008 elections using fake degrees; several politicians were given jail sentences. Holding a degree qualification was a precondition for contesting the 2008 poll.

The apex court's orders were based on its earlier verdict in Rizwan Gul Case passed in June 2010 [*discussed in above paragraphs*], which ordered the HEC and the ECP, to verify the degrees of all 1,095 parliamentarians and members of provincial assemblies.

In a continuing series of convictions, former federal minister Humayun Aziz Kurd was sentenced to one year in prison; Abdul Qayyum, a former MPA of the Khyber PK was imprisoned for three years. Ali Madad Jattak, a former provincial minister from the PPP, was sentenced to a two-year prison term by the Session Court in Quetta. Another former minister from Khyber PK, Aqil Shah, was given one-year jail term for his fake degree. Shah was minister of Sports & Culture.

Two other former members of the Khyber PK were convicted and sentenced for submitting forged degrees to the ECP in 2008. Sardar Ali Khan was jailed for three years, and Javed Khan Tarakai was sentenced to one year. Some politicians with fake degrees, who were sure to receive jail terms, had fled from their respective areas and their whereabouts went unknown. Courts declared them absconders, and verdicts were passed in their absence.

All the former lawmakers convicted for having fake or bogus university degrees were barred from taking part in the upcoming elections. All of the convicted parliamentarians were arrested in the respective courts immediately after sentencing because one former MPA from Punjab, Rizwan Gul of PML(N) had fled seconds after he was given a three-year sentence.

Jamshed Dasti, a former MNA of the PPP, was sentenced to three years in prison on 5th April by a district judge. He challenged the conviction in the Lahore High Court, which declared his conviction null and void three days later and ordered his release from jail.

However, the whole world laughed at us because next day in appellant tribunals, headed by the high court judges mostly, ALL [invariably all] the convicted fake degree holders were not only released from jails but were also allowed to contest the May 2013 elections.

On 14th April 2013, the ECP de-notified 11 former parliamentarians in fake degree case; those de-notified by ECP included three Senators, five Member Punjab Assembly, two from Sindh and one from Balochistan Assemblies.

Samina Khawar Hayyat, Shabina Khan, Rana Ejaz, Semal Kamran and Shumaila Rana of Punjab Assembly; Nadir Magsi and Bashir Ahmed from Sindh Assembly; Tariq Magsi from Balochistan were de-notified.

The former Senators included Israrullah Zehri, Rehana Yehya Baloch and Mir Muhabbat Mari.

What happened to them finally is not known.

Scenario 72

ARMY GENERALS EXTENDED [2010]:

On 17th August 1988, when Gen Ziaul Haq along with his 19 colleagues and two American top diplomats met an air crash allegedly after some mango crates, gifted to him by the *Bahawalpuri* admirers, exploded just after seven minutes of take-off, Gen Mirza Aslam Beg, the then Army Chief was tipped to announce for another Martial law. He avoided it.

Gen Beg went soft, highly disciplined and touched highest echelons of civility by choosing the democratic rule for the country. He asked the then Chairman of the Senate Mr Ghulam Ishaq Khan (GIK) to take over reins of the government and to announce general elections within ninety days.

General elections were held in November 1988; Benazir Bhutto came as the Prime Minister but they could not pull on with each other smoothly. The advisors to the PM Benazir Bhutto could not apprehend that they were able to hold the reigns of power simply because of this Army General. The things went worse and Gen Beg had to tip, suggest and advise the then President GIK [in 1990] for another elections. By distributing Rs:140 million among the PPP's opponents Gen Beg made sure that the Pakistan Muslim League (PML) should win with majority.

This distribution of 140 millions, snatched by the ISI from Hassan Habib the then Chief of defunct Mehran Bank, was stirred in the Supreme Court of Pakistan by Air Marshal ® Asghar Khan in 1996. So many judges picked up the case for hearing but the exercises ended in futile.

Once CJP Saeeduzzaman Siddiqui wanted to announce the decision in 1999 but then allegedly the army prevailed; the file was sent in the cold room. It is a separate and eloquent story which has been narrated in Volume One of this book in details which issue ultimately was taken up by the CJP Iftikhar M Chaudhry in early 2012 and announced the judgment [titled as ASGHAR KHAN CASE] in ending that year.

In nut-shell, the PML was made to win the elections of 1990 and Nawaz Sharif surfaced as Prime Minister as per *'Planning of the Agencies'*. What made Gen Beg angry all of a sudden within two years of Nawaz Sharif's first premiership, no body knows. Gen Beg started repenting on his decision of managing PML's victory and once gave a final shape to his plans of dissolving the government and to bring Ghulam Mustafa Jatoi as an interim Prime Minister.

When the intelligence reports reached PM Nawaz Sharif, he immediately announced nomination of Gen Asif Janjua as the new Army Chief. It was all against the norms and traditions then prevailing in the Army and the governments (because there were five months more with Gen Beg to serve as Army Chief) but it was taken as a wise step. PM Nawaz Sharif had also ensured that the news should get a wide publicity in media with comments and editorials with side stories.

A serving army Chief was told (in 1990s) five months earlier that he had to go home and then there came more hilarious moments in Pakistan's history *'when (on 24ᵗʰ July 2010) an Army Chief, Gen Ashfaq Kayani, was told five months earlier that his tenure stands extended by three years'*.

In the previous situation there was an emergency aroused for Nawaz Sharif of PML and in the second situation there were stakes held by President Zardari and PM Yousaf Raza Gilani, both belonging to the Pakistan Peoples Party (PPP).

But it has been happening in our history since very early days. Referring to an interview of Gen Faiz Ali Chishti, a veteran companion of Gen Ziaul Haq at the time of July 1977's coup, published in *daily 'Jang' of 20ᵗʰ June 1999*, a very factual analysis made by him points out that the responsibility of giving way to the army Generals generally goes to the inept and ineffective civil politicians. He said:

> *'The civilian rulers made Gen Ayub Khan a Commander in Chief in early 1950s. Was he a deserving General; No, the decision was not taken by the army itself but the then civilian rulers.*
>
> *In 1954 when his tenure of service was extended; who had done that. The then civilian rulers who might have sent some other deserving Generals home just because they liked Ayub Khan. Wrong it was.*
>
> *Gen Musa Khan's performance as Commander in Chief in 1965 War was zero. He deserved court martial on account of his follies on record but he was given extension.*
>
> *The military record of Gen Yahya Khan was having hundreds of pages describing stories, events and complaints regarding his 'loose*

character', but why was he promoted and taken so high, up to an Army Chief and then Chief Martial Law Administrator.'

A sad story but still available on record that Gen Gul Hassan was made the Army Chief jointly by Z A Bhutto & COAS Gen Yahya Khan on 20th December 1971 just after the debacle of East Pakistan. His tenure, however, was short-lived. He was ousted as army chief on 3rd March 1972 by the order of the Civilian Martial Law Administrator (CMLA) and the President Z A Bhutto. His retirement privileges and benefits were also taken away, an utter disgrace to the whole army as an honourable institution.

[Gen Tikka Khan was senior to Gen Gul Hassan. When the later was made the army chief, Gen Tikka Khan should have gone on retirement as per established army traditions but he had not.

Not only this, Gen Tikka Khan had humiliated the whole army by accepting a political slot of 'Minister of State' in Mr Bhutto's cabinet. It was OK if he was made a 'full federal minister'; but Mr Bhutto intentionally degraded the army by giving him a lesser portfolio and Tikka Khan was a party to it.

Gen Ziaul Haq was made the Army Chief on 1st March 1976 by PM Z A Bhutto while superseding a number of more senior officers. At the time of his nominating the successor to the outgoing chief Gen Tikka Khan the Lieutenant Generals in order of seniority were, Muhammad Shariff, Muhammed Akbar Khan, Aftab Ahmed Khan, Azmat Baksh Awan, Agha Ibrahim Akram, Abdul Majeed Malik, Ghulam Jilani Khan, and Ziaul Haq. But, Bhutto chose the most junior, dropping seven seniors to him.

Why was he [Gen Ziaul Haq] chosen even though he had never taken part in any war like Gul Hassan.

Gen Tikka Khan was offered extension by Mr Bhutto for a year in his service which he refused. *Before going he sent recommendations for new Army Chief saying that either of Gen Shariff and Gen Akbar Khan be considered. For Gen Aftab, Gen A B Awan and Gen Jilani it was written explicitly that the three were not fit for that slot (perhaps because they spent most of their services in intelligence directorates).*

For Gen Majeed and Gen Ziaul Haq it was stated that both were recently promoted, just gone on corps commander's postings but Mr Bhutto, being totally dishonest towards many, selected Gen Ziaul

Haq, the junior most, considering him the most docile. Mr Bhutto had suffered enough for that mistake.]

In July 2010, Gen Kayani was given three years extension in his tenure. He had succeeded Gen Musharraf as the COAS on 29th November 2007. PM Mr Gilani had extended Gen Kayani's term as Chief of the Army Staff making him the first four-star officer to receive a term extension from any democratic government.

Immediately after, the *daily 'Jang' dated 28th July 2010* commented:

'There was an apprehension that the vibrant judiciary would call him in the Supreme Court [though he had not done anything apparently wrong]'.

The media had raised their eyebrows on it that if Rehman Malik and Babar Awan could be called in the court being federal ministers then why not a retired General.

However, the announcement was done in utmost haste. The telecast was made all of a sudden and during such late hours of night leaving the people in astray. It was a broadcast of only two and a half minute, when the Prime Minister of Pakistan Mr Gilani, had affirmed an extension in tenure of the Army Chief Gen Ashfaq Kayani for three years effective from **29th November 2010** when he was likely to go on retirement in an ordinary course of nature. Next day the PM told the press that:

'Now the stability would prevail in the country because the President, the Prime Minister, the Army Chief and the Chief Justice of Pakistan, all will be retiring in 2013.

There will be no threat of martial law or any voice of mid-term elections in the country now'.

This statement itself had divulged a cogent hidden fact that there was definitely some danger or threat which caused this extension that too for an unprecedented period of three years.

WAS IT AN AMERICAN PROPOSAL?

The intelligentsia was ready to pass comments that it was done on immense pressure from their War on Terror ally called America because

Gen Ashfaq Kayani [allegedly] suited them more than any Pakistani General before, even more than Rehman Malik and President Zardari both; though the subsequent developments guided that Gen Kayani did not bother about America much.

Why such thoughts! Because just three months earlier, the Federal Defence Minister Mr Ahmed Mukhtar, had issued a press statement that no extension would be given to the Army Chief. What was the sudden emergency which had cropped up during the night of 24th July 2010 that the Ministry of information could not find enough moments to type a hand out of forty words and had to fax out a hand-written four line statement to prominent TV channels wishing PM's address to the nation in emergency. It was less than three minutes telecast.

Explore another proposition: Mr Zardari always acted upon advice of Rehman Malik or Husain Haqqani given on various subjects as [allegedly] both were the bonafide agents on the pay roll of the American CIA [*and they took it as pride rather to keep it as secret*] and constantly working on the US agenda but it had been the Pakistan's history.

Even Z A Bhutto was scared of this white 'friend'. Benazir Bhutto had availed the US blessings twice; America had forced Gen Mirza Aslam Beg and President GIK in 1988 to bring her as the PM though under some conditions. Similarly, it was America who had forced Gen Musharraf in 2007 to strike a deal [of NRO] with Benazir Bhutto to facilitate her coming back to Pakistan and to hold the elections of 2008 calling her the winner.

In 1999 when PM Nawaz Sharif had felt threats from his Army Chief Gen Musharraf, he had also sent Shahbaz Sharif to Washington to get a word of stern advice for his military commander.

Pakistan Army still remembers those moments of humiliation when, while drafting the Kerry Lugar Bill in September 2009 for aid to Pakistan, Mr Husain Haqqani had [allegedly & deliberately] got included certain embarrassing clauses in the draft which were not at all acceptable to the army. The result was that the Army immediately sent a note of anger and resentment to the PPP government. When the said bill was accented in October 2009 by the US Congress, the same evening a special meeting of Corps Commanders in GHQ was summoned and the KL Bill was rejected.

The government of Pakistan could not get more than $300 million aid, against a promise of $1.5 billion per year, under that KL arrangement till

2012; the US government withdrew its favours because Pakistan Army had declined to extend any cooperation required by virtue of that aid-bill. The GOP had got axed their own feet by making a false and cunning move through Husain Haqqani.

The angry army leadership over the KL Bill was then compensated by giving three years extension in the tenure of Gen Pasha, the ISI Chief while the Army Chief had already bagged the extension.

Whatever be the case; the said announcement of extension in Army Chief's tenure was made during an interval when the US Foreign Secretary Hillary Clinton was there on Pakistan's tour and soon after the US Army Chief Mike Mullin paid a sudden visit to Pakistan to advise the sitting government on two main issues that:

- *'Firstly Osama Bin Laden is in Pakistan;*

- *Secondly Lashkar e Tayyabah is expanding;*

  thus Pakistan should concentrate its efforts to handle these two acute problems at the ealiest'.

It was also a coincidence that when the three year's extension was announced for Gen Ashfaq Kayani, the next dawn brought another strange announcement from across the border that *'Hakim ullah Mehsood and Qari Fazalullah are still alive, they are not dead'.*

It was a challenge for Pakistan Army on one side but at the same time it was an eye opening bomb-shell for Pakistani media pointing fingers towards Army press releases which had brought dozens of columns in praise of uniformed people and their strategies on death news of the two.

After three days, another message was conveyed to the people of Pakistan through targeting one **Arshad Hussain** to death near Noshera in Khyber PK province. He **was the only son of Iftikhar Hussain, the sitting Information Minister of Khyber PK.**

Next day a suicidal-bomb blast took place near the same provincial Information Minister's residence claiming eight deaths and leaving about thirty persons injured. The government and the army were unable to read the message.

Coming back to sudden telecasts; it was a second occasion when the people of Pakistan had seen PM Gilani making a tele-announcement in alike hasty manner; with confused head and pale face. The earlier occasion was on 16th March 2009 when he had bowed his head before a moving mass of about a million people towards Islamabad and had agreed for reinstatement of the CJ Iftikhar M Chaudhry along with his fellow judges unconditionally. The people still believe that the cause of that defeated announcement was also sponsored by Gen Kayani.

The deep analysis of PM Gilani's verdict would take you nowhere. The think tanks opined that once again the Pakistan's Army was being dragged into politics in the name of Gen Kayani with whose efforts and cautious behaviour the Army was achieving success in keeping itself away from dirty politics of Pakistan after Gen Musharraf's devastating, distressing and demoralizing policies.

Whatever the case be, PM Gilani had in a way confirmed that in the absence of this extension, there was a strong likelihood of some casualty in respect of someone amongst the top three most probably either the PM or the President or the whole PPP.

The PPP had made a cogent achievement in political scenario then prevailing in Pakistan but the extension was also termed as a challenge for Gen Kayani because his appointment as an Army Chief was done by a military dictator himself whereas the extension granted was mostly considered as *'fresh political appointment of Gen Kayani'* done by political bosses for future political gains.

The time would reveal the truth behind the iron curtain of probabilities but the fact remains that till then Gen Kayani had proved himself as a very sensitive person as far as his professional skills and self respect were concerned. His past record had reflected that he did not believe in narrow thinking or tapered behaviour nor had he shown any undue favour for either pressure group; very deep inside and looking calm at face. Everyone was aware for his close association with Gen Musharraf but when the public opinion turned against that military dictator, Gen Kayani did not stand by him.

It was also a fact that had Gen Kayani refused to accept three years extension in his tenure, his person would have been taller and higher. He would have been capable enough to convey that his junior team members were equally sensible, responsible, dependable, accountable, more professional and more sincere & loyal for the country. As he had undertaken another long travel for three years he experienced many changes and would see more till his retirement.

After 2012's elections of America and having four more years for President Obama, 2013's general elections in Pakistan, new Parliament and new provincial governments, new Prime Minister, new President, new American government, reformed exit strategy for NATO forces from Afghanistan in 2014 [if it happened so] and what more unseen changes, nobody knows.

Once in early June 1958, the then President Iskandar Mirza, in a similar haste (as of PM Gilani in July 2010), by sending a hand-written note of only two lines, giving two years extension to the then Commander-in-Chief Ayub Khan, had opted and managed to call his own end within four months. Gen Ayub Khan had then extended his own rule till March 1969 - for eleven years.

Who knows what would happen next.

How the Americans had managed to bring the PPP regime up to the nerve-breaking point, extract of an article written by *Jamsheed K C, professor of International Studies at Indiana University,* appearing at internet media *on 22ⁿᵈ December 2009* is reproduced below:

> '*Conditions in Pakistan have been ripening, like the mango fruit eaten there, for another military coup d'etat. The economy has slumped, corruption is rampant, and terrorism is endemic. People are losing faith in the officials they brought to power.*
>
> *This time, the soldiers may not have to use guns and tanks. They can bide their time until the elected government descends into chaos, then march in as national savoir. But the country's judiciary is swiftly becoming a player to be reckoned with too.*'

[How correct that prediction was! One can see around in 2011-12; once again some people were shouting loud to call the army to save Pakistan.]

Professor Jamsheed kept on saying that on 16ᵗʰ December [2009] Pakistan's Supreme Court declared as unconstitutional the National Reconciliation Ordinance (NRO). The NRO was an amnesty granted in October 2007 by Gen Musharraf to politicians facing corruption and other criminal charges filed between January 1986 and October 1999. With that decision, all hell broke loose — politically speaking.

Interior Minister Rehman Malik himself was once facing arrest by the National Accountability Bureau (NAB) on corruption charges. President Zardari was facing the possibility of 12 corruption charges being reinstated. Worse, the Supreme Court had suggested that the government should ask Switzerland to reopen a money-laundering investigation against him that was once dropped on grounds of poor mental health. The judiciary was constantly humiliated for months because the ruling PPP simply flouted the apex court's orders on the pretext that why their opponents Sharif brothers were not being touched by the court.

So were demands by political opponents and the general public that PPP's inefficient administration be stripped of power. Pakistan's military had regained some of its prestige through considerable success by launching certain meaningful operations against Islamic militants within Swat and the Federally Administered Tribal Areas [FATA]. The Generals remained united as one group — the other was the judiciary.

Not unexpectedly, the military once more faced mounting pressure to restore order in Pakistan, even at the expense of democracy. Many among the entrepreneurial middle class and westernized upper class regard the military as the most viable and stable national institution.

As the Generals remained silent, Zardari's administration had been reduced to threatening people for SMS text jokes about its corruption with jail terms of up to 14 years. As Pakistan's primary ally and aid donor, the United States had indeed faced much difficulties coupled with embarrassment and disgrace while dealing with the Pakistan army directly. The US President Obama once said in 2009:

> 'So, despite its avowed aim of promoting democracy and human rights worldwide, the current U.S. administration may soon be stuck with having to accept an illegitimate Pakistani government led by Generals trying to restore order despite that in late July, Pakistan's Supreme Court declared illegal an earlier state of emergency declared by the military and it is likely to do so again.'

One could judge that when tens of similar threatening communications were fed through foreign media in continuity that US would prefer to negotiate with military bosses of Pakistan; and the US Secretary of State Hilary Clinton visited Pakistan to assure the rulers that nothing would happen till Gen Kayani remained in uniform, then of course, such like telecasts and extensions were the natural outcome and were considered appropriate with reference to the given context.

Still Pakistan could be seen as a colony; looking towards commands and forced advice from abroad.

As has been mentioned earlier; on 22nd December 2011, the Prime Minister Gilani roared in the Parliament emphasizing that he would not allow 'a state within a state' pointing towards army & ISI. In the first week of January 2012, when Mr Zardari was asked [*Ref: GEO News TV Interview*] to comment, he said that:

> 'He is a powerful Prime Minister. He has all the powers; he does not feel (he is) under anybody. If there is some (matter) which is annoying him, he has the right to take a position, and he has taken a position.'

When asked about the three-year extension given to Army Chief Gen Kayani, Mr Zardari said '*this is now a question in history*'.

However, in the '*TIME's 2010: persons of the year*', Gen Kayani appeared as:

> '**Highs:** Pakistan's army chief steered his country's military — long accused of abetting certain militant extremist groups, including the Afghan Taliban — toward confronting the jihadists in their midst. During the disastrous floods that ravaged Pakistan this summer, Kayani was seen as an energetic and effective figurehead of the relief effort even when the civilian government, led by unpopular President Asif Ali Zardari, in Islamabad, had been pilloried for its sluggish response.
>
> **Lows:** ...... In a surprise move, Kayani had his tenure extended by three years this November. The move has sparked concern in some quarters over the popular army chief's long-term ambitions. Pakistan has a long, troubled history of intervention and rule by military strongmen.'

There are more important things in history to be remembered.

GEN KAYANI – 3 YEARS AFTER:

Pakistan's Prime Minister Yousaf Raza Gilani once visited India for the India-Pakistan cricket semi-final after the visit was cleared by the Army. He was not able to board the flight had Gen Kayani not smiled. Gen Kayani, while in command, retained the support of the soldiers; largely because he stayed away from the media. He was never interested in publicity unlike his predecessor Gen Musharraf and had shown little interest in becoming the politician in uniform. This all went to his credit ensuring only with one extension as Army chief.

During Gen Kayani in chair, the politicians were able to focus on the civilian institutions of state and went for strengthening democracy in Pakistan. This policy also allowed the Army to consolidate its hold on matters of strategic importance. Gen Kayani went successful in improving relations with Afghan President Hamid Karzai from freezing to almost warm levels and ensured a level of cooperation between the two.

During the **last week of February 2013**, Gen Kayani, burst the bubble of hope of the anti-democracy elements for a military coup by supporting the continuation of the democratic process and transfer of power through impartial elections, besides emphasising the army's subservient role to a civilian government. He had invited prominent print and electronic media men on lunch and spoken out his heart during an off-the-record 4-hour briefing. Gen Kayani said that:

'*He fully supports the idea of holding a free, fair, and transparent elections leading to a smooth transfer of power in the country. He had assured the Chief Election Commissioner of full cooperation on the matter.*

The army has stood by the democratically-elected government during the past five years as required under the constitution.

That everyone must respect the mandate of the people and for this the army will provide the maximum help, but only that much which is asked for by the civilians.'

Gen Kayani was successful to dispel the speculations about a possible delay in the polls and the installation of a caretaker set up for a longer period. Gen Kayani's statements, indeed, reflected a paradigm shift in the thinking of the military commanders in regard to the role of the army in a state. Many media anchors recalled their Quaid who had, while reminding the army officers at Staff College Quetta on 14th June 1948, about the significance of oath of allegiance to the constitution, said:

"*I should like you to study the constitution, which is in force in Pakistan at present, and understand its true constitutional and legal implications when you say you will be faithful to the constitution.*"

It has never been considered fair to chastise Pak-Army because of the recklessness of 'some' individual Generals; Gen Kayani strengthened its credentials as supporter of the democratic system and the government by resisting all temptations. Equally laudable were the efforts of the superior judiciary that repeatedly vowed not to allow any unconstitutional move from any quarter, in addition to its unflinching faith in the democratic process.

Fortunately, Pakistan availed an independent media playing an admirable role in strengthening democracy.

The end message seemed to be that *'no one should try to play games with the transparency and fairness of the elections and the results must be accepted but the army will not impose itself in any way and this job has to be done by the civilians themselves.'*

In his briefing, Gen Kayani gave a long list of civilian failures during the last five years, almost a charge sheet against the politicians and the government and placed the blame of gigantic failures in many critical domains at the civilian doorstep. Not to intervene was constitutionally a constructive approach but in reality it brought the country to the verge of collapse; and Gen Kayani did not want to share the blame.

Examples of the civilians' failure that he quoted, in his own soft style were:

• The key issue of war against terrorism; do not blame the army as the civilians had not formulated a comprehensive anti-terrorism policy and they could not decide what to do.

• The army had not been consulted or taken on board about the political All Parties Conferences [APC] held on counter-terrorism.

• The civilians depended too much on ISI & MI and went scared of them too whereas the tasks should have been done by their own civilian intelligence agencies like IB and Police's Special Branch.

• Where are the civilian agencies? Total failure of the Interior & Home ministries; sometimes army guided the civilians to reform and take responsibility yet did not intervene to stop the decay.

• The army knew that these [incompetent] politicians will not be able to handle the gigantic issues like the war on terror, the Balochistan mess, the [religious] domestic extremism but they did not interfere so that the army may not be blamed.

Gen Kayani, in this context, reminded the Swat situation where he had to persuade President Zardari to take a decision. He also took ANP leader Asfandyar Wa. to the President and when the decision was taken to talk to Maulana Sufi Mohammed, the dialogue were held but when he violated the accord, an operation was launched. Then the civilians had to take over the responsibility which they did not.

Gen Kayani specifically mentioned the arrests made in Swat and complained that:

'For more than five years, Pak-Army is holding those people; the establishment either violating laws by doing so or risks more terrorism if they are released. But if those arrested persons are not convicted because of lack of evidence, the army cannot hold them forever.'

Gen Kayani said that an army operation could be launched in Balochistan if the civilians take that decision and order the army to do so. 'But once the operation is done and people are arrested, they will have to be tried and convicted by the police and courts for which the civilians are not ready.'

In short, Gen Kayani explained army's five years of non-interference and failure of the greedy politicians to cope with the disasters which could have been handled with good governance.

Albeit; Gen Kayani knew well that there had been Gen Musharraf's un-interrupted rule for complete eight years with complete dominance of the army including him; the persecution of selected politicians, the exploitation of the political system, physical threats to political leaders, their assassinations and mass murders, and importing WOT into this poor country at the cost of our meagre infra-structure were also equally responsible for leading Pakistan towards a failed state.

Shaheen Sehbai, in 'the News' of 1st March 2013, was right to say:

'....... So there was no way the army could avoid an election [of 2008] but there was no way the civilians could correct everything messy that the Generals were leaving behind.

Similar is the issue with the present elections. Gen Kayani is now saying that elections must be free, fair and transparent but the set-up that has been put in place is controversial, weak and fragile, weakest at the top.'

ANOTHER NRO PLANNED:

During the first week of March 2013, the media in Pakistan has been talking about another NRO being imminent like the one promulgated by former dictator Gen Musharraf which paved the way for Benazir Bhutto and Mian Nawaz Sharif to return to Pakistan and take part in 2008 Elections. Then it was thought to be a pre-requisite for fair elections. For elections of 2013 no Ordinance was needed as the 20th Amendment passed unanimously by the parliament was in saddles to ensure the fair elections conducted through an impartial non-political administration.

However, the real string pullers sitting far away in Washington DC and London had no concern with fairness of elections; they wanted any government in Pakistan but dependent on them; not on popular judiciary and the powerful military. *Usman Khalid of 'Rifah Org'* held in his essay *dated 7ᵗʰ March 2013* on internet media that:

> *"When NRO-1 was promulgated [in October 2007], no one, not even Gen Musharraf, had any idea that the end result would be the emergence of Asif Ali Zardari. The handlers of President Zardari – Altaf Hussain, Rehman Malik, Salman Farooqi and Hussain Haqqani etc had been the real rulers of Pakistan over the last five years.*
>
> *The same group coined NRO-2 to ensure 'no change in policies'; change of faces were tolerable. The stage was set for Nawaz Sharif to be the premier as the head of another 'coalition' and would ensure 'no change in policy', particularly foreign policy; through NRO-2."*

Nawaz Sharif's one to one meeting with the British Foreign Secretary at London, facilitated through Wajid Shamsul Hassan of London's High Commission, during last days of PPP's government is referred here for details.

During the gimmicks of 'caretaker set up' all the given names were only to be discussed in media whereas the real compromise had already been done on one name by both the ruling PPP and the opposition PML(N), that was Asma Jehangir, but she herself avoided to come forward, made an open announcement for that, thus saved her own life.

Asma Jahangir was the favourite of both the PPP and the PML(N) because she had for decades demonized the Pakistan Army as the 'enemy' of the political culture; once accused the ISI for her assassination. If she was appointed caretaker PM there was every likelihood of her being assassinated. Like the assassination of Benazir paved the way for the PPP to win the 2008 Elections and Asif Zardari becoming a despotic ruler of Pakistan to plunder the state with impunity, Asma's assassination could instigate yet another military rule in Pakistan.

The victims of violence in Pakistan, particularly the Shia community, had already propagated much for the military to protect them. Under the prevailing political dispensation which was hostile to the military as evidenced by the 'memo-gate' affair, the military went much constrained. At that crucial moment no one was talking about terrorism, poor people's funds illegally or fraudulently spent by the PPP & its allied parties, and of 'load shedding' that had wrecked life as well as the economy of Pakistan.

ISI CHIEF EXTENDED, TOO:

On 16th January 2010, *Arif Nizami* wrote that:

> '*Civilian control over the armed forces is a holy principle of democracy but has never been practiced in Pakistan even Mr Bhutto could not rein in the army after East Pakistan's debacle in 1971.*
>
> *Bhutto first succumbed to its demand that a film showing the surrender of Pakistani forces to India be withdrawn from PTV. Later, keeping the sensitivities of the army in mind, he decided to put the Hamoodur Rehman Commission Report in cold storage. Ultimately he was ousted and hanged by his handpicked army chief, Gen Ziaul Haq.*'

Much later, heavy mandated PM Nawaz Sharif tried to emasculate all institutions, one after another, and sacked his Army Chief Gen Jehangir Karamat [along with President and the CJP]. When Nawaz tried to sack the next Army Chief Gen Musharraf, he had to pay the price by being kicked out himself. Had his American and Arab mentors not pleaded with Gen Musharraf to send him into 10 years exile, he would have met the same fate as Mr Bhutto had seen two decades earlier.

Might be that under the Constitution Nawaz Sharif was perfectly within his rights as prime minister to sack his army chief but there were codes of conduct, rationale for so big actions and certain procedural formalities required to be obliged by all institutional heads. This time the army itself was determined to extend its armed blow to avoid further humiliation.

After NRO's decision of December 2009, a perception developed that the military would be getting rid of President Zardari and the acuity prevailed for quite long. After the SC's unanimous verdict declaring the NRO *ultra vires* of the Constitution, some forces, including some sections of the media, trumpeted high that the army and its intelligence apparatus were trying to get the presidency vacated.

The military, in fact, were too busy in dealing with the existential threat within from the Taliban but the flames were high. ISI had totally dissociated itself from political affairs beyond an iota of doubt thus there was no trust deficit between military and the government. Despite such clarifications, rumours kept on swinging with quotes from one Corps Commander's meeting on the Kerry Lugar Bill in ending 2009.

The fact remains that the GHQ had to take the unusual step of getting public approval through print and electronic media about its reservations about the KL bill when certain security clauses were added without consultations with it, the ISI or the Foreign Office. The government, on the other hand, insisted that the military was fully on board on the matter which was not correct.

Even then, Gen Kayani had assured both President Zardari and PM Gilani about their zero designs to undermine the democratic process though it was not at all required. President Zardari's close relationship with USA was another irritant not only with the army but also with general populace in Pakistan. PPP's corruption stories spread over media papers, their poor governance and a dull economic performance had disturbed all including the GHQ. The later could argue that the government's poor show had encroached upon its defence capabilities; referring to the ever prevailing internal insurgency especially.

Nawaz Sharif had time and again reiterated his support for a democratic system but his words apparently could not match with PML(N)'s deeds on ground. Nawaz Sharif, as a leader in waiting, would have lost every thing had the military moved in.

The governance and transparency were so ill managed, that not only the army but the media and the public at large had strong reservations about the PPP rulers. The dream of even an ounce of civilian control over the GHQ could be realised had the politicians set their own house in order; shredding off the self-interests and power-grabbing games were the foremost requirements.

On **30th December 2008**, the print and electronic media had displayed:

"In a major reshuffle in the army's top command, Chief of the Army Staff Gen Ashfaq Parvez Kayani brought in a new head of the all-powerful Inter-Services Intelligence (ISI) ...

Perhaps the most surprising of all such changes is the appointment of Lt-Gen Ahmed Shuja Pasha as the new Director General of ISI .... A highly professional soldier in his own right, Lt-Gen Pasha has, for the past over two years, been overseeing the ongoing security operation in the tribal areas and parts of the NWFP.

In his capacity as the Director-General military operations (DGMO) he was directly responsible for the launching and execution of all major security strikes in Fata and Swat, the latest being the major onslaught against religious extremists in the Bajaur tribal agency."

On **10th February 2010**, the government decided to extend the tenure of DG ISI Lt Gen Ahmad Shuja Pasha, for a period of one year. The decision was taken after the satisfactory performance of ISI in the war against terrorism.

The file was sent to the Presidency for a formal approval though the Army Chief did not need to send a summary for extension in the tenure of a 3-star General. A year earlier, Lt Gen Masood Aslam, Corps Commander for Peshawar, was given an extension by Gen Kayani, the Army Chief himself. The other extensions in the recent history of Pakistan Army were of Lt Gen Hamid Javed, Chief of Staff to former president Gen Musharraf, and the Chief of Strategic Plans Division, Lt Gen Khalid Kidwai.

Lt Gen Kidwai was due to retire in 2006, but was given extensions more than once due to the technical nature of his assignment. He continued to be the Chief of the SPD even after completion of his extended term as Lt General.

Then the top brass of Pakistan Army was set to undergo a reshaping process with the retirement of 12 three-star generals, including four corps commanders, during the year 2010, warranting more major promotions and the necessary reshuffles again. Three of the Lt Generals, including incumbent DG ISI, Gen Pasha, were scheduled to retire on 18th March or nearer. The other two were Lt Gen Tanvir Tahir & Lt Gen M Ashraf Saleem; Lt Gen Ahsan Azhar Hayat was going to retire in the mid-March.

Obviously and primarily the prime minister was the appointing authority of the ISI Chief and he could appoint anyone, civilian or uniformed; though it never happened before smoothly or if the PM had ever used his prerogative without danger signals. Traditionally, the COAS has been using this authority to appoint his spy chief.

The readable message in the above media report was that *"Gen Kayani ... has put in place a new team to implement his vision for reviving the prestige of the armed forces and for enhancing the security of the state."* Nothing new; the army has always been in charge of national security. Gen Pasha had 15 months with him to reach the age of superannuation; but if the 'required goal' was not achieved in 15 months, he was also to be considered for extension.

The same happened; he was needed for the sake of 'continuity' that without him the new security policy could not be implemented. The most charitable explanation for Pasha's extension was that Kayani and Pasha were together and fighting good of reorienting the Pakistan Army and changing its security outlook.

Gen Kayani mostly went contemptuous of the PPP government and its leader Mr Zardari, though never made it public even once; never wasted time negotiating with them as equals. During this nerve-war Gen Kayani always kept Gen Pasha by his side; as the Generals know the best and the 'bloody civilians' just don't get it. [*Gen Musharraf's journeys from one court to the other during April 2013 and after is a case study in this regard; isn't it?*]

During the same days, another issue played with the hearts of the general populace of Pakistan and that was the increased army spending.

Till end of the February 2010, the army budgetary expenditure was marked by over Rs:93 billion higher during that fiscal year. The normal defence expenditure rose by 12 per cent to Rs:166 billion during the first six months of the fiscal year 2009-10, from Rs:148 billion of the same period last year. Spending on public order and safety affairs also went up by 48 per cent to Rs:166 billion from Rs:139 billion.

The fact remained that additional expenditure on security operations in Malakand division and the tribal region had separately been made part of grants that increased from Rs:93.4 billion to Rs:134 billion in six months of the next fiscal year. The figure for the corresponding period during the previous year was Rs:40 billion.

The questions were raised that the Army Chief's decision to give extension in service to a couple of Lieutenant Generals on his own was a valid step or not; though under the rules Gen Kayani had the powers to promote senior officers without consulting the government. The intelligentsia had a safe corner that the decision was a part of the Pak-Afghan scenario on a larger canvas.

Prime Minister Gilani, however, preferred to convey an impression of 'no objection'. During Gen Musharraf's tenure the GHQ decided that heads of the department could give leave to their staff. This was done to provide relief to those who had to run from pillar to post to get their leave sanctioned. However, this power did not interfere with the government's authority to give its sanction to all other decisions including promotions or extensions.

The government's first and only white paper on defence written during the 1970s had strengthened the defence ministry's position as the main interface between the military and the civilian government. The first defence secretary was not only a civilian, he was a non-bureaucrat. To counter this move a centre-point was created in the form of the Joint Chiefs of Staff Committee [JCSC]. Unfortunately, neither institution could grow because of the military takeover in 1977.

The JCSC couldn't really stand up to the pressure of the military in the seat of power. Later, under Gen Musharraf, the army more or less killed the institution by changing one of the core principles for the JCSC that is the appointment of its Chairman by rotation. PM Nawaz Sharif, during his second stint, mistakenly or innocently contributed to the malaise by appointing Gen Musharraf as the Chairman when it was actually the naval chief's turn. In Pakistan's power politics it is the army chief who calls the shots.

The Indo-Pak history is witness to the fact that moves to alter the principles of governance always went costly. The Indians suffered as a result of this during the 1960s. Their defence establishment got into questionable human resource management in the armed forces which lost them the war of 1962 against China.

Gen Kayani might have signalled to PM Gilani that *'human resource management in the army comes under his purview and that he does not want politicians to decide on military issues'*.

Even in America those days, there were many [in Washington] in favour of an extension for the army chief. Some in the Obama administration continued to bet on the military horse rather than the civilian government. Within the army the preference was for certain officers, especially the ISI chief Gen Pasha; whether or not this personality-driven approach solved the Pak-Afghan problem to Washington's satisfaction was another theme.

Gen Pasha continued to hold reigns of the ISI. However, **on 25th April 2011**, Wikileaks documents had shown US investigators considered Pakistan's ISI to be a terrorist group itself.

Pakistan had been a key ally of the United States against the Al Qaeda & Taliban but deep mistrust between the two countries' intelligence agencies was laid bare during the last week of April 2011 with the leak of a 2007 US list of *"terrorist and terrorist support entities"* that included Pakistan's ISI. That was why, when a week later, a SEAL operation of 2nd May 2011 was launched in Abbottabad, Pakistan was not told even.

The ISI appeared with some 70 other groups, including Iranian intelligence and the Taliban, on a memo from the US camp for war prisoners at Guantanamo Bay that was released by the website of WikiLeaks. The exposure of the private US assessment had caused considerable strains in the relationship between the United States and ISI, which allegedly had longstanding ties to militants but also worked closely with the CIA; suggesting that it played a double game.

Let us hope if our civil & military elite would keep Pakistan first.

www.ingramcontent.com/pod-product-compliance
Lightning Source LLC
Chambersburg PA
CBHW022113080426
42734CB00006B/111